Macroeconomic Analysis

JAN WALTER ELLIOTT

University of Wisconsin, Milwaukee

WINTHROP PUBLISHERS, INC.

Cambridge, Massachusetts

Library of Congress Cataloging in Publication Data

Elliott, Jan Walter.
  Macroeconomic analysis.

  Includes bibliographical references.
  1. Macroeconomics. I. Title.
HB171.5.E486   330   74–26852
ISBN 0–87626–545–X

to Marilyn, Brian, Brad, and Todd

Contents

4

Production and Supply in the Economy   47

5

The Basics of Income Determination   62

6

Theory of the Consumption Function   84

Preface

This book on macroeconomics focuses upon the integration of theory with analysis of economic behavior over the near-term. Although many books on macroeconomics have appeared in recent years, the needs of macroeconomic analysis have not been well served. In books of an applied nature, the tools of macroeconomic theory have found extensive application in the formulation of economic policy prescriptions, often providing the foundation for professional advice about tax policy and expenditure actions of government policy makers and about the monetary stance of the Federal Reserve. Quite clearly, the value of applied macroeconomics is not exhausted by policy prescriptions. Indeed, the use of macroeconomic theory by managers of financial and non-financial corporations to aid in formulating projections about the near-term economic environment and the impact on that environment of possible economic change may well outweigh the use of macroeconomics in policy formulation in terms of the practical impact of macroeconomic theory on decisionmaking. An important concern of this book is with the less extensively discussed area of macroeconomic analysis.

Modern macroeconomic theory is the foundation for macroeconomic analysis. Therefore, this book presents macroeconomic theory at an intermediate level. However, to apply theory to the analysis of current economic situations and problems, several other topics must accompany the theoretical presentation. Among these, real-world measures of employment and unemployment, capacity, prices, and economic activity accompany the usual discussion of National Income accounting, and are given as much weight. The growing role of financial intermediaries in determining United States macroeconomic activity is also discussed as a foundation for the application of monetary theory to financial problems of the U.S. economy. Funds-flow channels are identified along with the market instruments of finance by which suppliers and demanders of money capital interact. This institutional detail enables the tools of theoretical analysis to be focused explicitly on the particular problem setting in the U.S. economy.

In addition, a presentation of empirical macroeconomic findings accompanies the presentation of theoretical models in the discussion of consumer and investment sector demand. This enables an appreciation of actual determinants of fluctuations in these sector demands. The particular needs of analysis also have inspired explicit coverage of investment demand in the housing and inventory categories, an often overlooked area of macroeconomics. The same concern has led to inclusion of a chapter covering empirical macroeconomic models that surveys a cross-section of differing contemporary empirical macroeconomic models and compares their forecasting performance. In addition, a chapter is devoted to the analysis of the economy in inflation, thus recognizing the continuing nature of the inflationary problem in the U.S. economy.

These topics and the overall focus of the present book allow it to serve in a flexible way the needs of courses that are aimed toward building skills in macroeconomic analysis. An introductory sequence in economics is assumed throughout the book, placing it essentially at the intermediate level in either economics or business administration programs. The flow of ideas through the book forms a basic requisite sequence with a number of possible options. The requisite sequence is chapters 1–2–4–5–6–8–10–14–15–16, which develops the macroeconomic theoretical model. Adding chapters such as 3, 7, 9, 12, 13, and 17 increases the analysis focus of the course. Adding chapters 18 and 19 treats policy applications, while adding chapter 11 covers international economics.

In addition to reflecting the intellectual bloodlines of Keynes, Patinkin and their followers, the present book is the result of the unselfish ideas of many colleagues and students. Professors Willard Carleton, David Smyth, and Frederick Bamford were particularly important in the development of the book, as they read the entire manuscript and offered many valuable suggestions. Professors Naim Sherbiny and Richard Westin also were kind enough to read and comment on portions of the manuscript, providing several suggestions as to important avenues by which the then-draft material could be kept from a premature demise. Although implication of these various individuals in the responsibility for errors that remain in the work is an attractive idea from the author's standpoint, it is unfortunately neither customary nor proper. There being no one else left, I must bear the responsibility for lapses in truth that remain in the work.

1
Introduction

A large, industrially advanced economy such as that of the United States frequently reaches out and directly touches the lives of its individual citizens, its business leaders, and its governmental officials. At income tax deadlines, job layoffs, antitrust suits, fuel shortages, and elections, those affected often find their curiosity aroused as to how and why the economy behaves in the manner it does. Perhaps more so than other groups, managers of business enterprises have a particularly keen and persistent need to develop and maintain a coherent overall perception of the state of the overall economy in which they operate. The dependence of product and labor markets upon overall economic conditions and the continuing problem of raising capital at reasonable rates in orderly markets are two areas of decision making in which practical minded business leaders require a workable perception of how their economy works.

One lesson learned clearly by twentieth century students of economics is that a useful perception of a complex industrial economy requires abstraction from the morass of detail involved. Some aspects of the economy must be ignored so that others can be focused upon carefully. Thus, some level of abstraction is necessary in pinpointing the modern economic thought process. The trick of economic model-building is to decide where such abstraction should occur and how extensive it should be—a subject we consider in this initial chapter.

The Framework of Macroeconomics— An Abstraction

As an apparatus for explaining behavior in the nation's markets for products, services, money capital, and other key economic variables, macroeconomic theory is today in a rather unsettled state. Economic theories that have held sway since the late 1930s for the explanation of employment levels and in assessing the impact of fiscal and monetary policy are under serious intellectual attack, and old theoretical notions about the determination of output and price levels are giving way to new ideas at a quickening pace. For contemporary students of macroeconomics, this condition has both positive and negative dimensions. On the negative side, the student has more ideas in need of personal evaluation and assessment than would be the case for a more settled subject. On the positive side, macroeconomics is made considerably more interesting, alive, and vital by the dynamic nature of its current development.

Although economists disagree about aspects of theory, they are in widespread agreement as to the structural properties of the economic stocks, flows, and markets about which macroeconomic theory pertains. Figure 1–1 illustrates this structure in a greatly simplified fashion.

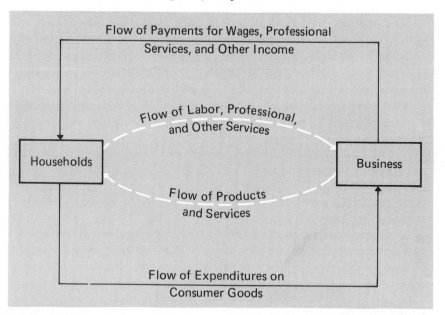

Figure 1–1
Circular Flow

The figure shows flows of money, products, and labor and other productive factors in a simplified economy having only a household and a business sector. To illustrate the essential flows, let us consider a circumstance where households withhold no income from product markets, spending each dollar of income upon consumer products and saving none. At the same time, the business sector retains no profits, returning each dollar of sales in payment for labor and other factors of production. In this highly simplified circumstance, money flows in an uninterrupted circle from business firms to households as payment for services purchased and back to business firms again as sales. As also shown in Figure 1–1, flows of labor and other factors move in the opposite direction to money payments. The family of transactions involving wage and related payments and labor and related services is referred to as the *labor market*. Similarly, the family of transactions involving payments made to business by households to acquire the flow of products and services is referred to as the *product market*. As a representation of an actual economy, Figure 1–1 is oversimplified. But it illustrates some important macroeconomic rules of thumb, including: (1) If the stock of money is fixed, a higher total flow of products and services requires a faster flow of money (greater velocity) between household and business sectors; (2) If the velocity or rate of flow of money between household and business sectors remains fixed, then an increase in the stock of money available will increase the total flow of products and services.

If, as in the United States, households and business firms engage in saving, then the circular flow of Figure 1–1 must be modified. Similarly, if product market expenditures are made by other than households, the circular flow is further altered. Finally, if a government sector exists, still further modifications in the circular flow are required.

Figure 1–2 shows a modified circular flow that accounts for these more realistic conditions, and thus it more nearly represents the structure of an advanced economy such as the United States. Hypothetical dollar flows are included in Figure 1–2 to further illustrate the flows involved. The household sector is now seen to have three outlets for its flow of income payments from business: (1) consumer expenditure; (2) consumer saving; and (3) taxes, which together completely dispose of available income flows. Similarly, the business sector receives sales in the form of new plant and equipment investment and government outlays in addition to consumer expenditure. Thus, the total income flow in the economy of Figure 1–2 is 1,150 rather than only the 800 of consumer spending. In addition, corporations are assumed to generate a flow of saving in the form of business net cash flow. Thus, note that inflows into the business sector of $800 + 200 + 150 = 1,150$ are exactly disposed of by the combination of factor payments by business (1,100) and business saving (50). The existence of a government sector produces a flow

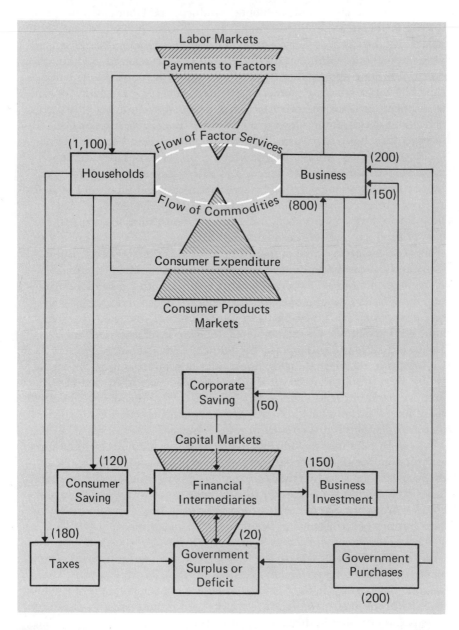

Figure 1–2
Three Sector Circular Flow

of tax revenues and a flow of government expenditures. Comparing the magnitude of the flow of taxes with that of government purchases establishes the net saving position of government. In Figure 1–2, government purchases exceed taxes by 20; thus a deficit exists on the governmental account. In Figure 1–2, the government can only spend more than it receives by borrowing funds in the same fashion that private investors must borrow. By the same reasoning, if taxes exceeded government purchases, the government sector would become a net saver and would provide funds to capital markets for investment.

Figure 1–2 also shows the role of banks and other financial intermediaries to be that of making the flow of private saving available to private and public demanders of funds. Thus, the financial intermediary sector of the economy receives saving flows and creates the financial instruments by which these funds can be supplied to demanders of money capital. The family of transactions involving suppliers and demanders of corporate money capital is called the *capital market*. This market and the previously outlined labor and consumer product markets are shown by the shaded triangles in Figure 1–2. For capital markets, the figure shows supplies of $120 + 50 = 170$ and demands of 150 (by business) and 20 by government for a total of 170.

Although still simple, Figure 1–2 illustrates some further rules of thumb beyond those emerging from Figure 1–1, as follows: (1) Financial intermediaries play an influential role in maintaining the rate of money flow by rechanneling nonspent income from household and business sectors into investment spending categories; (2) When the government budget moves into a deficit, the government becomes a demander of funds from capital markets, and when the budget is a surplus, the government functions as a supplier of funds; (3) Higher consumer saving rates slow down the circular flow of income unless this saving is entirely channeled through capital markets into increased investment; (4) Higher tax rates affect the circular flow in a manner similar to saving in reducing the amount of consumer income that is returned to the business sector through consumer expenditures.

Figure 1–2 shows the mechanical structure of three important macroeconomic markets depicted by the shaded triangles. But, it reveals little about the behavioral properties of these markets. For example, we know nothing about the possibility raised earlier that an increase in available money would slow down the rate of flow of money between household and business sectors. On the other hand, our macroeconomic theory deals with such behavioral questions by formulating logical and testable hypotheses about such questions in the context of analytical models. Because the role of models is central to the process of inquiry in economics, we now turn our attention to a discussion of models per se.

Models and the Real World

Stories abound in the physical sciences about uses of models to approach questions about the workings of the physical world. Typically, the process of model development in the physical sciences involves (1) an observation phase in which the model-builder gains impressions about and data from the process, (2) a model formulation phase in which a quantitative explanation of the observed data is developed, and (3) a verification phase in which comparisons are made between results implied by the model and results produced by the real physical system. If these comparisons show a close correspondence, then the model is often judged to be supported by the data. If such consistency is repeatedly found, the model usually gains acceptance as a useful quantitative representation of the real world system, ultimately becoming the basis for a physical law of behavior.

Such a generally accepted model may be used in several ways. The most common use is to make predictions about the response of the physical system to various stimuli. A second use is as a planning tool to generate "what if" data relative to the responsiveness of the system to individual external stimuli. A third possible use of such a model is to facilitate further understanding of the properties of corresponding physical systems by analysis of the composition of the model.

Models of advanced economies do not share all the attributes of models rooted in the physical sciences. For example, the experimental generation of data for observation and to aid the process of model development is usually not possible in the case of economic systems. To illustrate, we cannot instruct the U.S. economy to hold all its citizen's behavior constant while we change an economic policy variable in a known way. By contrast, controlled experimentation is usually a key way in which data are generated in the development of models in the physical sphere. Nonetheless, many of the elements involved in reasoning from models in the physical sciences apply in reasoning from models of the economy. We now consider such elements as they relate to economic models.

Place of Data in Model Development

One characteristic feature of constructing models of advanced economies is the necessity for these models to be framed in the same dimensions as the available statistical data. If we do not do this, the models are difficult if not impossible to test. Thus, it is reasonable to develop models for the United States that explain the GNP and/or its major components since it is possible to compare the results of these models with data actually produced by the economy. By contrast, the development of a model explaining the level of capital investments by government is untestable for all practical purposes since the U.S. national income accounting system does not break government expenditures into investment and expense categories.

An important characteristic of aggregate economic data is, as previously mentioned, its nonexperimental nature. Model-builders must take the data "as is," simply acknowledging the limitations of these data. Indeed, the limitations of nonexperimental data may be severe. Consider the evaluation of a model involving interest rates in the United States over the period 1960–1965. Many researchers would argue that insufficient fluctuation in interest rates occurred over this period to enable fully reliable comparisons between model results and actual results. In effect, extreme stability in interest rates is equivalent to having one sample point repeated again and again over the sample. No information is provided on other sample points. Unfortunately, no satisfactory solution to this problem exists except to await the generation of more data by the passage of time.

Model Development and Verification

We spoke earlier of the need to abstract in economic models. This aspect of economic analysis cannot be overemphasized. In large part, an economic model comes into being by virtue of decisions by the model-builder to forget about some presumably small and nonsystematic influences upon his model in favor of other influences thought to be of a major nature. If the model-builder's perceptions are correct, then the performance of his model will not suffer from the excluded variables. Indeed, it will instead profit by being a successful distillation that captures the essence of the working of the economic system without being entangled in unnecessary complexities. To illustrate this idea, consider the construction of a model that explains the amount of money in a (perhaps your own) personal checking account as of the end of each month. How many possible influences on the balance can you list? Perhaps dozens, including unplanned purchases, repairs to your personal property, unforeseen entertainment expenses, plus many routine, normal expenditures and receipts. The task of constructing a model of this balance initially involves sorting out the types of receipts and expenditures that can be counted upon to occur, i.e., the receipts and expenditures that occur systematically. Then, the effect of the unforeseen factors will have to be taken into account. Perhaps these factors constitute a certain fixed fraction of the total. Perhaps they can be related to some outside explanatory factor such as the time of year. The point is that there will be a clear need to emphasize a relatively small group of key explanatory factors in order to obtain a manageable model that can be an aid in structuring one's thinking about fluctuations in checking-account level.

Most economic models undergo a more-or-less continued process of development as research results produce new evidence about the association between the model and the world. This is particularly true of the Keynesian model, which has been extensively discussed, expanded upon, criticized, and evaluated in academic journals since its inception in the mid-1930s. The results of this developmental process have in part been a delineation along more specific lines of the original notions of Keynes. But, in part, the continuing process of debate has produced some generally accepted changes in the Keynesian model, such that the theoretical perception of the economy held by most economists is today not strictly Keynesian, even though it is distinctly Keynesian inspired.

One who is familiar with research in the physical sciences might wonder why an economic model such as the Keynesian model inspires continuing debate over the question of its appropriateness in explaining real world economic behavior. The important question at the root of this puzzlement is quite logical: Why can't the model be tested on the data of the economy and the final determination made as to whether it does or does not reflect these data?

The answer to this question is rooted in the earlier mentioned non-experimental nature of economic data. The inability to actually vary only one real world parameter in an economic system while holding all others constant leaves researchers with only imperfect methods to approximate this procedure. These methods are almost entirely statistical, involving analyses of the similarity in observed patterns of fluctuation that associate with individual variables in the economic model. Although results flowing from such statistical analyses establish inferences about the appropriateness of the model in representing the real world, they are never incontrovertible. Indeed, examples abound in economic research in which two theoretically incompatible models are both found to be statistically consistent with a single set of real world data. Such occasions point up the essential problem of model verification in a world confined to nonexperimental data—it is not possible to establish a test of an economic model under circumstances that can establish the applicability of a single economic model to the exclusion of all others.

This situation has led to a research style in economics that involves repeated testing of economic models in part and in total under varying circumstances over extended periods of time. Thus, as statistical evidence accumulates from varying sources giving consistent positive support for a particular economic model, that model tends to gain acceptance among economists. Similarly, accumulated negative statistical evidence is the basis for the discrediting of an economic model and its fall from acceptance. One of the more dramatic examples of this situation is found in pre-Keynesian theories of employment, which largely denied the possibility of serious unemployment of labor in a market economy for more than a short period of time. Both the bare fact of the lingering 1930s depression and the lack of face validity in the prescriptive solutions then offered by economists resulted in a serious discreditation of the pre-Keynesian model. At the same time, the apparent success of the Keynesian model in prescribing solutions to the pressing economic problem of the decade caused this model to gain rapidly in acceptance. In other circumstances where the real world situation is less dramatic, the process of acceptance of new economic models is ordinarily considerably slower as individual economists, analysts, and others are swayed by their own evaluation of the emerging statistical case for or against a particular economic model.

Models as Analytical Tools

Economic models customarily focus on the explanation of equilibrium positions. *Equilibrium* can be thought of as a condition where the various influences operating on an economic model entirely neutralize each other, creating a situation where no net forces are working to bring about a change in the performance of the model. To illustrate, consider the price of a particular firm's common stock upon release of news of an important new product discovery by that firm. The new information may be expected to sharply increase the perceived desirability of holding the stock. As a consequence, potential sellers of the stock would be less inclined to sell while potential buyers would be more inclined to buy. The current market price could not be maintained, as a net buying pressure now exists. Equilibrium has been disrupted, and the stock price begins to rise. As the stock price increases, potential sellers may be expected to be somewhat more inclined to sell at the higher prices while potential buyers may be somewhat less inclined to buy. These responses combine to reduce the net buying pressure, which in turn slows up the rise in price. After some point, the price will have risen to a point where sellers and buyers are equalized, such that no net buying pressure remains. At this equilibrium point, further price increases will not occur, since no net forces are now at work upon market price.

In this illustration, all other influences upon stock price except the announcement of the new product have been presumed to be held constant in describing equilibrium. The same is true of influences outside the model, such as speculative patterns of the variety that may lead to overshooting and undershooting in the actual price movements involved. Only if this "all else" constant or "one thing at a time" assumption is made, can equilibrium positions be described in simple, understandable terms in the context of a clearly understood economic model.

A critic of the entire idea of reasoning from economic models on a one thing at a time basis may contend that these models suffer fatally from assuming most economic influences to be constant in a world where they are not. The response to this criticism is thought by many to constitute the major strength of equilibrium analysis; namely, the capability to unravel the individual influences of key variables on the overall economic system by changing the value of key model variables one at a time and observing their differential effects upon an otherwise stable model.

Models in the Development of Economic Thought

The development of economic thought has not always relied on formal models in drawing conclusions about the economic state of the world. In the development of economic thought prior to the twentieth century, little use was made of the coldly logical implications of analytical structures comprised of assumptions and formal relationships among economic variables. Instead, economic thought was more philosophical in nature and tied closely to ethical, political, and moral beliefs. Indeed, the topic was commonly referred to as political economy and usually considered to be a branch of the moral sciences.

In the twentieth century, this orientation has undergone a rather sharp change. In particular, the economics of national income has evolved into basically a tool of analysis that enables the analysts to impose a personal political and moral overlay upon a basically value free analytical model. Thus, the role of the formal analytical economic model in economic reasoning has been greatly enlarged, while the role of assertions as to what is "right," "wrong," "good," or "bad" has been greatly reduced. The current state of this process of evolution is often referred to as the age of positive economics.

Economic Models and Management Decisions

Positive economic analysis is well suited to serve the needs of management decision makers in large organizations. These managers must deal regularly with decisions affected by their assumptions about factors such as profit expectations by business, preferences toward liquidity by firms and individuals, tendencies toward consumer saving, and intentions by corporations to increase their level of plant and equipment investment. At the same time, current analytical models of the U.S. economy contain these and other similar factors within a coherent, logical framework. Thus, the contemporary economic model is a highly relevant tool for organizing and integrating perceptions and predictions such as those listed in this chapter. For example, the contemporary economic model implies that a perceived national trend toward higher liquidity positions by firms and/or households would lead to higher interest rates, reduced capital expenditures, lower consumer spending, and a lower level of employment. In many decision making contexts, such "if-then" information could provide highly useful data to the decision makers. However, the reliance by a real world manager upon the conclusions of an economic model will almost certainly be affected by the extent to which the manager understands and believes the model from which such implications derive. A former president of U.S. Steel is reported to have accompanied a major announcement of a round of product price increases with the assertion that when it comes to important decisions, top executives must be their own economists. This is an interesting point to ponder. For the manager, it suggests that the advice of economic staff specialists and outside consultants must be somehow weighted by the responsible policy maker, prior to its impact on decision making. It seems clear that the better the understanding of economic theory and its application by the policy maker, the more effective will be the policy maker's use of staff inputs in making decisions and formulating policy. The development of this type of practically oriented understanding of economic concepts is the main task of this book. To pursue the specifics of this task, we initially consider the statistical measures available to economic analysts to determine the current and past course of business activity, beginning with a consideration of the national income accounts and their derivative measures.

Discussion Questions

1. In the circular flow diagram of Figure 1–2, the level of investment spending appears to involve only the business sector, i.e., it is spending undertaken by business creating sales in the business sector. To what extent is this statement correct? Does this aspect of investment mean that we may largely ignore such expenditures in assessing economic conditions?

2. Referring to Figure 1–2, what is the essential function of financial intermediaries in the flow of total incomes and expenditures?

3. Overheard: "Economic model building involves making simplifications and leaving out some variables in order to focus on others. Thus, economic models are inherently unrealistic." Evaluate this statement.

4. What is a positive economic model? What other kinds of models are there?

5. John K. Galbraith has recently suggested that much of standard economic theory is nonobjective due to its zest to preserve a politically free model structure that is positive or objective in nature. Galbraith's objection is that this represents an extreme political position that lacks the realism associated with true scientific objectivity. Comment.

2

The National Income Accounts

This chapter begins a consideration of the functioning of the economy of the United States. Overall economic conditions provide the environment in which business strategy is set. In modern corporations, this economic environment cannot be ignored in strategic and tactical management decisions. Product markets are too big, product lines too diverse, and labor and capital markets too national in scope to allow it to be otherwise. Thus, concern with the level of economic activity and its near-term path is widespread in modern management decisions. The same concern is present among all those interested in maintaining a critical facility regarding aggregate economic behavior. When questions about the level of economic activity are discussed at gatherings of managers and in connection with specific business decisions, there is no way to avoid talking in terms of the definitions set forth by the U.S. Commerce Department. This is easily understood. This department collects the information and makes most of the estimates by which the performance of the U.S. economy is determined. Therefore, aggregate economic analyses of the type in which we are interested must necessarily be framed in the terms set forth by the Commerce Department.

Total Performance

Overall economic behavior usually refers to an assessment of the economy's overall performance. We begin our consideration of national income accounting definitions with a consideration of overall performance measures.

12

The *Gross National Product (GNP)* is a frequently heard term. It is the national income accounting system's measure of gross spending, and it estimates the total amount spent on final goods and services currently produced in the United States. Figure 2–1 shows the path of the GNP in the United States since 1929, as well as a breakdown of this total into its major components—consumer spending, investment spending, government purchases and net exports. It is interesting to note the dominance of consumer spending in the GNP total and the somewhat erratic nature of the investment spending category. We shall have more to say on both these points in later chapters on consumer and investment spending. For now, we focus on the definition of the term and consider aspects of its statistical measurement.

Note the word "final" in the above definition. We eliminate from the GNP the value of all intermediate goods purchased for inclusion in other products. We thereby eliminate multiple counting of these intermediate goods, leaving the GNP as a measure of spending on goods and services sold to end users. The concept is rather straightforward. If a good is sold to a buyer for resale, either directly or in processed form, it is an intermediate good. If it is sold for end use, it is a final good.

The reference in the definition to goods sold in the United States indicates that we are measuring domestic output exclusively. In effect, the money that other nations spend on U.S. goods represents an addition to this measure, while the money that U.S. persons spend upon the output of other nations is not spending on U.S. output and therefore should be excluded. Thus, we adjust our GNP measure by adding the excess of our exports over our imports to the remainder of the spending. The reference to dollars *spent* in the definition implies that the acquisition of goods and services for which no market transaction occurs is not included. Thus, the services of housewives and of do-it-yourselfers are not included.

The GNP definition stipulates spending on current aggregate production rather than aggregate sales. If 900 billion of goods and services were produced in a period and 910 billion of goods and services sold in the period as final product, resulting in a reduction of inventories by 10 billion, the GNP would measure the 900 billion production figure. The GNP definition thereby creates a distinction between GNP and final sales of goods and services whenever inventory change is non-zero. In times of rapidly changing sales, the production distinction can have an important effect upon the GNP statistic that can be a source of confusion in the reading of the record. To illustrate this point, consider a level of production of 100 in period one with sales of 200 in the same period. Assume this is followed by production of 300 in period two and sales of 200 in this period. The GNP figure would show the sharp jump from 100 to 300, even though sales of final goods remain constant over the two periods. Because of this attribute of the GNP,

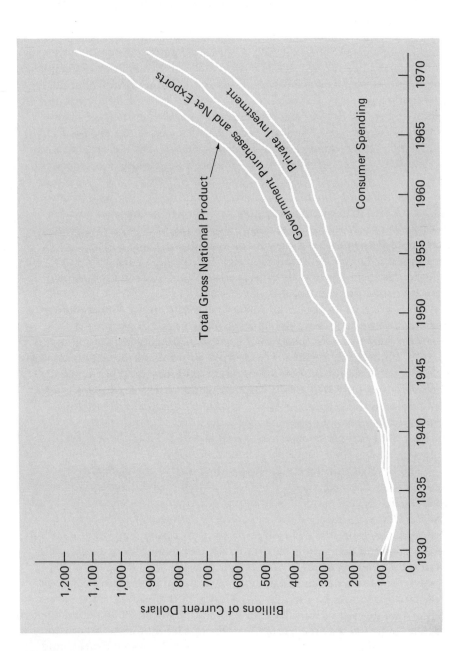

Figure 2–1

GNP in the United States

analysts usually look at both final sales and GNP figures to form judgments about the course of economic activity.

Our "current production" stipulation implies that the sale and purchase of used goods and services is not a part of the GNP per se. Thus gross sales of antiques and used automobiles are not a part of this measure. On the other hand, if an antique or other used good is resold by a dealer for more than its cost to the dealer, the net difference is considered value currently added to the good and accordingly does count as part of the GNP.

The "production" part of the definition implies the addition of labor, capital, material, and other value to the product. Accordingly, the purchase and sale of securities and other financial instruments are not a part of the GNP. These transactions represent only a change in consumer asset accounts. The same is true of transfer payments. However, where services are performed as a part of the exchange of financial instruments, the value of the service is added to the GNP. Thus, the broker's fees on the exchange of stock add to the GNP whereas the value of the stock exchanged does not.

Income and Expenditures—A Crucial Identity

When the GNP has changed by 5 percent over some period of time, our definition now makes it clear that the total level of spending on final goods and services produced in the nation has changed by 5 percent. As the circular flow diagram in Chapter 1 shows, these expenditures accrue completely as incomes to those involved in the production process. As long as our accounting is precise, every dollar spent on the GNP will accrue as a dollar of income. From a national income accounting viewpoint, we are looking at the same collection of transactions from both the income and sales sides of the economic counter. If we define *Gross National Income (GNI)* as the total income claims made on GNP, the statement

$$\text{GNI} \equiv \text{GNP}$$

summarizes the central property of our accounting system—that all expenditures on end use products are accounted for as some form of personal or nonpersonal income.

Total Expenditures

Let us now turn to the specific way in which we count expenditures in the system and the ways in which we accumulate information on income earned. Table 2–1 shows the primary accounting breakdowns of expenditures. The

Table 2–1

National Output Statistics   1973

	DOLLARS (BILLIONS)		
1. Personal Consumption Expenditures			805.0
Durable Goods		131.1	
Nondurable Goods		336.3	
Services		337.6	
2. Gross Private Domestic Investment			201.5
Fixed Investment		194.0	
Nonresidential	136.0		
Residential	58.0		
Change in Business Inventories		7.4	
3. Net Exports of Goods and Services			4.6
Exports		101.3	
Imports		96.7	
4. Government Purchases			277.2
Federal		106.9	
State and Local		170.3	
Total Expenditures on the Gross National Product			1,288.2

Note: Details may not add to totals due to rounding.
Source: Economic Report of the President, 1974.

first category, personal consumption expenditures, includes the spending on goods and services by individuals and nonprofit institutions and the value of food, clothing, housing, and financial services received by them as income in kind.[1] The first of three major subcategories under consumer goods is durable goods, defined basically as a good yielding its services over an extended period, such as a year. These consist of automobiles and parts, furniture, appliances, home electronics, and some sporting goods. Of these, automobiles are the largest, most durable in terms of serviceable life, and most volatile single durable good. Only the value of new car sales are included according to our current production definition. Used car sales basically represent past production. However, the increase in value associated with reconditioning and resale of used cars represents current production and thus adds to the GNP. A further illustrative numerical breakdown of consumer durables is given in Table 2–2, which shows details of the durable goods category.

     Nondurable goods include items with usable lives of approximately less than 1 year. Food, clothing, gasoline, and other consumable goods are

1 This is paraphrased from the explanatory notes of U.S. Department of Commerce, *Business Statistics, A Biannual Supplement to the Survey of Current Business, 1973,* U.S. Government Printing Office, Washington, D.C., 1973.

Table 2–2

Personal Consumption Expenditures   1973

	DOLLARS (BILLIONS)	
1. Durable Goods		131.1
Automobiles and Parts	57.9	
Furniture and Household Equipment	54.7	
Other	18.5	
2. Nondurable Goods		336.3
Food and Beverages	161.5	
Clothing and Shoes	69.8	
Gasoline and Oil	29.0	
Other	76.0	
3. Services		337.6
Housing	114.5	
Household Operation	48.0	
Transportation	23.4	
Other	151.6	
Total Consumer Goods Spending		805.0

Note: Details may not add to totals due to rounding.
Source: Economic Report of the President, 1974.

in this category. Table 2–2 shows the specific breakdown of nondurables. Services include the spending on nonphysical goods that generally are used up upon or immediately after purchase. Entertainment, professional services, housing costs, and commercial transportation spending are some of the items in this category, as further shown in Table 2–2.

The second broad expenditure category of Table 2–1, gross private domestic investment, consists of the new acquisitions of capital goods by private business and nonprofit institutions and the change in business investment in inventories. The first breakdown, fixed investment, is further divided into nonresidential and residential. The nonresidential category includes spending by profit-seeking and nonprofit institutions on construction and producer's durable equipment. This largely consists of business investment on plant and equipment, but also includes nonprofit institutional investment.[2] The second breakdown of fixed investment, residential investment, includes the spending on new housing units, including private dwelling units and apartment dwellings. As this categorization indicates, the purchase of a house is not considered in the accounting system to be a consumer

2 A related series, plant and equipment spending, is essentially concerned with measuring only the profit-seeking portion of nonresidential fixed investment and is therefore smaller than the latter series.

expenditure, but instead a business investment. The reasoning for this definition apparently is that the extremely long time over which a house yields its service would create a distortion if counted as a consumption-type expenditure at the time the house was purchased. Therefore, the accounting system treats a purchase of a home as a business expenditure and considers that the homeowner in effect "rents" the home to his consumer half by his business half. Therefore, a rental value is imputed to owner occupied houses. This nonreal expenditure is considered a purchase of a rental service in the consumer goods category, which generates a flow of imputed income receipts. In this way, a house is treated in the same general way as a factory.

The final breakdown of the investment category is the change in business inventories. The inventory change account is the key ingredient in the accounting identity between aggregate expenditures and aggregate incomes. If a business adds to inventories by creating output for which there is no customer, it has paid out incomes to the various factors of production in anticipation of a later retrieval of income at the time of sale. In the meantime, it would seem that our identity between spending flows and income flows has gotten out of balance. This is not so, however, because of the treatment of inventories. Inventories are considered as a business investment at the time they are created. Therefore, at the time the firm completed the product, the accounting system considers it has purchased the unsold good for its inventories. In this way, inventory investment becomes the buffer between production, income generation, and sales.

The change in business inventories is considered an investment expenditure and is a part of gross private domestic investment. Historically, inventory change has produced disproportionately large effects on the GNP, mainly because it is the *change* in a variable, rather than the variable itself. To illustrate the point, if inventories of business are successively 60 billion, 68 billion, and 65 billion, the inventory change series will show first +8 and secondly −3, a swing of 11 billion in the GNP accounts between the second and third periods.

The third broad spending category in Table 2–1 is net exports of goods and services. It is derived by subtracting U.S. imports from U.S. exports. *U.S. imports* are the purchases by U.S. residents of goods and services produced abroad, while *U.S. exports* are purchases of U.S. output by other nations. Including net exports as part of the GNP results in its formulation as a measure of total spending on current U.S. production, since we are adding the value of U.S. exports and subtracting the value of imports. As shown in Table 2–3, the exports portion of this figure consists largely of the sale of merchandise and services. However, also considered as an export is the income on investments made abroad. The flow of business profits can be thought of as payment for the continuing purchase of entrepreneurial and capital services by other nations.

Table 2–3

International Sector Statistics   1973

	DOLLARS (BILLIONS)		
1. Exports of Goods and Services			101.3
Merchandise		70.3	
Military Sales		1.8	
Income on Investments		8.9	
Private	11.9		
Government	− 3.0		
Other Services		20.3	
2. Imports of Goods and Services			96.7
Merchandise		69.6	
Military Expenditures		4.6	
Other Services		22.5	
Net Exports			4.6

Source: Economic Report of the President, 1974.

As further shown in Table 2–3, imports consist of goods and services as well as military expenditures abroad. Military expenditures are considered an import, the reasoning being that money spent for military purposes abroad is the purchase of national security, and therefore is a quasi-service expenditure by the government. Net exports are often referred to as the balance of trade, as they reflect net commercial-type transactions. They should not be confused with the balance of payments accounts, which also consider transfers of funds and other financial flows not connected with the purchase and sale of goods and services.

The final major category in Table 2–1 is government purchases, divided between federal and state and local expenditures. Both figures basically represent the purchase by government of goods and services. As such, government purchases do not represent all governmental outlays. In addition to the purchases shown in the GNP accounts, governments transfer funds to persons and abroad for social security and other welfare programs. They also make interest payments, finance certain government supported enterprises, and make grants-in-aids to other governmental units. Government purchases of the type included in the GNP are defined to include products purchased from private firms and also the direct cost of the services of individuals on government payrolls. This means that the cost to a city government of retaining a consulting firm and the costs of keeping an employee on the payrolls are considered in the same category in the Commerce accounting system. This introduces a significant exception to the "market-valued" part of the GNP definition. In the case of government outlays, we lump together the market price of goods and services purchased from the private economy with (1) the cost of running the bureaus and offices of government and (2) the costs of maintaining the nation's civil service and other public employee staffs. The latter government outlays are not market transactions in the sense of most of the other transactions included in the GNP. Therefore, a precise definition of the GNP should indicate it measures total spending upon current marketed domestic production *and* the costs of nonmarketed public service.

Total Incomes

Having now generally reviewed the accounting for total expenditures, we turn to the alternative expression of this activity—the aggregate income produced by this spending. Commerce breaks gross national income into two major parts. The first part, called *national income,* is the total payments to all the basic contributors to or factors of production, including labor, managerial, capital, and other inputs.[3] Accordingly, national income measures the total personal and nonpersonal income payments made to all business and personal income earners. The remaining part of gross national income (not included in national income) represents the part of total spending that is not accounted for as income earned. Its primary ingredients are excise and other business tax payments and depreciation payments.

Specifically, the Commerce breakdown is shown in Table 2–4. Items 1 through 5 represent the components of national income. Items 6 through 9 are the nonincome payment adjustments that form the bridge between National Income and GNP. The first item in Table 2–4, compensation of employees, covers wages, salaries, and supplements and includes all monetary compensation of employees and salaried managers, commissions, tips, bonuses, and payments in kind. The second item, proprietor's income, includes the earnings and other income of sole proprietorships, of partnerships, and producers' cooperatives. Capital gains and losses are excluded. The third item, rental income of persons, consists of the earnings of persons from the rental of real property, except the earnings of persons primarily engaged in the real estate business. Earnings of this latter group would be counted as regular business income under either proprietor's income or corporate profits. Rental income of persons also includes the imputed value of the rental income on owner-occupied houses. As indicated earlier, in the accounting for dwelling units as an investment good, a stream of returns in

3 Commerce defines national income as follows: "National Income is the aggregate earnings of labor and property which arise from the current production of goods and services by the Nation's economy." (*Business Statistics,* 1967, p. 5.)

Table 2–4

National Income Statistics   1973

	DOLLARS (BILLIONS)	
1. Compensation of Employees		785.3
Wages and Salaries	691.5	
Supplements to Wages and Salaries	93.9	
2. Proprietor's Income		84.3
Professional and Business	57.5	
Farm	26.8	
3. Rental Income of Persons		25.1
4. Corporate Profits and Inventory Valuation		109.2
Corporate Profits before Tax	126.5	
Inventory Valuation Adjustment	−17.3	
5. Net Interest		50.4
Total National Income		1,054.2
6. Payments of Indirect Business Tax		117.8
Federal	21.0	
State and Local	96.8	
7. Transfers, Subsidies to/from Business		4.2
Business Transfer Payments	4.9	
Less: Subsidies Less Current Surplus on Government Business	0.7	
8. Retained in Business as Depreciation Allowances		109.6
9. Statistical Discrepancy		2.3
Total Gross National Income (and Product)		1,288.2

Note: Details may not add to totals due to rounding.
Source: Economic Report of the President, 1974.

the form of imputed rental payments are included both as a form of income and as a consumer goods expenditure. This allows for measurement of the consumption of dwelling unit services over time, as well as a form of return on investment. The rental income of persons category accounts for real and imputed rental income earned as secondary income by persons engaged in other primary income earning pursuits.

The fourth item, corporate profits and inventory valuation, is primarily the pretax earnings of corporations organized for profit, exclusive of capital gains and losses and intercorporate dividends. Corporate profits also includes net receipts of dividends and branch profits from abroad, as reflected in the balance of payments statistics. In general, it is safe to say that the definition of profits used in this category is in accordance with federal income tax regulations. The second item, inventory valuation adjustment, measures the difference between the change in business inventories valued at average prices during the period and the change in business inventories valued at their book value. This adjustment is made to profits to remove the inventory profit or loss that occurs in business accounting when the book cost of goods removed from inventories differs from the current cost of replacing those goods in inventory.[4] Valuation in current prices of the costs of inventories used up puts sales and costs on a consistent basis, a requirement for deriving estimates of output in current prices.

The fifth item, net interest, includes three primary kinds of interest payments. First, it includes the actual interest paid by business firms to persons net of the interest received by business from all sources. Secondly, it includes the net interest received by persons from abroad. Finally, it includes imputed interest on personal accounts with financial intermediaries in those cases where earnings are not paid out each year as interest or where financial services are received in kind. In this definition, we should note that we include in general only the interest paid to consumers. Interest paid to business firms by other business firms or by persons accrues as regular profits or proprietor's income. For example, most interest payments by firms to banks would be intrabusiness sector transactions and therefore would not be included in this account.

There are two kinds of interest payments not dealt with in Commerce's definition of net interest. The first is interest payments made by consumers to consumers. The second is the interest payments made by governments to consumers. Both these categories are not considered payments for the nation's factors of production; hence they are excluded from our national income estimate. This omission serves to emphasize the concept embodied in our definition of national income—basically a measure of the total income earned by and paid to the factors of production by business firms and governments. As such, the consumer-to-consumer payments clearly are not appropriate for inclusion. The omission of government-to-consumer payments from these interest income figures reveals a somewhat problematic byproduct of our national income concept. On the one hand, the idea of national income as factor payments appears to exclude payments by governments made for purposes other than the payment for public service rendered.

---

[4] It should be noted that this valuation adjustment applies to all business inventories, including corporate as well as noncorporate inventories. Farm inventories are the only exception, being calculated at average prices during the period. This all-inclusiveness means that it is not conceptually correct to regard the corporate profits plus inventory valuation figure as "adjusted corporate profits." It is rather a hybrid figure that could be described as adjusted corporate profits plus the adjustment factor for the unadjusted earnings of proprietorships and partnerships. It would be conceptually more pleasing to divide the valuation figure into corporate and noncorporate and apply each to the correct kind of income, thereby resulting in adjusted incomes in both categories. As it now stands, when the valuation figure is positive, the adjusted corporate income figure is understated and proprietor's incomes overstated. The reverse is true when the valuation is negative.

However, as a by-product, we have the situation where a lender adds to national income if he lends to private profit-seeking organizations (via net interest). But if he lends to public institutions, he does not add to national income, and the interest receipts are counted as transfer payments instead of interest income.[5]

While items 1 through 5 in Table 2–4 represent payments by business to the factors of production, they do not represent the total division of the nation's sales dollar. Three other categories of payments are made. The first of these is the payment of indirect business taxes at the federal, state, and local level. These taxes are levied on bases other than profits and include excise taxes, property taxes, and the miscellaneous taxes, fees, and charges imposed by states and municipalities. By accounting for these taxes outside national income, Commerce recognizes them as being a form of taxes in which the business firm acts as a collection agency for the public, transferring the tax receipts periodically to the governmental recipient.

The seventh item in Table 2–4, transfers, subsidies to/from business, contains two parts. The first part, business transfer payments, consists of the nonwage-nonincome payments made by business firms. These payments consist of gifts to nonprofit institutions, consumer bad debts, personal injury payments by business except those to employees, theft losses, and cash prizes. The second part, net subsidies less surplus on government business, consists of the subsidies paid by the federal government to firms, plus the operating deficit (or minus the operating surplus) on the operation of federal, state, and local government enterprise. A *government enterprise* is taken here to be a government organization that collects revenues from users for the specific purpose of paying the costs of the operation of the organization. Examples would be the Tennessee Valley Authority and the Post Office Department.

Since business transfers are a nonincome payment, they are added to the national income figure in building an estimate of gross national income. The net government subsidies item, however, is subtracted in building the total since it represents a flow of income in excess of the market value of output for these services; likewise, if a profit were realized on these enterprises, it would be added in building the total, since it would be "public profit," thereby treated analogously with corporate profits.

The eighth item in Table 2–4, depreciation allowances, consists of the depreciation charges of corporate and noncorporate business firms and the depreciation write-offs of nonprofit institutions. Also included are capital outlays charged to current expense and write-offs of fixed capital due to

[5] To make matters worse, if we were to include government-to-consumer interest payments as interest income, we would be in the position of having to add these to our GNP side in order to maintain the basic concept that gross income and gross product are identical. This could be done by adding these to the government purchases of goods and services (the purchase of money use).

accidental damage. The predominant element is the depreciation write-offs. The definitions applicable to depreciation are in close accord with those used for tax purposes, since the data are measured from tax return information.

Two Statistical Routes to the GNP

Items 6 through 8 in Table 2–4 constitute the gross national income or gross national product elements that are not part of our national income. As such, they are the adjustments necessary to form the accounting identity between these two gross figures. The ninth item, statistical discrepancy, implies that more than one estimate has been made and that all do not coincide. This is indeed the case. Estimates are separately prepared for gross national income and gross national product. The statistical discrepancy measures the final difference in these two estimates. For the GNP estimate, data are collected on spending activities in each of the categories in the GNP breakdown. From these data, an estimate of the GNP is prepared. At the same time, data on each of the national income categories are collected leading to an estimate of national income. Data are analyzed on depreciation, business transfers and government subsidies, and indirect business taxes, enabling an estimate of gross national income to be built. Then, the results from the two routes are compared. When differences in the results obtained by the two routes have been reduced to a tolerable level, the estimate is complete. The spending estimate is taken as the benchmark, so that the statistical discrepancy is shown in the income figures. A review of the historical statistical discrepancy series verifies that the final divergence between spending and income estimates has been quite small in comparison with the size of the estimate.

Measures of Consumer Buying Power

From the GNI and GNP totals, we can extract measures of the income flowing to persons and of the income available to them for spending. These measures are called, respectively, personal income and disposable personal income. Personal income provides a useful contrast with national income. Whereas the latter is concerned with measuring payments to the factors of production, the personal income figure is concerned with measuring the money flowing to the consumer, either earned as a factor of production or received as a transfer.

Extracting Personal and Disposable Income

Table 2–5 shows the steps in extracting personal income from national income. Corporate profits are subtracted since they are factor payments not flowing into the personal sector. Contributions for social insurance, both by employees and employers, are subtracted since they represent a portion of national income withheld from payment to persons. The remainder of national income thereby represents a sum paid out to persons. However, additional personal payments are made that are not a part of national income, and these must be added in to obtain our measure of money flowing into personal accounts. The first of these is government transfers to persons. These payments consist of social insurance and government welfare payments. As such, they add money to personal accounts. The next item, interest paid by government and by consumers, similarly adds to spendable funds in the hands of persons although it is not a factor payment. It must therefore be added to our total. Dividend payments are the part of corporate profits distributed to persons. Since we have earlier subtracted out total corporate profits, we must now add back dividends as that portion of profits that do flow into personal accounts. Alternatively, we could redefine the corporate profits figure as retained corporate profits by subtracting dividend payout from the total. Then, we could merely subtract this retained profit figure from national income, resulting in a single adjustment rather than the two-part method employed in Table 2–5. As earlier described, business transfer payments represent income-like transfers by business to personal accounts;

Table 2–5

National Income and Personal Income   1973

		DOLLARS (BILLIONS)
National Income		1,054.2
Less: Corporate Profits and Inventory Valuation	109.2	
Contributions for Social Insurance	92.2	
Plus: Government Transfers to Persons	112.5	
Interest Paid by Government and by Consumers	37.1	
by Consumers 22.5		
by Governments 14.6		
Dividends	27.8	
Business Transfer Payments	4.9	
Personal Income		1,035.5
Less: Personal Taxes		152.9
Disposable Personal Income		882.6
Less: Personal Outlays		828.7
Personal Consumption Expenditures	805.0	
Interest Paid by Consumers	22.5	
Personal Transfers to Foreigners	1.2	
Personal Saving		53.8

Note: Details may not add to totals due to rounding.
Source: Economic Report of the President, 1974.

they are therefore a necessary final addition in our process of personal income estimation.

The composition of personal income makes it clear that it is a pretax measure of buying power. If we subtract personal tax payments, we obtain a measure of the aftertax income flowing to personal accounts. This figure, called *Disposable Personal Income (DPI)*, is a measure of effective net consumer buying power. Table 2–5 shows this adjustment. DPI is widely considered to be a basic economic yardstick for measuring fluctuations in consumer purchasing power.

Personal Outlays and Saving

Having generated disposable personal income, we can use the national income data to make an accounting for this income to spending and saving categories. As Table 2–5 shows, the spending categories are grouped under the heading Personal Outlays. Three items comprise personal outlays. The largest, personal consumption expenditures, has been defined previously. In addition, interest paid by consumers are included, as are personal transfers to foreigners. This latter category includes gifts made by persons in the United States to foreign persons and organizations and other nonpurchase transfers of funds. Thus, personal outlays consist of purchases, interest obligations, and personal transfers abroad by consumers. The portion of disposable personal income not committed across these three categories is defined as personal saving. Defined this way, saving in GNP terms is a residual value obtained by subtracting personal outlays from DPI.

This saving flow can be thought of as the total amount of current income allocated by the consumer to uses other than personal outlays. In the GNP accounts, saving is the flow of nonconsumed income. If we refer to these nonpersonal outlay accounts as the asset accounts of the consumer, then the total change in these asset accounts would be equal to the saving flow. The national income accounting system does not attempt to equate the total change in consumer asset accounts and the level of saving flow. However, some of the primary asset accounts that would be affected by the saving flow are demand deposits, time deposits, savings deposits, holdings of bonds and other financial instruments, and contractual savings accounts such as insurance trusts. Conceivably, if a complete accounting could be made of the change in these asset accounts, it would equate with the size of the saving flow.

Intersector Relationships

From the concepts and terms now developed, an analysis is possible of the flows of funds among the consumer, business, governmental, and international sectors. Such an analysis reveals cash-flow relationships among business, private, and public spending activities. Table 2–6 shows this analysis. In the consumer sector, inflows consist of the receipts of disposable personal income. Outflows consist of personal outlays. For the data in the table, the

Table 2–6

Intersector Relationships   1973

	DOLLARS (BILLIONS)	
Consumer Sector		
Inflow: Disposable Personal Income	882.6	
Outflow: Personal Outlays	828.7	
Net Consumer Sector Funds Flow		+53.8
Government Sector		
Inflow: Personal Taxes	152.9	
Corporate Taxes	56.3	
Indirect Business Taxes	117.8	
Contributions for		
Social Insurance	92.2	
Total Receipts	419.2	
Outflow: Purchases of Goods and Services	277.2	
Interest Payments by Government	14.6	
Transfer Payments	115.1	
Subsidies less Surplus on		
Government Enterprises	0.7	
Total Outlays	407.6	
Net Government Sector Funds Flow		+11.6
Business Sector		
Inflow: Gross Retained Earnings	134.7	
Undistributed Profits 42.4		
Inventory Valuation −17.3		
Depreciation 109.6		
Outflow: Gross Private Domestic Investment	201.5	
Net Business Sector Funds Flow		−66.8
International Sector		
Flows to: Imports	96.7	
Transfers to Foreigners	3.6	
Total Flows to International Sector	100.3	
Flows From: Exports	101.3	
Net International Sector Funds Flow		−1.0
Statistical Discrepancy		+2.3

Note: Details may not add to totals due to rounding.
Source: Adapted from *The Economic Report of the President,* 1974 (U.S. Department of Commerce, Office of Business Economics.

consumer sector was a net saver, with inflows greater than outflows. Consumer asset accounts were thereby enlarged. It is possible, although highly unusual, that the consumer sector could operate as a source of funds to other sectors by dis-saving. This might be expected in the case of a sudden sharp downturn in disposable incomes, which consumers were reluctant to immediately follow by cuts in spending.

The governmental sector shows the flows associated with the combined activities of federal, state, and local governments. The inflows in Table 2–6 consist of four sources of government tax revenues. Outflows contain the major categories of government spending and transfer activities. If total government inflows exceed outflows, the governmental sector is a net recipient of funds. (A gross governmental budget surplus occurs.) If outflows exceed inflows, the governmental sector is a source of funds in an overall cash flow sense. (An overall budget deficit occurs.)

Inflows to the business sector consist of undistributed corporate profits, adjusted for inventory valuation, and depreciation write-offs. This sum, identified as *gross retained earnings,* is essentially the net cash flow of business firms. As such, it summarizes the funds flowing from production activities. The amount of money spent by corporations on new plant and equipment, residential construction, and inventory investments, represents the outflow of funds from the business sector. When business outflows are greater than inflows (the normal case), the balance represents the employment of new capital by the business sector. This amount consists of newly issued equity capital, i.e., new stock issues, as well as newly issued debt instruments. Alternatively, we could decompose the total gross private domestic investment into that amount financed internally, gross retained earnings, and the remaining amount of external financing.

Flows to the international sector consist of imports, in payment for which funds flow abroad, and transfers by government and by persons. Flows from abroad consist of the payments by other nations for the purchase of U.S. exports. In years when exports exceed imports plus transfers, the international sector provides an inflow of funds. It is thereby a source of funds to the system in the same way as business investments in excess of cash flow are a source of funds. Thus, the imports and transfers are shown in Table 2–6 with positive values, indicating a form of saving, and the exports are given a negative value, indicating a form of investment. Finally, the statistical discrepancy equates the inflows and outflows. The general relationships in Table 2–6 are typical for a growing economy, in which the consumer sector normally generates positive savings, thereby subtracting from the flow of funds available to other sectors. By contrast, the business sector usually generates negative savings, thereby adding to the funds available to other sectors. Although this situation usually accompanies economic growth, we should not look upon it as showing that the business sector is a fountain of funds and the consumer is a drain upon fund flow. As the circular flow diagram of Chapter 1 indicated, the relationship between the two relative to the functioning of financial intermediaries makes the business sector's ability to function as a "source" of funds dependent upon the consumer sector's willingness to incur positive savings and to supply these savings to the business sector either directly or indirectly through financial intermediaries. Thus, the business sector does not create new money that is absorbed by the consumer sector, but instead it recycles the money that flows as nonspending in the consumer sector.

Although the GNP and its derivative measures of income are the most widely published measures of general business activity, a number of other measures of aggregate business activity are available. In addition, a variety of associated measures of prices and employment are regularly available to economists and analysts of business activity. Our discussion in the next chapter turns to some of the more important of these measures.

Discussion Questions

1. Gross national income and gross national product are defined as being equal to each other in the accounting structure of the United States. Does this mean that no one saved anything in the sense that expenditures and income were equal?

2. What differentiates personal income from national income? Do you see any unique uses for one not contained in the other? What about value judgments contained in each?

3. Explain accounting differences in the treatment of
    (a) interest paid and received on corporate bonds.
    (b) interest paid and received on government bonds.
    Take a position for or against these differences.

4. From the chapter, what did you gather constitutes the rationale for imputed rent on owner-occupied homes?

5. Build an argument that the GNP understates the true value of domestic production of final goods and services.

6. Which of these add to the dollar value of GNP? Explain as clearly as possible and take a strictly accounting viewpoint, assuming no changes in behavior.
    (a) The government grants a 5 percent pay raise to all civil service workers.
    (b) General Motors grants a 5 percent pay raise to all employees, while maintaining product prices unchanged.
    (c) Ford grants a 5 percent pay raise to all employees and passes the cost along by a 5 percent increase in product prices.

3
Other Measures of Economic Activity

In the previous chapter we outlined the major features of the GNP accounting system in the United States. The data produced as parts of this system are currently in such widespread use that it is easy to confuse the GNP and derivatives as a *measure* of economic activity with the true actual *level* of economic activity. While the GNP measure is a single-dimensional quantitative magnitude, the actual state of economic activity is multidimensional, encompassing such facets as intensity of intermediate and final production, need for labor, general briskness of markets, and dynamics of price movements, and in addition is not easily quantifiable in all its various dimensions.

In this chapter we consider measures of economic activity that cover dimensions of economic behavior other than the total spending dimension of GNP data. Our discussion will deal with physical output measures, employment measures, price measures, and leading, coincident, and lagging indicators. We begin by considering a measure of physical production.

Measuring Industrial Production

The *Index of Industrial Production* is published monthly in the *Federal Reserve Bulletin* (FRB) by the Board of Governors of the Federal Reserve System, Division of Research and Statistics. It measures changes in the physical quantity of output of manufacturers, minerals, and electric and gas utilities. The major market breakdowns in the index are shown in Table 3–1.

Table 3–1

Market Groupings—Index of Industrial Production

	1973 INDEX (1967 = 100)	PERCENT WEIGHT
Consumer Goods	131.7	28.53
Automotive Products	136.8	2.84
Durable Home Goods	140.3	5.02
Nondurable Consumer Goods	129.0	20.67
Equipment	106.7	20.42
Business Equipment	122.6	12.74
Defense and Space Equipment	80.2	7.68
Intermediate Products	131.1	13.26
Construction Products	134.2	5.93
Miscellaneous Intermediate Products	128.6	7.34
Materials	129.3	37.79
Durable Goods Materials	130.1	20.91
Nondurable Goods Materials	129.1	13.99
Fuel and Power, Industrial	123.9	2.89
Total Weighted Index	125.6	100.00

As seen, the index measures intensity of production in four major market segments: consumer goods, business and defense equipment, intermediate products, and materials. Production indices are developed for all major components of each of these segments. Table 3–1 shows a first level breakdown of the four segments. Data are actually gathered and published in part on a more detailed breakdown than this first level.

The component and sector indices are then built by weighting each individually measured index by the percent of expenditures it represented as of the base date of the index. For example, for a base of 1967, i.e., 1967 = 100, the expenditure proportions in that year would establish the weights. The weights used for various production categories are shown in Table 3–1. These show that the materials sector carries the heaviest weight in the index, followed by consumer goods. At the same time, better than 40 percent of the weight of the index attaches to nondurable consumer goods and materials for durable goods (steel, aluminum, etc.). Thus composed, the FRB index measures intensity of industrial activity in various stages of the economy's production cycle for the same time period. There is no concern with double-counting as with the GNP since the FRB measure is not one of dollars of output but rather intensity of business activity.

Accordingly, some interesting differences may be noted between the FRB index and the GNP. First, we have noted that the index of industrial production reflects output movements at intermediate as well as final stages within manufacturing and mining industries, whereas the GNP deals only with final goods. By measuring the output of intermediate goods, the index tends to discern imbalances in the manufacturing-to-retail pipeline that might not show up in the GNP figures until a later date. A second clear difference between the two is the concept of an index, which is a unit-free measure as compared to the dollar-measured GNP. A third major difference is found in coverage. The index of industrial production does not cover production on farms, in the construction industry, in transportation, or in various trade and service industries. The industries that are included in the index produce approximately 35 percent of the value of GNP-type output in the United States, according to the Commerce Department.[1] The FRB index is not as broad-gauged a measure of economic activity as the GNP. On the other hand, by its focus on production activities primarily in the physical product area, the index offers a more useful measure of these specific activities than can be obtained from the GNP or its immediate spending breakdowns.

Measuring Employment

The total number of job seekers who are employed represents an additional measure of aggregate economic activity. A larger labor force is normally required to produce a larger GNP, given a particular state of technology. A fundamental relationship may therefore be expected to exist between employment levels and output levels. While true enough over the long-run, short-run changes in GNP levels are often not followed directly by proportionate changes in employment. If GNP is rising, the initial reaction of many firms may be put in a "fuller" week and move to overtime scheduling until the output increase is assumed permanent. Only if the output increase is persistent can employment adjustments be expected. When output is falling, the cost of employee separations and layoffs entice many firms to maintain employment and adjust hours worked as long as possible. When the decline in output is generally expected to persist, these adjustments will have to be translated into employment changes. This hours-worked buffer has the effect of making the timing of the influence of output upon employment somewhat variable over the short-run, which in turn makes short-run output–employment relationships more unstable than most analysts and policy makers would prefer.

Attention is often focused in business conditions analyses upon unemployment rather than employment. While employment figures measure the number of people at work, unemployment figures deal with this number in relation to the total work force. This means that measuring the work force

1 See *Business Statistics*, 1967, p. 14.

is necessary in measuring unemployment. Let us therefore turn our attention to the definition and measurement of the work force and from that, unemployment. Table 3–2 shows the derivation of the work force from the total population of the nation. As seen, two major groupings in the population are not part of the work force. The first group consists of children and the physically or mentally disabled. The remainder represents the working age able-bodied population who are seeking jobs. This group is defined as the *work force*. The percent of the total population represented by the work force is often referred to as the *participation rate*. Factors that can be seen to directly affect the participation rate include the age group composition of the population, changes in the custom of working wives, average retirement ages, and the size of the military force.

The total labor force splits into those employed and those unemployed. Thus, the definition of unemployment used in the U.S. accounting system becomes clear. Those members of the working age able-bodied population seeking but not finding jobs are classified as unemployed. Likewise, the percent unemployed refers to those seeking jobs but unable to find them. The percent unemployed is the most commonly publicized measure of employment. The figure is sometimes misinterpreted to refer to the portion of the population seeking but not finding jobs rather than the percent of the work force in such a position. The difference can be significant. For example, in 1969, 1.4 percent of the population was unemployed, but 3.5 percent of the labor force was unemployed, whereas for the 1973 data in the table, 2.1 percent of the population and 4.9 percent of the labor force was unemployed.

Table 3–2 indicates that several more variables beside output and pop-

Table 3–2

Labor Force, Employment, and Unemployment in the United States   1973

	THOUSANDS	PERCENT	
Total Population	210,404	100.0	
Less: Children and Disabled	62,141	29.5	
Work Age Able-bodied Population	148,263	70.5	
Less: Armed Forces Personnel and Population Not Seeking Jobs	59,549	28.3	
Total Civilian Labor Force	88,714	42.2	(100)*
Employed	84,409	40.1	(95.1)*
Unemployed	4,304	2.1	(4.9)*

* Percent of the labor force.

Source: Economic Report of the President, 1974.

ulation influence employment and unemployment statistics, including the size of standing military units (which absorb individuals who would otherwise be part of the work force), the tendencies of secondary workers (dependent on others for subsistence) to seek jobs, retirement patterns, and the work load of those employed via the effect on new employment demand. To illustrate, it is not unusual to find strong general business conditions met by a rise in the proportion of the work-age population seeking jobs, often housewives and teen-agers. Thus, the impact on employment and unemployment statistics of output changes is masked under these circumstances. When output begins to drop off, it is not unusual to see this same proportion fall as supplementary workers head back to housewife and student roles. This indicates that employment statistics must be considered carefully in light of factors such as these in order to draw reasonable implications as to their meaning.

Unemployment data are often used to draw implications about the fullness of production. An issue often discussed in connection with employment analyses is a consideration of general movements in prices in the economy. In considering the status of general prices, several economy-wide statistical measures are available for review. Three of the most widely published are the GNP implicit deflator, the consumer price index, and the wholesale price index, which we now discuss in that order.

Measuring General Prices: The GNP Implicit Price Deflator

The GNP implicit price deflator is the broadest based price index available for general products and services in the United States. It is calculated as the weighted average of prices for goods in each major spending category in the GNP. Price indices for each component in a spending category breakdown similar to that of the GNP are estimated and published quarterly by the Commerce Department in connection with the GNP statistics. The major categories in the GNP deflator are shown in Table 3–3. These separate price indices are weighted by their relative percent shares of the currently estimated GNP to arrive at the overall GNP implicit price index. Table 3–3 shows that a close correspondence exists between the GNP expenditure categories and the categories involved in the implicit deflator. The major exception is in the investment category. No price-index estimate is made for the change in business inventories. Since inventory change is a component in the GNP's gross private domestic investment category, a weighted average value cannot be explicitly calculated for this overall category. Instead, price indices for the components of fixed investment (nonresidential structures,

Table 3–3

GNP Implicit Price Deflators

	1973 INDEX (1958 = 100)	
Personal Consumption Expenditures		145.1
Durable Goods	114.5	
Nondurable Goods	146.8	
Services	160.0	
Fixed Investment*		153.3
Nonresidential Structures	194.4	
Producers' Durable Equipment	129.6	
Residential Structures	170.5	
Exports		150.5
Imports		157.8
Government Purchases of Goods and Services		191.4
Federal	186.5	
State and Local	194.5	
Total Gross National Product		153.9

* Separate deflators are not available for total gross private domestic investment, change in business inventories, and net exports of goods and services.

Source: Economic Report of the President, 1974.

producers' durable equipment, and residential structures) are combined into a fixed investment price index that is used to represent the entire gross private domestic investment category. This amounts to assuming that the missing investment category—changes in business inventories—has the same price movement as the weighted average of all other investment categories. In addition, a price index for the GNP category of net exports is not estimated. Instead, indices for exports and imports are formulated and weighted by the relative expenditure proportions in these two categories.

The government purchases sector of Table 3–3 illustrates one important difficulty in preparing estimates such as the GNP implicit deflator. Recall from Chapter 2 that government purchases includes the cost of non-marketed public services such as the Internal Revenue Service. Arriving at a price index for federal government purchases therefore implies successful estimation of the "price" change for these nonmarketed services. Moreover, if increases in productivity in these services occur, the quality of such services has increased. If no change in the price occurs, a quality increase lowers the effective price of the service. Therefore, in calculating whether or not an effective price increase has occurred in such nonmarketed public services, it is necessary to separate quality induced price changes from "pure" price changes. We shall not pursue this problem further, but our recognition of it should counsel caution in the interpretation of small changes in the GNP implicit deflator.

Our overall interpretation of the implicit price deflator's movements must match its broad definition if we are to generate meaningful information from its analysis. If the deflator rises by 5 percent, then the estimated average price of all goods and services comprising the GNP has risen in price by that amount. Indeed, such a rise could occur in a period when the cost of living, which refers to only consumer prices, was falling or remaining constant.

Measuring Consumer Prices: The CPI

Prices are popularly of most concern as they affect the consumer. The *Consumer Price Index (CPI)* maintained by the U.S. Department of Labor measures only the price movements of goods bought as consumer items. To do this, a "market basket" of 400 goods and services that are typically purchased by urban wage earners and clerical workers is priced on a comparative basis each month in various locations throughout the country. Types of goods and services involved in the index are new and used cars, furniture and other durables, nondurables, consumer services, food items, rental and home ownership services, fuel and utilities, household furnishings, apparel, transportation, medical care, services, and recreation.

The specific basket of goods that is the basis for the consumer price index is changed from time to time to reflect changes in consumer living standards. Generally speaking, this basket is designed to reflect the expense of all major items upon which the consumer spends a portion of his income. Several different breakdowns of the index are regularly published including a breakdown of prices by type of good or service, a breakdown by category of expense, and a geographical breakdown of prices in various parts of the country. Table 3–4 shows the index broken down by major category of consumer expense.

Several of the eight major categories of expense in Table 3–4 are mixtures of durable goods that last for several years and nondurables or services with very short useful lives. Monthly computation of the index creates a problem with the durable portion of such categories since it is not reasonable to reflect the entire amount of an increase in price in the index when the durable good may be purchased only once every 2 or 3 years. The transportation category is a case in point. It contains the cost of automobile use by consumers that involves the price of newly purchased automobiles. But, since a typical consumer buys a car only once every 2 or 3 years or more, a fractional part of the automobile value is included in the index for a particular year or month. Thus, only a fraction of any price increase in auto-

Table 3–4

Consumer Price Index

	1973 INDEX (1967 = 100)
Food	141.4
Housing	135.0
Apparel and Upkeep	126.8
Transportation	123.8
Medical Care	137.7
Personal Care	125.2
Reading and Recreation	125.9
Other Goods and Services	129.0
All Items	133.1

Source: U.S. Department of Labor, Bureau of Labor Statistics.

mobiles is contained in the index. This fractional system is applied to all goods with service lives longer than the time period of the index and is applied in reverse to items purchased more than once in the index time period, e.g., bread, milk. The result of this procedure is essentially to weight the costs of each category of expenditure in Table 3–4 by the fraction it absorbs on the average of the typical consumer's budget.

In constructing the index, resource limitations require at least two less than comforting computational simplifications. The first deals with the measurement of quality changes. As with the GNP deflator, when the quality of a good or service in the consumer's "basket" is increased, any accompanying price increase for the good or service must be adjusted to take the increased quality into account. So the actual price of a good could steadily increase but if this were accompanied by a steady increase in quality, the calculated CPI component might well be unchanged. Thus, quality changes are an important influence on calculated price movements.

The measurement of quality changes by the Bureau of Labor Statistics is reportedly done in essentially a survey fashion based on statements furnished by the involved producers. For example, automobile manufacturers furnish information on the portion of a particular model price change that they feel is due to quality as opposed to "pure" price. The Bureau then decides whether to accept or modify this recommendation. This procedure may not be without bias and could cause the index to inaccurately reflect true price change.

The second important computational simplification in the index has to do with the use of fixed weights for combining the individual component indices. As earlier outlined, these weights are intended to reflect budgetary proportions of the typical consumer. In computing the index, the weights are maintained at fixed values for periods of several years. To the extent that systematic trends exist either over time or with respect to general business conditions in the actual proportions of the consumer's budget allocated to the various CPI components, the calculated index will inappropriately weight individual prices in arriving at the total price index. To some observers, such systematic trends seem a distinct possibility.

The quality accounting and fixed weight limitations of the CPI suggest its primary use should be as a rough gauge of general consumer prices. Accordingly, small month-to-month changes in the index should not be the basis of conclusive statements about current changes in price trends. Rather, patterns of change that persist over several months are a sounder basis for defensible interpretations. This observation is strengthened by an additional characteristic of the CPI—some of the individual component indices are only estimated quarterly, while others are estimated monthly. Thus, the reported CPI will often tend to have a bumpy character on a month-to-month basis. The basic point is important enough for restatement: Interpretations of small short-run changes in the CPI should be made with extreme caution due to the basic limitations of the CPI as a measuring device.

The consumer price index is the most common basis for statements as to the change in the cost of living. This makes the index a key data source for analyzing inflation as it affects the consumer. A 5 percent rise in the CPI is usually interpreted as a 5 percent rise in the cost of living. With cost-of-living escalator clauses in many major union contracts, small ripples in the CPI can result in increasingly large waves in the economy. Increases in the CPI result automatically in some wage increases that in turn result in higher unit costs and lower corporate profit margins. This may lead to price increases undertaken to restore profit margins, resulting in further increases in the CPI. This circular pattern can be a source of inflationary pressures in which the CPI plays a central role.

Measuring Wholesale Prices: The WPI

The *Wholesale Price Index (WPI)* encompasses a series of indices measuring the change in prices for various materials, commodities, and other goods sold at the wholesale level to manufacturers for further processing into end-use items. The indices are published monthly by the U.S. Department of Labor's Bureau of Labor Statistics and are widely used to indicate changes in the profit margin positions of producers due to production cost increases. They are often interpreted as a signal of probable future price changes at the end-user level. That is, when the WPI is rising substantially, the suggestion is that some price increase at the end-use level will be necessary to restore producer profit margins to former levels.

The WPI is broken down in several ways. Two such breakdowns are shown in Table 3–5 and Table 3–6. In Table 3–5 wholesale prices are categorized according to the type of commodity involved irrespective of the industrial segment in which the commodity is used. This provides a picture of the cost situation for specific product areas and indicates which commodity areas are having the greatest influence on overall patterns of consumer prices. The combined index for all commodities is calculated by weighting each component index by weights that reflect its revenue proportion. Thus, the index for all commodities in Table 3–5 is a single measure of the general pattern of all wholesale prices.

Table 3–6 presents a breakdown of the WPI by stage of processing. The component indices in this table show wholesale prices appropriate to industrial segments in crude materials, intermediate, and finished goods production stages in the economy irrespective of the type of commodity involved. The index for each component in Table 3–6 reflects the commodity prices for all commodities appropriate to that industry component. This breakdown enables influences on overall wholesale prices to be traced to their origin in the stages of production. It is often used as the basis for statements about how near or distant measured changes in overall wholesale prices are from end-user prices.

Table 3–5

Wholesale Price Indices, by Major Commodity Groups

	1973 INDEX (1967 = 100)	
Farm Products		176.3
Processed Foods and Feeds		148.1
Industrial Commodities		127.0
Textile Products and Apparel	123.8	
Hides, Skins, Leather, and Related Products	143.1	
Fuels and Related Products and Power	145.5	
Chemicals and Allied Products	110.0	
Rubber and Plastic Products	112.4	
Lumber and Wood Products	177.2	
Pulp, Paper, and Allied Products	122.1	
Metals and Metal Products	132.8	
Machinery and Equipment	121.7	
Furniture and Household Durables	115.2	
Nonmetallic Mineral Products	130.2	
Transportation Equipment, Motor Vehicles and Equipment	119.2	
Miscellaneous Products	119.7	
All Commodities		135.5

Source: U.S. Department of Labor, Bureau of Labor Statistics.

Table 3–6

Wholesale Price Indices, by Stage of Processing

	1973 INDEX (1967 = 100)	
Crude Materials		174.0
Foodstuffs and Feedstuffs	179.6	
Nonfood Materials, Except Fuel	161.5	
Fuel	164.5	
Intermediate Materials, Supplies, and Components		131.9
Materials and Components for Manufacturing	127.8	
Food Manufacturing Materials	146.0	
Nondurable Manufacturing Materials	121.5	
Durable Manufacturing Materials	133.7	
Components	121.4	
Materials and Components for Construction	136.7	
Finished Goods		129.5
Consumer Finished Goods	131.2	
Foods	146.4	
Other Nondurable Goods	125.9	
Durable Goods	115.8	
Producer Finished Goods	123.5	
All Commodities		135.5

Source: U.S. Department of Labor, Bureau of Labor Statistics.

As in Table 3–5, the All Commodities index in Table 3–6 is a weighted combination of the stage of processing components, and it produces the same value as that of Table 3–5 for the commodity components. This equality must hold since both are alternative presentations of the same basic price data matrix, which is classified on a two-dimensional stage of processing and commodity-type basis. That is, each primary price index applies to a particular commodity used in a particular stage of processing. Cumulating along the stage of processing dimension gives the Table 3–6 breakdown while cumulating along the commodity dimension gives the Table 3–5 categories.

Generalizations on Price Indices

Our discussion of price indices has indicated at least three characteristics of these indices that appear to be generally shared by broadly based price indices. The first is that they are based upon samples of information, both geographically and from the standpoint of the goods and services covered by the index. This interposes a sampling error in the calculation of any general price index. An illustration of this error is found in the estimation of the consumer price index. In trying to estimate changes in nationwide consumer costs, we must seek a sample that is geographically representative. In addition, the sample must be representative of the typical basket of goods. It should be clear that the best of indices will always contain an element of sampling error related to these factors.

The second characteristic common to price indices is the adjustment for product or commodity change. As our discussion of the CPI illustrated, if we are to correctly measure the change in the price of a good over time, the actual selling prices must be adjusted to account for any product changes that occurred. We have observed that this adjustment defies the precision many analysts would like and imparts a similar lack of precision to the index itself.

The third characteristic is the dependence of the indices upon a scheme of fixed weights to combine various components in the index. All the indices now discussed except the GNP implicit deflator rely upon such fixed weights. As our CPI discussion pointed out, to the extent the true weights vary nonrandomly with some pertinent variable such as the level of business activity, a fixed weight index will incorrectly weight component part estimates. In summary, our discussion has indicated some of the limitations of price indices by highlighting the imperfect nature of these indices. It is well to keep these limitations in mind when attempting to interpret changes in published indices.

The NBER Economic Indicators

The National Bureau of Economic Research, or NBER as it is commonly called, is an organization that has for decades been concerned with the formulation of measures of overall business activity. The NBER has generated and studied many hundreds of economic time series on variables related to overall economic behavior. The bureau's approach to the study of economic indicators has been pragmatic and not directed by adherence to any branch of economic theory. Indicators of economic change are judged by the Bureau to be important if they correspond closely with fluctuations in the general course of economic activity. Indicators are classified into those that lead the course of business, those that are coincident with the course of business activity, and those that lag behind the course of general business. In judging the performance of a series, the NBER focuses upon its behavior at the points where expansionary peaks and recessionary troughs occur. A series that consistently corresponds with economic peaks and troughs is assigned high relevance by the NBER. We now consider some of the indicators developed and maintained by the NBER, beginning with the leading indicators, followed by the coincident and lagging indicators.

An important leading indicator of trends in general business is the average work week of production workers in manufacturing. This measure has proven more sensitive than other employment based measures in measuring developing changes in output levels, as producers typically have shown a preference for hours worked adjustments rather than employment adjustments during early phases of business upswings and downswings. Thus, significant changes in weekly hours worked usually signal upcoming changes in output and, eventually, in employment. Since the series is published monthly in the *Business Conditions Digest,* it offers current evidence on likely changes in aggregate output.

Two related measures of considerable importance in deriving indications of impending output changes are the level of new orders for durable goods and contracts and orders for plant and equipment, both of which are available in *Business Conditions Digest* and elsewhere. These series represent new purchase commitments for producers' machinery and equipment. They differ in details of coverage and in data sources. Each represents a proxy for the demand forecasts and forward market expectations of producers. As market projections and general expectations change, producers are likely to reflect these changes in their new equipment purchase commitments as well as in their production plans and schedules. Since both series are available monthly, they add further current evidence on the direction of output trends.

Another leading indicator is the new building permits issued for private housing units. Also available monthly, this series reflects the expectations of real estate investors and families as to future economic conditions. Since housing has been an important source of volatility in the overall GNP in recent years, a direct gauge of probable upcoming spending patterns in this segment of investment activity becomes a useful source of information about overall economic conditions.

The leading indicators now discussed share the property of directly measuring movements in variables that comprise the level of business activity. Other less direct indicators of economic activity considered to be key leading indicators by the NBER are claims for unemployment insurance, new business formations, change in the value of business inventories, industrial prices for materials, stock prices, corporate profits, ratio of manufacturing prices to costs, and the change in consumer installment debt.

Rises in industrial materials prices and rises in the ratio of prices to unit labor costs both historically associate with current short-term general expenditure changes and with later increases in aggregate output levels. We may draw from this the suggestion that the two price measures may be a useful gauge of current expenditure intensities. A second feature of the price, unit wage-cost ratio, is that the denominator is a function both of changes in hourly wage costs and hourly labor productivity. That is, cost per man-hour divided by units per man-hour yields cost per unit. This means that increases in output per man-hour will lower per unit labor costs and raise the price-cost ratio. Since increases in output per man-hour have often accompanied expansions in production levels, the price-cost ratio would tend to rise in response, even if no rise occurred in product prices.

Consumer installment debt is a leading indicator primarily because increases in this series denote increases in the pool of spendable money by consumers. Also, since this debt is usually incurred during the process of purchase, a close correspondence can be drawn between increases in debt levels and increases in spending. However, of potentially greater importance is the indication that changes in consumer installment debt provides concerning the general expectations and attitudes of the consumer. During periods where outstanding credit is either declining or growing at an abnormally slow pace, the consumer is exhibiting a cautious attitude toward increasing his debt burden, an attitude that likely carries over into other spending plans and activities. The interested reader is invited to analyze this and each of the other leading indicators in the *BCD* publication wherein historical patterns are graphically presented.

The NBER's coincident indicators rise and fall concurrently with the level of general business, reaching their peaks and troughs at about the same time as the peaks and troughs in general business. The coincident indicators the Bureau considers most reliable are the number of employees in nonagricultural establishments, the unemployment rate, the constant dollar GNP, the Federal Reserve Board Index of Industrial Production, Personal Income, Manufacturing and Trade Sales, and Sales of Retail Stores. Considering this list, the question may occur, "If the GNP and the index of industrial production, etc., are coincident *indicators* of general economic activity, what is the definitive *measure* of that activity to which the indicators apply?" The Bureau's response generally is that there is no single quantitative measure that captures all aspects of general business fluctuations. Instead, the NBER relies upon agreement among most of the indicators that a change in the direction of business activity is occurring in formulating a conclusion that the course of general business is changing.

In reviewing the coincident indicators, the real GNP and the level of personal income are related measures flowing from the national income accounting system. Similarly, the measures of total nonagricultural employment and unemployment rate are clearly related measures as indicated in our earlier discussion. The two sales series provide an indication of the intensity of activity at the final goods level of the economy, somewhat similar to the GNP although more restrictive in coverage. The Index of Industrial Production captures a still different dimension of productive activity as our earlier discussion of this measure indicated.

The NBER lagging indicators provide confirmation of changes in business activity, thereby aiding in the assessment of when a substantial change in business activity has occurred. The major lagging series of the NBER are the unemployment rate for persons unemployed 15 weeks or longer, business spending on plant and equipment, the book value of manufacturing and trade inventories, the labor cost per unit of output, the level of commercial and industrial loans outstanding, and bank rates on short-term business loans. Among these, the employment series captures the growth or decline in the level of lingering unemployment, often a result of substantial fluctuations in production levels. Plant and equipment spending by business is the result of an extensive planning process in which proposals are prepared, plans drawn, contracts let, and finally, expenditures made. This imparts a lagging property to these expenditures that constitutes an important source of confirmation for conclusions about shifts in the level of business activity.

Inventories provide further confirmation due to their role as a buffer between production and sales. When market demand falls off, inventories often rise due to the failure of production levels to correctly anticipate the decline. Labor costs per unit lag general business fluctuations due presumably to the existence of substantial fixed labor costs such that output changes and unit labor cost changes move in opposite directions to an important degree. Finally, the bank loan and interest rate series are lagging indicators presumably due to the contractual nature of loan commitments and to a lesser extent interest costs. As business declines, business loans are terminated or reduced upon expiration in larger numbers. Thus changes in these financial variables are added confirmation of previous output changes.

Of the NBER series, the leading indicators are of most interest since they are of some predictive value. To provide a single summary measure of the 12 leading indicators, the NBER maintains a composite index that combines all the leading series. The composite of leading indicators is a common summary measure of the NBER data.

Plant Utilization Rates

The rates at which plant capacity is utilized in manufacturing and related industries is an often used measure of overall business activity. Capacity utilization is measured in the fall and in the spring as part of the McGraw-Hill Plant and Equipment survey. The results of this survey are published in *Business Week*. In the survey, manufacturers are asked to compare their actual operating levels with desired levels, both of which are expressed in percent of physical capacity. Thus an industry may have an actual operating rate of 93 percent of capacity and a desired rate of 91 percent, meaning that the typical firm in that industry is operating at a level of output above that at which it would prefer to operate for maximum efficiency. Such a condition would be expected to build pressures for expansion of plant if the level of operations was considered to be more than temporarily high. Operating levels substantially below desired levels would likewise dampen the firm's investment plans if it was considered more than temporarily low. In addition to the McGraw-Hill survey, the Commerce Department maintains a similar index of capacity utilization.

With the array of business indicators and measures available to the analyst of modern business, it is perhaps to be expected that a particular set of data will not produce an uncontested interpretation. Some analysts who place greater emphasis on indicators suggesting weakness will hold pessimistic positions. The opposite position will be held by those who place greater emphasis on measures that happen to be upward pointing. Although a considerable degree of art remains in the interpretation of any specific array of indicators, more sophisticated analysts typically incorporate as broad-gauged a grouping of measures as possible into their projections—and then remain cautiously unsure of their results.

The discussion of national income accounting and other measures of business activity in this and the previous chapter has revealed major ingredients in the system of data that regularly reports on performance of the U.S. economy. In the next chapter, we turn to the beginning of a consideration of principal channels and mechanisms that economists believe are influential in explaining performance of the U.S. economy. We initiate this discussion by considering the explanation of equilibrium in the aggregate economy.

Discussion Questions

1. Can you think of a circumstance where the Index of Industrial Production could fall while the GNP was rising? Explain.

2. Consider a businessman who produces a made-to-order line of machinery. Is the GNP or the Index of Industrial Production more relevant for the formulation of a close-up perspective as to where the economy is headed with respect to his product?

3. What impact do you think the widespread availability of day-care centers would have on the statistics of employment? Make your assumptions explicit in your answer.

4. Consult some data on (a) real GNP and (b) total employment. Graph these data, both on a quarterly basis and an annual basis. Do you find any unusual patterns? Is the relationship more stable on a quarterly basis or on an annual basis? Can you explain why?

5. Assume that a gasoline shortage has caused a great abbreviation in the service provided by retail gasoline dealers, in effect lowering the quality of

the total product sold by these dealers. If the price of gasoline remains constant during the period when the quality declines, what should the impact be upon the price index for gasoline used in the consumer price index?

6. Which is a better measure of inflation, the GNP implicit price deflator or the consumer price index? Why?

7. Consult the data on leading economic indicators in *Business Conditions Digest*. Can you find instances where the leading indicators called a "false" signal of an upcoming business reversal? Can you find reasons for the indicators giving false signals?

8. Of what use are lagging indicators?

9. Stock prices are considered a leading indicator. Why do you suppose they have played this role historically in the United States?

10. Consult data on wholesale prices and on consumer prices. Is it true that wholesale prices invariably rise and fall in advance of consumer prices, such that wholesale price changes are a signal for upcoming consumer price changes? Does there seem to be any regularity in the lead that wholesale prices exhibit over consumer prices? Do you think wholesale prices are a useful, practical gauge in judging probable changes in future consumer prices?

4

Production and Supply
in the Economy

"What determines the level of the GNP?" This question occupies our discussion in this chapter and the next several that follow. In this chapter, we consider the nature of the decision to increase or decrease output levels by the nation's business firms under conditions where slack exists in the full utilization of labor and other inputs. We begin by considering production decisions at the level of the firm and industry and then at the level of the entire economy. The general nature of supply in the U.S. economy is discussed. Finally, a simple and provisional aggregate supply model is formulated as the basis for further discussion of output determination in the economy. In Chapter 16, we return to this subject in light of the intervening flow of macroeconomic ideas to develop a more precise view of labor market influences upon the production and employment levels in the economy. However, our concern with aggregate supply cannot await that later point because supply behavior plays an important role in the determination of the level of the GNP in any particular time period.

Production and Supply by Firms

Our first concern is with understanding the basic reasons why business firms change the prevailing level of output. To consider this question, we initially focus on the decisions of a typical producer in the economy and assume that the actions of such a typical producer will reflect the actions of the entire array of producers that comprise the supply side of the nation's mar-

47

kets for goods and services. The theory of microeconomics has given extensive consideration to the production decisions of individual producers in various market environments.[1] One of the central propositions of the microeconomic theory of production is that increases in output over a short-run period will be accompanied by falling marginal productivity of labor and rising marginal costs. Accordingly, producers contemplating an increase in output must also contemplate that rising marginal costs of production will accompany the change.

To make our discussion more specific, we consider the simplified case of a producer that has only two productive resources involved in its production process. These are (1) a flow of capital services coming from a stock of capital assets. Both the stock of assets and the flow of capital services are assumed to be fixed in the short-run and variable in the long-run. And (2) a flow of labor services that constitute the only variable productive resource in the short-run. The cost curves for such a producer are shown in Figure 4–1. The marginal cost curve shows how unit costs change as output changes, while the average cost curve shows the way average unit costs change with output. As seen, marginal costs tend to rise with output increases, primarily due to the less efficient use of additional labor as output is increased. That is, as the fixed capital stock is used more intensively, the variable labor resource is less and less productive.

If we now assume prices are taken by the individual producer to be beyond his control and fixed at P_0 in the short-run, either by the operation of competitive markets or because they are administered in a manner partially independent of demand, then we may find the output level that provides maximum profits for the producer. In Figure 4–1, output level Q_0 is the profit maximizing output level. At Q_0, the level of output is sufficiently high to raise the marginal production costs to the level of product prices. At output levels less than Q_0, the production of an additional unit of output adds to revenues by the amount of the product price, while adding to total costs by the amount of the marginal costs. Since all output levels lower than Q_0 are accompanied by the condition that price is greater than marginal cost, the production of such units increases profits by adding more to revenues than to costs. Profits are maximized by the production of all units in which price exceeds marginal costs. Output levels greater than Q_0 reduce total profits because they add more to costs than they add to revenues.

We define pure profits as the excess of revenues over costs, i.e., we state:

Pure Profits = (Quantity)(Price) − (Quantity)(Average Cost)
          = (Quantity)(Price − Average Cost)

[1] For an extensive consideration of this subject, see Richard Leftwich, *The Price System and Resource Allocation*, 5th ed., Dryden Press, Hindsdale, Ill., 1973.

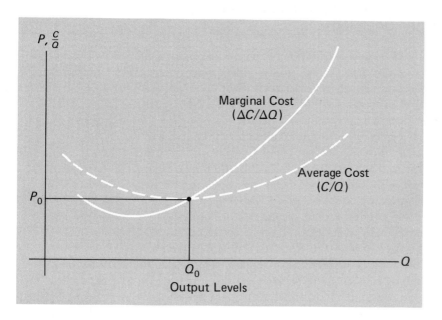

Figure 4–1

Production Levels in the Firm

When price equals average cost, no pure profits exist. The word "pure" is vital to our understanding of the meaning of production at price equals average cost. The average cost curve in Figure 4–1 is assumed to contain the opportunity cost associated with producing in the particular industry the producer is concerned with. This opportunity cost is the profit available to the producer from employing the firm's productive resources in the most profitable alternative employment. If the firm can earn a profit above these costs, then its productive resources are being employed in the most profitable alternative use available. If a firm's revenues do not cover these costs, then it is operating at a loss in terms of its potential earnings, even though its level of earnings may produce a positive accounting profit.

An individual producer in a market system where entry of new producers into various industries and exit of existing producers is easy cannot expect to earn pure profits on other than a temporary, transitory basis. The existence of pure profits in a particular industry will spur the entry of new producers into that industry, which will tend to push down prices and lower the level of profits toward the break-even normal level. In an industry realizing less than normal profits, the exit of some producers in search of a normal return will reduce the supply and push the price up toward normal profit levels.

Economy-wide Production and Supply Decisions

We now consider the question "What factors cause the economy's suppliers of products and services in general to increase their level of production under conditions where resources are not fully utilized?" Figure 4–2 helps answer this question. In this figure, we consider an increase in demand for the product of a typical firm, which increases the market price of its product. If the typical firm continues to maximize profits, it will expand its output level along its marginal cost curve. Output will increase from Q_0 to Q_1 in response to the market price from P_0 to P_1. Thus, Figure 4–2 shows that increases in demand in particular industries and for particular firms will initially increase output as prices rise. The price and output expansion in Figure 4–2 produces pure profits for the producers involved. With total sales now equal to $(P_1)(Q_1)$ and total costs equal to $(AC_1)(Q_1)$, the level of pure profits is given by the shaded rectangle in Figure 4–2.

But what if the increase in demand is more general than just for a few firms or a few select industries? Suppose the increase in demand we have now considered exists in all industries. Profits rise above normal levels

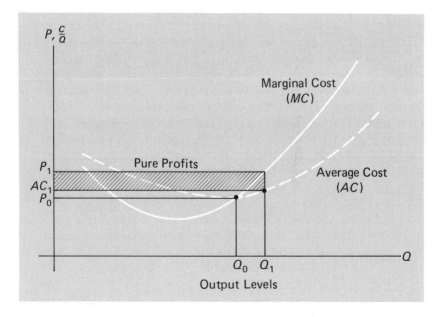

Figure 4–2
Shifts in Demand and Prices

across the entire economy, and output is increased in all industries along the marginal cost curves of the producers in each industry. The implication is that economy-wide increases in demand for products and services are accompanied by increases in production, higher prices, and higher profits for business firms. While true enough at first glance, side-effects are created by an economy-wide expansion in demand that may alter this result. The first is the impact on materials and other such costs that an expansion in output in all industries may have. If materials are in limited supply, an economy-wide increase in demand may push up their prices, increase the costs of industry in general, and reduce the pure profits.

The second effect is upon wages. If the demand for labor throughout the economy increases, wage rates may be pushed up as producers face a tightening labor market, particularly as full-employment is approached. Shortages in various labor categories may emerge that will increase the upward pressures on wages. A wage increase will further contribute to reducing the level of pure profits. Accordingly, the side effects of an economy-wide increase in demand may undo the initial increase in business profits.

Figure 4–3 shows one possible outcome of these reactions to an increase in demand in the economy. The pressures on wages and materials

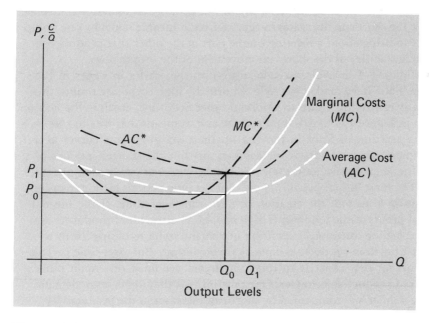

Figure 4–3
Shifts in Output Levels

maximizing level of production along a now lower marginal cost curve. Such a shift could at least in part offset the upward shift in the cost curves associated with the upward pressures on wages.

Figure 4–5 shows recent U.S. patterns in both output per man-hour and output in manufacturing. Output per man-hour is a measure of the average productivity of labor. When it is rising, the average unit labor cost is falling, if wage rates are held constant. Figure 4–5 shows that labor productivity and output levels have generally moved together in the United States. Accordingly, it is not unreasonable to assume that the short-run expansion of output will at least partially relieve wage induced pressures on unit costs by increases in labor productivity.

Perhaps the most important influence upon the short-run response of producers to changes in demand can be found in the characteristic shape of the marginal cost curves of individual producers, as illustrated by Figure 4–6. This figure reflects the situation where the typical producer's marginal costs are substantially constant until their capacity level of output, Q_c, is reached, at which point marginal costs increase rapidly. In this circumstance, a minor increase in product prices, such as from P_0 to P_1, will associate with a large increase in the profit-maximizing level of output from Q_0 to Q_1. Such minor increases in prices may occur indirectly, by the reduction of customary discounts, by the deletion of product "extras," or by the reduction in product quality by a small amount. As such, small price increases may not result in noticeable pure profits and may not induce labor to demand wage increases to restore their "fair" share of national income. If increases in productivity associated with increases in demand should offset any wage increases associated with higher general demand for labor, the cost curves would remain reasonably constant as demand increases. Given flat curves as in Figure 4–6, the short-run effect of increases in demand is to cause substantial additional output to be produced at only slightly higher prices.

As output in the typical firm is expanded beyond the range where marginal costs are approximately flat, we should expect to see more rapidly rising prices, increases in wages above productivity, and rising average and marginal costs.

Supply Behavior in the United States

In the United States, there is reason to believe that producers do respond to increases in demand under less than full employment conditions as if their marginal cost curves were flat and shaped like that shown in

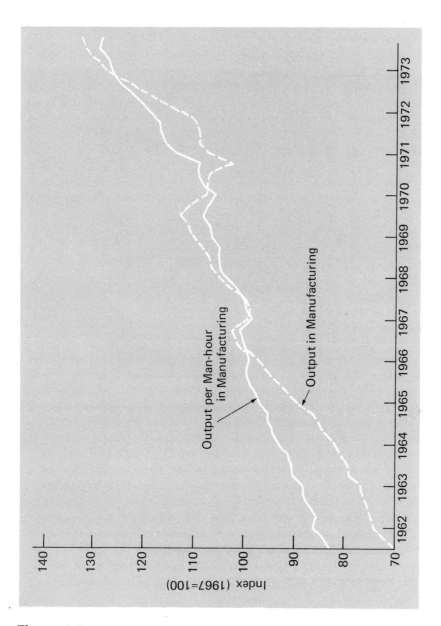

Figure 4–5

Trends in Output per Man-hour

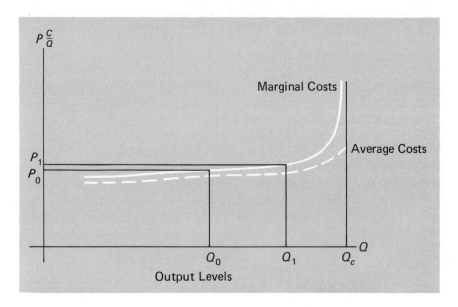

Figure 4–6

Cost-Output Relationships

Figure 4–6. Table 4–1 shows some data relevant to this point. Comparative changes in production levels, wage rates, productivity of labor, unit labor costs, product prices, and average capacity utilization rates are shown for two periods in the United States, involving both moderate levels of capacity utilization and high levels of capacity utilization. Over the 5 year period 1961–1965, the table shows that production in the private sector increased by better than 25 percent. During the same period, the increase in hourly wages was approximately the same as the increase in labor's output per man-hour, thus resulting in unit labor costs that rose by an average of less than four-tenths of 1 percent per year over the period. This suggests that unit costs remained approximately constant over the period, while output rose substantially. In other words, the wage increases tending to shift up unit cost curves were almost entirely offset by the productivity increases tending to shift the unit cost curves down.

Prices were pushed up only slightly in the 1961–1965 period, rising by less than 1 percent per year while output increased by better than five times that amount. This experience is consistent with the view that in general production took place over regions of marginal cost curves that were approximately flat. However, over the same period of 5 years, substantial ad-

Table 4–1

U.S. Trends in Costs, Prices, and Capacity Use

| | CUMULATIVE CHANGE FROM: | |
	1961–1965	1965–1969
Private Production	+25.4%	+17.3%
Average Wage Rates	+18.8%	+31.0%
Private Output per Man-hour	+16.4%	+ 9.7%
Unit Labor Costs	+ 1.8%	+19.5%
Prices, Private Sector	+ 4.9%	+14.2%
Average Capacity Utilization Rate	83%	89%

Source: Economic Report of the President, 1974.

ditions to capacity and modernization of existing capacity occurred in the United States. This means that changes in the scale of production are intermingled with movements along short-run curves. This blurs any precision we could attach to conclusions drawn from Table 4–1. But it does not detract from the assessment we have now made of the net effect of output expansion, costs, prices, and productivity over the period.

The 1965–1969 period is in sharp contrast to the earlier period. The average rate of capacity utilization has increased from the earlier 83 percent to 89 percent, a rather high level by historical standards. The rate of growth in output is lower than the earlier period while the increase in hourly labor cost is only one-third offset by increases in productivity. The result is a sharp increase in unit labor costs, as upward wage pressures on unit cost curves dominate downward productivity pressures. In addition, a more than 14 percent increase in product prices is required to bring about an increase in output of 17 percent, a result that contrasts sharply with the earlier period and roughly suggests a rising pattern of marginal costs.

Our discussion of the data of Table 4–1 in general indicates that it is consistent with recent U.S. experience to suggest that business firms in the economy behave over time as if their marginal cost curves were rather flat until high rates of capacity utilization are reached, where they then behave as if such curves were upward sloping. In addition, Table 4–1 suggests that when utilization rates are not high, cost curves may be quite stable during output expansions, due to the pressures of wage increases being offset by expansions in labor productivity.

Our discussion so far has focused mostly on the impact of increases in demand upon unit costs, prices, and output decisions of producing firms. For the United States, all appearances are that increases in demand bring about different responses from suppliers than decreases in demand bring. The response of firms to decreases in demand is not likely to be symmetrical to their response to increases in demand. In particular, firms cannot expect their hourly labor costs to decline due to a decrease in the demand for labor. Indeed, these costs may rise for reasons such as the role of organized labor in negotiating regular hourly wage increases regardless of decreased demand for labor and increased unemployment levels. In addition, output per man-hour is influenced by a generally improving level of technology as improved machines, equipment, and techniques are employed and as production becomes generally more capital intensive by employing more capital per hour of labor employed. These factors may offset the tendency of output per man-hour to fall during output contractions as a result of the less efficient use of quasi-fixed labor inputs.

Table 4–2 shows production, labor cost, price, and other data for two recent annual periods in the United States during which private output declined on an annual basis. As seen, during both periods of output decline, hourly labor costs rose. Also, output per man-hour increased somewhat although the rate of increase was less than proportional to the increase in wage rates. As a result of larger wage increases than productivity increases, unit labor costs rose, leading to somewhat higher prices even though output levels declined. This result can be explained by reference to Figure 4–7. In this figure, we again refer to a typical firm producing on the reasonably flat portion of its marginal cost curve. The increase in unit labor costs causes an upward shift in the marginal cost curve from MC to MC'. As a result of this shift in marginal costs, the typical producer cannot supply his product markets at an acceptable profit when prices are P_0. As a result, upward pressures are placed on product prices even though product markets are weak. If product prices do not rise, say because of price controls or social pressures to keep them at P_0, many producers with cost curves similar to those shown in Figure 4–7 will refuse to supply the market, and shortages of the product will develop.

Table 4–2

U.S. Trends in Output, Costs, and Prices in Recession

| | ANNUAL CHANGE FROM: | |
	1957–1958	1969–1970
Private Production	−1.4%	−0.5%
Average Wage Rates	+4.3%	+7.6%
Private Output per Man-hour	+3.2%	+1.1%
Unit Labor Costs	+1.1%	+6.4%
Prices, Private Sector	+2.1%	+4.8%
Average Capacity Utilization Rate	80%	82%

Source: Economic Report of the President, 1974.

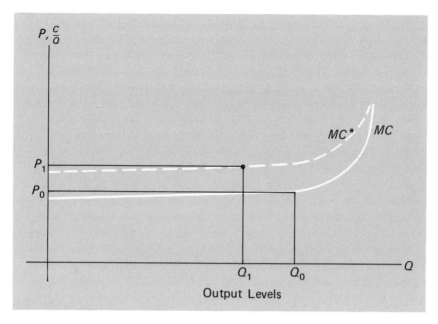

Figure 4–7

Marginal Costs and Output in Recession

These shortages will not be the result of the inability to acquire inputs for the production process. They will simply reflect the unwillingness of a producer in a market economy to supply markets at a personal loss.[2]

We may assume that the situation shown in Figure 4–7 will lead to higher prices sufficient to allow the producer to realize a normal return to his invested resources. Thus, in Figure 4–7, an increased price level of P_1 leads to production of the smaller output level Q_1. While we can not be conclusive on the strict applicability of the Figure 4–7 case to the two recessionary situations shown in Table 4–2, we do find that the logic expressed via the figure is at least consistent with the results produced in the two recessionary periods considered.

A Conclusion on Aggregate Supply

To proceed with our analysis, we assume that marginal cost curves are generally flat over an initial range of under-capacity production. The

---

[2] The price controls in the United States from 1971 to 1974 produced several such examples. To illustrate, cases were reported of farmers destroying young chickens because the cost of raising and bringing them to market outweighed the controlled market price.

result of this is to cause short-run increases in demand to elicit nearly proportional increases in real output and minor increases in price, given that increases in wage rates and material costs do not intervene to shift cost curves upwards. In other words, we assume for now that increases in the demand for labor and other materials at less than capacity levels of output will not push up wages or material prices by an appreciable amount, and that the resulting stability in cost curves leads to a pattern of supply behavior in which increased demand is met by proportionately large output changes and proportionately small price changes. As capacity in various industries in the economy is reached, our assumption must be changed. Increases in demand in the range close to capacity utilization will cause only small and temporary increases in output while causing proportionately large changes in prices, wages, and unit costs. Although we expect that supply relationships are not the same when output is decreasing as when they are increasing, we shall on many occasions treat them as if they were attempting to point out the consequences of this simplification wherever it occurs.

This view of the expected behavior of producers can be summarized by Figure 4–8 in a way useful in our later analysis. In (a) of this figure, the level of demand in the economy in relation to the level of production is shown. Our assumption that suppliers will respond to increases in demand by similar increases in output when production is short of capacity leads to the 45° line relating the two, that is, the relationship between demand and production is one-to-one. If producers find that demand is increasing, they will respond by increasing production on a proportional basis. In other words, if the total level of demand increases by 30 billion, production will similarly increase by 30 billion. At the same time, (b) shows output increases will require only minor price increases until capacity is approached, where prices will have to be increased at a faster pace to induce further output changes. At demand level E_c, productive capacity has been reached, as output is equal to $Q_c = E_c$. Any further expansion in output is impossible. Additional demand will only result in prices being increased proportionately in order to ration the fixed amount of physical output. Although expenditures and dollar-valued production can continue to increase proportionately even beyond capacity levels, the increase in value of production is totally due to price increases once the point $E_c = Q_c$ has been passed.

The shape of the price-production curve in (b) directly reflects the cumulated marginal cost curves of producers throughout the economy. It will be approximately horizontal over the region of output where a predominant number of producers are producing along an approximately horizontal firm-level marginal cost curve. The price-production curve will begin to rise more sharply as more and more producers begin to confront the sharply rising regions of their marginal cost curves.

In Chapter 16, we consider the question of output and employment

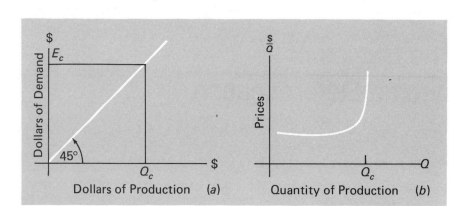

Figure 4–8

Spending, Production, and Prices

determination in more detail in the context of a specific model that focuses upon conditions of supply and demand in the nation's labor markets. For now, Figure 4–8 provides a simple albeit provisional model of the supply behavior of producers in the economy. It becomes useful in the explanation of economic activity when it is related to a model of demand in the economy. In the next chapter, we consider the structure of such a model of aggregate demand.

Discussion Questions

1. What conditions would be necessary for the normal level of profits throughout the economy to undergo a long-run increase? Explain.

2. If marginal costs in the economy are generally rising, what, if anything, can you say about the pattern of the marginal product of labor?

3. If marginal costs are approximately horizontal over a low capacity-utilization range of production, what is implied about the marginal product of labor over this range?

4. Update Table 4–1 for the most recent Commerce Department data. What patterns and implications can you draw from your analysis?

5. Can you think of circumstances where many firms in the economy would not be willing to respond to an increase in demand by increasing output?

6. If marginal costs in the typical firm in the economy are not approximately horizontal over an initial range, but rise steadily throughout all output regions, how is the price-production diagram in Figure 4–8(b) affected?

5

The Basics of
Income Determination

One of the features of the U.S. national income accounting system discussed in Chapter 2 was the production nature of the measure. Whatever the business firms in the country and other producers decide to produce determines the GNP. The total amount of products and services actually demanded and purchased by the nation's consumers, investors, and governments is one step removed from the GNP. If spenders decide to increase their level of expenditure but producers decide not to increase their level of production, nothing happens to the GNP. The only effect on our income accounting statistics is that the level of inventories declines. Of course, it is not realistic to propose that the nation's business firms will make their decisions about output changes with no eye to their level of market demand. The relationship between changes in total market demand and total production levels has an important bearing on our view of how the equilibrium level of the GNP is determined over a period of time. Conditions in money capital markets and other markets also have an effect on equilibrium in markets for products and services. In this chapter, we consider the nature of product market equilibrium and its relation to demand and supply in related markets. We also consider the implication of an important interrelationship between the level of production and the level of total demand —the product market multiplier effect.

Total Demand and Product Market Equilibrium

Final sales of goods and services in the United States are broken into four categories: (1) Consumer Expenditures (C), (2) Fixed Investment (I), (3)

Government Purchases (G), and (4) Net Exports (EX). If we denote the level of final sales as E_f, we may write

$$E_f = C + I + G + EX \qquad (5\text{-}1)$$

Expression 5–1 is true by accounting definition. We may think of E_f as measuring the total level of intended final demand in the economy as long as we are willing to assume that those who demand goods in these four categories are able to actually spend the amounts they intend to spend. That is, intended spending will equal actual final sales as long as an insignificantly small number of purchasers are turned away by producers unwilling or unable to furnish the products and services demanded. It is crucial to recognize that final sales are not the same as the GNP. The difference is inventory investment. In Expression 5–1, I is defined as fixed investment. The comparable term in the accounting GNP identity, gross private domestic investment, contains inventory investment as well. If inventories are growing, then the level of total production, GNP, will exceed the level of final sales, E_f. If inventory levels are dropping, then final sales are rising above production levels. Denoting the level of inventory investment, or inventory change, as INV, we have the following relationship between final sales and GNP:

$$GNP = E_f + INV \qquad (5\text{-}2)$$

With our assumption that final sales approximates intended final spending, Expression 5–2 may be interpreted as showing that when intended final spending is above total production, the result will be falling inventories. Similarly, inventories will rise when production levels exceed intended spending. To be more precise in our discussion of inventories, we should recognize that some additions to inventories by business firms are intentional, in order to expand finished goods inventories or to put more goods into production. (Inventory investment includes work-in-process.) Accordingly, we can partition inventory investment into a planned or intended portion, INV_f, and an unplanned or unintended portion, INV_u, such that $INV = INV_f + INV_u$. With this further delineation, we may slightly rewrite Expression 5–1 as

$$E_f = C + I + G + EX + INV_f \qquad (5\text{-}3)$$

which also leads to a slight restatement of Expression 5–2 as

$$GNP = E_f + INV_u \qquad (5\text{-}4)$$

Expression 5–3 adds to the total intended spending on final goods the

amount of intended investment in inventories by business firms. Expression
5–4 similarly shows that the difference between total intended spending and
total production is not the total level of inventory investment, but the unintended portion of this total.

To illustrate this distinction, consider a situation where a GNP of
500 is produced. Intended consumer spending is 250, intended fixed investment is 150, intended government spending is 110, and intended inventory
investment is 5. Total intended spending is 515. Thus, inventories actually
fall by 15, the amount by which demand exceeds production. Since intended
inventory investment was +5 while total inventory investment was −15,
a level of unintended inventory investment of −20 actually occurred in the
period. Such a situation indicates that production decisions of business
firms underestimated the actual level of demand. During such periods when
E_f is greater than GNP (INV_u is negative), the level of business inventories
falls below desired levels. When GNP is greater than E_f, then INV_u is positive and production levels are running ahead of sales in the entire economy.
As a result, inventories rise above the levels desired by business.

Imbalances between production and sales represented by either positive or negative levels of unintended inventory investment are of key significance in our discussion of aggregate equilibrium because they can be
expected to precipitate changes in the level of output produced. As inventories fall below desired levels because demand exceeds production, market
projections and sales forecasts have in general been too low, and some firm-
ing of prices occurs. As a result, production schedules are increased, thereby
enlarging the level of the GNP. If inventories rise above desired levels,
then production exceeds final sales, and sales forecasts have been too high.
As this becomes apparent, production levels are cut back, thereby decreasing
the size of the GNP. A continual process of such adjustments retains a balance between production levels and sales levels over time.

We are not implying by this discussion that all upward or downward
movements in the GNP are touched off by imbalances in sales and production. If business in general forecasts an increase in demand, a larger GNP
will result without the motivation of less-than-desired inventories. However, we could expect the larger GNP to be sustained only in the case that
the higher forecasts were on target, so that a market existed for the larger
output levels. The reverse is true when business in general anticipates a
decrease in demand. A smaller GNP would logically be produced and sustained only in the case the forecasts proved correct.

We have now discussed two mechanisms motivating changes in the
level of GNP: (1) unintended inventory change, as a signal of production-
sales imbalances and (2) changes in forecasted market demand. The GNP
is at a sustainable level when inventories are at desired levels, when sales
and production are in balance, and when forecast sales and actual sales are

equal. More specifically, we may describe the condition for equilibrium as

$$E_f = \text{GNP} \tag{5-5}$$

which corresponds to the condition that $INV_u = 0$. Expression 5–5 describes a situation where the amount of production flowing from the economy's business firms matches the amount of spending taking place by consumers, investors, and governments. No motivation is present for producers to change their level of production. This condition is graphically illustrated in Figure 5–1. In this figure, the 45° line summarizes the behavior of suppliers in responding to demand changes, as discussed in Chapter 4, and the line DD represents the total level of intended spending $(E_f)_0$, which at this point we assume to be constant. At all production levels to the left of GNP_0, intended spending exceeds production levels, inventory levels will be drawn down below intended levels, and we may expect output to be increased in response. To the right of GNP_0, production levels are above demand, unplanned inventories accumulate, and we may expect production to be reduced in response. Only at GNP_0 are production levels in balance with demand, thereby generating no motivation for change.

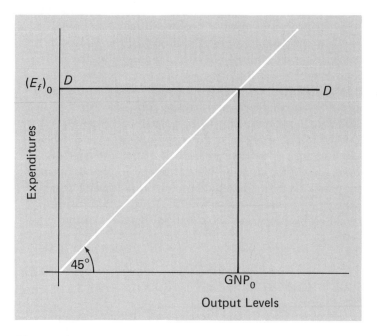

Figure 5–1
Aggregate Equilibrium

Inventory-Sales Relationships in the United States

In the United States, if producers planned to add 10 billion to inventories, but if the actual GNP rose only 4 billion above final sales, then the level of measured inventories would rise by 4 billion, but would remain 6 billion below the desired level. The national income accounting system would show a rise in inventories, but would result in a ratio between inventories and output levels that is less than that generally desired by business. In the case of a drop in final sales below the current GNP, the situation would be reversed. Output would be greater than spending, inventories would rise above intended levels, and the ratio of inventories to sales would rise to abnormally high levels.

Because of the value of inventory-sales ratios in judging the balance between output and inventory accumulation, data on such ratios are maintained by the Department of Commerce for various industrial sectors in the United States—for manufacturing, wholesale, and retail trade, and overall for all groups. In Figure 5–2 the overall ratio is plotted along with the corresponding change in the real GNP, both measured quarterly. Figure 5–2 shows that periods of rapidly rising GNP correspond well with periods when the inventory-sales ratio is falling, presumably to lower than desired levels, and vice versa for periods of slowly rising or falling GNP. Points $P_1 - P_6$ and $T_1 - T_5$ are of special interest. Points $P_1 - P_6$ represent the most significant peaks in the inventory-sales ratio. Undoubtedly, inventory-sales ratios were above normal levels at these points, and a portion of the total investment in inventories was unintended and from the producers' point of view, excessive. Associated with all these points is a slow or negative rate of current and recent past growth in the GNP. Points $T_1 - T_5$ represent the most significant troughs in the inventory-sales ratio, when inventories were presumably below desired levels and an unintended disinvestment had occurred. These latter points correspond to periods in which current and recent past growth in GNP had been at a rapid rate. The same general correspondence is apparent throughout the figure, thus illustrating the position of inventory buildups and depletions in signalling output expansion or contraction.

Supply-Demand Interaction: The Multiplier

Equilibrium in the economy has been described as a balance between levels of production and levels of demand. In the United States, levels of production and levels of demand are not independent. A large proportion

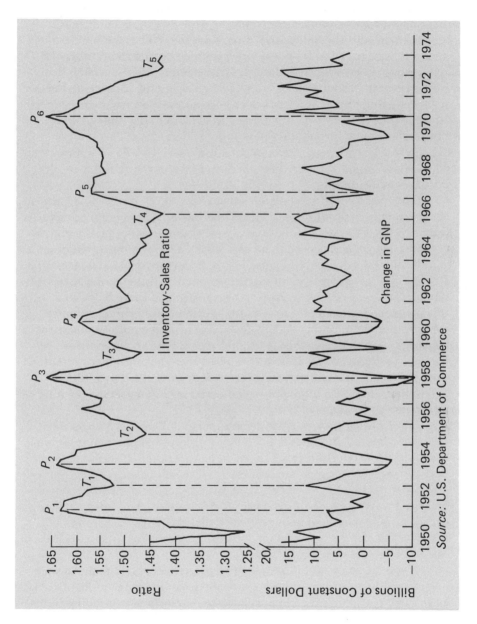

Figure 5–2

Inventory-Output Relationships

of the income created in the production process is paid out to wage earners, lenders, owners, and other factors of production. Indeed, the income flowing from production of the GNP forms the basic flow of spending power for most expenditures on the GNP. Consumer spending is the largest, most significant case in point. If the consumer normally spends more on goods and services as his income is enlarged, then an important connection is apparent between production levels and levels of spending. In general, the act of enlarging production tends to enlarge income flow and thereby enlarge the level of spending. An enlarged level of spending usually can be expected to lead to further increases in production levels. The result of this interaction between production and demand is that the total impact on the GNP of an initial increase in spending is some multiple of the initial spending increase.

The effect is illustrated graphically in Figure 5–3. In this figure, the level of intended spending is shown as rising with the level of output and income. This illustrates that levels of spending and levels of production are not independent, but depend upon each other in the determination of the equilibrium level of each. In Figure 5–3, if the level of demand is given by D_0, the equilibrium level of output/income is Y_0. If the level of demand should shift up by ΔD to D_1, the fact that the demand curve is not horizontal and independent of supply causes the new equilibrium level to be a multiple of the initiating shift in demand. The new equilibrium level of income, Y_1 is thus greater than it would have been had no interaction been present. The ratio $\Delta Y/\Delta D$ is usually referred to as the multiplier.[1] A multiplier of 5 means that an independent shift in total demand by 1 billion will induce a total of 5 billion in total output and income before the interaction runs its course.

The fact that the aggregate demand curve in Figure 5–3 slopes up at a rate less than 45° indicates that a dollar in additional production and income will not produce an entire dollar in new spending. If this were the case, the slope of the aggregate demand curve would be one, or 45°, and any initiating spending increase would cause income and spending to rise forever. A slope of less than 45° means that some nonspending, or saving, occurs during each round of income, such that the multiplier process will run its course in time, as the original increase in spending eventually leaks out of the income spending flow into saving.

A specific analysis of this interactive process as applied to the income and expenditure categories of the United States is illustrated in Figure 5–4. In this figure, the impact of an increase of 100 units in new spending is con-

---

[1] The reader may wish to verify that if D_0 in Figure 5–3 were perfectly horizontal, then ΔY would equal ΔD, and the ratio would equal 1, producing no multiplier effect.

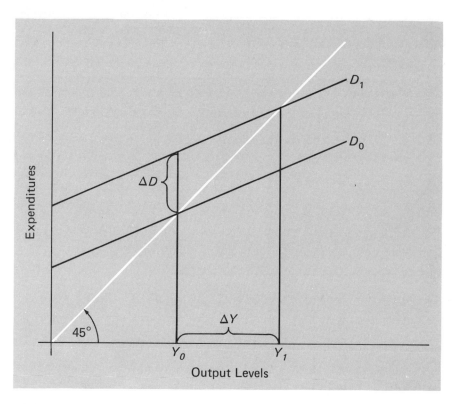

Figure 5–3
Multiplier Effects

sidered. The figure does not reveal the reason for this increase, but we can suppose it to be the result of an upgrading of business expectations, leading to an additional amount of investment spending due entirely to exogenous or outside factors. The immediate result of this expenditure increase is an increase in incomes of the same amount. If we apply the approximate percentage composition of gross national income as that shown in Table 2–4 in Chapter 2, a representative distribution of the 100 units to income recipients shows that total factor payments would rise by about 72 units, largely composed of increased payments of wages and salaries. Business payments of indirect business tax would rise by 8 units. Finally, the remaining 20 units of gross national income would be retained by business as pretax profits. Upon completion of this initial distribution of incomes, a secondary distribution would occur, as further shown in Figure 5–4. The rise of 72 units in factor payments would generate additional tax liabilities by in-

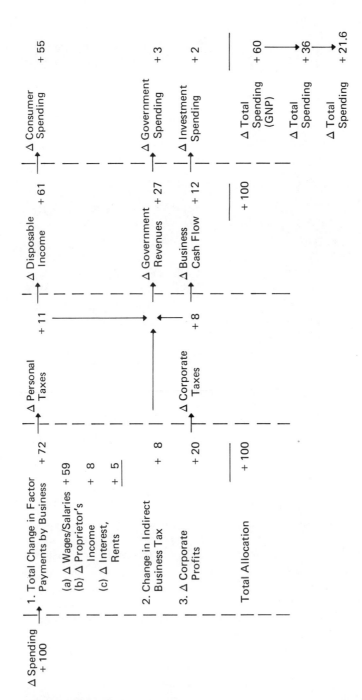

Figure 5–4

creasing personal and other incomes of the factor payees. If we assume this liability to be 15 percent of the increase in income, a secondary distribution of 11 units would occur by the personal income earners to government. Corporations would make a similar secondary distribution due to corporate income tax liabilities. If we assume this liability to be 40 percent of profits, then 8 units would be distributed to government by business. Thus, after the secondary distribution, the income generated by the 100 units in production has been resolved into three primary flows: (1) the disposable income flow, held by consumers; (2) the tax revenue flow, held by government; and (3) the business cash flow, held by business. The nature and extent of the operation of a multiplier process in the U.S. economy is determined by the extent to which changes in the size of these three flows correspond with changes in the spending flows of the income recipients.

Consumer spending is usually seen by economists as reacting systematically and positively to changes in the flow of disposable income. This income relationship is the cornerstone of any significant income expenditure multiplier, due to the large fraction of an increase in aggregate income that is channeled into consumer accounts. However, the consumer income expenditure flow is not the entire reason for a multiplier. Nearly 40 percent of an increase in the GNP typically is distributed among nonconsumer accounts. This means it is important to consider the extent to which changes in the sizes of the two other major income flows generate changes in spending flows by their recipients.

Economists are much less in agreement on the strength and stability of government and business income spending relationships than they are on the relationship between disposable income and consumer spending. Regarding the government taxes-spending relationship, a non-zero multiplier component requires that either local, state, or federal governments systematically adjust spending plans over the course of a budgetary period as that period's actual tax revenues become clear. For example, downward adjustments in spending in the form of (a) the postponement or delay of ongoing programs, or (b) the enactment of latent cost savings in the operation of governmental units might be a logical expectation as a response to the case where less tax revenue was flowing into the government pool than anticipated. The resulting budget deficit, by providing "cannon fodder" to the political opposition, could become intolerable to the incumbent political unit. In the case of state and local governments, spending is largely constrained by tax revenues, due to the unavailability of debt financing for these governments.

Upward adjustments in spending plans in response to additional tax revenues rely on a similar behavioral connection. For example, additional tax revenues (greater than anticipated) would (a) allow marginal programs that had formerly been postponed or delayed to go forward; or (b) enlarge the magnitude of an impending surplus, which would cause the governmental unit to be vulnerable to charges of "fiscal drag" on the economic system; or (c) facilitate cost increases in the operation of governmental units that would otherwise be intolerable. If such a spending-revenue relationship is quantitatively significant, it will add to the value of the overall induced spending associated with an increase in incomes and thereby enlarge the impact of the multiplier. In Figure 5–4 a small positive value for this induced governmental spending has been assumed for illustrative purposes.

The multiplier impact of a spending change is further enlarged if a relationship exists between the size of business cash flows and business investment spending. The significance of business cash flow in investment and some related empirical evidence is discussed in Chapter 8. It suffices here to point out that if business tends to increase investment spending as internal funds generated via cash flow are increasingly available, then a component of induced spending will be associated with increases in the business cash flow pool. Figure 5–4 shows a hypothetical value for such induced expenditures.

The total of these induced spending activities establishes the multiplier that operates in the economic system. In Figure 5–4 the 100 unit initial increase in the GNP generates 60 units of induced spending, which in turn generates an additional 36 units of spending (assuming the same relationships reapply), which in turn generates 21.6 units, and so forth. The total amount of this induced spending can be found by considering the following analytical formulation

$$dY = dE_a + dE_i \qquad\qquad (5–6)$$

where dY is a change in total GNP, dE_a is an initiating or autonomous change in expenditures, and dE_i is the spending induced by the initiating change. Following our discussion, we may formally state that

$$dE_i = b(dY) \qquad\qquad (5–7)$$

where dE_i and dY are as before, and b represents the marginal propensity to spend, or the total of all induced consumer, business, and government spending as a proportion of the initial spending, that is,

$$b = \frac{dE_i}{dY}$$

Then, combining 5–6 and 5–7, we obtain

$$dY = dE_a + b(dY) \qquad\qquad (5–8)$$

which gives

$$dY(1 - b) = dE_a$$

or

$$dY = \frac{1}{(1 - b)} \times dE_a \tag{5-9}$$

The expression $1/(1 - b)$ represents the relationship between an initiating increase in spending and the relating total increase in income and is therefore a multiplier in the arithmetic as well as conceptual sense of the word. The larger the induced spending attributable to increases in the income flows, the larger is the multiplier, since a larger fraction of the initiating spending is returned to the economic system at each round. For the example given in Figure 5–4, a total of 60 units in spending was induced by an increase of 100 units in initial spending, therefore the effective value of b is 0.6. This makes the multiplier equal to $1/(1 - 0.6) = 2.5$, meaning that the total GNP increase generated by the initiating 100 billion would be 100 times 2.5 or 250 units.

The income-expenditure multiplier now discussed applies in two differing ways to relate an initiating change in expenditures to a total resulting change in income. The first deals with a one-time change in the initiating expenditure that is made in the initial period and then withdrawn. The general effect of this type expenditure is shown in Figure 5–5(a). The initiating expenditure, $\Delta E_a = 100$, is withdrawn after period 1. However, its induced effect remains. Assuming $b = 0.6$, in period 2, induced expenditures of $E_a(b) = 100 \times 0.6 = 60$ remain and create additional income and expenditures in period 3, and so on. When the multiplier process is complete, the total amount of new income created is $E_a(1/1 - b) = 250$, as given in Expression 5–9. However, as illustrated in Figure 5–5(b), when the multiplier process is complete, the level of income would have returned to its original level. The single period expenditure increase has no permanent effect on equilibrium.

The second way in which the multiplier applies is with respect to a change in E_a that is permanently maintained over time. The effect of this type of expenditure increase is shown in Figure 5–6. As seen, the initiating expenditure $\Delta E_a = 100$ is carried through over each of the time periods, forming a base of income. For $b = 0.6$, the induced amount of expenditure in the second period, $\Delta E_a * b$, adds to this amount in the second and each successive period, creating a total of $\Delta E_a + \Delta E_a \times b = \Delta E_a(1 + b) = 160$ of income in the second and each later period. In the next period, the total amount is increased by the increment $\Delta E_a * b^2$, giving as the total income

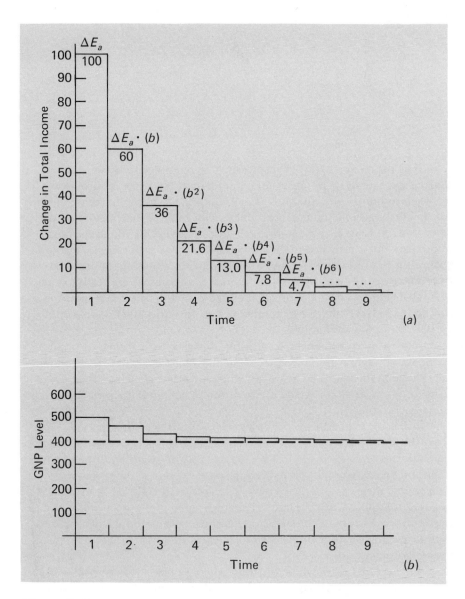

Figure 5–5

Multiplier Effects

level $\Delta E_a(1 + b + b^2) = 196$. The new equilibrium position in Figure 5–6 will reestablish at a *level* that is $E_a(1/1 - b) = 250$ higher than the previous level. The difference between the one-time and sustained expenditure change is thus whether or not the resulting equilibrium value is affected.

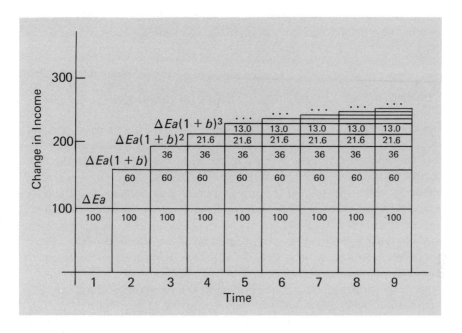

Figure 5–6
Cumulative Multiplier Effects

We also have a correspondence between the amount of new income generated in the case of a single expenditure injection and the change in equilibrium level in the case of a sustained injection.

Multiplier and Time Period

The multiple spending-income effects of an initiating change involve reference to a time period. For a given spending change, we would expect a larger multiplier effect to operate over the course of a year than over the course of the initial calendar quarter. Therefore, we necessarily must speak of the same-quarter or impact multiplier, or the 1 year multiplier, with the awareness that the successive terms in the multiplier process are truncated beyond the time period under consideration. The length of the time period we consider can also be expected to have an effect upon the stability of the multiplier associated with an initiating change. When we recall that the value of b was the sum of the response patterns of various spending groups, it follows that stability in these patterns can be expected to be greater averaged over longer periods such as a year than over periods as short as a quarter. While the quarterly marginal propensity to consume by all consumers has been found in statistical studies to be relatively volatile, giving rise to a similarly volatile multiplier, the pattern over the course of an entire year can be expected to be more stable, and the pattern over 5 and 10 year periods even more stable.[2]

Equilibrium in Goods and Financial Markets

The aggregate equilibrium conditions so far discussed have been concerned with the interaction of supply and demand in markets for goods and services. No indication has been given as to the impact of conditions in the nation's markets for money capital upon GNP levels. However, most economists believe that the markets for money capital and the markets for goods and services are interrelated, so that conditions in one can act on the other. For example, assume that the supply of money is deficient relative to the demand, causing both rising interest rates and some rationing of available credit. As a result, some borrowers of capital for investment purposes are discouraged by rising borrowing costs, while others cannot find available credit at the current interest rate. The result is a reduction in goods market expenditures below the levels that otherwise would have prevailed, leading to a similar reduction in production activities and incomes. Where the supply of money capital exceeds the demand, we expect lower interest rates and more aggressive lending policies by financial institutions. Such a condition would be expected to increase spending by some business and other income recipients.

The most direct relationship between the two markets can be seen in the highly credit dependent areas of spending activity. Spending on new housing, on state and local governmental construction, and some automobile spending are widely believed to be sensitive to rising interest rates or other imbalances between supply and demand conditions in money capital markets. Although we return to this point in several later chapters, it is important to recognize at the outset of our analysis that the markets for goods and services cannot be in an equilibrium while markets for money capital are in a state of change. As a consequence, we cannot comprehensively evaluate conditions in one market without evaluating conditions in both.

Equilibrium in Factor Markets

A third major market in the nation is that for factors of production including markets for materials used in the production process, markets for labor and services for all types, and markets for all other factors of produc-

---

[2] For a more extensive discussion, see Chapter 7.

tion. This array of related markets is dominated by the labor markets in terms of social importance and general concern. The labor market may be said to be in equilibrium when suppliers of labor are in general satisfied with levels of employment at the prevailing wage rate and demanders of labor services are satisfied with the flow of labor services at the prevailing wage rate. Neither shortages or involuntary unemployment exists in such an equilibrium position. A similar definition applies with regard to the nation's markets for materials.

We now consider whether disequilibrium conditions in the markets for factors of production can be expected to react upon aggregate goods-money market conditions, a question we return to in some detail in Chapter 16. To proceed, assume a shortage of some categories of skilled labor exists at prevailing wage rates. Can the existence of this condition be expected to generate important forces affecting conditions in the markets for goods and services? [3] Recalling our discussion in the previous chapter, a skilled-labor shortage may be expected to lead to bidding up the market wage rate. Production costs and profit margins would decline. This decline, in turn, results in decisions to reduce production schedules. Thus, a connection exists in this case between labor market disequilibrium and goods market equilibrium. A more direct relationship is suggested by the proposition that extreme demand-over-supply disequilibrium conditions in the labor market, by preventing utilization of labor planned by producers, may lead to an involuntary cutback in production levels, income levels, and, therefore, spending levels. In this latter proposition, however, the assumption of extreme disequilibrium conditions is of vital importance, since smaller labor shortages can be offset by overtime, inefficient use of other substitute resources, and so forth.

If we consider the opposite kind of labor market disequilibrium, that of supply over demand, our reasoning must be altered. Consider more available workers in a given skill category than demanded at the market wage, resulting in unemployment. Only if we employ the unlikely assumption that such a condition would lead to lower wages, alterations in production costs, etc., can we establish a counterpart of the first factor analyzed in the case of the demand-over-supply disequilibrium. Since the second reason in the earlier case was essentially a capacity limitation, our reasoning is even more strained, as it is necessary to suppose that the ready availability of workers in a given skill category would cause an upward revision in production schedules by driving down the market wage. We are led to the

---

[3] The situation posed here and discussed in the following paragraphs implies that the disequilibrium condition is not immediately resolved by adjustments in wage rates, but rather is maintained over a short-run period of time, during which labor shortages and pressures on wage rates exist, but do not succeed in eliminating the disequilibrium.

conclusion that the effects of supply-demand imbalances in labor markets are likely to be unsymmetrical in their effects upon goods market equilibria, having important potential effects in the case of demand-over-supply disequilibrium and less effect in the case of supply-over-demand disequilibrium.

Much of what we have said regarding the possible effect of labor market disequilibrium upon goods market equilibrium also applies when we consider the impact of disequilibrium in markets for materials. Shortages of such materials as steel, copper, and aluminum could (1) create delays in normal delivery times and (2) cause general increases in prices. Both of these factors may cause postponements and other unintended adjustments in production plans. Clearly, extreme demand-over-supply imbalances in materials markets could cause intended and unintended cutbacks in production, incomes, and, therefore, spending. However, the asymmetry observed in the case of labor market disequilibrium is not as evident in the case of materials markets. If we consider the case of an oversupply of aluminum, leading us to assume (1) a cut in the price and (2) shorter than normal delivery time, then this decrease in cost to the aluminum user[4] may generate positive adjustments in production schedules.

We have seen that money market and goods market equilibria are interrelated, and that labor and materials market conditions have important impacts on goods market equilibrium. Equilibrium in the economic system thereby exists when the factors of supply and demand in goods and services markets are in equilibrium concurrently with the factors of supply and demand in the money market and where important imbalances do not exist in labor and materials markets.

In our discussion of labor force equilibrium, we have considered the impact of excess demand for labor on goods market equilibrium. Our understanding of the full meaning of economic equilibrium can be enhanced by understanding the meaning of capacity for the economy and by considering the potential impact that attainment of capacity may have on equilibrium.

Labor Force Capacity

Labor force capacity is defined as that level of real GNP wherein a maximum percentage of all job seekers are employed. The term "maximum percentage" implies that we do not require that every person seeking a job be employed in order to classify the labor force as fully employed. In the

---

4 The cost decrease would take the form of reduced inventory costs as well as reduced material costs, since average inventory levels would fall.

economy at any particular point in time, a certain fraction of the work force will be temporarily unemployed due to job changes or for seasonal reasons. This transitory unemployment is a necessary by-product of job mobility and seasonally produced products and therefore is expected even in a fully utilized economy. Given this transient group of unemployed workers, our definition implies that labor force capacity level of output has been reached when all remaining job seekers are employed.

When the labor force is being utilized at or near full employment, further economic expansion in the form of larger real GNP production is constrained by growth in this capacity. In such a situation, the factors affecting growth in labor force capacity are of concern in analyzing possible future equilibrium levels of GNP. There are two primary ingredients affecting the capacity labor force. The first has to do with the maximum number of man-hours available at full employment. The second deals with the productivity of those man-hours.

Considering the maximum number of available man-hours, we find as important determinants (1) the total number of people seeking jobs and (2) the average man-hours worked per person. The total number of people seeking jobs is fundamentally influenced by (1) the movement of the population into job-seeking age groups and (2) the prevailing wage rate relative to the level of prices (the "purchasing power" wage). However, this magnitude is also influenced by such factors as changes in enrollments in colleges and universities, which has the effect of delaying entry into work seeking status on the part of this group, size of the military force, which directly affects available individuals, and patterns of employment seeking by wives and dependents. With regard to this latter factor, it will be recalled from Chapter 3 that the work force is defined as that proportion of the population who are seeking jobs. This means that an individual can define himself either in or out of the labor force by deciding to seek employment and thereby either add to or subtract from the capacity labor force. The housewife who alternately seeks outside employment and employment in the home is an example of this factor, which has the effect of making the size of the labor force and labor force capacity somewhat more volatile than it would be otherwise. The average man-hours worked is affected by long-term institutional trends as well as by the short-run pace of economic expansion. In the short-run, business firms often choose increases in hours worked over increases in employment as a first response to increases in demand, particularly until they can judge whether or not increases in demand are likely to be of a continuing nature. In addition, work stoppages, overtime, and the composition of output between consumer and other sectors of the economy can account for short-run fluctuations in average man-hours worked.

The second major ingredient in determining labor force capacity is the productivity in the employment of a given number of total man-hours. From our definition of labor force capacity as a full-employment production level, it is clear that the productivity of the available man-hours is a determinant of capacity output. Productivity of the labor force is affected by patterns in technological change that alter production methods, by the extent of exploitation of existing technological innovation by industry, in the skills and education of the work force, and in an array of other factors, a discussion of which would take us beyond our purpose at this point.

Our discussion of labor force capacity has sketched factors that affect the maximum output associated with full employment of the labor force. Although only impressionistic, our conclusion is that this effective capacity, susceptible to alteration by changes in an array of determinants, is likely to be somewhat variable over time. In addition to this volatility, it is clear that the use of overtime, third shifts, underqualified labor, and so forth, can cause the point where labor force capacity is reached to be difficult if not impossible to determine empirically. Rather than the idea of a point along the real output spectrum into which the economy rams as it grinds to a halt, the more meaningful notion is that of labor force capacity as a zone of real output levels in which conditions are abnormally tight and employment is at or near maximum levels. As population progresses and technology advances, this labor force capacity zone is associated with higher and higher levels of real output over time. As such factors as population participation rate, weekly hours worked, and military requirements change, the position of the zone is subject to fluctuation of a short-term nature. For example, if employment conditions were extremely tight in a certain time period resulting in more widely advertised employment opportunities for nonmembers of the work force, then the participation rate may rise and the labor force capacity zone pushed toward higher levels. The same would be true if tight conditions were met by a rise in man-hours worked per week.

Physical Plant Capacity

Besides a potential constraint on output levels imposed by maximum labor utilization, a second constraint exists in the form of the economy's stock of plant and equipment. We may define physical plant capacity as that level of real output at which the economy's stock of plant and equipment is fully utilized. As in the case of labor force capacity, our definition is of a point on the output spectrum whereas the more nearly correct notion is of a range of output in which in general plant and equipment is being utilized at higher than desired rates, where standby equipment is being operated, marginal plant facilities used, and so forth. As in the previous case, it is convenient to discuss this capacity zone as if it were a point.

The major determinants of physical plant capacity output levels are (1) the amount of plant and equipment in place and (2) the productivity of existing equipment and facilities. The amount of equipment in place is affected by the level of spending on new plant and equipment by business and the rate of scrappage of existing equipment and plant. It is an interesting characteristic of physical plant capacity that the business investment spending that adds to this capacity level, through the multiplier pushes actual GNP levels up toward capacity levels.

The productivity of existing equipment and facilities is influenced by several factors. Perhaps most fundamental is the level of labor utilization applied to existing facilities. Normally, as more man-hours of labor are applied to an existing stock of plant and equipment, the per unit or average productivity of the equipment will rise. Thus, we would expect that normal growth in the labor force would account for some rise in the productivity with which a given capital stock is utilized. This will only occur up to a point, however, at which existing plant and equipment is sufficiently saturated so as to choke off further gains. As technology progresses, more efficient machines and better techniques for production are developed. Both of these enable the productivity of the economy's stock of plant and equipment to be improved as capital expenditures are undertaken to take advantage of such improvements.[5]

Although statistics measuring physical plant capacity and its utilization are not as well developed as those on labor force capacity, statistical series on capacity are available from the Commerce Department and from McGraw-Hill. The McGraw-Hill survey of plant and equipment spending measures the level of capacity utilization desired by business and the level of capacity utilization actually attained by business. The desired rate in this series is the ideal rate at which business would like to operate and is expressed as a percentage of actual physical capacity. Thus, when an industry reports a desired operating rate of 92 percent of capacity it is in effect reporting that it ideally wants to maintain 8 percent of physical plant capacity on hand as standby equipment to handle production bulges, equipment breakdowns, and so forth. While not measuring physical plant capacity directly, the McGraw-Hill series yield an inference about physical capacity attainment in the form of the gap between desired and actual operating rates.

[5] In fact, the investment expenditures made by business can be categorized into those that affect capacity by expanding the amount of equipment and facilities in place and those that affect capacity by improving the efficiency of the existing capital stock by exploiting technological change.

Capacity Interrelationships

Labor force capacity utilization and plant capacity utilization are related. This derives from the assumption of diminishing returns in the use of both labor and capital resources. As utilization of the labor force approaches capacity, the employment of marginal laborers and the inefficient marginal use of existing laborers can be expected to contribute to declining marginal productivity of labor and to rising unit labor costs, as discussed in Chapter 4.[6] As the marginal productivity of labor declines with further employment, it is rational for business to substitute now relatively more productive capital resources for labor until the marginal productivity of the capital resources per dollar has been reduced and equated with the marginal productivity of labor per dollar.

If our assumptions are reasonably correct, then we are suggesting that the expansion of production initially by the employment of more labor can be expected to generate pressures for use of more capital and the purchase of new capital as the productivity of labor at the margin is reduced. In the identical manner, we would expect the approachment of plant capacity to stimulate additional use of labor resources, in response to a decline in the marginal productivity of capital. The two rates of capacity utilization are thus related in such a manner that the near realization in the use of either stimulates a higher rate of utilization of the other.[7] Labor force capacity pressures have the effect of spilling over upon plant capacity utilization and vice versa.

Our discussion now turns in the next chapters to an analysis of the basic factors in the aggregate demand for goods and services. We have discussed goods market equilibrium from a very general perspective. It now enhances our understanding to look behind those aggregative shrouds to the spending groups that comprise the total. The spending category that is quantitatively the most important includes those outlays made by people in the economy in their role as consumers of goods and services. It is to a consideration of that spending category that we now turn.

---

[6] This latter assumes that productivity of the nth overtime hour is less productive than the productivity of the $(n-1)^{th}$ hour.

[7] However, since we reasoned that near capacity labor force utilization may stimulate additional investment spending as well as additional utilization of existing equipment, the impact on capacity utilization of plant generated by near capacity labor force utilization is reduced.

Discussion Questions

1. What role does the 45° line play in the determination of aggregate goods market equilibrium? Does it carry any behavioral significance, or is it primarily a graphic device?

2. Does a rise in inventories always indicate an upcoming decrease in output, due to an excess of production over demand? Explain.

3. What behavioral conditions in the economy must hold in order for an increase in expenditures to have no multiplier effect? Would you ever expect to find such circumstances in the U.S. economy?

4. What would be the effect on the U.S. multiplier if governments redistributed all their tax revenues to the business and consumer sector? Would the multiplier rise or fall?

5. The Department of Commerce maintains a statistical series on the capacity output level in the United States. Find out how this level of capacity is determined through time, and comment upon its use, given the discussion of capacity in this chapter. You may wish to consult the *Economic Report of the President*.

6. What could it mean to speak of economic equilibrium in goods and services markets at an output level greater than capacity?

6

Theory of the Consumption Function

In this and the following chapter, we consider the largest and dominant category of expenditures in the economy—those made by the nation's households and other consumers. In this chapter, a theoretical structure of the consumption function is developed that relates the level of income, prices, and interest rates to the level of consumer expenditures. In the following chapter, a specific analysis of key national income accounting categories of consumer spending is made that focuses on the application of theoretical ideas to the specific product and service markets in the United States. We begin with the development of a theoretical framework for consumer behavior.

A Conceptual Framework for Household Consumption

From a broad, theoretical viewpoint, we may usefully consider consumer spending from the level of the typical household. The resulting view of aggregate consumption evolves from aggregating household behavior over the entire economy. Basically, a household has a flow of income over time and is faced with the continual decision as to how this income will be allocated between expenditures and saving. We may wish to think of this decision as the choice between consumption now and consumption later. Thus, at its roots, saving is a store of purchasing power for later conversion into goods and services.

We proceed by forming a definition of saving as simply nonspending. More specifically, we assume that consumer disposable income, Y, can be entirely divided into consumption, C, and saving, S, as follows:

$$Y = C + S \qquad\qquad (6\text{--}1)$$

If we divide both sides of 6–1 by the price level, P, we can form the matching identity between real (constant purchasing power) disposable income, Y_r, real consumption, C_r, and real saving, S_r, as follows:

$$\frac{Y}{P} = \frac{C}{P} + \frac{S}{P} \qquad\qquad (6\text{--}2)$$

or, equivalently

$$Y_r = C_r + S_r \qquad\qquad (6\text{--}3)$$

which gives this residual definition of saving as

$$S_r = Y_r - C_r \qquad\qquad (6\text{--}4)$$

To focus more explicitly upon the idea of saving as consumption postponed to the future, we shall consider a two period framework in which t is the present period and $t + 1$ is a future period over which all household spending and saving plans are carried out. For purposes of simplification, we shall not look beyond period $t + 1$ in our analysis. In this framework, we assume consumers make spending and saving decisions to maximize their total satisfaction over both periods. The level of total consumer satisfaction is affected both by the products and services consumed in time t and the products and services consumed in time $t + 1$. Furthermore, we can envision several combinations of present consumption and future consumption that will lead to the same total level of satisfaction over the two periods. This notion leads to the indifference map shown in Figure 6–1. The curve S_1 in Figure 6–1 shows the combinations of present real consumption, C_t/P_t, and future real consumption, C_{t+1}/P_{t+1}, that give the same level of total satisfaction. Accordingly, the household is indifferent between present-future consumption combination A and present-future consumption combination B. However, every combination of present and future consumption lying along the higher indifference curve S_2 is preferred to a combination lying along S_1. This is seen by reference to points C and D in comparison to point B. Point C involves the same amount of future consumption as point B but more present consumption, thus it is clearly preferred. Similarly, point D involves the same amount of present consumption as point B but more future con-

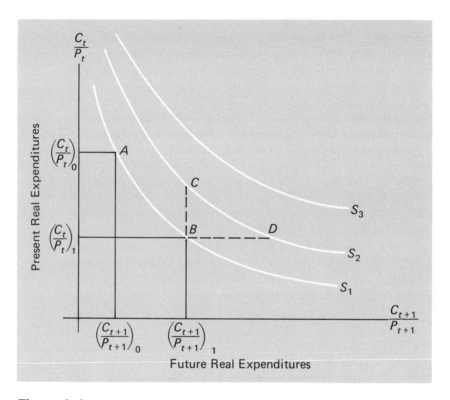

Figure 6–1

Consumer Indifference Map

sumption, and so is preferred to *B*. The same reasoning applies to all comparisons between lower and higher indifference curves. The indifference curves are shown convex to the origin, indicating a diminishing marginal rate of substitution between future and current consumption by the household. This means that as current consumption is decreased, a greater and greater volume of future consumption is required in order to keep the level of total satisfaction constant. Similarly, as future consumption is decreased, a greater and greater volume of present consumption is required to maintain the same level of consumer satisfaction.

This pattern suggests that the postponing of present consumption in favor of future consumption is similar to a luxury in the mind of the typical household. With a high level of present consumption, the household is willing to trade off a proportionately large amount of current goods for goods in the future, due to a relatively low level of satisfaction associated with the marginal goods and services consumed in the present period.

So far, our discussion has only been concerned with the characteristics of present-future consumption indifference curves. We now consider the combinations of present and future consumption that can actually be purchased by the household with its limited income. To do this, we need to recognize (1) that prices may differ between the present and future period, such that the consumer's purchasing power may be altered between the two periods, and (2) that money may be borrowed or loaned by the household over the present-future period. For sake of discussion, we assume that the typical household knows its current income level, Y_t, its future income level, Y_{t+1}, the current price level, P_t, and the future price level, P_{t+1}. In addition, the interest available to the consumer is denoted as r. To simplify the discussion, we assume the consumer can either borrow or lend at r, that is, there are no financial "middlemen" to create differences between lending and borrowing rates. From this, we may assemble an expression for the maximum amount of goods and services the consumer unit could purchase if it spent all its income earned over both periods on current consumer goods. The expenditure of all currently earned income would result in the purchase of a quantity of goods and services equal to Y_t/P_t. In addition, the household could borrow against its income in period $t + 1$. It could borrow an amount B, where

$$B + Br = Y_{t+1}$$

Solving this for B gives

$$B = \frac{Y_{t+1}}{1 + r}$$

The maximum amount of borrowing, B, is less than Y_{t+1} by the amount of the required interest payment, Br. The amount of present purchases possible from B is given by B/P_t, or equivalently by $Y_{t+1}/P_t(1 + r)$. Accordingly, the maximum amount of goods that can be purchased in the present period by our household if it borrows the maximum amount against future income is given by summing these present and borrowed components as follows:

$$M_p = \frac{Y_t}{P_t} + \frac{Y_{t+1}}{P_t(1 + r)} \tag{6–5}$$

On the opposite extreme, we can form an expression for the maximum amount of goods the household could purchase if it made no purchases in the present period, but saved all its income for purchases in the future period. The present period's income could be loaned out at r until period $t + 1$, producing $Y_t r$ in interest income. This produces

$$Y_t + Y_t r = Y_t(1 + r)$$

in purchasing power in the future period. The amount of goods this income could purchase is given by $Y_t(1 + r)/P_{t+1}$, since it involves the purchase of goods at future rather than present prices. The future income adds an amount of future purchases equal to a maximum of Y_{t+1}/P_{t+1}. The maximum future purchases is thus given by

$$M_f = \frac{Y_t(1 + r) + Y_{t+1}}{P_{t+1}} \tag{6-6}$$

Rather than either of the extremes given by M_p or M_f, the household will usually allocate some portion of present income to consumer purchases, lending out the remainder for purchases in the future, or borrow against a portion of future income in order to extend present purchases beyond present income. That is, purchases will usually be allocated by the household such that present purchases are less than M_p and future purchases are less than M_f. All such possibilities are shown in Figure 6–2. In this figure, the maximum present purchases, M_p, are shown as the intercept on the vertical axis while the maximum future purchases, M_f, are shown along the hori-

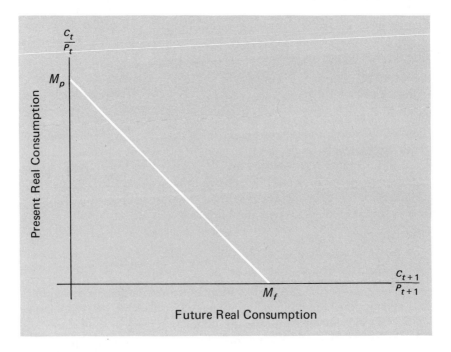

Figure 6–2
Budget Curve

zontal axis. Both are boundary points for the household's purchase combination. Connecting them shows all feasible combinations of present and future consumption, given the prices, income levels, and interest rates of the household involved.

Whereas the present-future indifference map of Figure 6–1 shows the level of satisfaction associated with all purchase combinations, Figure 6–2 shows the feasible purchase combinations. Relating these two constructs yields the particular feasible purchase combination that maximizes the level of consumer satisfaction. We assume rational consumers will consume and save according to such a maximizing criterion.

In Figure 6–3, the indifference map is superimposed on the budget curve. Recalling that curve S_3 is a higher level of satisfaction than S_2, and that S_2 is higher than S_1, the objective of maximizing consumer satisfaction graphically translates into a problem of reaching the highest possible indifference curve given the budget constraint. This occurs at point A, where the budget and indifference curves are tangent. The consumer's budget will not

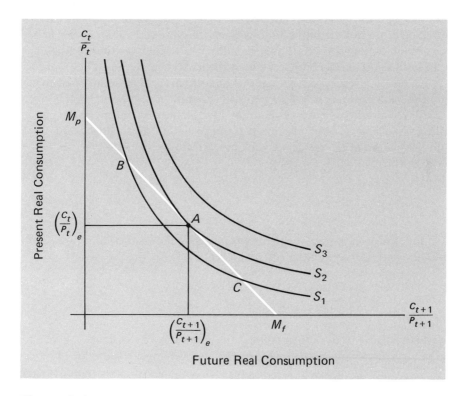

Figure 6–3
Consumer Equilibrium

allow any higher level of satisfaction, such as curve S_3, and the consumer will not settle for any lower level of satisfaction such as level S_1 produced by purchase combinations B or C.

If the consumer were at point B, the level of satisfaction could be increased by cutting back on current consumption and increasing future consumption, that is, increasing present saving. This downward movement along the budget curve increases the level of satisfaction, since the purchase combination is moving outward on the indifference map from S_1 toward S_2. This increase in satisfaction continues until point A is reached. After point A, further decreases in present consumption in favor of future consumption move the consumer back down to a lower indifference curve, since the marginal satisfaction of current consumption compared with future consumption has increased to the point where no further shifts are warranted in the consumer's mind. Accordingly, we may expect the consumer to settle upon the purchase combination A where the budget curve reaches a point of tangency with the highest possible indifference curve.

Our earlier development of Expressions 6–5 and 6–6 indicated that the consumer's budget position is affected by current and future prices, by current and future income levels, and by prevailing interest rates. To see how these variables impact on consumer spending and saving positions, it is helpful to form a specific algebraic version of the budget curve shown in Figure 6–2. We notice several properties of this budget curve: (1) It relates real consumption expenditures in t, C_t/P_t, to real expenditures in period $t + 1$, C_{t+1}/P_{t+1}, in terms of the maximum total purchases possible given the prevailing prices and interest rates; (2) It is linear; and (3) It is a downward sloping function of C_{t+1}/P_{t+1}. Accordingly, the budget curve has the following form:

$$\frac{C_t}{P_t} = a - b \frac{C_{t+1}}{P_{t+1}} \tag{6-7}$$

In a linear curve, the value of a is given by the vertical intercept, which in our case is equal to M_p. We therefore know that

$$a = M_p = \frac{Y_t}{P_t} + \frac{Y_{t+1}}{P_t(1 + r)} \tag{6-8}$$

Another property of our linear curve is that the value of the slope, b, given by the ratio of a change in the value of C_t/P_t to a change in the value of C_{t+1}/P_{t+1}, remains constant for all movements along the curve. In our case, this ratio is always equal to the ratio between the two intercepts, M_p and M_f. Thus, we may state

$$b = \frac{M_p}{M_f} = \frac{\left[\dfrac{Y_t}{P_t} + \dfrac{Y_{t+1}}{P_t(1+r)}\right]}{\left[\dfrac{Y_t(1+r) + Y_{t+1}}{P_{t+1}}\right]} = \frac{P_{t+1}}{P_t(1+r)} \qquad (6\text{–}9)$$

We now substitute Expressions 6–8 and 6–9 into 6–7 to give the specific version of our budget expression as[1]

$$\frac{C_t}{P_t} = \left[\frac{Y_t}{P_t} + \frac{Y_{t+1}}{P_t(1+r)}\right] - \left[\frac{P_{t+1}}{P_t(1+r)}\right]\frac{C_{t+1}}{P_{t+1}} \qquad (6\text{–}10)$$

This budget expression can help us to understand the influence of income, price, and interest rate fluctuations upon current real consumption expenditures.

Effect of Income on Consumption

We first consider the impact of income changes on real consumer expenditures. In doing so, we take the approach of "one thing at a time" by holding all other variables constant except income and then finding the way in which current consumption behaves as income changes. With P_t, P_{t+1}, Y_{t+1}, and r held constant, Expression 6–10 shows that changes in Y_t impact on the budget equation by changing its intercept. An increase in Y_t enlarges the intercept without affecting the slope. Figure 6–4 shows the effect graphically. Because we are holding prices constant, a change in either nominal income or nominal consumption is equal to a real change; accordingly, we have simplified the notation in Figure 6–4 such that $C_r(t)$ refers to both a nominal and a real change in current consumption, $C_r(t+1)$ refers to a similar change in period $t+1$ consumption, and Y_r refers to the level of real income.

In Figure 6–4(a), the effect of an income increase from $Y_r(0)$ to $Y_r(1)$ is seen to be an outward shift in the budget line and an increase in real consumption from $C_r(0)$ to $C_r(1)$. The distance between $Y_r(0)$ and $Y_r(1)$ is greater than the distance between the resulting $C_r(0)$ and $C_r(1)$ values. This indicates that consumer spending increases by only a fraction of the income increase in this case. The household saves a portion of the income increase and increases expenditures by the remainder, that is, it allocates a portion

---

[1] We could divide through this expression by P_t and make other algebraic simplifications. However, this would obscure some of the basic relationships we wish to consider. Thus, for discussion we shall leave the equation in its present unreduced form.

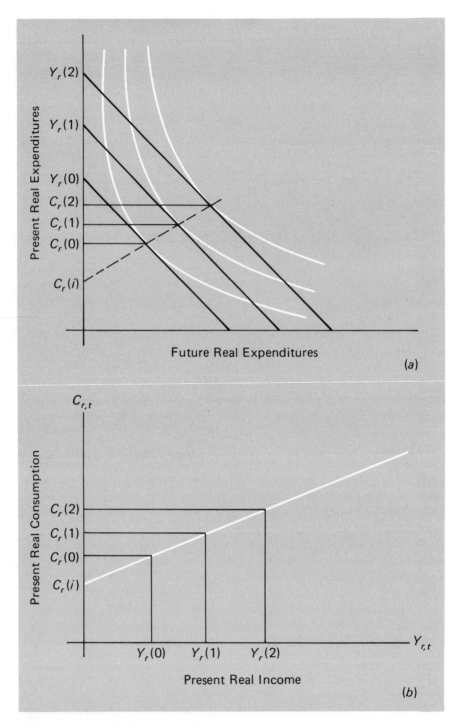

Figure 6–4
Income-Consumption Relationships

to current consumption and a portion to future consumption. In Figure 6–4(b), the real income level is related to the level of real consumption to form the consumption function. This consumption function is a plot of the consumption levels that solve the household tradeoff between current and future consumption at various income levels. We thus assume the consumer is in a maximum satisfaction equilibrium at each and every point along the consumption function.

The point $C_r(i)$ in Figure 6–4(a) and (b) represents the level of consumption that would take place in period t if present income were to fall to zero but future income remain unchanged. If we set $Y_t = 0$ in Expression 6–10, we find that the intercept becomes

$$a = \frac{Y_{t+1}}{P_t(1 + r)} \tag{6-11}$$

which means the budget line would not fall to zero. Consumers would borrow against income in period $t + 1$ or draw down existing assets for the purpose of maintaining a minimum level of present consumer expenditures. The consumption function in (b) thereby has a positive intercept equal to this zero income level of consumption. If present income became zero and future income was also known to be zero, then we find that the remaining portion of the constant term given by Expression 6–11 would become zero and that the budget line would fall to the origin, giving a zero level of consumption for a zero value of both Y_t and Y_{t+1}. Thus, for a short-run income collapse that does not carry into the future, we find the consumption function to have a positive intercept, implying a present maintenance of consumption expenditures. However, for a present income collapse that is long-run and carries into the future, we find a proportional consumption response and a consumption function with no intercept term. Accordingly, we expect a short-run consumption function to have a positive intercept while a long-run consumption function should be more nearly proportional. We will have more to say on this topic in the next chapter.

The consumption income solutions in Figure 6–4(a) enable the construction of a saving function. This construction is shown in Figure 6–5. Recalling our definition of saving as income less consumption, we can plot income levels against the saving levels associated with the household solution of its present-future consumption expenditure decision. For example, at $Y_r(0)$, a level of saving of $Y_r(0) - C_r(0)$ occurs. The intercept of this function is the negative level of saving equal to the level of consumption spending that would take place at zero income levels. The curve then rises by the increasing level of nonspending that takes place at each successively higher income level.

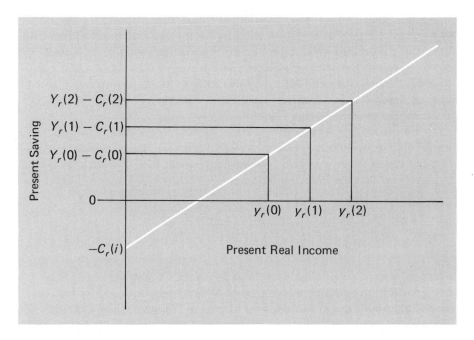

Figure 6–5

Saving Function

Impact of Interest Rates on Consumption

Unlike income levels, interest rates impact on both the intercept and the slope of the consumer's budget equation. If we now fix income levels and prices for t and $t + 1$, we may trace interest rate effects upon consumption in the same way we traced income effects. A look back at Expression 6–10 shows that an increase in the rate of interest, r, reduces the size of the intercept term in the budget equation. It also reduces, or flattens, the value of the slope. The change that results from an increase in interest rates is shown in Figure 6–6.

In (*a*) of this figure, interest rates are increased from r_0 to r_1, thus shifting down the budget line and at the same time pivoting it into a flatter position. The downward shift represents the reduction in maximum present purchases due to the higher cost of borrowing against future income. The household cannot raise as much present purchasing power now as before the interest rate increase. The flatter slope of the budget curve represents the higher future reward to the household from deferring present consumption, lending more income at the increased rate until period $t + 1$, and then capitalizing upon the increased earnings by higher purchases in the future period.

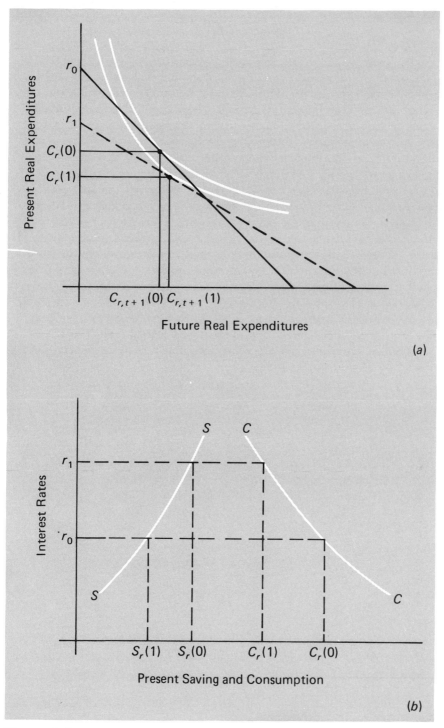

Figure 6–6

Interest Rate Effects on Consumption

In Figure 6–6(a), the present level of consumption declines as a result of the interest rate rise. Since we have fixed the current level of income, the level of saving rises with the falling consumption. At the same time, the level of future consumption, $C_{r,t+1}$, rises. The higher interest rate thus motivates the consumer to save a higher percent of present income and to defer some current expenditure until the future. In Figure 6–6(b), the saving and consumption relationships that derive from (a) are shown. An upward sloping saving interest rate function is accompanied by a downward sloping consumption interest rate schedule. However, this is not the only possible result of an increase in interest rates. Because we have a change in both the slope and the intercept of the budget equation, the net effect of an interest rate increase will depend upon the shape of the consumer indifference curves. Figure 6–7 illustrates another outcome. In this figure, a second set of consumer indifference curves causes the same increase in interest rates from r_0 to r_1 to create no change in the level of consumption or saving. The consumer indifference curves in the case of Figure 6–7 are shaped such that after the budget line shifts, the resulting optimal indifference curve involves the same level of consumer spending as in the initial position. This pattern indicates a strong consumer preference for current consumption expenditures,

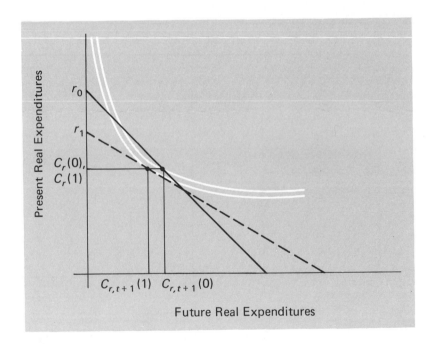

Figure 6–7

Interest Rate Effects

such that the additional incentives to save represented by the higher interest rate are insufficient to cause the new equilibrium to occur at a lower level of current consumption.

Notice in Figure 6–7 that the preservation of current consumption levels in the face of the rise in interest rates involves a reduction in future consumption from $C_{r,t+1}(0)$ to $C_{r,t+1}(1)$. This is not a necessary result, but evolves from the circumstance that the equilibrium occurs to the left of the pivot (or crossover) point between the old and new budget lines. Had the equilibrium occurred to the right of the pivot point, the solution would have involved more future consumption.[2] Essentially, the reason for this result is that a solution to the left of the pivot point involves a level of current consumption that is greater than current income, thus involving some borrowing against future income.[3] In this case, the increase in interest rates lowers the total income available for current expenditure. More must be borrowed against future income, thus lowering the level of future consumption. To the right of the pivot point, money is being loaned out for future use, since positive saving occurs. Accordingly, more money is available for future use due to the higher lending rates, and if the equilibrium occurs in this region, the result will be more future consumption as a result of the higher interest rate.

A third possible interest rate effect is illustrated by Figure 6–8. In this figure, the indifference map shows a preference structure that causes current consumption to increase in response to an increase in interest rates from r_0 to r_1. In this circumstance, the consumer has a strong preference for future consumption. The equilibrium solution to the right of the pivot point indicates positive saving is occurring at the solution point. The higher interest on this saving enables the intended future consumption schedule to be met with less current saving. Current saving thus declines. The decline in current saving associates with an increase in current consumption.

Liquid Assets and Consumption

So far in our discussion, we have considered only current and future income as sources of purchasing power. In addition to income flows, most households have available a stock of liquid assets, including money balances and near-money financial assets such as bonds. These liquid assets are a poten-

---

[2] The student may wish to demonstrate this by modifying Figure 6–7.
[3] The point where the r_0 and r_1 curves cross corresponds to the point where $Y_{t+1} = C_{t+1}$ and where $Y_t = C_t$, i.e., where no saving occurs in either the present or the future period.

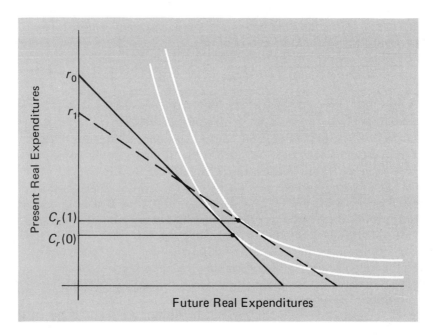

Figure 6–8

Interest Rate Effects

tial source of added purchasing power, in either the present or the future period. They add to the total amount of present maximum consumption, M_p, by the amount of their liquidation value and to the future maximum consumption by this amount multiplied by $(1 + r)$. The effect on the budget line is shown in Figure 6–9. In (a) of this figure, a stock of liquid assets equal to L is added to the present and future income flows. This increases the maximum possible present purchases by an amount L/P_t, giving a new total possible purchases of $M_p + L/P_t$. In the future period, this L earns the rate of interest, but is convertible into commodities at the future price, P_{t+1}. The amount added to M_f is thus given by $L(1 + r)/P_{t+1}$. We retain our assumption of all else constant by fixing Y_t, Y_{t+1}, P_t, P_{t+1}, and r. Then, Figure 6–9(a) shows that the effect of the addition of L is exactly the same as an increase in income in that it shifts out the budget line, leading to increased present consumption.

In Figure 6–9(b), the effect of the addition of liquid assets on the consumption function is shown. At the same present income flow, the addition of L now associates with a higher level of consumption, as the consumption function shifts up from C to C'. Basically, the reason for this result is the impact the existence of L has on the satisfaction the consumer derives from

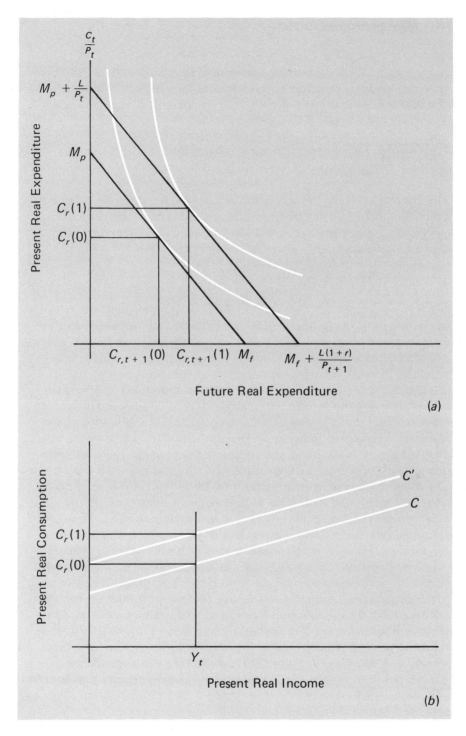

Figure 6–9
Wealth Effects on Consumption

present saving. With the buttress of a stock of liquid assets, the satisfaction deriving from existing saving flows is reduced. Accordingly, consumption is increased and, since present income, Y_t, is unchanged, saving is reduced.

Aggregate Consumption and Product Market Equilibrium

The discussion in this chapter has focused on the typical household or consumer. If we aggregate the budget equations and indifference maps of these households, the aggregate consumption function results. Our discussion indicates that this function is of the following general form:

$$\frac{C_t}{P_t} = f\left[\frac{Y_t}{P_t}, r, \frac{L_t}{P_t}\right] \qquad (6\text{--}12)$$

In our discussion of the income effect on consumption, we found a positive income-consumption relationship regardless of the shape of the consumer indifference map. The same is true of the impact of liquid assets on consumption. However, the interest rate effect on consumption was seen to depend upon the particular shape of the individual consumer indifference map. This makes the net effect of interest rates on consumption difficult to evaluate, given the large number of individual households in back of our aggregate consumption function. Perhaps as a result of this situation, evidence on the statistical importance of interest rates in aggregate consumption expenditures is quite inconclusive.

If we think of an economy consisting entirely of consumers, the consumption function of Expression 6–12 leads to a statement of aggregate equilibrium. This one-sector economic equilibrium is shown in Figure 6–10. If interest rates are at r_1 and the real wealth position is $(L/P)_0$, then the consumption function is positioned at level A. Since consumer demand equals total demand, the equilibrium position occurs at real income level $(Y/P)_A$. If the interest rate increases from r_1 to r_2 (assuming the new consumer equilibrium position involves more present saving and less current consumption), the consumption function shifts down from position A to position B, reducing equilibrium real income from $(Y/P)_A$ to $(Y/P)_B$. If we return to position A and consider in isolation an increase in consumer wealth positions from $(L/P)_0$ to $(L/P)_1$, we find the new consumer equilibrium position involves more consumption in the present for a given level of present income. The consumption function shifts from position A to position C, where the new equilibrium income has increased to $(Y/P)_C$.

In the U.S. economy, the practical importance of interest rate and wealth movements on the position of the consumption function depends on

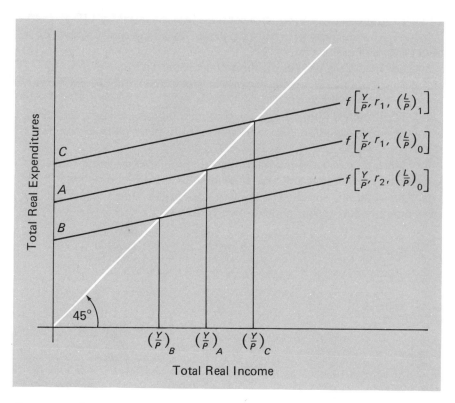

Figure 6–10
Aggregate Consumption Function

the specific shape and character of that function and is more of a statistical question than a theoretical one. In the next chapter, we shall be concerned with the statistical realities of consumption function analysis as it applies to key national income categories of consumption expenditure. We shall also consider empirical results that bear on the crucial explanatory variables in statistical consumption functions for the U.S. economy.

Discussion Questions

1. What would it imply about consumer behavior if the indifference map of Figure 6–1 sloped out from the origin, i.e., was concave to the origin, rather than the shape shown in the figure?

2. How would the slope of the consumer budget equation be affected by

a 10 percent increase in prices with constant interest rates? By a 10 percent increase in interest rates with constant prices? By a 10 percent increase in both prices and interest rates?

3. How would the level of consumption be affected by a 5 percent increase in prices and a 2 percent increase in prices, given income levels constant?

4. When interest rates change, the consumer budget equation "pivots" around a particular point. Can you show that this pivot point corresponds to the point where $Y_t = C_t$ and $Y_{t+1} = C_{t+1}$?

5. Which do you find more plausible—that the level of saving rises as interest rates rise or that the level of saving falls as interest rates rise?

6. How, if at all, would an increase in stock prices impact upon consumption spending in the model presented in this chapter?

7

Analysis of Consumer Spending

This chapter is concerned with the factors affecting consumer spending in the United States. Since this diverse category accounts for upward of 60 percent of total GNP, analyses of the economy are importantly influenced by the analyst's conclusions about patterns of consumer spending. Our discussion will focus on three distinct national income categories of consumer spending: (1) automobiles, (2) other durables, and (3) nondurables and services. We shall discuss variables affecting these expenditures that provide indicators useful for short-run analysis of consumer spending.

Consumer Spending and Business Decisions

Regardless of the particular product area of a firm, its market outlook is not likely to remain unaffected by significant changes in consumer spending behavior. Besides direct producers of consumer's products, producers of investment goods will shortly feel a reaction from any substantial shifts in consumer spending as consumer goods firms alter plant expansion and equipment purchase plans.

As the multiplier effect operates on overall income levels, virtually all producers of goods or services for which income is a significant demand determinant will be affected. Even producers of goods or services purchased by governments may not remain insulated from shifts in consumer spending patterns. Assume, for example, that a sharp decline occurs in consumer spending, in turn producing a greater decline in total aggregate income. The income decline lowers the total level of tax revenues, moving governmental budgetary positions toward deficit positions. If this revenue decline threatens to produce a serious deficit, then cutbacks in government spending might well be the response. The proportion and primacy of consumer spending relative to total spending in an economy such as the U.S. economy causes conditions in the consumer sector to set the pace for the entire economy. Although inconsistencies in general market conditions between the consumer sector and other sectors sometimes persists over the short-run, in general, these inconsistencies are eventually resolved in favor of the consumer sector.

For purposes of analysis, it is useful to dissect the consumer category into partitions containing goods and services having closely related demand determinants. This enables a common framework to be applied in the analysis of each sector. A widely used partitioning for forecasting purposes includes a two-part breakdown of durable goods into automobiles and all other durables and a combination of the remaining two national income categories, nondurable goods and services into a single category.

Spending on Automobiles

Fortunately for analysts, formulating informed impressions of the total level of new car purchases in the immediate future is somewhat easier than determining when or if an individual will purchase a new car. While the latter's decision may appear more responsive to social or psychological variables than to measured and available economic statistics, the aggregation of those individual decisions into more than 30 billion in expenditures reflecting 9 or more million new car purchases produces an aggregate variable more susceptible to analysis. However, as the U.S. energy crisis of 1973–1974 illustrates, noneconomic factors can play an important role in automobile demand. On this occasion, the prospect of fuel shortages created a decline in new automobile demand of 30 to 40 percent from previous levels. As a first step in this analysis it is useful to consider some general characteristics of the demand for automobiles that influence the choice of specific variables for study.

As a durable good, the automobile is more durable than any other good in its category in the sense that it yields its total services over a greater period of time. Also, a more highly organized and active used market exists for automobiles than for any other durable good. These two factors indicate the asset-like character of the automobile. In turn, this asset-like quality affects the way in which the outlook for automobile purchases is analyzed.

A second general characteristic affecting analysis of automobile demand is the number of credit purchases. Typically, greater than 60 percent of all new car purchases in the United States are made on credit. The influence of credit conditions upon new car markets must therefore be taken into account, as will be seen following.

Automobile Stocks

The asset-like character of automobiles implies an important explanatory role for the stock of existing automobiles. As sales of new cars occur, units are added to the stock of cars. At the same time, scrappage of old units withdraws cars from the road. The net effect represents the change in stocks of autos over a time period. As population and incomes grow, a larger stock of automobiles is normal. Growth in the actual stock at either a greater or smaller pace than this "normal" would tend to either saturate the consumer's basket of goods with automobiles, thereby weakening new sales, or create a gap between actual stocks and long-run stocks, which would strengthen sales. This means that years when sales of automobiles are above long-term trends can normally be expected to weaken prospects for further above-average years, other things being equal. Likewise, abnormally weak years retard the growth in the stock of automobiles and help strengthen the basis for future demand. Although these stock adjustment influences may be entirely offset by increases in income, decreases in prices, or changes in other relevant variables, such pressures can be expected to be present in markets for new automobiles in the United States.

This stock adjustment effect has been formally incorporated into several popular econometric models dealing with demand for automobiles. In a model developed at the University of Pennsylvania's Wharton School, the stock of automobiles at a point in time is measured by the weighted sum of the preceding 40 calendar quarters of expenditures on new automobiles, under the assumption of a declining scheme of weights.[1] The statistically measured relationship in the Wharton model between changes in automobile stocks and changes in new expenditures is negative, thereby reflecting the type of stock adjustment effect we have now discussed.

Earning Power and Credit

The theory of consumer spending as outlined in the previous chapter focuses attention upon consumer incomes as a principal determinant of consumer spending. In analyzing demand for automobiles, this proposition must be tailored to take into consideration special characteristics of the automobile market. One such characteristic is the extensive use of credit by new car purchasers. A credit purchase of a new car (1) often does not require an

[1] See M. K. Evans, *Macroeconomic Activity: Theory, Forecasting, and Control,* Harper & Row, New York, 1969, p. 170.

advance buildup of liquidity, (2) depends on income regularity as well as upon income level, (3) is likely to be sensitive to retail credit conditions. The first of these characteristics suggests that levels of consumer liquid assets are not likely to be of much importance in sizing up conditions in automobile markets. Statistical studies in which reliable results have been obtained have repeatedly verified this notion, finding little or no relation between liquid asset changes and changes in spending under a variety of differing model specifications.[2]

Qualifications for automobile financing almost unanimously require that the borrower be employed at a job that seems likely to offer persistent employment. Therefore, as unemployment rates grow or decline, the market of eligible new car purchasers and, in turn, actual sales will be affected accordingly. However, this does not imply that total or per capita levels of income are not also important. Income levels represent the basic flow of funds from which repayments will come. Therefore, we should expect total demand to be affected by the size of total income flows. In the final analysis, the lender's evaluation of a potential borrower's ability to meet monthly payments is affected by both the employment and income dimensions of personal financial strength.

Recent empirical studies of automobile demand have found important explanatory roles for both employment measures and income measures. The Wharton automobile forecasting equation includes personal disposable income net of transfer payments, as well as the unemployment rate. In a highly detailed econometric investigation by the Brookings Institute, the equation dealing with automobile demand contained a very similar income term, but did not contain an unemployment variable.

Buying Attitudes

Purchases of new cars often represent highly postponable expenditures. Although car stocks and income and employment conditions affect consumer decisions to postpone or undertake a new car purchase, they do not entirely satisfy one's intuitive perception of the elements involved. Consumer attraction to new styles, attitudes toward income and job prospects, and general confidence are determinants of automobile purchases, in addition to special factors such as fuel shortages or highway congestion. The Survey Research

2 See, for example, L. R. Klein and J. B. Lansing, "Decisions to Purchase Consumer Durable Goods," *Journal of Marketing*, 20:2 (October 1955), p. 120; Janet A. Fisher, "Consumer Durable Goods Expenditures, with Major Emphasis on the Role of Assets, Credits, and Intentions," *Journal of the American Statistical Association*, 58:3 (September 1963), p. 654; and Evans, *Macroeconomic Activity*, pp. 41–44, 176.

Center (SRC) at the University of Michigan has developed indices measuring consumer buying attitudes, intentions, and confidence. If the SRC index correctly measures consumer intentions toward automobile purchases, then these data should have important explanatory powers in models of automobile demand. In fact, if the SRC attitude index is added to a statistical equation for automobile demand containing only disposable personal income, the index adds appreciably to the statistical results. On the other hand, when the SRC attitude index is added to an equation containing disposable income net of transfers, stock of automobiles, new car prices relative to other consumer goods, and the unemployment rate, it does not add to the explanatory powers of the equation.[3] This implies that unemployment rates and the SRC index often explain much the same kind of variation in automobile sales. However, when unusual factors such as legal restrictions affecting driving, fuel shortages, or work stoppages impact upon consumer attitudes, the substitutability of the two measures may break down, and in such a case the SRC data may prove more effective.

Prices

In addition to the factors discussed so far, elementary demand analysis suggests that the demand for automobiles should be influenced by new car prices. The theory also suggests that the prices of other goods upon which the consumer may spend his available dollars should affect the level of demand. Both the Brookings and Wharton models reflect this thinking by employing a ratio of new car prices to total consumer prices. This ratio proved statistically significant in the Wharton model but largely insignificant in the Brookings study.[4] Both the Wharton and Brookings statistical studies have concluded by their use of the price ratio that prices of new cars relative to prices of all consumer goods is an important consideration in the analysis of new car markets.

To summarize, major econometric models of the U.S. automobile sector find the demand for automobiles depends on (1) disposable income, (2) automobile stocks, (3) prices of automobiles relative to other consumer goods, and (4) unemployment rates or attitude surveys.

---

3 See Evans, p. 169.
4 See Evans, p. 168 and J. S. Duesenberry, G. Fromm, L. R. Klein, and E. Kuh, *The Brookings Quarterly Econometric Model of the United States,* Rand McNally, Chicago, 1965, p. 684.

Spending on Other Durables

The "other durables" category, which results from subtracting new car purchases from total durable goods purchased, contains expenditures for furniture, major appliances such as TV sets, minor appliances such as mixers and electric can openers, and other miscellaneous household goods of a durable nature. Besides an automobile, the items in the category represent the "capital equipment" of a household. The household asset quality of most of the goods in this category produces some similarity between factors important in their purchase and those important in the purchase of automobiles. One such similarity is the importance of existing stocks of goods in determining present demand. As in the case of new car stocks, we may expect short-term above-trend patterns of other durables expenditures to add disproportionately to asset stocks, thereby creating a depressing influence on future expenditures. Behind this expectation is the notion of a normal stock of other durable goods largely affected by the number of family units and general income levels toward which the actual stock tends to adjust. This expectation finds statistical support in both the Wharton and Brookings studies where the stock of other durables was found in both cases to be a highly statistically significant explanatory variable for new expenditures in the category.

As with demand for automobiles, disposable income represents the basic cash flow of consumers pertinent to the other durables category. In accordance with this notion, the Wharton and Brookings studies both find total disposable income as a highly significant purchasing power variable.

Besides the effect of income and stocks of goods, prices of other durables relative to all consumer prices might be expected to affect demand as the comparable ratio did in the case of automobile demand. We would not, however, expect the effect to be as pronounced since the other durables category contains a number of items carrying both large and small price tags whereas the automobile category consisted of only one large item, which is typically shopped for extensively regarding price. The Brookings study included a ratio of relative prices in their model, although its explanatory value was insignificant. The Wharton study omitted this variable. This leads to the conclusion that relative prices are not as statistically important in analyzing other durables as they are in analyzing new car demand.

Several larger items in the other durables category are frequently purchased on credit, furniture and TV sets being examples. This suggests that credit conditions might have an important influence on other durable expenditures. However, there is no statistical support for this hypothesis, except insofar as disposable income acts as a surrogate for credit worthiness (which it surely must to some extent).

Thus, the evidence of two extensive empirical studies suggests only disposable income and stocks of other durables as key statistical determinants of spending in this category. Adding this to the earlier conclusion regarding automobile expenditures produces the durable goods expenditures model shown in Figure 7–1. Although highly general, it reflects the consensus of our discussion of the empirical results of major econometric models of the U.S. economy. In Figure 7–1, durable goods have been characterized as asset-like because their purchase is postponable, and because they often comprise the capital stock for family units. Their common purchase by the use of credit and their high unit cost relative to nondurables makes them more susceptible than other consumer goods to careful shopping and deliberate choice. Nondurables and services, on the other hand, comprise thousands of small purchases and household expenses, many of which are bought from habit or expedience. Our discussion now turns to analysis of this category.

Spending on Nondurables and Services

When the national income accounting system's nondurables category is added to the services category, the sum (call it NDS) reflects greater than 50 percent of the total GNP. The nondurables portion represents clothing, food, household incidentals, plus thousands of other items of small unit price and short service life. Services include rental payments, medical costs, recreational expenses, and countless other expenditures for items used up essentially upon purchase. The NDS category, relatively free from the asset-like characteristics of durable goods, reflects the kind of goods and service that most consumption function analysts have in mind in constructing models of consumer spending.

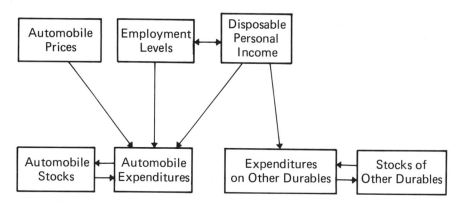

Figure 7–1

Summary—Durable Goods Markets

In Chapter 6, the theory of household consumption derived in a general way an explanatory role for income in consumer spending. With respect to the empirical role of income in consumer spending, Keynes offered the observation that "men are disposed, as a rule and on the average, to increase their consumption as their income increases, but not by as much as the increase in their income." He also postulated that "A man's habitual standard of life usually has the first claim on his income, and he is apt to save the difference which discovers itself between his actual income and the expense of his habitual standard." [5] These two products of Keynes' intuition have been subjected to repeated empirical tests individually and in combination with other hypotheses in the years since Keynes, in search of evidence on the specific nature of income-spending relationships, first expressed them. In general, these later theoretical and empirical results have verified the essential statistical validity of Keynes' hypotheses and have extended and added to his analysis in several directions. We now turn our attention to some of these results that have proven to be of greatest applicability.

Relative Income Effects

Studies of spending patterns by various income earning groups over a fixed time period verify the common-sense notion that lower income groups spend a larger percentage of their income in a given year than higher income groups. This pattern suggests that income growth over time should enlarge upper income groups relative to lower income groups and cause higher average levels of savings and lower average levels of consumption. These tendencies toward higher savings proportions over time would represent a growing leakage of purchasing power out of the economy, which would in turn necessitate continually growing levels of income independent expenditures such as investment spending in order to provide growing incomes.

Fortunately for economic growth, the picture provided by these income class studies of ever increasing savings proportions is not verified by available evidence on long-run patterns over time in consumption-income relations. A study by Kuznets of long-run patterns in the consumption-income ratio over the period 1869–1929 and a more recent study by Goldsmith covering the period 1897–1949 both revealed evidence of a remarkable degree of stability in the ratio over time.[6] Other even more recent studies have generally reached the same conclusion.

[5] J. M. Keynes, *The General Theory of Employment, Interest, and Money,* Harcourt Brace, New York, 1936, pp. 96, 97.
[6] S. Kuznets, *Uses of National Income in Peace and War,* NBER, New York, 1942; and R. W. Goldsmith, *A Study of Saving in the United States,* Vol. 1, Princeton University Press, Princeton, N.J., 1955.

The apparent contradiction between evidence drawn from income class studies and from time series analysis of consumption-income ratios was reconciled by arguments appearing at about the same time by Duesenberry and Modigliani.[7] Although the methods of the two analyses differed, they both resulted in the same form of the consumption function. Duesenberry's argument has received more continuing analysis and so will be outlined here. The first proposition is that a consumer's purchase propensities are not independently determined by his absolute income level but instead are related to his strata on an income class scale. This property, if present, leads to the expectation that the lower income strata will save small proportions of their income, even though that strata corresponds to higher and higher levels of real (purchasing power) income over time. A second proposition in Duesenberry's model is that income-consumption relationships are not statistically the same when they are rising as they are when they are falling.

The first proposition views the consumer as establishing his consumption standards basically with a view toward the consumption patterns of those above and below him in the income strata. This view helps explain the results of income class studies that consistently show that lower income strata consumers tend to save relatively low and constant income proportions, even though their incomes are rising over time. The asymmetry of income-consumption relationships yields a ratchet effect in which contractions in total income tend to lead to proportionately smaller contractions in consumer spending, as consumers base their adjustments on formerly achieved income levels and strive to preserve former standards of consumption. However, rises in income are likely to be met with nearly proportional rises in consumption expenditures unless these rises are considered temporary.

Figure 7–2 shows the effect graphically. In this figure, the broken line represents a perfectly proportional response of consumer spending to income change, i.e., the ratio of consumer spending to consumer incomes is constant along the line LRC for all income levels. By contrast, the two short-run consumption functions, C_1 and C_2, show a falling ratio of consumption to income as income is rising and a rising ratio as incomes are falling. According to the relative income hypothesis, the short-run curves are primarily applicable to income changes not expected to persist over any long period of time. A recession is an example. If recessionary income declines are considered temporary, consumers will reduce their consumption along the flatter short-run family of curves, allowing the ratio of consumption to income to rise by

---

[7] See J. S. Duesenberry, *Income Saving, and the Theory of Consumer Behavior,* Harvard University Press, Cambridge, Mass., 1949; and F. Modigliani, "Fluctuations in the Saving-Income Ratio: A Problem in Economic Forecasting," in *Studies in Income and Wealth,* Vol. 2, NBER, New York, 1949.

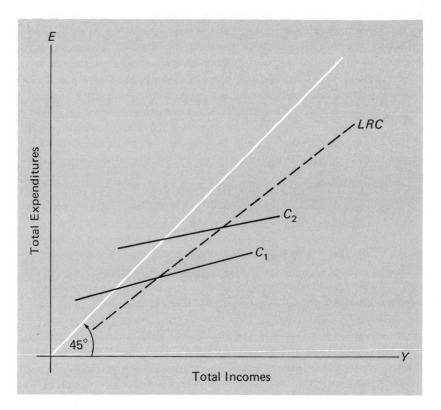

Figure 7–2
Relative Income Effects

reducing their saving. This could also apply to income increases that are considered temporary by the consumer. When income changes are considered continuing and persistent, the relative income model perceives the consumer response to be nearly proportional, moving along the long-run curve represented by *LRC* in Figure 7–2. This is the same result that derives from the model of household consumer behavior in Chapter 6 for the cases where an income decline is assumed to be in the present period only as compared to both the present and future periods. As a result, the relative income model provides a further rationale for that earlier conclusion.

Statistical tests of the relative income model tend to confirm statistically the type of process postulated by the model. However, as is more than occasionally the case in economics, alternative explanations of income-consumption behavior have been offered that also can be shown to be consistent with observed statistical results. One such alternative is the permanent income model of consumer behavior developed by Milton Friedman and others.

Permanent Income Effects

The permanent income model of consumer spending evolves from a view of consumers as being importantly habit based in their purchase decisions and led in these decisions in an important way by their perceptions of their long-run or permanent income flow. T. M. Brown has explored the impact of such influences upon consumer spending, and concluded that the effects of inertia-like forces is likely to be of principal importance in consumer spending.[8] The emphasis on habit patterns in Brown's analysis has been given more specific meaning and developed extensively by Milton Friedman.[9] Friedman has developed a model of consumption expenditures based on a model of both permanent income and permanent consumption. Permanent income is not observable in Friedman's analysis, but is partly masked by random or "noise" components contained in measured income statistics. The permanent income component of measured income is hypothesized as that portion that is expected to occur regularly over time essentially as a result of the perceived earnings rate on the present value of the consumers' stock of wealth and accumulated earning power on personal "human captial." Unanticipated or irregular income receipts are assumed to have an unpredictable impact on current spending in the permanent income model, since they cannot be expected to have an important impact on this perceived permanent income flow. Friedman isolated this permanent component of income by formulating it as a weighted average of past measured income levels, where the weights decline exponentially. The deviation of permanent consumption from measured consumption was considered to be essentially random, once the level of consumption is corrected for the investment-like character of consumer durables purchases. A basic proposition of the permanent income model is that the ratio of permanent income to permanent consumption is independent of the level of permanent income and is highly regular over time. This does not imply the ratio of permanent consumption to permanent income is constant over time. On the contrary, it is seen to depend on the rate of interest, i, on the level of household liquid assets and wealth, w, and on the age and other such characteristics of households, u. This gives the general expression:

$$C_p = k(i, w, u)Y_p \qquad\qquad (7–1)$$

[8] T. M. Brown, "Habit Persistence and Lags in Consumer Behavior," *Econometrica*, 20:3 (July 1952), pp. 355–371.
[9] M. Friedman, *A Theory of the Consumption Function*, NBER, New York, 1957.

where C_p and Y_p are permanent consumption and permanent income respectively. This expression largely corresponds with the theoretical analysis of the previous chapter in formulating an explanatory role for interest rates and consumer wealth in current consumption spending. In his statistical tests of the permanent income model, Friedman essentially assumes that i, w, and u move slowly in comparison to changes in Y_p and accordingly that the ratio of C_p and Y_p is quite stable through time.

Friedman considered the consistency of his permanent income propositions with both income class and time series evidence on income-saving relations. In both cases, he interpreted the evidence as favorable to his model. His time series analysis employed annual data developed by Goldsmith over 1897–1949 from which an average ratio of consumption to income was calculated to be 0.877. A simple range of 5 percent on either side of this average contains 39 of the 53 yearly observations and shows no particular pattern. Six of the 14 points lying outside the range correspond to the irregularities of wartime years, periods which Friedman expects were characterized by both a positive transitory income component (temporarily high income levels) and a negative (transitory) consumption component (rationing, etc.), which together would explain the low ratios observed.

In addition to the evidence of the long-term income ratios, Friedman made more extensive statistical tests of the permanent income model involving specific statistical approximations of Y_p and C_p. Regressions of Y_p upon C_p produced results similar to the evidence from the income-consumption ratios, implying a long-run ratio of permanent income to permanent consumption of about 0.88. In addition, the permanent income model fit the data well, explaining about 96 percent of the fluctuation in permanent consumption by permanent income over the period 1905–1951 with war years excluded. In general, the tests run by Friedman on the permanent income model were interpreted by him as providing support for the model structure. However, a recent study using the same data arrives at conflicting empirical conclusions, a result that raises questions about the empirical case for the operation of the permanent income model.[10]

Regardless of the conclusiveness of the empirical evidence, Friedman's work underscores Brown's less specific concepts of the influence of habits and past patterns of behavior upon current spending. The suggestion is that large changes in income over short periods are not likely to be met by proportionate changes in consumption. For example, over the course of a quarter, a sharp decline in consumer incomes is not likely to solicit a similar change in consumer spending unless the change is viewed as permanent. Over the course of a quarter, discrepancies between measured and perma-

---

[10] See J. M. Holmes, "A Direct Test of Friedman's Permanent Income Theory," *Journal of the American Statistical Association,* 65 (September 1970), pp. 1,159–1,162.

nent income might even be expected to produce measured income-consumption changes in the opposite direction, a result occasionally found in quarterly income-consumption statistics.

Effects of Liquid Assets and Wealth Positions on Consumption

The theoretical discussion in Chapter 6 and the formulation of Friedman's permanent income framework have both suggested an important theoretical role for consumer liquid asset and general wealth positions in consumer spending. Basically, the previous discussion has indicated that buildups in stocks of liquid assets and wealth in general reduce the marginal satisfaction of additions to these stocks and lead to enlarged purchases of consumer goods.

The empirical evidence on the effect of liquid asset positions generally supports the theoretical role assigned to them. In the study of consumption spending incorporated into the Brookings model, Suits and Sparks found a significant statistical role for household liquid assets in equations for nondurables and services.[11] Other consumption studies have yielded similar results; for example Patinkin summarizes and reports on the results of 12 consumption function analyses that dealt with liquidity measures.[12] Of these, ten were significant in the model in which they appeared. On the other hand, analyses by Klein and Evans have not found a significant role for liquid assets in statistically estimated consumption functions.[13] Nonetheless, the general consensus of the growing body of empirical evidence on the role of liquid assets in consumer spending is that liquid assets do contribute importantly to the explanation of fluctuations in consumer spending.[14]

A related component of wealth, capital gains, has also received attention as a possible determinant of consumer spending.[15] Both realized and

[11] See Duesenberry, Fromm, Klein, and Kuh, p. 208.

[12] D. Patinkin, *Money, Interest, and Prices,* 2nd ed., Harper & Row, New York, 1965, pp. 656–657.

[13] M. R. Evans and L. R. Klein, *The Wharton Econometric Forecasting Model,* 2nd enlarged ed., Wharton School of Finance and Commerce, University of Pennsylvania, Philadelphia, 1968.

[14] An excellent account of the detailed studies in this area is contained in R. Ferber, "Consumer Economics, A Survey," *The Journal of Economic Literature,* 2:4 (December 1973), pp. 1,303–1,342.

[15] See K. B. Bhatia, "Capital Gains and the Aggregate Consumption Function," *American Economic Review* 62 (December 1972), pp. 866–879.

unrealized capital gains have been found in some studies to explain important proportions of consumer spending fluctuations. This is a provocative finding, as it suggests that rising security markets may positively shift the consumption function. In this way, increases in security prices lead to higher levels of aggregate consumption and income, presumably because consumers feel richer during rising stock markets and opt for larger levels of current consumption compared to future consumption.

Total wealth holdings, including liquid assets, capital gains, and other asset holdings, has been studied by other researchers. Theoretical and empirical support for the role of wealth has been found by Ando and Modigliani, who emphasize the role of wealth in balancing income streams over working-age cycles.[16] In their model, consumption depends on the total purchasing power available to the consumer, on the rate of return on new funds, and on the position of the consumer in his working age career. In the life cycle framework, the consumer is seen to redistribute available financial resources over the working age cycle in order to obtain the most desirable long-range pattern of consumption. Other models have been proposed containing specific roles for wealth holdings. However, statistical studies made in the context of overall econometric models have not produced strong support for the use of all-encompassing wealth variables in consumption analysis.[17]

Other Consumption Determinants

Economists have discussed several additional consumption determinants. One such determinant is income distribution. As income is distributed away from high-saving upper and towards lower income strata, the overall consumption-income ratio will rise. Shifts in age groupings can have a similar effect. If increasing proportions of the population fall into family forming and high-spending age groups, the consumption-income ratio can be expected to rise. These two factors, which reflect clear and distinct influences upon consumption spending, also are typically subject to only rather small change during any one- or two-year period. This minimizes their statistical importance for short-term analysis. Accordingly, econometric

---

[16] A. Ando and F. Modigliani, "The Life Cycle Hypothesis of Saving: Aggregate Implication and Tests," *American Economic Review*, 53:1 (March 1963), pp. 55–84.

[17] However, a contrary view is maintained in a model developed by F. de Leeuw and E. M. Gramlich known as the Federal Reserve–MIT econometric model. ["Channels of Monetary Policy," *Federal Reserve Bulletin* (June 1969), pp. 472–491.] In this approach, wealth plays a substantial role in consumer activity. For a discussion of this model see Chapter 17.

model-building largely ignores income distribution and population age groupings in short-term models.

The same conclusion applies to the overall influence of interest rate fluctuations in aggregate consumer spending. Although Chapter 6 has derived a clear-cut theoretical role for interest rate fluctuations in consumer spending, econometric studies have in large part not confirmed this role as being of much practical consequence. This result may in part reflect the finding in the previous chapter that the impact of interest rates on consumption depends on the shapes of household indifference curves. A wide diversity in the shapes of individual household indifference curves could lead to the effect of interest rate fluctuations being almost entirely neutralized over the entire economy. In any event, the Wharton, Commerce, and Brookings econometric models agree in not using interest rate levels to explain consumer spending.

Stability of Income-Consumption Relationships

The usefulness of the consumption function as a tool in economic analysis is importantly dependent upon its stability from one time period to the next. If we can depend upon the income-consumption relationship to be highly stable, we can predict the way in which the consumer will respond to independent shifts in demand. On the other hand, if the consumption function shifts wildly and unpredictably over time, it cannot be expected to be of great value as a tool for practical economic analysis. One way to formulate a crude impression on this question is to calculate the ratio of the change in consumer spending compared to the corresponding change in income over successively longer periods. This is done in Figure 7-3 for the post-World War II period in the United States.

The figure shows the quarterly ratio of consumption change to income change, the annual change in consumption compared to the annual change in income, and also a 5-year moving change in consumption compared to the corresponding 5-year moving change in income. These ratios of incremental income-consumption change cannot be strictly interpreted as estimates of the slope of the consumption function, since no attempt has been made to hold constant the effects of other consumption determinants. But even so, a rough indication of the stability and pervasiveness of the income-consumption relation is provided by the plots in Figure 7-3. These plots show that the incremental consumption-income ratio becomes more stable as both consumption and income are averaged over longer time periods. The standard deviation of the 5-year series is only 0.044 as compared to a value of 2.135 for the standard deviation of the quarterly series. The general picture is clear. The longer the time period involved, the more stable we can

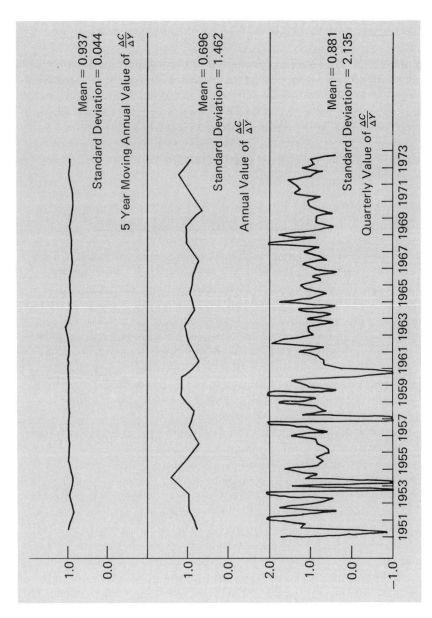

Figure 7–3

Stability of Income-Consumption Relationships

expect the consumption function to become. We find the most instability over quarterly periods, and accordingly the simple consumption function must be expected to be somewhat less useful for analysis over this period than for longer periods. Figure 7–3 also suggests the possibility that other consumption determinants may be more important over shorter periods such as a quarter than over longer periods. This is the conclusion reached by many analysts and the view reflected in part by the multivariate specification usually found in short-run econometric models of the U.S. economy. For longer periods, the impact of many nonincome variables found important in explaining fluctuations in consumption over the short-run can be expected to decline and the role of income to increase.

Empirical Models for Nondurables and Services

Perhaps the most stringent test of conceptual models of consumption is the extent to which predictive econometric models employ them in forecasting and simulation. Among major econometric models, only the Wharton model directly reflects the permanent income hypothesis. In fact, the Wharton model-builders specifically derive their equation from the permanent income framework, with appropriate modifications to account for statistical problems of parameter estimation.[18] The income term in the Wharton equation is a declining weighted average of current and three past quarterly percent changes in income, on the reasoning that the consumer's permanent income will be influenced greatest by recent past income experience. In addition, the Wharton model includes a four-quarter moving average of past consumption expenditures. This reflects the influence of past attained consumption standards upon current consumption expenditures. This influence is measured to be positive, indicating the "reverse saturation effect" of past attained levels of consumption.

The Brookings study is not directly comparable with the Wharton study since three equations were developed to represent nondurables and services expenditures rather than the single equation of the Wharton model.[19] The Brookings results are similar to the Wharton results in the emphasis in each equation given to the sum of past expenditure patterns (measured by a four-quarter moving average of past expenditures). Beyond that, substantial differences exist. First, the influence of current income is direct, linear, and exclusive of past income levels, thereby representing a simple income-consumption hypothesis, as compared with the permanent income model ex-

18 See Evans and Klein, pp. 21–22.
19 Duesenberry, Fromm, Klein, and Kuh, p. 684.

pressed in the Wharton results. In addition, the Brookings study incorporates relative consumer price ratios as explanatory variables. However, the coefficients are not strongly significant statistically, which suggests only a weak role for relative prices in nondurables and services analysis. Finally, the Brookings analysis includes variables measuring liquid asset holdings and total population in the model for consumer services. The population variable essentially accounts for secular trends in consumption expenditures. The liquid assets variable measures the influence of this component of wealth holding upon service expenditures and finds this influence to be significant. This gives statistical support for the liquid asset hypotheses discussed earlier.[20]

An early model developed at the University of Michigan and published in 1962 by Daniel Suits provides additional evidence on the determinants of nondurables and services expenditures.[21] In the Michigan model, the income variable employed reflects a simple linear income-consumption hypothesis as in the Brookings study. In addition, the most recent quarter's level of expenditure is included in the model, reflecting a standard of living effect. Finally, a lagged liquid assets variable is included, providing further support for the explanatory value of liquid assets in consumer spending.

A further empirical illustration of consumption relationships is provided by a model developed under the direction of the U.S. Commerce Department.[22] Like the Brookings study, the income hypothesis of the Commerce model is simple and linear. A living standard effect is measured by an eight-quarter moving average of past consumer spending, similar to the terms in the Wharton and Brookings studies. Population is also employed as an explanatory variable as with the Brookings study.

Analysis of Nondurables and Services—
A Summary

The empirical results now considered have uniformly emphasized the importance of current and past income changes in explaining changes in current consumption expenditures. They have also emphasized the importance of past patterns of consumption expenditures as a reflection of the impact

---

[20] However, the data period of the study encompassed are the major post-World War II recessions, which raises somewhat the probability that liquidity variables would be significant.

[21] D. B. Suits, "Forecasting and Analysis with an Econometric Model," *American Economic Review,* 52:1 (March 1962), pp. 104–132.

[22] See *Survey of Current Business* (May 1966), p. 30.

of attained standards of living upon current spending. This consensus is shown in the summary diagram of Figure 7–4. In addition, the structure of major econometric models supports an important explanatory role for liquid assets in short-run fluctuations in consumption, particularly in regard to service type expenditures. This influence is also shown in Figure 7–4. Finally, population has been used in some models to reflect secular trends in consumption expenditures.

In this and the previous chapter, we have considered both theoretical and empirical contributions to the understanding of the diverse category of consumption expenditures. The largest portion of remaining private demand for goods and services is in the category of Gross Private Domestic Investment. In the next chapter, we consider a large and closely watched portion of these expenditures—those made on fixed investment other than housing.

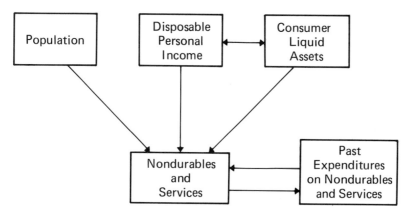

Figure 7–4
Summary—Nondurable and Services Expenditure

Discussion Questions

1. In what basic way are the markets for automobiles and the markets for television sets similar? In what ways do they differ? Explain.

2. How does "relative income" differ from "permanent income"? In what ways do these two concepts represent similar influences.

3. Suppose a household's wealth position suddenly increased due to an inheritance, while its income remained unchanged. How, if at all, would this impact upon its permanent income?

4. Can you think of a circumstance where an increase in income over a calendar quarter might lead to a zero or negative change in consumer expenditure? Can you find any evidence in the U.S. national income data in which this either occurs or is approximated? Could the circumstances you have described apply to an annual period? Explain.

5. The empirical studies reviewed indicate a feedback effect of income on consumption over time. Referring to Figure 7–4, explain why and how this occurs.

8

Theory and Analysis of Fixed Capital Investment

In the United States, fluctuations in capital investment have historically been pivotal ingredients in the direction and magnitude of general economic fluctuations. The key position of capital investment in overall income determination stems from the character and position of these expenditures in the macroeconomic marketplace. Fixed capital investment is a large component of the GNP, usually accounting for more than 10 percent of the total. Moreover, fixed investment is usually viewed as less dependent on the current level of economic activity than upon expectations about the future course of economic activity. This means we usually find consumption expenditures react importantly to independent fluctuations in investment, but not vice versa. Investment is thus normally seen as the catalyst in economic fluctuations with consumption being more the respondent. In addition, the future orientation of investment expenditures often makes these expenditures a barometer of the market expectations of the business sector. New expenditures on plant expansions and equipment are a dollar-and-cents show of faith by the nation's producers in the upcoming prospects for the economy.

The national income accounting breakdown of gross private domestic investment contains three rather distinct elements. These are business fixed capital investment, residential construction, and inventory investment. Because these three expenditure flows are separable both theoretically and in terms of the factors important in their statistical explanation over time, we shall consider them separately in our discussion. In this chapter, we take up the largest of the three—business fixed investment. In Chapter 9 we consider investment in residential construction and in inventories.

Investment Opportunities and the Marginal Efficiency of Investment

Macroeconomic investment theory most directly deals with expenditures in the fixed capital investment category of the national accounts. This category includes outlays for new business plant and equipment and for non-profit facilities and equipment. In addition to the focus of the theory upon fixed capital investment, these expenditures usually receive more attention in analyses of economic fluctuations than the other components of gross private domestic investment, probably reflecting the important quantitative position of the fixed investment category. The crucial role of investment in overall economic fluctuations has led to a rich development of theory dealing with these expenditures. Empirical testing of models of fixed investment has also been extensive.[1]

Investment Opportunities in the Firm

We begin with a view of the investment decision in the individual firm. This view sees investment expenditures as representing the purchase of a stream of cash returns, R_1, spaced over future time periods. Considering time periods $1, 2, \cdots n$, the return from an investment outlay can be expressed as

$$R_1 + R_2 + \cdots + R_n \qquad (8\text{--}1)$$

Analyzing the value of the return from a specific investment opportunity is essentially a matter of placing a single value upon this stream of future returns such that the value can be compared with the investment outlay. The question of assigning a meaningful value to a stream of time-spaced returns such as shown in Expression 8–1 requires consideration of the total size of the R_1 values and consideration of their distribution over time. The time distribution of returns is important because in modern economies, money has a time value. Since money can be loaned out at interest, a dollar today is worth more than a dollar tomorrow. This means we cannot simply add the components of the returns stream shown in Expression 8–1 over

[1] See, for example, J. R. Meyer and E. Kuh, *The Investment Decision,* Harvard University Press, Cambridge, Mass., 1957; Kuh, *Capital Stock Growth: A Microeconometric Approach,* North Holland Publishing Co., Amsterdam, 1963; L. R. Klein, "Studies in Investment Behavior," *NBER Conference on Business Cycles,* New York, 1951, pp. 233–277; and D. W. Jorgenson and C. D. Siebert, "Theories of Corporate Investment Behavior," *American Economic Review,* 58 (September 1968), pp. 681–712.

time, but must add them in such a way that we correctly account for the earning power of money received in future periods.

Discounted present value techniques offer an acceptable way to accomplish this objective by discounting future-valued returns to the present by an appropriate interest rate and summing the discounted components to obtain the present value of the stream, which we denote by PV. PV is given as follows:

$$PV = \frac{R_1}{(1 + i)} + \frac{R_2}{(1 + i)^2} + \cdots + \frac{R_n}{(1 + i)^n} \qquad (8\text{--}2)$$

where i is the opportunity cost for use of funds for investment. In Expression 8–2, each component represents the amount of money required now to reproduce the amount of return R_t at future time period t. For example, an amount of money equal to $R_2/(1 + i)^2$ is required presently to produce R_2 amount at time period 2. Accordingly, in Expression 8–2 if we have PV funds available now, depositing this amount in an account earning at i rate of interest allows the withdrawal of R_1 funds at the end of the first time period, R_2 at the end of the second time period, and so forth, until, upon withdrawal of R_n funds at the end of the nth period, the account is just depleted.

A numerical example provides further illustration. Suppose you are offered a 3-year contract in which you are to receive $100 after the first year, $1,000 after the second year, and $10,000 after the third year. The offering price of this contract is to be $9,000. The decision is whether to buy the contract or not. On the surface, the contract offers a total of $11,100 over 3 years for the outlay of only $9,000, for a profit of $2,100. But, this view does not account for the opportunity cost of the investment, which is the earning power of the $9,000 over the 3-year period. Suppose you can earn 8 percent on your money over this 3-year period. Then, according to Expression 8–2 you would have to deposit $100/(1.08) = $92.59 presently to reproduce the $100 at the end of the first year. Similarly, $1,000/(1.08)^2 = $857.34 is required now to reproduce $1,000 2 years hence, and $10,000/(1.08)^3 = $7,941.74 is required now to reproduce $10,000 after 3 years. The total outlay at present of $8,891.67, if deposited at the available 8 percent, would enable the same pattern of earnings to be reproduced as that offered by the contract, but at a lower outlay. Clearly, your 8 percent earning opportunity is superior to the proposed contract, and the contract should be declined. If the earning rate available to you dropped from 8 percent to 6 percent, the situation is reversed. At this lower earning rate, a total of $9,380.64 is required to reproduce the earnings stream—more than the offering price of the contract. The contract is now a better deal than your 6 percent earning opportunity.

The $8,891.67 and the $9,380.64 in this illustration are the present value, PV, of the contract under the conditions where the discount rate is 8 percent and 6 percent respectively. They illustrate the important property of Expression 8–2 that the present value of a stream of returns declines as the rate of discount rises, and vice versa. Falling rates of interest in general have a tendency to increase the present value of all investment opportunities, whereas rising interest rates in general reduce the present value of investment opportunities.

Our discussion indicates that the present value of an individual investment opportunity can be compared directly with the required outlay, with projects being judged profitable when the present value exceeds the cost. Assuming an individual firm continuously has available to it an array of investment projects yielding various PVs and requiring various outlays, or Cs, then a ranking of all available investment opportunities can be prepared in the order of the net of PV over C. If the availability of funds to the firm is unlimited at a cost of i, the discount rate, the firm will profit from engaging in all the investment projects for which $PV > C$, in which case the point where $PV = C$ locates the most profitable volume of investment outlay. Further investment beyond this point does not earn at the opportunity cost of money use, i, and thus is not as profitable as investing further funds at i.

Alternatively, the same analysis can be restated in terms of comparisons of the rate of return on individual investment projects with the opportunity cost of funds. In our earlier illustration, if the available earning rate had been 7.5 percent rather than 6 percent or 8 percent, the calculation of the present value of the contract shows that it is neither positive nor negative but identical to the $9,000 cost. This is a backhand way of saying that the contract offers a 7.5 percent compounded rate of return over the 3-year period. In general, we can set the value of PV equal to C in Expression 8–2 and solve that expression for the rate of discount. The resulting rate just equates the present value of an investment with its cost. We shall refer to such a calculated rate as the internal rate of return or just the investment's rate of return. The internal rate of return can also be thought of as the maximum money use rate the firm could face and still produce a profitable investment.

If a firm's investment opportunities are ranked according to their internal rate of return, the resulting schedule shows the marginal earning rate associated with various levels of capital expenditure by the firm. A hypothetical investment opportunity schedule for an individual firm is shown in Figure 8–1. In this figure, a small volume of investment equal to I_1 can be made at an extremely high rate of return, with the marginal efficiency of further additions falling off. Once the level of investment I_1 is attained and incorporated into the firm's capital stock, the next highest

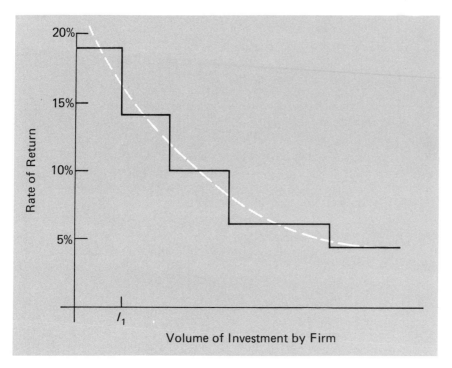

Figure 8–1

Hypothetical Investment Opportunity Schedule for a Firm

return investment establishes the marginal efficiency of further additions to the firm's capital assets. The broken line in Figure 8–1 illustrates the smoothed shape of this investment opportunity schedule and shows a falling marginal efficiency of additions to the firm's capital stock through new investment expenditures.

Investment Opportunities in the Economy

If we lump together the investment opportunity schedules for all firms in the economy, we may refer to the resulting curve as the *Marginal Efficiency of Capital,* or *MEC,* curve. The MEC is illustrated in Figure 8–2. Its downward slope reflects the general pattern throughout the economy that we have discussed at the level of the firm. Increases in investment by all firms both use up high-earning available investment opportunities and increase the capital base. Both lead to a falling marginal return on further additions to capital. Thus, the MEC slopes down to the right.

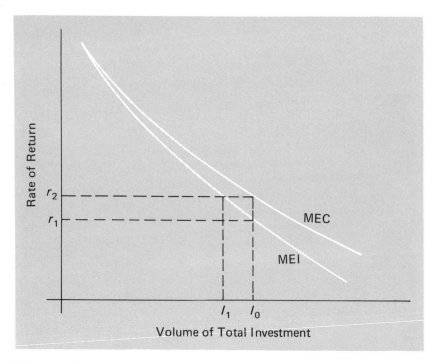

Figure 8–2
An Economy's MEC and MEI Schedules

In our discussion of the individual firm's investment opportunity schedule and its aggregation into the economy's MEC, we have not taken into account possible effects of demand pressures upon the sector of the economy that produces capital goods such as plants and machinery. The capital goods sector in the U.S. economy is largely made-to-order in character. The inventory positions of producers in this sector are relatively small and in some cases zero. The effect of this is to accentuate the effect on capital goods productive capacity of shifts in the demand for capital goods. Invariably, when the demand for capital goods rises, the effective delivered price also rises, and the delivery lead time increases. Both these increases reduce the actual rate of return on individual investment projects. Because individual firms cannot plan on this without also forecasting the investment plans of all other firms, we have not considered it to be a factor in the formulation of the investment opportunity or MEC schedules. However, as the level of investment proceeds in a particular time period, individual producers will find prices and lead times increasing according to the intensity of the overall level of capital goods demand, and they will have to revise downward the projections of return on investment in their investment opportunity schedules. Some investment plans may be cancelled or postponed until prices decline and lead times are shorter. As a result, the effective aggregate investment curve that accounts for these revisions in plans lies below the MEC curve. We shall label this curve the *Marginal Efficiency of Investment* curve, or the *MEI* curve.

The MEI is shown in Figure 8–2 along with the MEC. If we hold constant the level of aggregate investment at I_0, we see that the effect of higher capital goods prices and delivery stretch-outs at that level of investment is to reduce the rate of return on marginal investments from r_2 to r_1. Alternatively, if we consider the volume of investment for which the marginal rate of return has dropped to r_2, we find the effect of the higher prices of capital goods and delivery stretch-outs has reduced the level from I_0 to I_1. We should expect the problem of higher prices and longer lead times to worsen as the level of investment grows, such that the gap between the MEC and the MEI grows with higher investment. Of course, if prices and lead times in the capital goods industry were fixed, the MEC would equal the MEI. Since this is not generally the case, we shall concentrate our attention on the MEI as the effective aggregate investment demand schedule.

The Cost of Capital in Investment Decisions

While the MEI schedule shows the benefits associated with employing greater amounts of money capital to produce successive additions to the nation's stock of capital assets, it does not reveal anything about the costs of employing the money capital involved. In general, these costs are not inconsequential. Indeed, they are generally taken as establishing the lower boundary for acceptable investments. The question of the costs and benefits associated with new or continued employment of money capital by corporations has been extensively developed in the literature of corporation finance.[2] The generally accepted framework of this literature encompasses the view that all forms of money capital available to the firm have a use cost that must be taken into account when considering the appropriate cut-off point for investment.

More specifically, the typical firm is seen as financing its investments from a pool of capital that consists partly of internal funds, partly of new equity, and partly of debt. Figure 8–3 illustrates the point. This figure shows

[2] For a survey, see J. C. Van Horn, *Financial Management and Policy*, 3rd ed., Prentice-Hall, Englewood Cliffs, N.J., 1974, Chapters 3–4.

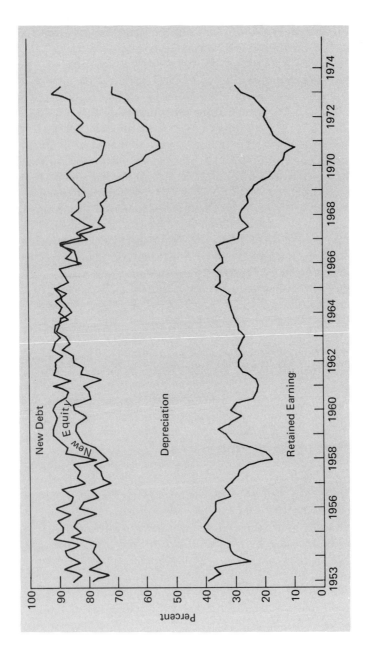

Figure 8–3

Proportions of Corporate Capital

the proportions of new capital raised by U.S. corporations over time. Internally generated capital is broken into retained earnings and depreciation, which helps show that the largest continuing supply of money capital comes from the funds freed by depreciation write-offs, with the second largest amount coming from retained earnings. Together, these two comprise corporate saving and equal an average of about 80 percent of the new capital raised over time. New debt capital averages about 14 percent of new capital needs, while the remaining 6 percent of capital is raised by new equity issues. Figure 8–3 shows that the proportions of capital employed by corporations is generally rather stable but is influenced by cyclical factors such as the recessionary period of 1970. In that period, a decline in corporate profits and a stable flow of depreciation reduced the proportion of internally generated funds from 74 percent in 1969 to about 55 percent in the middle of 1970. Accordingly, corporations were forced to raise larger amounts of capital externally in debt and equity markets in order to finance their investment programs.

Since firms normally raise funds internally and in debt and equity markets, it is not appropriate to consider the use cost of only particular types of capital, but rather the cost associated with the entire pool. Thus, a dollar of investment capital can be thought of as having an average cost that reflects the fractions normally raised in the categories of Figure 8–3. Such an average use cost of funds can be found by weighting the specific costs of debt, equity, and retained earnings by their normal proportions. The remaining category of depreciation is generally assumed to carry the same cost as average dollar of new money capital, since it is assumed to have been produced by a combination of all forms of capital. The resulting weighted average measures the average use cost of new corporate capital, which we designate as r. If we define r_d, r_{eq}, and r_{int} as the costs of debt, equity, and retained earnings respectively, we may state:

$$r = f_d \cdot r_d + f_{eq} \cdot r_{eq} + f_{int} \cdot r_{int} \qquad (8\text{--}3)$$

where f_d, f_{eq}, and f_{int} are the fractions of debt, equity, and retained earnings and where

$$f_d + f_{eq} + f_{int} = 1 \qquad (8\text{--}4)$$

Debt costs, r_d, are the market costs of new corporate debt. They are often represented by yields on new or existing corporate bonds, and they represent an explicit cost to corporations for the use of borrowed funds. In the United States, value of r_d is affected by corporate income tax rates since interest costs on money borrowed by corporations is deductible from tax liabilities. Thus, the correct r_d for our consideration is the after-tax market costs of new debt.

Equity costs and the costs of retained earnings are not market costs in the view of most corporation finance analysts.[3] Instead, they are seen as opportunity costs reflecting the profits foregone by investors when a corporation employs the investor's funds in its investments, rather than returning funds to shareholders for their investment. These opportunity costs consist of the return investors in corporate stock could earn if they invested their funds in the best investment alternative having similar risks as corporate stock. Accordingly, the cost of equity, r_{eq}, is defined as the required return on corporate stock established by the alternative investment opportunities available to corporate shareholders.

If it were not for taxes on dividends and transactions costs, the cost to the firm of reinvesting retained earnings, r_{int}, would be exactly equal to r_{eq}. It would make no difference whether the corporation was contemplating the use of funds from newly issued stock or using funds generated internally. Either type of funds belong to the firm's shareholders and accordingly the best stockholder alternative investment governs their use. However, taxes place a liability on funds transferred to stockholders as dividends. Thus, with a 40 percent marginal tax rate on dividends, the payment of a $10 million dividend by a corporation only results in 6 million of investable funds by the stockholder. This tax leakage creates a difference between opportunity costs associated with funds generated internally compared with costs for funds raised by new equity. If stockholders can at best earn 15 percent on other comparable investments, i.e., if $r_{eq} = 15$ percent, then they could earn $(0.15) \cdot (16) = 0.9$ million on 6 million of after-tax dividends, abstracting from transactions costs. To do as well as this, the firm could earn at the lower rate $0.9/10 = 9$ percent and produce the same volume of earnings. Accordingly, the cost of retained earnings may be given as this indifference point:

$$r_{int} = r_{eq}(1 - tx) \tag{8-5}$$

where tx is the marginal tax rate on dividends.

As Expression 8-3 states, the overall cost of capital is obtained by weighting the costs of debt, equity, and retained earnings by their relative proportions in the corporate financial mix. Although an individual firm may be able to raise virtually unlimited amounts of debt and equity capital in customary proportions at essentially unchanged market costs, if a large number of corporations in the economy attempt to increase their debt and

---

[3] For a detailed discussion see Van Horn, pp. 93–103 or H. Beirman and S. Smidt, *The Capital Budgeting Decision*, 3rd ed., Macmillan, New York, 1971, pp. 152–160.

equity capital flows by substantial amounts over a short period of time, they will undoubtedly push up the market cost of debt. In addition, the need to attract a large number of new shareholders to provide a proportionate share of equity capital will require the attraction of investors with higher opportunity costs, thus increasing the cost of equity capital and the derived cost of internal funds. As shown in Figure 8–4, the result of these pressures must be a rising overall marginal cost of capital. Furthermore, there is reason to believe that the marginal costs of capital for the entire economy rise rather slowly over an initial range, and then more rapidly as shown in Figure 8–4. For small amounts of total capital raised, a larger than normal proportion (if not all) is produced by internal funds, since these funds flow into corporations as a by-product of operations. Over this initial range, minimum demands are placed by corporations upon capital markets. Therefore, fluctuations in corporate demand for capital over this range of internal funds will have little effect upon debt costs or required return on stock and thus equity costs. However, when total capital requirements by corporations begin to exceed the level of internally flowing funds, the pressures on capital markets build rapidly, and the prices of debt and equity capital can be expected to increase in relation to the increase in demand for corporate

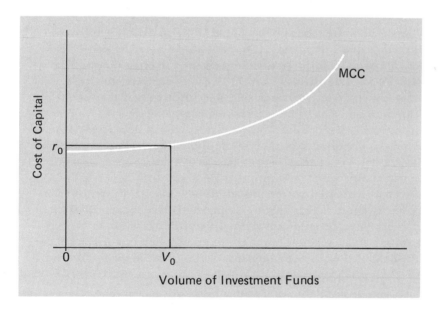

Figure 8–4
Aggregate Cost of Capital

capital.[4] Figure 8–4 shows this pattern. Over an initial range OV_0, most of the capital requirement of corporations is met through internal funds, such that the capital market impact of increased demand for investment funds is minor and the curve is nearly flat. Beyond V_0 internal funds are exhausted and additional capital acquisition involves raising funds in debt and equity capital markets. In this region, the greater the market demand by corporations, the higher the market cost, for a given market supply curve for corporate capital. We label the curve in Figure 8–4 the *Marginal Cost of Capital* curve, or the *MCC* curve.

The marginal cost of capital and marginal efficiency of investment curves establish the equilibrium level of investment in the economy. Figure 8–5 depicts the process. Since the MEI shows the marginal return on various levels of investment and the MCC shows the marginal cost of the associated investment funds, the intersection of the two curves shows the position where the marginal return for investment has just fallen to its associated marginal cost. At the intersection of the MEI and the MCC, all the acceptably profitable investments have been undertaken. In Figure 8–5, the level of investment I_0 and the cost of capital r_0 are the equilibrium level of investment and the overall cost of capital respectively.

Influences on Investment via the MCC

As Figure 8–5 indicates, the position of the MCC curve has an important impact on the equilibrium level of investment. We now consider some of the more important influences upon investment that occur due to shifts in the MCC. A common influence on the MCC is independent fluctuations in market interest rates on bonds and other debt capital that occur for reasons other than being induced by movements along the MCC to differing investment levels. Such changes in the market cost of debt have a direct impact on the overall cost of capital and thus shift the entire function. Moreover, as the cost of debt changes, to a certain degree a change occurs in the opportunity cost of holding corporate stock, since corporate debt may be considered an alternative upon its adjustment for risk differences by investors. For example, higher debt costs can be expected to increase the required return on stock, as long as we view the required return to stock as maintaining a stable relationship to the required market return on debt. Figure 8–6 shows the effect of an independent increase in the market cost

4 Since investment spending may be expected to induce consumer spending, a similar set of pressures is transmitted indirectly to capital markets by induced changes in the demand for money by consumers to facilitate changes in consumer spending. We take this subject up in Chapter 14 and for now ignore such effects.

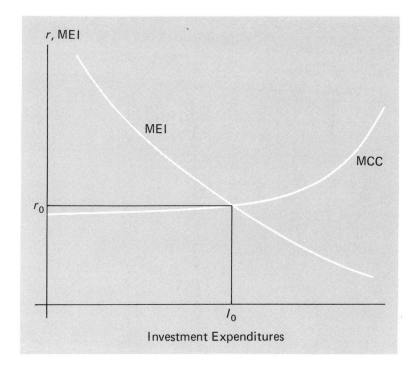

Figure 8–5

Investment Equilibrium

of debt upon the MCC and upon investment. The initial level of investment I_0 is disturbed by the interest rate induced increase in the MCC function from MCC_0 to MCC_1. The higher cost of capital reduces the equilibrium level of investment to I_1, where the resulting cost of capital has increased from r_0 to r_1. However, the increase in r is not as great as the shift in the MCC function, due to the effect of the decline in investment upon the demand for capital funds. Whereas the curve at point I_0 has shifted upward by an amount $(r^* - r_0)$, the actual increase in r is less than this amount, i.e., r_1 is less than r^*. In general, we may expect the direct and indirect effects of a change in the market cost of debt to bring about a movement in equilibrium investment in the opposite direction.

A closely related effect upon the MCC occurs by a possible revision of the required return on corporate stock. If stockholders in general revise their perception of the level of risk associated with investment in stock, they will revise their required return on equity accordingly. For example, suppose that an economic event such as an international currency crisis

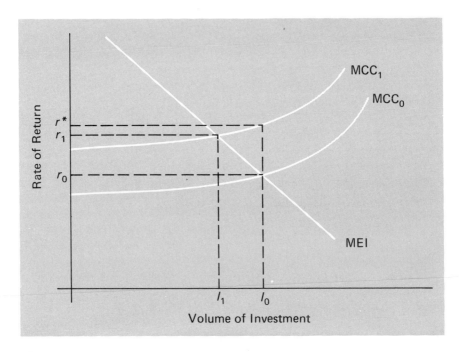

Figure 8–6

Increase in Interest Rates

causes corporate stocks to be judged to be significantly more risky. A higher level of perceived risk by investors causes an upward revision of the required return to equity. Stock prices decline in order to align the now higher required return with the expected market return. As the required return to equity increases, the cost of both equity and retained earnings increases as well. The overall cost of capital increases accordingly. The effect on investment is identical with that shown in Figure 8–6. Similarly, the adoption of a more bullish attitude on the part of investors such that stocks are generally perceived to be less risky shifts the MCC downward, lowers the cost of capital for all levels of investment, and increases the equilibrium level of investment.

Since the cost of debt capital, r_d, is adjusted for taxes, changes in corporate profits taxes impact upon the overall cost of capital and thus upon the position of the MCC. However, the same change in corporate taxes will alter the cash flow produced by new investment by altering the tax charge associated with each dollar of cash flow generated by investment projects. Thus, the impact of a change in corporate taxes upon our investment model shifts both the MCC and the MEI in the same direction. Figure 8–7 shows

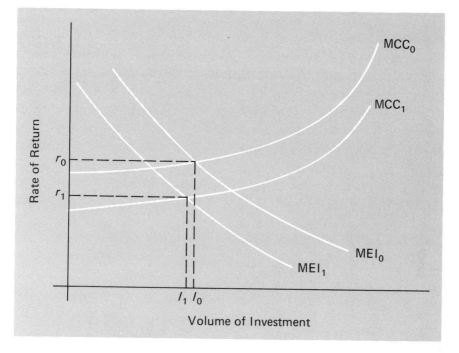

Figure 8–7

Corporate Tax Effects

the effect of an increase in corporate taxes. The initial position of the MEI and MCC curves at MEI_0 and MCC_0 produce an equilibrium level of investment equal to I_0 and a cost of capital of r_0. The tax increase reduces the after-tax cost of debt for a given market cost, thus lowering the MCC curve to MCC_1. However, the negative effect of the tax increase on return on investment calculations also shifts the MEI downward to MEI_1. The impact on investment depends on the relative impact of these two shifts. In Figure 8–7, the impact on the MEI is greater than the impact on the MCC and the equilibrium level of investment falls.

A change in either corporate profits or depreciation write-offs has an impact on the shape of the MCC curve. If corporate profits increase, a larger volume of investment funds can be generated before corporations need to raise funds heavily in capital markets. A decline in the corporate demand for capital market funds increases the point where debt and equity cost increases begin to increase the cost of capital at a faster pace. Figure 8–8 shows this effect. In this figure, the initial position of the MCC and MEI at MCC_0 and MEI_0 produce an equilibrium level of investment of

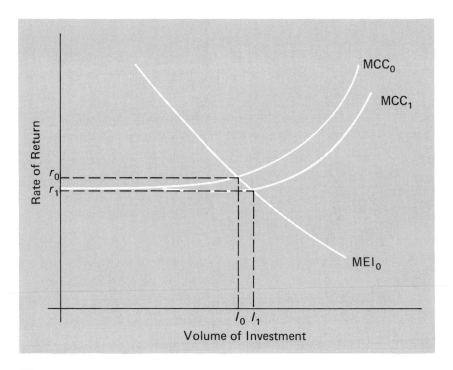

Figure 8–8

Increase in Internal Funds

I_0. An increase in profits or depreciation shifts the MCC outward for higher volumes of investment by postponing the region of heavy capital market demand. The result is a decline in the cost of capital and an increase in the equilibrium level of investment to I_1. This indicates we may expect increases in the flow of corporate internal funds to have a positive impact on equilibrium investment.

Influences on Investment via the MEI

As a measure of the marginal return on new investment, the MEI is subject to influences having to do with the projection of future outcomes of current investment. In the evaluation of the expected return on investments, managers and financial planners throughout the economy must hold a premise about the pace of economic activity over the future time period of the investment. These product market expectations can have an important impact upon the analysis of the prospective return from new capital expenditure. For example, assume you are developing an estimate of the internal rate of return on a substantial plant expansion project. Assume also that at present the current plant facilities are comfortably but not overly utilized. Will there be sufficient market demand to enable the new facilities to be operated at 50 percent of capacity, 70 percent of capacity, or 90 percent of capacity? The rate of return you calculate will be importantly affected by this premise. Accordingly, whether the investment ranks high or low in a firm's investment opportunity schedule depends importantly upon the expectation held about future product market demand. As expectations across the economy are revised, the position of the MEI will be altered, leading to a change in the level of investment spending. Figure 8–9 illustrates the circumstance where the expectation about future product market demand has been revised upward. The MEI shifts from its initial position of MEI_0 to the position MEI_1, leading to an increased level of investment spending from I_0 to I_1. In addition, the cost of capital tends to rise by an

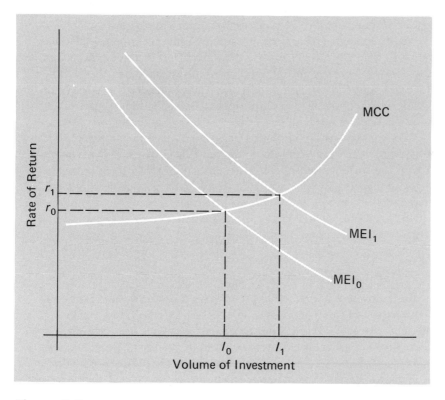

Figure 8–9

Expectations and the MEI

amount that depends upon whether the original equilibrium occurs on the relatively flat portion of the curve or in the upward sloping region.

The Investment Accelerator

At least to some degree, corporate decision makers must be influenced in the formulation of their investment related expectations about future product market demand by levels of current product market demand. If we assume the effect of present conditions upon expected future conditions is important and persistent over time, then we find reason to expect the MEI to shift outward as in Figure 8–9 in response to an increase in the present level of demand. This pattern forms a relationship between present levels of product market demand and levels of investment spending. This general idea is known as the investment accelerator effect.

Perhaps the most applicable context in which to think about the investment accelerator is during those time periods in the economy when market demand conditions are undergoing a cyclical change. Suppose that product market demand conditions are becoming considerably stronger due to a general economic recovery from a slump. This emerging product market strength logically has an impact upon the future market expectations of investment decision makers and leads to an outward shift in the MEI. To the contrary, there are occasions where we may consider the accelerator impact of current product market conditions to be negligible. If a period of unusual weakness or strength characterizes the current economy for what are widely believed to be temporary reasons, those formulating product market expectations may completely ignore this condition. The energy crunch in the United States during late 1973 and early 1974 is a case in point. Although the impact of the Arab oil embargo during that time created a small recession in U.S. product markets, business investment was not noticeably affected by this weakness, which during that period was widely believed to be temporary.

A Profits Accelerator

The amount of net return expected from a new investment depends upon a variety of factors besides the levels of expected product market demand. The expected level of prices compared to costs is one such factor. If business investors feel that they can maintain product prices in a favorable position relative to labor and other costs, they will calculate higher rates of return on possible investment opportunities than if they expect wages and other costs to rise in relation to product prices. Increases in prices relative to costs make each unit of output produced by a new capital investment yield more net return. Over the entire economy, a favorably revised price-cost expectation thus leads to an outward shift in the MEI and to an increase in investment spending, in the same fashion as was shown in Figure 8–9.

If the current relationship between prices and costs has an important impact upon expected future price-cost relationships, we have a second kind of accelerator effect at work upon investment spending. We call this effect the *profits accelerator*. Suppose corporations in general experience a decline in their profit margins due to increases in all costs at a faster pace than market and social conditions will allow prices to increase. Suppose also they do not see this condition as temporary, but a product of long-run influences upon the business sector. The expected rate of return on most investments will be downgraded as a result, leading to a leftward shift in the MEI and a decline in new investment spending. On the other hand, if a general expansion in business activity improves profit margins and these increases are seen by business as a normal part of the expansion, then they may be figured into new investment projections, shifting the MEI outward and increasing the equilibrium level of investment.

Since fluctuations in product market demand and fluctuations in profit margins often occur in the same direction and in comparable magnitudes, the product market and profits accelerators become essentially a single accelerator effect under these conditions, producing a component of induced demand for investment goods. Under certain highly mechanical assumptions, the impact of an accelerator upon equilibrium in the general economy can be highly destabilizing, causing demand to increase even further in response to an initial increase, feeding upon itself until a boom of uncontrolled proportions occurs, and accentuating a downward movement in demand by causing a further reduction in investment demand in a downward spiraling fashion. In our discussion, we shall not consider such models further, as they have not been of significant value in understanding business fluctuations in advanced economies such as the United States.

Investment Spending and Product Market Equilibrium

The discussion to this point has emphasized factors that affect the level of investment spending. Because investment is a large and significant component of the GNP, these factors are transmitted to other sectors of the economy and have an impact upon general product market equilibrium. To see some of these effects, we expand the simple one sector product market equilibrium model of Chapter 6 to include an investment sector. In a two sector model, both consumers and investors make expenditures on goods and services. Aggregate equilibrium occurs where the total demand for goods and services equals the level of current production, at which point no unanticipated inventory change occurs. Denoting intended and actual consumer spending by C, intended investment spending by I, saving by S, and total income by Y, and where $C + S = Y$, equilibrium occurs where

$$C + I = Y = C + S \qquad (8\text{--}6)$$

or equivalently, where

$$I = S \qquad (8\text{--}7)$$

The left-hand side of 8–6 is total intended spending, while the right-hand side shows the disposition of total income from production into consumer spending and saving accounts. When intended spending equals actual production and income levels, product market equilibrium occurs. Expression 8–7 shows this condition is equivalant to one in which intended investment exactly equals saving.

Our discussion of investment has emphasized the importance of factors that affect the marginal cost of capital (MCC) curve and factors that affect the marginal efficiency of investment (MEI) curve. The marginal cost of capital was seen to be primarily an upward sloping function of the level of investment, as well as a function of independent shifts in market interest rates, which we define to include the market cost of debt and the opportunity cost of equity capital. The term "independent shifts" is important in understanding the role of market interest rates in the MCC function. As investment increases, market interest rates rise as movement occurs along the MCC. Thus, interest rate changes are in part induced by investment changes. However, shifts in interest rates also occur that are not directly related to current fluctuations in investment. Changes in consumer saving patterns or in government spending and taxing programs are examples of sources of investment–independent shifts in i and in the MCC. Thus, the level of investment and the rate of interest are in the final analysis jointly determined. At this point, however, we shall deal with the interest rate as if it were largely predetermined. In Chapter 14, we consider interest rate determination in more detail. For discussion purposes, we denote the market interest rate as i. In addition, we assume for purposes of simplicity that the proportion of capital raised internally and externally remains constant, and that the cost of equity capital rises and falls in proportion to the cost of debt. Accordingly, we may summarize our discussion as

$$\text{MCC} = S(i, I) \qquad (8\text{--}8)$$

The marginal efficiency of investment was essentially found to be a function of the rate of investment and the prevailing expectation about future return on investment. This gives

$$\text{MEI} = D(exp, I) \qquad\qquad (8\text{--}9)$$

where exp stands for the expectational influence on the position of the MEI. The equilibrium level of investment occurs where MCC = MEI. Setting 8–8 equal to 8–9 results in an expression in i, exp, and I. If this expression is solved for I, we obtain the following expression for the equilibrium level of investment:

$$I = I(i, exp) \qquad\qquad (8\text{--}10)$$

A less general version of this investment function can be obtained by relying upon the accelerator relationship as the principal determinant of expectations. If expectations are principally determined by the level of current output, Y, then we have

$$I = A(i, Y) \qquad\qquad (8\text{--}11)$$

In Figure 8–10, equilibrium is depicted graphically for the two sector model. For purposes of focusing upon the addition of investment, we have shown a simple consumption hypothesis in which consumption is a function of only income. In addition, we assume for the time being that prices are constant. Figure 8–10(a) depicts the investment function given by Expression 8–10, while (b) shows the accelerator model of Expression 8–11. In both (a) and (b), the consumption function is shown sloping up to the right with the investment function added to it in the vertical direction. In (a), the initial equilibrium position is found at Y_0 income level when the equilibrium market interest rate is at i_0 and the level of expectations is at exp_0. If the market interest rate should fall from i_0 to i_1, the MCC falls, causing the new equilibrium level of investment to rise for the given level of expectations. The investment function shifts up from position A to position B. Because of the upward sloping consumption function and the multiplier effect upon total income, the level of Y is increased by more than the increase in the investment function, shifting from Y_0 to Y_1, a greater amount than the difference between expenditure level A and level B. Thus, the fall in the market interest rate has produced a general effect upon the economy that is transmitted to the consumer sector, resulting in an increase in consumer spending from the initial level of C_0 to the new level C_1.

Similarly, an increase in the level of expectations from exp_0 to exp_1 increases the equilibrium level of investment and shifts the investment function up from the initial position A to the new position D. At D, the in-

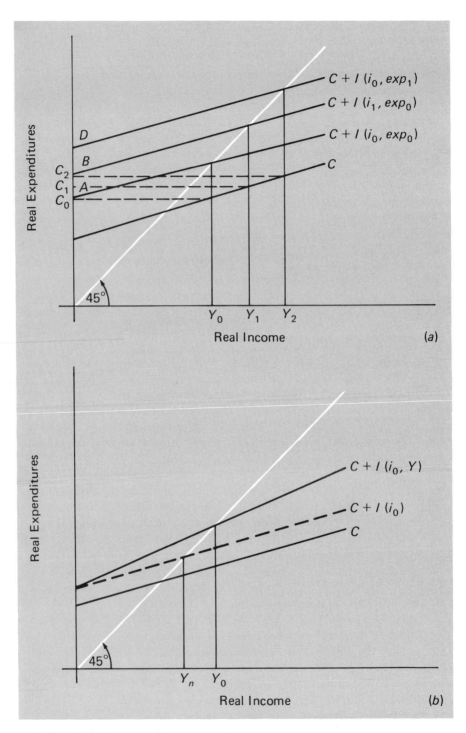

Figure 8–10

Two-Sector Model

creased expenditure again induces, via the multiplier, an increase in consumer spending from C_0 to C_2. Interestingly, the implication of this is that an increase in the expectations of business investors has the effect of increasing consumer incomes and expenditures. Similarly, an erosion in business expectations leads to a decreased level of consumer spending and incomes.

Figure 8–10(b) shows the effect of investment in the accelerator model. In this figure, both the consumption function and the investment function slope upward as income increases, illustrating an increase in both consumption and investment as income increases. The equilibrium level Y_0 is where the level of income has risen just enough to offset the basic and induced components of both consumption and investment demand. In contrast, the income level Y_n shows the level of aggregate equilibrium in the absence of an accelerator effect and illustrates the increase in aggregate income that comes about due to the accelerator impact.

Either version of the model in Figure 8–10 is useful in providing a framework for considering the overall product market influence of factors that impact on equilibrium levels of investment spending, either because of their influence upon the MCC curve or their influence upon the MEI. In the same way, factors that impact upon the investment function can be evaluated as to their possible impact upon induced investment. Thus, our two-sector model provides something not contained in our separate analyses of each sector—the framework for considering the logical implications for one sector of influences upon equilibrium in the other sector.

Empirical Models of Capital Investment Spending

Empirical studies of investment made in conjunction with aggregate econometric models of the United States have produced both common and contrasting findings. Our discussion focuses upon the Commerce, Wharton, and Brookings empirical results. These analyses were conducted specifically at the aggregate level and directed toward prediction.

The first of these models was developed as part of a project undertaken at the U.S. Department of Commerce.[5] This model explains fluctuations in fixed investment in terms of (1) business investment anticipations, (2) output in the private sector of the economy, and (3) personal consumption expenditures. In addition, an index of time acts as a catchall for unspecified influences. Finally, past (two-quarter lag) deviations between actual

[5] See the exposition of this model in *The Survey of Current Business* (May 1966), pp. 30–37.

and anticipated investment are included. The business investment anticipation referred to is a survey made by the U.S. Department of Commerce into the expected investment plans of large U.S. firms. It is made for two quarters ahead. The use of investment anticipations as an explanatory variable reduces reliance upon theoretical assumptions and associated explanatory variables. Presumably, the impact of fundamental explanatory variables is already reflected in the anticipated expenditure and is superfluous in the model itself except as the extent of realization of these plans is affected. Both the consumption expenditure and private output variables are included in the Commerce model as explanatory variables to measure an accelerator influence.

In the Wharton model, nonresidential fixed investment is broken into manufacturing, commercial industries, regulated and mining industries, and farm investment. The manufacturing investment segment is typical of the findings of the Wharton research. In that segment, investment is found to be a function of (1) capacity utilization, (2) output in the private sector, (3) corporate cash flow, (4) the yield on corporate bonds, and (5) the actual capital stock.[6]

In contrast to the Commerce model, the Wharton approach gives explicit attention to the time lag between investment decisions and investment expenditures. The view taken is that the major influence of the explanatory variables is upon the decision to invest, rather than upon expenditures themselves. This results in a time-lag relationship between changes in the explanatory variables and changes in expenditures. The specific form of the time pattern of influence is of further interest. Each explanatory variable is actually a seven-quarter weighted average of actual values, where the weights start at two-quarters lagged, rise in value to five- and six-quarters lagged where the weights reach a maximum, and fall to nine-quarters lagged.

The variables used in the Wharton equation show statistical support for accelerator and cost of capital measures in the explanation of fluctuations in investment. The use of a weighted average of past output changes indicates that accelerator influences have statistical explanatory power. In addition, the use of a capacity utilization measure suggests that the evaluation of the return on new investment is affected by the current rate of plant use to a statistically important degree. Finally, the weighted average of past corporate cash flow is found to be significant in the Wharton equation, along with the cost of corporate debt. Both these are ingredients in the formulation of the marginal cost of capital and give rise to shifts in the position of the MCC curve. Thus, some evidence is provided by the

[6] The particulars of this and the following discussion can be found in M. K. Evans, *Macroeconomic Activity: Theory, Forecasting, and Control,* Harper & Row, New York, 1969, pp. 135–136.

Wharton model as to the relevance of cost of capital fluctuations in explaining fluctuations in investment spending.

Further evidence on the influence of these variables can be obtained by reviewing elasticities of cash flow and interest rates in the Wharton investment equation. The cash flow elasticity (ratio of percent change in investment expenditures to percent change in cash flow), computed at its peak—was 0.23, i.e., a 2.3 percent change in investment follows from a 10 percent change in cash flow. A similar computation of interest rate elasticity produced an inelastic value of 0.50. Thus, unlike the Commerce project, the Wharton model finds an important explanatory role (though inelastic) for two cost of capital factors in investment analysis.

The final term in the Wharton model is a measure of recent past patterns of change in the capital stock. The significance of this term implies that periods of above average growth in the nation's capital stock have been a source of weakness for future investment expenditures, *ceteris paribus*. This finding is consistent with the concept of diminishing returns to the use of capital over relatively short-run periods of time. Given the addition of capital in distinct lumps by firms, other input adjustments (e.g., certain skilled labor categories) can be expected to lag behind, thereby altering efficient input proportions. This lowers returns from additional capital use until input combinations fully adjust. For example, a firm that has just made a large addition to plant capacity will need a full complement of trained staff in order to operate the addition successfully. As this staff is assembled and familiarized with the new operational environment, the plant cannot be operated efficiently. The capital stock variable in the Wharton expression measures this general effect.

The nonresidential fixed investment category in the Brookings study is broken into durable and nondurable manufacturing, public utilities, and all other. We shall here consider as representative the manufacturing-durable goods component. The predictive model in the Brookings study actually consists of two parts—one concerned with investment intentions and one with actual spending, or "realizations." [7]

In the two-part breakdown, the Brookings approach differs sharply in concept from either of the two previous alternatives. Whereas the Wharton model gave extensive treatment to the nature of the time lags involved in the influence of explanatory variables, the Brookings model used single past values of variables, but defined two distinct stages, an intended investment stage and a realized investment stage. In this breakdown, the major impact of influential explanatory variables is upon intended investment. Actual investment outlays result from a process of adjustment toward

[7] See J. S. Duesenberry, G. Fromm, L. A. Klein, and E. Kuh, *The Brookings Quarterly Econometric Model of the U.S.*, Rand McNally, Chicago, 1965, pp. 690–691.

intended levels. This two-step approach enables measurement and analysis of the time lags involved between changes in influencing variables and resulting changes in investment expenditures.

In the Brookings model, investment intentions are influenced primarily by relationships between output and the price of capital services. A ratio of aggregate output to the use cost of capital services appears in the model lagged several quarters. The user cost of capital services measures the total cost of using capital inputs. This cost is the sum of (1) the opportunity or use cost of the money committed to capital investment, (2) the cost of actual depreciation in the capital stock associated with physical wear-out and technological obsolescence (not to be confused with accounting depreciation), and (3) the adjustments to these costs that result because of the tax status of depreciation expense and the associated changes in accounting write-offs that result from new investment expenditures.

The statistical coefficients on the lagged values of the output-cost ratio are all positive, which statistically supports the theoretical role ascribed to both output and capital costs. The realizations equation shows that anticipated investment enters actual investment expenditures in two places, concurrently and in lagged form. The time-lagged effect contained in the Brookings study is generally consistent with the time distribution of the influences involved in the Wharton study.

In addition to output-cost ratios, the Brookings intentions model contains the difference between lagged investment intentions and further lagged values of depreciation in the capital stock, which can be interpreted as a measure of net investment or additions to the stock of capital. The last term in the intentions model is the stock of capital lagged three quarters, which supports an important empirical role for past values of the capital stock in the fashion of the earlier stock adjustment mechanism.

Short-run changes in output and profits are seen in the Brookings study to produce some changes in previously laid investment plans, due to flexibility in delivery dates on new equipment and flexibility on the part of firms in making partial commitments on major capital programs. The Brookings results imply that the influence of profits and output upon the realization of anticipated investment is relatively current, involving no more than two-quarter lagged changes in profit and output. This suggests a statistically significant role for an output-profits accelerator effect over short-run periods.

Summary of Empirical Results

Taken together, the Commerce, Wharton, and Brookings studies suggest several variables are consistently influential empirically in explaining short-run fluctuations in business plant and equipment investment. Recent levels of product demand or output are influential in all three models, providing evidence consistent with an accelerator influence on investment in which aggregate output and demand changes transmit an effect upon new investment that reacts upon aggregate output and so forth, resulting in a multiplier-accelerator interaction. Figure 8–11 illustrates this influence graphically by the feedback loop involving GNP, private output, investment expenditures, and back to the GNP. Interest rates are a factor in both the Wharton and Brookings models, presumably due to their role as a determinant of the marginal cost of capital. The Wharton model focuses on market rates of interest on long-term bonds while the Brookings approach employs a measure of the user cost of capital services, a more inclusive concept. As shown in Figure 8–11, we conclude from these results that long-term interest rates as a determinant of fluctuations in the cost of capital are a second major influence upon investment expenditures.

Finally, the Wharton model emphasizes the role of corporate cash flow in explaining investment fluctuations, while the Brookings study finds an important role for profits in converting anticipated expenditures into realized expenditures. Since profits and cash flow measures are related partially by definition, but also behaviorally, we may interpret these two findings as representing a single influence, which we take to be as a measure of the role of internal funds flow in the cost of capital. Accordingly, the third

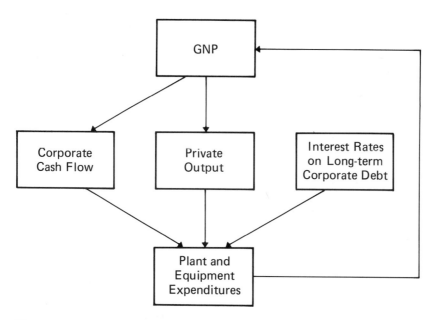

Figure 8–11

Summary: Empirical Determinants of Plant and Equipment Outlays

major influence upon investment expenditures shown in Figure 8–11 is corporate cash flow.

Although business fixed investment is the largest of the GNP investment categories, it is by no means the only significant factor in an investment analysis. Often as not, fluctuations in housing expenditures or fluctuations in inventory investment will mark the difference between an on-target assessment of economic conditions and an unenlightened outlook. In the next chapter we take up these categories of investment expenditures.

Discussion Questions

1. What is the difference between a firm's investment opportunity schedule and the MEC?

2. What is the major distinction between the MEC and the MEI?

3. Can you think of an influence that affects both the MEI and the MCC? What is the direction of each effect and the net effect upon equilibrium investment?

4. What is the likely impact of a surge of foreign money capital into U.S. capital markets upon the level of U.S. investment? Explain.

5. How, if at all, would an upward revision in the perceived risk of owning corporate stock impact on markets for consumer goods? Be specific, and explain fully.

6. What form of capital (internal funds, debt, equity) do you think would typically be the most expensive to corporations, that is, which would contribute the most to the overall cost of capital?

7. What, if any, are the implications for economic equilibrium if the slope of the consumption is 0.7 and the slope of the investment function is 0.4?

A Problem in Capital Investment

A recent article in a leading business publication contended that the United States faces a capacity crunch in many of its basic industries over the mid-1970s decade. According to the Federal Reserve Board, the nation's 12 basic materials industries (including steel, cement, copper, aluminum, textiles, and paper) operated in the second quarter of 1973 at about 95 percent of available capacity, which is the highest rate in the 25 years since the inception of the statistics. Analysts point out that even though companies in these basic industries are spending many millions of dollars for new plants and equipment, price increases have eroded the purchasing power of these expenditures, and legal pollution requirements have caused a considerable volume of the expenditures to be directed to noncapacity creating projects. Many firms involved cite an inability to finance expansion as the main cause of their capacity problems. This financing problem is attributed to a high cost of borrowing as well as to low levels of profits.

According to some economists' calculations, the net effect of these and other factors is to create a level of manufacturing employment in mid-1973 that is 2.3 percent below what it was in 1969. A similar effect is apparently at work on capacity. For instance, a spokesman for the American Paper Institute recently stated that capital expenditures by the paper industry for 1973 will be 24 percent ahead of 1972, but that expenditures for capacity expansion will actually decrease.

Do you feel that the arguments in this analysis are (1) logical, (2) consistent with the theory studied? What do you feel should be done about the type of capacity problem studied here? Why?

9

Investment in Housing and Inventories

Beside the purchase of new plant and equipment, investment occurs when new housing expenditures are made and when business adds to its inventories. These categories account for roughly one-third of gross private domestic investment and are often an important source of cyclical instability in the economy. In this chapter we consider these investment categories beginning with residential construction.

Residential Construction

Expenditures on residential construction in the GNP accounts include outlays for new single and multiple private housing units and for additions and improvements to existing housing units. The pattern of these expenditures in the recent U.S. economy is shown in Figure 9–1. Also shown in the figure for comparison purposes are the corresponding movements in nonresidential fixed investment and in the GNP minus residential expenditures. All three series are measured in constant dollars and shown as a ratio of their 1946 value for ease in comparing relative proportionate movements. The real GNP less residential construction shows the level of economic activity in the remainder of the economy and provides an opportunity for cyclical comparisons between the course of general economic activity and the course of residential construction activity. Figure 9–1 shows that residential construction has charted a rather independent course from the remainder of the economy over the period of the data. This suggests that residential construc-

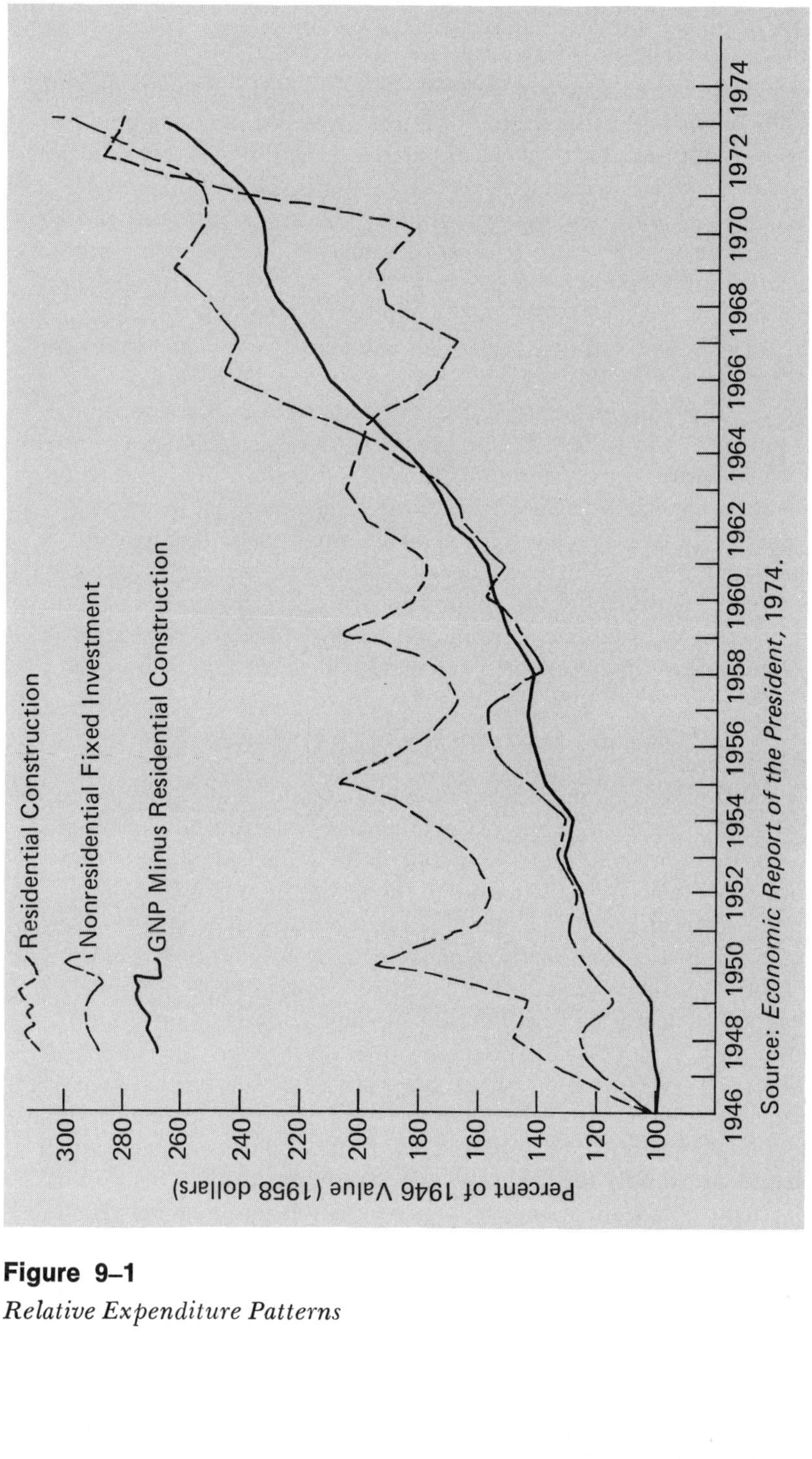

Figure 9–1

Relative Expenditure Patterns

tion expenditures should not be considered to be similar to consumer expenditures in responding to overall income levels, but rather are more nearly independent sources of fluctuations in spending.

The jagged pattern of residential construction shows that these expenditures have been a source of cyclical instability in the economy, tending toward a boom or bust existence for producers in these markets. There are several possible reasons for this type of pattern. Lead times between the decision to build and the availability of rental units are often more than a year in apartment building and only slightly less for single-family units. Also, changes in vacancy rates tend to be translated rather slowly into changes in rental rates and home prices. Finally, vacancy rate changes affect expected returns from new investment only as they become common enough to be the basis of new real-estate analysis. These factors add up to a rather lengthy time delay between (1) decisions to invest in new construction, (2) the impact of this new construction upon return on investment, and (3) new decisions to invest. The impact of significant changes in levels of new construction upon rates and prices and therefore upon return on investment may in fact be sufficiently slow and uncertain that investors cannot effectively take such levels into account when evaluating new investment opportunities. Therefore, construction markets may be characterized by a degree of overshooting and undershooting by investors as a result of their inability to formulate accurate projections of future markets. For example, periods of high occupancy rates and high rental prices draw forth an increased level of building that lowers occupancy rates, pushes down prices, and discourages new construction until demand catches up and vacancies are reduced.

In addition to possible origins of the jagged pattern of Figure 9–1 in such real market factors as rental prices or vacancy rates, a study by Guttentag suggests that financial factors may contribute to the instability in construction.[1] This stems from the nature of the supply of money for housing and the impact of financial variables upon new housing expenditures. New housing expenditures are greatly dependent upon availability of mortgage credit. If credit is not available or is excessively costly due to high interest rates, new construction will be deferred by some consumers until more favorable times.

The thrust of Guttentag's work proposes a relationship between fixed (plant and equipment) investment patterns and mortgage availability that sees the total mortgage credit available as a residual flow contingent upon the demand and supply for business fixed investment loans. This residual theory recognizes that the money market typically assigns a higher risk to

---

[1] See J. M. Guttentag, "The Short Cycle in Residenital Construction," *The American Economic Review*, 51:3 (June 1961), p. 292.

mortgage loans than to long-term loans for fixed investment. This is typically reflected in a positive spread between market interest rates on bonds and on mortgages. This presents no particular distortions if both interest rates fluctuated freely, since the two sections of the money market represent alternative risk return combinations for lending agencies. However, the mortgage market is characterized by two major components—an FHA and VA insured segment and a nongovernment insured or conventional component. The FHA/VA insured segment entails a maximum rate of interest that may be charged, while the conventional segment is generally without regulation beyond certain state limits on mortgage interest rates. The effects of the FHA/VA maximums during times of rising interest rates is to cause the normal spreads between FHA/VA rates and fixed business investment interest rates to narrow or evaporate completely, which in turn induces lenders in the FHA/VA segment to pursue other now-more-attractive opportunities. Thus, the narrowing of the spread reduces the sources of supply of FHA/VA funds.

Although the FHA/VA ceiling interest rates could be adjusted by legislative action to preserve a normal spread, this is generally not done. In the latter part of the 1968–1969 period of rising interest rates, the yield on corporate bonds rose above the FHA/VA ceilings, having the effect of sharply reducing supplies of these funds. This made conventional mortgages the only active segment of the market. Conventional mortgage down payments are usually larger than for FHA/VA loans, which further discourages some demand for housing. However, recent tight money experience suggests that the effect is overshadowed during periods of sharply rising interest rates by still other regulatory constraints upon interest rates applicable to the principal mortgage lending institutions—savings and loan associations and mutual savings banks. The maximum interest rates these institutions can pay on savings accounts and for business certificates of deposit is regulated primarily by the Federal Home Loan Board.[2] Unlike commercial banks, fractional reserves cannot be used to expand loans to a multiple of deposits in the savings and loan sector. Therefore, mortgage lending capacity is directly proportional to savings accounts and deposits held by the institution. As with the spread between mortgage and other rates, the rates paid by savings institutions are usually somewhat higher than those paid by banks on time deposits: When interest rates rise, the maximum rates allowed by regulatory authorities are not necessarily adjusted to maintain normal relationships between savings associations and commercial banks, who are similarly regulated. For example, in 1969 maximum rates payable by banks on both sav-

2 Certificates of deposit are short-term notes given by banks and savings institutions to businesses or by firms with short-term financial needs to firms with excess short-term liquidity.

ings accounts and business certificates of deposit rose relative to those of savings institutions, lowering the spread below normal levels. As a result, certificates of deposit and savings accounts moved from savings institutions to banks in significant amounts. This drain from the savings institutions similarly reduced their ability to extend new conventional mortgage loans. The final effect was to substantially reduce this remaining segment of the overall mortgage supplies.

Another factor in the operation of the mortgage market during periods of dynamic interest rates is that of disintermediation, a term coined by the financial community. When market rates of interest on U.S. Treasury bills, corporate bonds, and other financial instruments rise relative to amounts paid for deposits in financial intermediaries such as banks and savings and loan associations, it becomes increasingly attractive for holders of these deposits to switch to direct money market instruments instead (such as bonds). During situations such as 1969, when bond yields were over 9 percent while savings deposits typically yielded a maximum of 5 percent, many savers moved directly into the supply side of the bond market to participate in the higher yields. This reduced the flow of deposits into savings institutions as well as banks.

As long as regulations governing FHA/VA mortgage maximums and maximum interest payments on savings deposits and certificates of deposit remain sticky in response to increases in market rates of interest, we may expect to see the supply of funds available for mortgage loans sharply curtailed during periods of rising rates, thereby causing a rationing of reduced supplies among borrowers and curtailing housing construction expenditures.

The jagged pattern of residential construction shown in Figure 9–1 implies an independence of construction expenditures from aggregate income levels, which further suggests that income is not a fundamental determinant of residential construction expenditures. That is the view taken by many forecasters and analysts. Econometric models such as the Wharton model include income as an explanatory variable for construction expenditures based on the hypothesis that income levels act as a realizations proxy in the case of residential construction, affecting the timing but not the long-run level of construction expenditures. To further analyze this and other propositions about the nature of residential construction, attention now turns to a consideration of major findings of the Wharton, Commerce Department, and Brookings analyses of residential construction.

Empirical Studies of Residential Construction

Studies by Wharton researchers have produced the conclusion that three-quarters is empirically the best lag structure in the impact of residential construction decisions upon construction outlays. These decisions, in turn, are hypothesized to be influenced by disposable income levels, by the cost of housing relative to rental costs, and by the difference between long-term and short-term interest rates. The role of disposable income in this structure is described as basically expectational, influencing the extent to which planned investments in new residential construction are actually undertaken. In using a ratio of construction costs to rental costs in their model, the Wharton researchers find construction spending is stimulated by rising rental prices relative to construction costs and retarded by falling rents or construction costs, after the three-quarter realization lag. This influence undoubtedly results mainly from the effect on return-on-investment in apartment buildings. As rents rise proportionately to construction costs, returns would likely rise.[3] Also, some renters might be led to become houseowners through new home construction.

The interest-rate term in the Wharton model measures expected money market tightness, via the reasoning that if monetary conditions are expected to tighten, then short-term rates will show the effects initially and create an unusual gap between short and long rates. Long-term rates presumably close this gap only slowly if the monetary tightness should continue and be extensive. The gap between the two thus becomes a measure of short-term monetary conditions in the economy.

The Commerce Department model consists of two equations, one for housing starts and a second for actual expenditures. According to the results of this model, 41 percent of current housing starts produce the associated actual expenditure in the following quarter, and 10 percent of starts produce the expenditure two quarters later. These percentages correspond roughly to housing unit completion rates for the quarters following a housing start. The percentages appear to be rather stable over time. In the Commerce Department's approach, these percentages are used to weight current and lagged housing starts to produce a three-quarter weighted average of recent housing starts. Along with seasonal dummy variables, this housing starts term is relied upon exclusively to explain expenditures. Accordingly, the variables considered influential in ultimately explaining housing expenditures in the Commerce model all influence housing starts. In this model, starts are determined by mortgage interest rates, rental prices relative to con-

---

[3] When a standard discounted rate of return model is used, such as

$$C = \frac{R_1}{(1+r)} + \frac{R_2}{(1+r)^2} + \cdots + \frac{R_n}{(1+r)^n}$$

where
$$\begin{aligned} C &= \text{Construction cost} \\ R_1 \cdots R_n &= \text{Rental returns net of costs} \\ r &= \text{Rate of return on investment} \end{aligned}$$

it is clear that we cannot state flatly that an increase in an index of C over an index of R_t will raise r. Nonetheless, since the time horizon, n, is relatively long, it appears to be the usual result.

struction costs, and vacancy rates. Unlike the financial variable in the Wharton model that measures money market expectations, the financial variable in the Commerce model directly measures the cost of mortgage money. The statistical significance of the term provides evidence that the direct cost of mortgage funds is important in explaining fluctuations in housing starts. A ratio of rental costs and construction costs is included in the model as in the Wharton model. The Commerce result further indicates that increases in rental costs relative to construction costs associate with increases in construction activity after a time lag. Wharton estimated the appropriate lag at three-quarters. Commerce assumes such cost changes affect housing starts after a one-quarter lag and that starts thus influence expenditures with a current, one, and two greater distributed lag effect, according to a 0.41, 0.49, 0.10 weighting scheme. This produces a somewhat more current impact upon expenditures than in the Wharton model.

The Commerce model gives explicit recognition to the role of vacancy rates in housing starts. However, the variable employed, two-quarter lagged deviation from trend in vacant units, is not statistically significant at even 10 percent levels of significance. Therefore, an important empirical role for the variable in explaining housing starts is not clearly confirmed in the Commerce model.

The housing sector of the Brookings econometric project is similar to the Commerce model in its basic approach, structuring the problem into a housing starts component and an expenditure component. Several types of related housing equations are included in the Brookings housing sector, including new residential construction, improvements and modifications, and nonresidential nonbusiness construction. We shall consider only the new residential construction equation as illustrative.

Considering the explanation of housing starts, similarities with the Commerce model are apparent in the use of one- and three-quarter lagged housing starts and the direct use of a cost-of-funds measure. Like both previous empirical models, the ratio of rents to construction costs is included. As in the Commerce model, the term affects housing starts after a one-quarter lag. The number of vacant housing units is employed lagged one-quarter and found to be statistically significant. This result suggests vacancy levels are important in analyzing the residential construction outlook, presumably because of their role in rental property return-on-investment calculations. The cost-of-funds measure in the Brookings equation is a short-term money market rate, the yield on 3-month U.S. Treasury bills. This variable adds evidence to the earlier results regarding the empirical significance of cost-of-funds in analyses of the housing market. In addition, the Brookings model for housing starts contains a basic demographic variable, the change in the number of households and a measure of residential housing scrappage rates.

The three econometric models of construction reviewed are in complete agreement about the influence of two forces on new expenditures. Relationships between construction costs and rental costs are significant in all three models. Such relationships are likely to be important influences upon short-term fluctuations in residential construction. The second area of agreement among the models is upon the influence of interest rates on new expenditures. All three models employ measures of interest rates as part of the explanatory mechanism. In addition, both Wharton and Brookings include vacancy rates as explanatory variables. These findings are summarized in Figure 9–2. As this figure indicates, the variables used to explain residential construction in major econometric models are largely independent of current income, a conclusion that confirms our earlier discussion of this question.

Inventory Investment

The last remaining GNP investment category is inventory investment, measured as the change in stocks of materials, work-in-process, and finished goods inventories during a period. The dollar amount of total inventory investment is small compared to nonresidential fixed investment or residential construction. However, the category is one of the most volatile among the GNP accounts and has often been pivotal in its relationship to general business fluctuations. Table 9–1 shows the relationship between changes in inventory investment and changes in total GNP for post-World War II

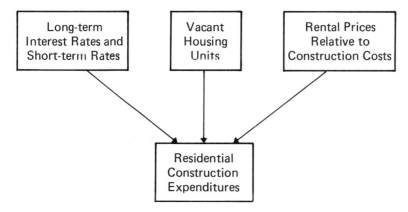

Figure 9–2

Summary: Residential Construction

Table 9–1

Post-war Recessions and Inventories

RECESSION DATES	CHANGE IN REAL GNP	CHANGE IN REAL INVENTORY INVESTMENT
	(BILLINGS OF 1958 DOLLARS)	
1948.4–1949.4	− 5.4	−10.9
1953.2–1954.2	−14.3	− 7.4
1957.3–1958.1	−17.7	− 8.6
1960.1–1961.1	− 7.6	−13.0
1969.3–1970.1	− 8.0	− 7.5

Source: U.S. Department of Commerce, National Income Statistics.

recessions, where recessions are defined as two or more successive declines in real GNP. It illustrates that at least three of the recessions, 1948–1949, 1960–1961, and 1969–1970 were almost entirely accounted for by drops in inventory investment. A study of aggregate inventory relationships by Klein and Popkin in fact indicates that if 75 percent of the fluctuations in inventory investment could be controlled, the economy would not have experienced a single post-World War II recession.[4] This general notion leads some analysts to characterize the U.S. post-World War II recessions all as inventory recessions. In any event, the historical pattern of inventory investment and general business conditions makes it clear that a successful analysis of general business will rest significantly on the analysis of inventory investment.

The nation's business firms hold inventories for several basic reasons. Among these, finished goods inventories provide for business transactions in areas of the economy that sell from inventories (e.g., consumer soft goods). This demand will fluctuate proportionately with sales, since higher levels of sales typically lead to higher needs for transactionary stocks. Finished goods inventories also provide a buffer against short-run sales-production imbalances. Given costs of adjusting production levels and carrying inventories, appropriate buffer levels of finished goods inventories can be stipulated to provide protection against short-run demand shifts. We shall refer to this as finished goods buffer demand. Similarly to finished goods, materials inventories are held to provide inputs for current production levels, to act as a buffer between materials order lead times and changes in production and also occasionally as a speculation on changes in market prices. We may define total transactions and buffer inventory demand as the sums

[4] L. R. Klein and J. Popkin, "An Econometric Analysis of the Postwar Relationship Between Inventory Fluctuations and Change in Aggregate Economic Activity," Part 3 of *Inventory Fluctuations and Economic Stabilization,* Joint Economic Committee, Washington, D.C., 1961, pp. 71–86.

of demand for finished goods and materials in each area. Finally, work-in-process inventories are held in direct proportion to current production.

In Chapter 5, the conditions for aggregate equilibrium were described as those in which sales and production were in balance so that finished goods buffer stocks were at intended levels. That analysis indicates that independent increases in aggregate demand may initially lower inventories through unintended draw-downs of finished goods buffers. In general, our equilibrium framework suggests that total investment in inventory buffers will fluctuate inversely with expansionary or contractionary movements in the economy. In an accounting sense this is always true by definition as long as we measure expansionary and contractionary disequilibria as excesses of aggregate sales over aggregate production and vice versa. However, this does not mean that total inventory investment will necessarily move inversely to aggregate equilibrium, but only that the buffer component of inventory demand will do so. The total demand may rise or fall in response to aggregate demand shifts depending on the corresponding movement in transactions demand for inventories and work-in-process demand.

While jointly predicting these demand components is extremely hazardous, it is possible to develop informal impressions as to the expected relationship between inventory investment segments and changes in business activity. The expected direction of movement in various inventory components in response to various demand-output relationships is summarized in Figure 9–3. Three representative situations are shown for illus-

Figure 9–3

Expected Change in Intended Inventory Investment

TYPE OF INVENTORY INVESTMENT	DEMAND CHANGE-OUTPUT CONSTANT	PROPORTIONAL DEMAND AND OUTPUT CHANGE	DEMAND CONSTANT-OUTPUT CHANGE
Finished Goods Transactions	Same direction as demand	Same direction as demand output	Unchanged
Finished Goods Buffers	Opposite direction of demand	Unchanged*	Same direction as output
Materials Transactions	Unchanged	Same direction as demand, output	Same direction as output
Materials Buffers	Same direction as demand	Unchanged*	Opposite direction of output
Work-in-Process	Unchanged	Same direction as demand, output	Same direction as output

* Except for recovery to desired levels in some cases.

trative purposes. They reflect a variety of alternative business situations. Looking horizontally across Figure 9–3, the intended investment in finished goods for transactionary purposes is expected to rise and fall with levels of aggregate demand, without regard to levels of output. Finished goods buffer stocks, on the other hand, can be expected to directly reflect unanticipated changes in the relationship of demand and production, rising when production exceeds demand and falling when demand exceeds production. Unlike finished goods, materials transactionary stocks can be expected to respond principally to production levels. Therefore, shifts in market demand not accompanied by production changes would leave these stocks unaffected. Expectational effects upon stocks of materials related to anticipated changes in production due to demand-production imbalances are expected to be in the direction of the anticipated production correction. For example, if aggregate demand increases over production, an increase in orders for materials stocks can be expected to accompany plans for production increases and vice versa for decreases in demand below production levels. Finally, work-in-process inventories are a direct reflection of output levels and can be expected to change accordingly.

For the particular situations illustrated by the column headings of Figure 9–3, the total inventory change is the sum of the five components in the figure. When demand begins to rise in excess of production, as illustrated in the first column, intended finished goods transactionary inventories and materials buffers are increased. However, finished goods buffers are reduced. The total effect is a reduction of inventories below intended levels; however, this may correspond to either an increase or decrease in actual levels, depending on the extent of the buffer effect. During the early phases of a business expansion before production has caught up with rising demand, the negative buffer effect may dominate and cause the actual level of inventories to decline. However, more common is the situation where inventories rise with the rising demand, but not to intended levels.

During periods when both demand and production are rising proportionately, Figure 9–3 indicates we should expect inventories to rise for transactionary and work-in-process purposes. This normally is the least difficult situation to analyze, in the absence of special factors such as recovery programs from past periods of extreme inventory positions or major work stoppages. The third situation, involving output changes relative to demand is seen to generally produce inventory changes in the same direction, except for the opposing effects of materials buffer stocks, which may be expected to react negatively to the emerging output-demand gap.

The general propositions of Figure 9–3 do not take into account special influences upon inventories such as the special properties of the made-to-order industries in the economy or the impact of high rates of inflation. Inventories of finished goods in the machine tool and defense sector are virtually nonexistent. Materials inventories are present, but the major investment in inventories is in the work-in-process category. As new orders are received, the contract items are put into production, which adds directly to inventories. Thus, changes in economic activity in this sector directly change inventories in the same direction. Finally, when contract items are delivered, payment is completed, and inventories decline at the same time the major portion of the expenditure is recorded, offsetting its aggregate effect. These special characteristics of the made-to-order sector essentially produce inventory-output-demand relationships opposite to those in the remainder of the economy, which further complicates the problem of analyzing overall inventory relationships.

A second potentially important special influence upon inventory investment is the actual and expected rate of inflation in the prices of final goods and raw materials and components. If the business sector in general expects raw materials prices to rise over the near term, they may find it quite profitable to build stocks of materials and other inputs at current prices. In these cases, the cost of carrying additional inventories is more than offset by the lower purchase price obtained by current purchase. Thus, inflationary expectations on the part of business can lead to a desire to hold larger inventory levels for reasons quite apart from the transactions or buffer demands shown in Figure 9–3. In 1973 and early 1974 in the United States, many corporations were actively engaged in programs of inventory accumulation for exactly this reason, and corporate profits during this period were aided measurably by the effect of these programs.

Empirical Studies of Inventory Investment

We again focus on the Commerce, Wharton, and Brookings studies as representative of the major results of empirical research on the determinants of inventory investment. The Commerce model explains inventory investment as a function of (1) private production except for housing, inventories, and consumer service expenditures; (2) past levels of inventory investment; and (3) unfilled orders for durables. Also, an index of time is included to account for undefined trend effects, and a dummy variable accounts for the special effects of strikes on inventories.

The first of these terms is a measure of inventory sensitive output in the economy. It excludes governmental output since this output is not inventoried in the usual sense. Then, inventory investment itself is subtracted to obtain a measure of final goods produced. Finally, expenditures on services are subtracted since they consist largely of noninventoried production.

Our earlier discussion indicates this variable should measure the transactions demand for inventories. Its statistical significance provides empirical support for the influence of this transactions demand. Past inventory investment reflects the effects of past buffer levels upon current investment. Past patterns of abnormal inventory accumulation can be expected to reduce current inventory investment by saturating buffer stocks.

Unfilled orders for manufacturer's durable goods exerts a positive and significant effect on inventory investment in the Commerce model. This variable measures the backlog of new made-to-order business in the economy. As the volume of new orders increases, the level of output and work-in-process inventories should rise, which is the result demonstrated empirically in the Commerce model.

The Wharton model divides total business inventories into manufacturing and employs two equations for prediction. We shall consider the manufacturing equation as representative of Wharton's approach. Manufacturing inventory investment is explained by fluctuations in (1) sales in manufacturing, (2) past values of inventory investment, and (3) recent changes in unfilled orders for durable goods. Also included is a variable to account for the special effects of strikes. In this scheme, a one-quarter lag characterizes the effect of manufacturing sales upon inventories. As in the Commerce case, past inventory investment reflects the impact of past buffer levels on current investment. Unfilled orders for durables again is found to be a significant determinant, presumably also as a measure of the impact of the made-to-order segment on overall inventory levels.

Finally, the Brookings study contained several different versions of equations for (1) manufacturing durable goods, (2) manufacturing nondurable goods, (3) trade, and (4) agricultural inventories. We shall consider the manufacturing sector for purposes of comparison with the two earlier models. In this sector, investment is explained by (1) lagged values of inventory investment, (2) current output levels, (3) defense expenditures and obligations, (4) unfilled orders for goods, and (5) output capacity relationships. As in the Commerce case, an index of time is also included.

The manufacturing sector contains made-to-order manufacturing as well as other producers. The explanatory variables shown (actually drawn from two equations, for durables and nondurables) relate to both these segments. As in both earlier cases, past inventory investment measures buffer effects of past inventory positions. The appearance of the output variable again demonstrates the general empirical relevance of output measures in inventory investment. The same is true of unfilled orders, which are significant in all three studies. Brookings also uses defense expenditures as a second reflection of the special impact of this part of the made-to-order segment. The effect is twofold, (1) a positively measured impact on inventory investment when new defense obligations (contract initiation) are made, and (2) a negative impact when actual expenditures occur. This is wholly consistent with our earlier discussion.

The last major influence expressed in the Brookings study related output and capacity utilization levels (product of the two). This apparently measures the impact on inventory investment of over or under capacity utilization. Higher rates of capacity utilization and production associate with higher levels of inventory investment in Brookings' results.

The areas of agreement among major econometric models in the explanation of fluctuations in inventory investment center around three major influences. As depicted in Figure 9–4, these influences are (1) aggregate private output measures, which were found to be important in all three studies reviewed; (2) past patterns of inventory investment, reflecting the impact of buffer stocks, also present in all three cases; and (3) unfilled orders for hard goods, reflecting the special impact of the made-to-order segment, and also present in all three studies. As indicated by Figure 9–4, the influence of output upon inventory investment adds to the overall multiplier effect in the economy, since inventory change adds to aggregate output. The significance of past inventory investment patterns indicates that influences resulting from past inventory decisions influence current inventory investment. The significance of unfilled orders also emphasizes the importance of the made-to-order segment on overall inventory investment levels.

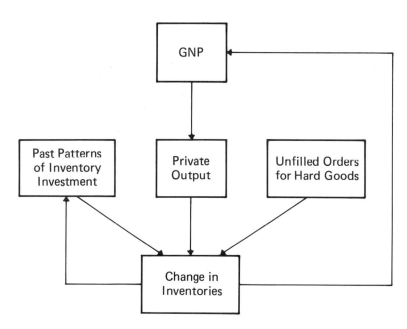

Figure 9–4

Summary: Inventory Investment

Analysis of Investment—Conclusions

In this and the previous chapter, we have explored representative empirical research in all three major categories of gross private domestic investment. Figure 9–5 shows the combined summary of these discussions, as they were depicted in Figures 8–11, 9–2, and 9–4. In Figure 9–5, the level of private output is seen to influence both plant and equipment and inventory investment, a relationship that produces an output accelerator effect as discussed in Chapter 8. Interest rates are seen as an important empirical determinant of investment in the plant and equipment and residential construction categories, due to their role as a measure of the use-cost of funds and perhaps as a measure of general capital market conditions.

Although our consideration of the residential construction and inventory investment components of the total GNP investment category has identified several factors that have a special impact on these expenditures apart from those that impact upon plant and equipment expenditures, it has not indicated that the investment model of the previous chapter is inappropriate as a broad characterization of the entire investment category. The simple acceleration version of this model is given by

$$I = I(i, Y) \tag{9-1}$$

where i is the market interest rate and Y is the level of income. While this oversimplified structure does not incorporate a sufficient array of factors to instill much faith in it as a predictive structure, its simplicity and essential correctness make it attractive as a representation of investment in the macroeconomic setting with which we are basically concerned. Clearly, the forecasting and analysis of short-run fluctuations in real business and economic conditions requires explicit accounting for the effects of variables such as those shown in Figure 9–5. But, for purposes of following the logic of macroeconomic relationships to their conclusions, the simple function of Expression 9–1 is valuable as a collection point for observing the impact of omitted variables such as those of Figure 9–5 that shift the investment function.

This discussion ends our analysis of expenditures in private domestic markets for goods and services. In the next chapter, we turn to a consideration of government expenditures, government taxes, and the impact of these expenditures on economic activity.

Discussion Questions

1. Consult some recent statistical data on movements in the GNP and movements in residential construction. Do you see any support for the contention that residential construction moves in opposite directions from the general economic pattern?

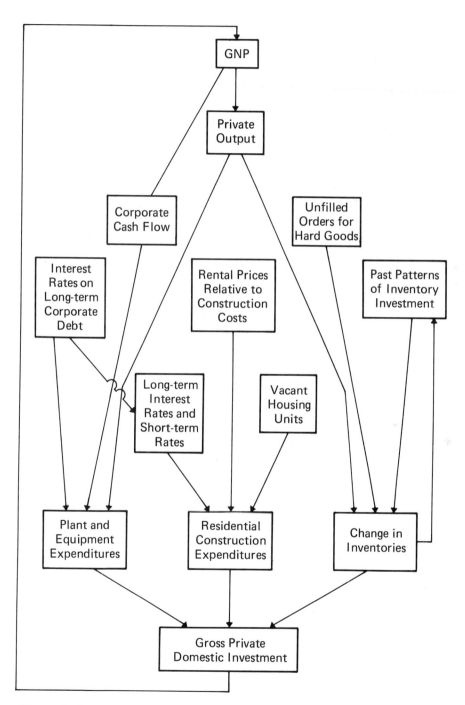

Figure 9–5

Summary: Gross Private Domestic Investment

2. Can you find statistical evidence of a recent time period when mortgage rates were historically high and construction spending was also historically high, i.e., above its long-run trend?

3. What do you suppose would be the effect of a complete removal of the FHA/VA ceilings on mortgage rates?

4. What do you suppose would be the effect of a law that tied the rate on savings and loan deposits to the bank rate on time deposits according to a fixed parity, such as 1 percent above bank time deposit rates?

5. When would you expect corporate speculation in their own inventories to be more than a temporary phenomenon, i.e., can you outline circumstances wherein corporations would have an interest in permanently increasing their inventory-to-sales ratio?

6. As the economy comes out of a recession into an expansionary period, should the level of inventories be rising or falling, according to the fundamental factors involved? What does the statistical evidence show to be the case for the five expansionary periods following the recessions dated in Table 9–1?

10

Economic Impact of Government

Chapters 6 through 9 have examined conceptual and analytical ways to represent by a few major functional relationships the aggregate expenditures of millions of consumers and hundreds of thousands of business investors. By comparison, analysis of influential variables affecting government expenditures appears to be a comparatively easy task, since the decision makers involved are relatively few in number and are generally required to stipulate their spending plans in advance in the highly visible form of state, local, and federal government budgets. Yet, few aggregate econometric (or other forecasting) models explain government expenditures in terms of a set of influential predetermined variables. The same is true of all major theories of aggregate income. Rather, in such models government expenditures are usually considered not to be influenced by current levels of variables such as consumer expenditures, investment expenditures, or the GNP. Consequently, the conceptual and analytical tools of macroeconomics usually focus on the *effects* of government expenditures rather than on their determinants. That is the approach of this chapter, which first focuses upon broad effects of government within a general theoretical framework and then considers specific conclusions related to empirical analysis of the impact of government upon the U.S. economy.

Government Revenues and Outlays in the United States

For the purpose of analyzing the determinants of the GNP, the government sector consists of the federal government, the various state governments, and

169

local and municipal governments. These governments purchase products such as buildings, roads, defense weapons, educational facilities and personnel, waste disposal systems, and recreational facilities, which they supply for public use. They also pay the cost of providing a variety of regulatory, protection, and other services to the public. In the process, governments make a large amount of direct expenditures in private markets and maintain a large number of employees on public payrolls. In both these ways, governments influence aggregate economic activity. Besides direct expenditures, governments also transfer funds, collecting them from the public and redistributing them to needy parties, primarily for social security and related welfare programs. Also, governments redistribute funds through interest payments on public debt, which are paid to bondholders out of tax revenues drawn from the general public.

Table 10–1 contains gross spending categories for both federal and state and local governments in the United States. Of the four main categories in which outlays are considered, the Purchases of Goods and Services, category 1, is typically the largest. The federal portion is largely composed (75–85 percent over the 1960s) of national defense. For example, of the expenditures on goods and services made by the federal government in calendar 1969, 79.3 billion were for national defense and 22.7 billion for all other federal government purchases of goods and services. In the purchase composition of state and local governments, two areas stand out. These are education and the cost of state and local licensing, regulation, and municipal services. These two expenditure areas account for approximately 75 percent of total state and local government purchases. Besides purchases of goods and services, the remaining major categories in Table 10–1 are (2) transfers, which include all social security and related program payments; (3) interest payments on federal, state, and local bonds; and (4) subsidies less surplus on government enterprise, an adjustment measuring both transfers made to firms by governments and the profit or loss on government operated businesslike services such as the U.S. Post Office.

The outlays in category 1 of Table 10–1 either enter private markets directly as expenditures made by governments for the purchase of privately produced output or enter the economy indirectly as income payments to government employees for their services. While not actually a market expenditure, these income payments are counted as an expenditure in the national income accounting definitions. Since the income payment portion is one step removed from GNP-type expenditures, it is not likely to be as potent in its economic impact as the former expenditures.[1]

---

[1] The effect of the income payments defined as government expenditures is analogous to taxes in its "one-step-removed" impact on the economy and can be considered as a negative tax.

Table 10-1

Government Outlays

| | | BILLIONS OF CURRENT DOLLARS | | | | | |
		1950	1955	1960	1965	1969	1973
1. Purchases of Goods and Services	Federal	18.4	44.1	53.5	66.9	98.8	106.9
	State*	19.5	30.1	46.1	70.1	111.2	170.3
	Total	37.9	74.2	99.6	137.0	210.0	277.2
2. Transfers	Federal	14.4	14.4	23.4	32.5	52.4	95.5
	State	3.5	3.7	5.1	6.9	11.6	19.5
	Total	17.9	18.1	28.5	39.4	64.0	115.0
3. Interest Payments	Federal	4.5	4.9	7.1	8.7	13.1	15.9
	State	0.3	0.5	0.7	0.5	−0.2	−1.3
	Total	4.8	5.4	7.8	9.2	12.9	14.6
4. Subsidies less Surplus on Government Enterprise	Federal	1.2	1.5	2.5	4.3	4.6	5.4
	State	−0.9	−1.6	−2.2	−3.0	−3.5	−4.7
	Total	0.3	−0.1	0.3	1.3	1.1	0.7
Total	Federal**	38.5	65.0	86.5	112.4	168.9	223.5
	State	22.3	32.7	49.6	74.5	119.0	183.8
	Grand Total	60.8	97.6	136.1	186.9	287.9	407.3

Note: Details may not add to totals due to rounding.
Source: Economic Report of the President, 1974.

* Includes all state and local governmental bodies.
** Excludes Grants-in-Aid to states.

Categories 2, 3, and 4 in Table 10-1 are not expenditures in the GNP sense. Rather, they are income-like transfers that subtract from total purchasing power in some areas of the economy and add to purchasing power in other areas. For example, federal payments under social security laws provide monthly income for elderly, widowed, and other special categories of citizens and subtract from the income of general wage earners. These payments affect the economy to the extent that the consumption expenditures of donors and recipients are affected by them. Thus, the behavioral tendency to consume out of transfer payments determines the impact on the economy of governmental outlays (and associated receipts) in categories 2, 3, and 4.

Receipts by governments are obtained from four major categories, as shown in Table 10–2. The first category, personal taxes, includes all income and other taxes and governmental fees paid by persons and nonincorporated businesses (which are treated essentially as persons for tax purposes). As seen, the majority of these taxes are collected at the federal level. Corporate profits and indirect business taxes represent the total of all taxes paid by corporations. While nearly all corporate profits taxes are levied at the federal level, the majority of indirect business taxes are collected at the state and local level. The indirect business tax category encompasses excise, property, and all other taxes and governmental fees except income taxes. The fourth category measures total contributions for social insurance made by persons and by employers. Collections under the federal program represent the major portion of this category.

The total of these four receipt categories is the gross revenue of the government sector of the economy. Subtracting total outlays from total receipts produces the overall combined surplus or deficit position of all governments combined. This figure measures the aggregate net effect of all governments. A positive difference (surplus overall budget position) means governments collected more money from the public than they returned through expenditures, transfers, or other outlays. A negative difference (deficit position) means just the opposite. State and local governments are largely constrained from incurring budgetary deficits by law. A review of the historical pattern of state and local spending also indicates an absence of overall surplus positions of any significant proportions, probably due to continual expenditure pressures. Therefore, the majority of the overall governmental surplus or deficit position is generally attributable to the federal government.

Various government spending and taxing programs affect the economy in different ways. Generally, spending has the most direct effect on output and employment levels, while taxes that operate through income have an indirect effect. In general, the receipts and outlays of governments do not offset each other dollar for dollar in their effect on the economy—a balanced budget is not a neutral economic policy. We now consider these and related ideas on a conceptual level. Later, we shall explore the empirical impact of government activities upon the U.S. economy.

Expenditures, Taxes, and the GNP

Government spending on goods and services directly adds to the level of aggregate demand in the private sector.[2] Accordingly, the basic impact of

---

[2] However, as earlier mentioned, a significant portion of G (government expenditures) is composed of income payments made to government employees on civilian and military staffs and is therefore not a direct addition to the expenditure stream in the strict sense of that term.

Table 10–2

Government Receipts

		BILLIONS OF CURRENT DOLLARS					
		1950	1955	1960	1965	1969	1973
1. Personal Tax and Other Receipts	Federal	18.1	31.4	43.6	53.8	94.8	114.5
	State and Local	2.6	4.1	7.3	11.8	21.7	38.4
	Total	20.7	35.5	50.9	65.6	116.5	152.9
2. Corporate Profit Taxes	Federal	17.0	20.6	21.7	29.3	36.6	49.8
	State and Local	0.8	1.0	1.3	2.1	3.4	6.4
	Total	17.8	21.6	23.0	31.4	40.0	56.2
3. Indirect Business Tax	Federal	8.9	10.7	13.5	16.5	19.0	21.0
	State and Local	14.5	21.4	31.7	45.9	67.0	96.8
	Total	23.4	32.1	45.2	62.4	86.0	117.8
4. Contributions for Social Insurance	Federal	5.9	9.3	17.7	25.1	46.9	80.1
	State and Local	1.0	1.8	3.0	4.5	7.3	12.0
	Total	6.9	11.1	20.7	29.5	54.2	92.1
Total Receipts	Federal	49.9	72.1	96.5	124.7	197.3	265.4
	State and Local*	18.8	28.3	43.4	64.4	99.4	153.6
	Grand Total Receipts	68.7	100.4	139.8	189.1	296.7	419.0
	Total Outlays (from Table 10–1)	60.8	97.6	136.1	186.9	287.9	407.3
	Surplus	7.8	2.7	3.7	2.2	8.8	11.7

Note: Details may not add to totals due to rounding.
Source: Department of Commerce, Office of Business Economics.

* Excludes Federal Grants-in-Aid.

government spending on national income is similar to that of new investment or that of an autonomous increase in consumer expenditures. Figure 10–1 shows the effect on aggregate income of adding government expenditures to private expenditures. For purposes of simplicity, we assume in this figure and the discussion that follows that the level of intended investment (I) is independent of income, that consumption (C) is a simple function of only income, and that prices are constant. According to the last assumption, all magnitudes in the figure are measured in real or constant dollar magnitudes. In Figure 10–1, a level of intended private investment equal to AB is added to the level of consumption, producing a private sector equilibrium position of Y_0 in the absence of government spending. The addition of an

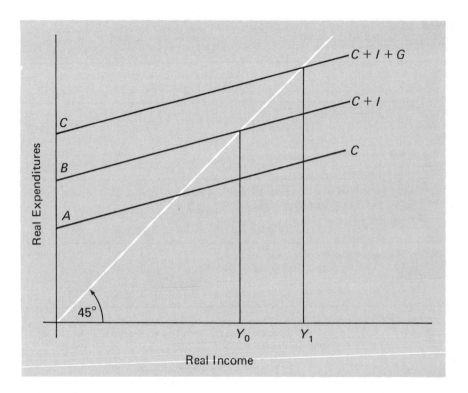

Figure 10–1

Government and Aggregate Income

amount of government spending equal to BC operates through the income consumption multiplier to increase the equilibrium level of real income to Y_1, where the increase in Y given by $(Y_1 - Y_0)$ is greater than the level of added government spending BC by the amount of the multiplier.

The effect of adding tax receipts to this picture depends somewhat upon the kind of tax involved, with lump-sum taxes impacting differently on equilibrium than income taxes. However, all taxes involve a reduction in spendable income. If the tax is assumed to be levied on the basis of income, the effect will be to reduce available or disposable income below aggregate income by creating a leakage of a fraction of income into tax categories at each round in the circular flow of income. Thus, if the consumer normally returns 80 percent of an increase in spendable income back into the economy in the form of increased spending, then an income tax of 30 percent levied upon consumer incomes will lead to an expenditure of 80 percent of the 70 percent of take-home income, or 56 percent of the gross income. The effect of the tax is to reduce the slope of the consumption function from 0.8 to 0.56 and lower the resulting multiplier from 5 to 2.27. Figure 10–2 shows the effect graphically. We start with an initial position of $C_0 + I + G$ and equilibrium income of Y_0. If an income tax is imposed upon consumer incomes, the effective slope of the consumption function is reduced, rotating the entire aggregate demand schedule down to $C_1 + I + G$ and reducing the equilibrium income to Y_1.

By comparison, if nonincome taxes are levied, no effect takes place on either the slope of the consumption function or the multiplier. Presumably, if consumers behave normally in response to a lump-sum tax, they will pay part of their tax out of their saving and part by reduced purchases. Moreover, the absolute amount by which saving and consumption is reduced is invariant with changes in income level. With a marginal spending ratio of 80 percent, a 10 billion lump-sum tax should cause consumption at any income level to be reduced by 8 billion and saving to be reduced by 2 billion. The effect is shown graphically in Figure 10–3. The initial equilibrium position of $C_0 + I + G$ where income is Y_0 is shifted down by AB where this

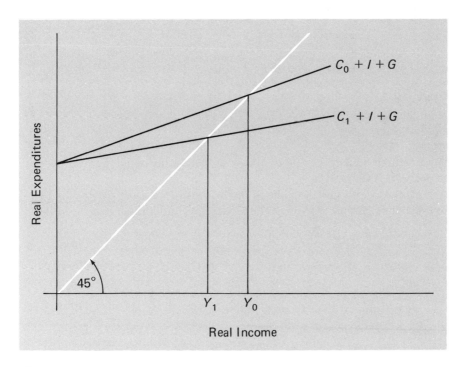

Figure 10–2
Effect of Taxes

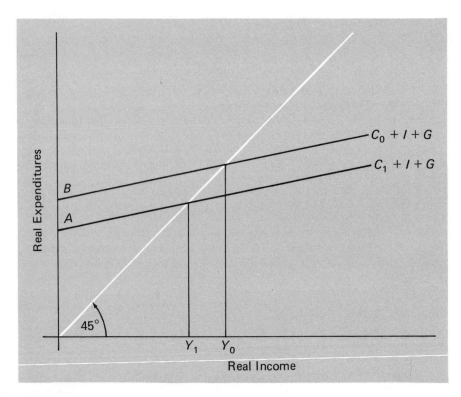

Figure 10-3

Lump-Sum Taxes

amount equals 80 percent of the lump-sum tax. Accordingly, the equilibrium income level is reduced to Y_1.

These tax and spending effects can be considered more specifically by the use of an algebraic version of the model now under discussion, as follows:

$$C = C_a + bY_D \qquad (10\text{-}1)$$

$$I = I_a \qquad (10\text{-}2)$$

$$G = G_a \qquad (10\text{-}3)$$

$$Y = C + I + G \qquad (10\text{-}4)$$

$$Y_D = (1 - t)Y - TX_a \qquad (10\text{-}5)$$

Expression 10-1 shows consumption, C, as a linear function of disposable income, Y_D, where C_a is the level of income-independent consumption and b is the slope of the consumption function, often called the marginal propensity to consume. The value of Y_D is defined by Expression 10–5 to be the after-tax portion of gross income, Y. Taxes are of two forms. TX_a is a fixed lump-sum tax that subtracts a constant amount from Y, while the income tax rate, t, reduces income by an amount tY. Thus, total taxes are given by $TX_a + tY$, and Y_D is equal to Y less total taxes. Both intended investment, I, and government spending, G, are assumed to be given by the fixed amounts I_a and G_a respectively. Finally, equilibrium occurs where total expenditures equal total income, as shown by 10–4. If we substitute Expressions 10–1, 10–2, and 10–3 into 10–4, we can restate this equilibrium condition as

$$Y = C_a + bY_D + I_a + G_a \qquad (10\text{–}6)$$

Substituting Expression 10–5 for Y_D gives

$$Y = C_a + b(1 - t)Y + I_a + G_a - bTX_a \qquad (10\text{–}7)$$

Rearranging gives

$$Y - b(1 - t)Y = C_a + I_a + G_a - bTX_a \qquad (10\text{–}8)$$

or

$$Y = \frac{1}{1 - b(1 - t)} \cdot [C_a + I_a + G_a - bTX_a] \qquad (10\text{–}9)$$

Expression 10–9 illustrates our earlier discussion of the impact of government spending and taxing on the economy. The bracketed portion of Expression 10–9 shows the components of current intended expenditure and tax leakage that are independent of current income. These are referred to as autonomous components of aggregate demand. The $1/1 - b(1 - t)$ term in Expression 10–9 shows the multiplier modified to take into account the leakage due to an income based tax. As in Expression 10–9, it is convenient, to think of equilibrium Y as resulting from a multiplier applied to the total level of autonomous demand. To illustrate, if $C_a = 30$, $I_a = 150$, $G_a = 380$, $TX_a = 75$, $b = 0.8$, and $t = 0.25$, then the multiplier in our expression is 2.5 while the net autonomous expenditures and tax leakages are 500. Equilibrium income occurs at $Y = (2.5)(500) = 1,250$. At this level, $Y_D = (0.75)(1,250) - 75 = 862.5$, which when inserted into the consumption function gives $C = 720$. Adding to the value of C the other intended expenditures I and G gives $720 + 150 + 380 = 1,250$ of total intended expenditure, which is the exact amount of total production. This illustrates that $Y = 1,250$ is indeed an equilibrium position where total production/income levels are in precise balance with total intended expenditure.

A closer look at Expression 10–9 reveals that the impact of government spending and lump-sum taxes are upon the autonomous component of the model, with no effect on the value of the multiplier. Thus, changes in either G_a or TX_a will be subject to the multiplier but will not affect its value. On the other hand, the influence of the income tax rate, t, is directly upon the multiplier, with increases in t reducing the multiplier and decreases in t raising it. Accordingly, income tax rate changes affect the economy by altering the multiplier process that acts upon autonomous components of demand.

Since government expenditures and taxes enter our model in different structural ways, their influence on the economy is not exactly offsetting. The easiest way to see this is by setting $t = 0$ in Expression 10–9, i.e., assuming no income taxes. Under this assumption, the multiplier in our numerical illustration increases from 2.5 to 5.0 and the equilibrium level of Y increases from 1,250 to $(5)(500) = 2,500$. We now assume that the level of government spending is increased by 10, from 380 to 390, and that a new lump-sum tax of 10 is also imposed, increasing the value of TX_a from 75 to 85. The revised total level of autonomous demand is now given by $30 + 150 + 390 - 68 = 502$, which is greater than the original amount by 2. Applying the multiplier of 5 to this difference shows that the equilibrium level of income is increased by $(2)(5) = 10$ as a result of the addition of 10 in both government spending and lump-sum taxes.

The balanced addition of government spending and taxes is not neutral but expansionary by the same amount as the budget increase. The reason for this non-neutral effect is that the government spending change increases the level of autonomous demand dollar-for-dollar whereas the equal change in taxes reduces autonomous demand by only a fraction of its value. The lump-sum tax represents not a reduction in spending but a loss of purchasing power by consumers. Given a stable marginal propensity to consume, b, our model shows that a reduction in saving occurs as well as a reduction in consumer spending, as the tax is paid partially from reduced purchases (bTX_a) and partly from decreased saving $(1 - b)TX_a$. The non-neutral effect of equal changes in government spending and taxing is often referred to as the balanced budget multiplier. In the case we have considered, the balanced budget multiplier is unity, a result that follows directly from our model of Expression 10–9 under the assumption that $t = 0$. To see this precise result, consider the change in equilibrium income that results from a small change in government spending. Denoting this ratio as dY/dG_a, we have

$$\frac{dY}{dG_a} = \frac{1}{1 - b}$$

A similar expression for a change in income resulting from a small autonomous change in lump-sum taxes is given by

$$\frac{dY}{dTX_a} = \frac{b}{1 - b}$$

If we make a balanced budget change in both G and TX, then $dG_a = dTX_a$ and the total effect on Y is the net value of the two effects. This total effect is given by

$$\frac{dY}{dG_a} - \frac{dY}{dTX_a} = \left[\frac{1}{1 - b} - \frac{b}{1 - b}\right] = \left[\frac{1 - b}{1 - b}\right] = 1 \qquad (10\text{-}10)$$

which shows that equilibrium income rises by the exact amount of the initial balanced budget change in government spending and taxes.

A second view of the balanced budget effect of government upon the economy can be obtained by assuming that at least some taxes are income based. In this case, when $t \neq 0$, the evaluation of balanced budget effects is more complicated than in our previous discussion, since the matching of expenditure increases by tax increases involves an increase in the tax rate rather than in a lump-sum amount. Nonetheless, the same principle holds in the case of these more complicated calculations: an expenditure change by government and an equal and opposite tax change is not neutral in its combined economic effect.

In a world of income taxes, a concept related to this balanced budget principle is the tendency for governmental budgets to move into surplus positions as the equilibrium level of income rises. In our model, the total level of taxes, TX, is given by

$$TX = TX_a + tY \qquad (10\text{-}11)$$

If we continue to assume that government spending is autonomous, the budgetary position is given by B, where

$$B = TX - G_a \qquad (10\text{-}12)$$

or

$$B = TX_a + tY - G_a \qquad (10\text{-}13)$$

A positive value for B indicates more tax revenues than expenditures, which is a budgetary surplus, while a negative value for B indicates a deficit in the government account. In our earlier example, $TX_a = 75$, equilibrium $Y = 1,250$, $t = 0.25$, and $G_a = 380$. Therefore, $B = +7.5$, as tax revenues of 387.5 exceed the 380 of expenditures. Now suppose that a negative shift in investment demand occurs in the private sector, such that I is decreased from the initial value of 150 in the earlier example to a value of 130. This decrease of 20 in autonomous demand decreases equilibrium Y by $(2.5)(20) = 50$. In turn, a reduced amount of tax revenues of $(0.25)(50) = 12.5$ results from this income decline, thus lowering the total level of tax revenues from 387.5 to 375 and converting the surplus of 7.5 into a deficit of 5. Thus, the role of income shown in the budget Expression 10–13 makes it clear that increasing income levels tend to move government budgets into surplus positions while declining income levels tend to move government budgets into deficit positions, if all else is held constant.

The expenditure-taxing concepts now discussed can be seen graphically by considering a slightly modified representation of Expression 10–9. Y may be divided as follows

$$Y = Y_D + TX \qquad (10\text{--}14)$$

Similarly, Y_D may be expressed

$$Y_D = C + S \qquad (10\text{--}15)$$

where S is savings, defined as the residual obtained after subtracting C from Y_D. Combining these two expressions gives

$$Y = C + S + TX \qquad (10\text{--}16)$$

Expression 10–16 shows that aggregate income can be expressed as the sum of consumption expenditures, tax payments, and the saving residual. Since equilibrium occurs where Y equals intended spending, which is given as $C + I + G$, we may write

$$C + S + TX = C + I + G$$

and

$$S + TX = I + G \qquad (10\text{--}17)$$

which indicates that equilibrium involves a balance between aggregate private and public leakages and new public and private expenditure inputs. In our model, the left-hand side of 10–17 consists of variables assumed earlier to relate behaviorally to aggregate income as follows:

$$S = Y_D - C = Y_D - C_a - bY_D = Y_D(1 - b) - C_a$$

or, by substituting Expression 10–5 for Y_D

$$S = (1 - t)(1 - b)Y - C_a - (1 - b)TX_a \qquad (10\text{--}18)$$

and, as before

$$TX = tY + TX_a \qquad\qquad (10\text{–}19)$$

The two leakages represented by 10–18 and 10–19 are illustrated graphically in Figure 10–4. For convenience in illustrating the point, TX_a has been set to zero. This simplifies interpretation of the graph with no real loss in meaning. As seen, the level of savings grows as income grows, reflecting a constant marginal rate of both consumption and savings and is negative at

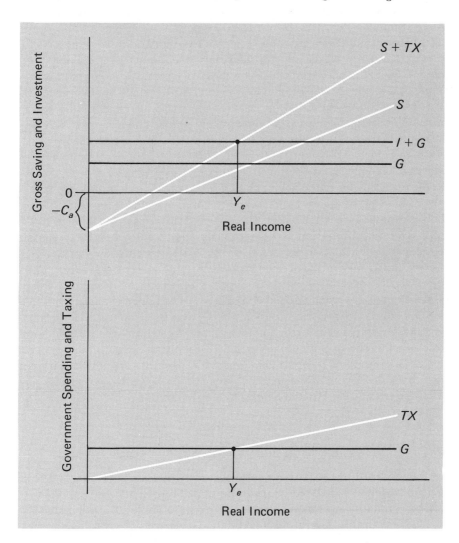

Figure 10–4

Taxing and Government Spending

low levels of income (dissavings), representing an autonomous level of consumption at zero income. Taxes also grow with income and are added to the S function to show the total public and private leakage, $S + T$. New public and private expenditures G and I are assumed to be autonomous and are shown as horizontal lines.

Following 10–17, Y_e is the level of output that produces a flow of private savings and tax revenues just sufficient to offset the input of new I and G expenditures. The equilibrium Y_e balances private inputs and leakages with public inputs and leakages. Implied by Y_e is both a private and public input-leakage surplus or deficit position. The lower part of Figure 10–4 shows the level of G and TX associated with the Y_e equilibrium. As seen, Y_e occurs where $G = TX$. This is the special case where aggregate economic equilibrium associates with a balanced governmental budget position. However, the $G = TX$ result also indicates that new private inputs are exactly equal to private leakages, i.e., that $I = S$ in the private sector. The two other logical possibilities insofar as public-private sector relationships are concerned are shown in Figures 10–5 and 10–6. In Figure 10–5, the relationships are aligned such that aggregate equilibrium, Y_e, occurs at a level where $TX > G$, thereby producing a surplus in the governmental budget position. At the same time, Expression 10–17 requires that $I > S$ in the private sector at the equilibrium. This illustrates a situation where the expansionary pressures generated by the $I > S$ condition in the private sector are absorbed by the governmental sector surplus position. In this sense, the budgetary surplus has a contractionary impact on the no-government equilibrium in the private sector. Figure 10–6 illustrates the opposite situation, in which aggregate equilibrium occurs at an output where $G > TX$ and $S > I$. The budgetary deficit in the public sector is expansionary since it offsets excess private saving. In the absence of the government sector, equilibrium in the private sector would have to contract until $S = I$. Figures 10–5 and 10–6 illustrate that economic equilibrium positions and governmental budgetary positions are quite separable, such that equilibrium in the economy does not imply a balanced, surplus, or deficit position in the government budget in and of itself.

Governmental Impact in the United States

Although illustrative of governmental economic effects, the graphic and algebraic model now analyzed is an oversimplified representation of specific U.S. governmental effects on economic activity. As Table 10–1 and Table 10–2 have indicated, several sharply different categories of government outlays and forms of taxes exist that do not lend themselves to the easy classifications of the earlier example. For example, the category Government Purchases of Goods and Services (category 1 in Table 10–1) is the only category of government outlays that directly enters into calculation of the GNP.

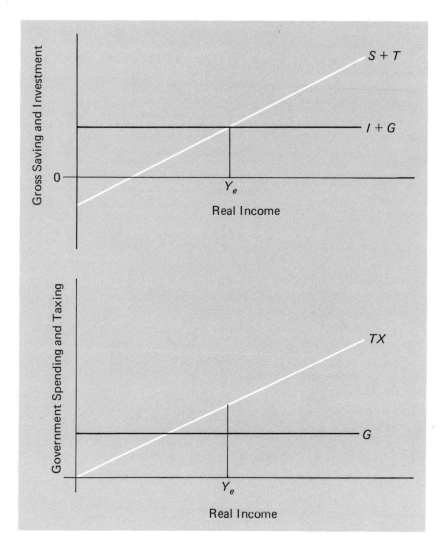

Figure 10–5
Public Surplus at Equilibrium

Transfers, interest, and subsidies formally only redistribute income among groups of citizens. If recipient and donor groups have approximately the same income expenditure propensities, the effects of these transfers would be neutral. But this is probably not a reasonable assumption considering the specifics for the United States. The largest transfer category, social security payments, is principally received by elderly, widowed, and unemployed persons, who may be presumed to spend close to 100 percent of their monthly

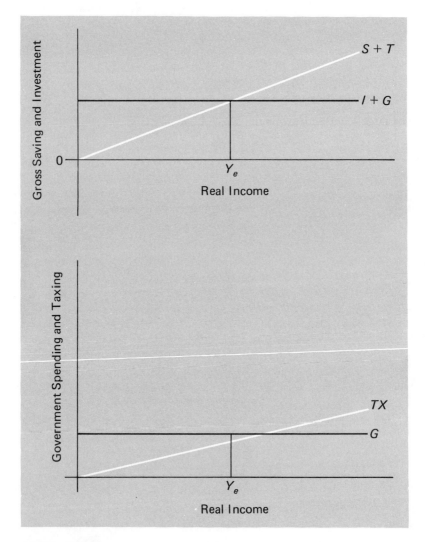

Figure 10–6

Public Deficit at Equilibrium

receipts. At the same time, the donor group consists of a broad cross-section of U.S. wage-earners and others. Collection of payments from these groups almost certainly cuts their consumer expenditures by less than 100 percent. The aggregate effect of these transfers undoubtedly is to raise overall consumption-income ratios and the marginal propensity to consume since the increase in consumption by recipient groups more than offsets the decrease by donor groups.

Regarding the four major categories of tax revenues given in Table 10–2, some possibly important deviations exist from the simple tax function given by Expression 10–19. Whereas personal tax receipts approximately follow this pattern as do social security contributions (to a lesser extent), other major tax categories may be more closely related to special variables. Indirect business tax is levied on the output of private business firms and is likely to be largely determined by the level of private output. Corporate income taxes are levied on corporate profits and will be largely determined by the complex array of corporate output, cost, and price changes that together determine corporate profits.

These illustrative comments suggest that actual prediction of tax revenues and assessment of the total effects of governmental outlays upon the economy is likely to be complicated, involving a detailed analysis of the effects upon and effects of relevant private sector variables. Upon this premise, realistic analysis of the quantitative impact of government on the U.S. economy can be best undertaken in the context of an econometric model that explicitly measures the relevant relationships. The Wharton econometric model is sufficiently disaggregated to accommodate measurement of a variety of private sector-governmental relationships. It therefore enables conclusions about the effects of governmental expenditure, taxing, and other policies upon the economy. We now consider some of these conclusions. In considering the Wharton results, it should be borne in mind that they have been obtained by applying the measured coefficients of the model's equations along with baseline projections of the autonomous variables. This produces a baseline estimate of GNP for a succession of time periods. Against this baseline, a change is introduced in one governmental variable, with all other autonomous variables unchanged, and the effect on aggregate output and other variables is observed. From these results, aggregate income multipliers (ratios of resulting aggregate income to initiating permanent change) are constructed for various governmental variables.

A number of these multipliers are shown in Table 10–3. Since they have been derived from the Wharton model through simulation, the results are not free of the peculiar characteristics of that model, i.e., they may contain effects not present in the actual economic system they are intended to represent, or they omit significant influences inherent in that system.[3] In the final

3 That is, an econometric model of differing structure may be expected to produce different estimates of the same multipliers when the identical assumptions and givens are employed. However, a survey of eleven econometric forecasting models made recently by Fromm and Klein that includes the Wharton model shows that several other models produce quite similar results, which suggests that the results of the Wharton model may reflect a more general finding than only for the Wharton structure. For details, see G. Fromm and L. R. Klein, "A Comparison of Eleven Econometric Models of the United States," *American Economic Review*, 63:2 (May 1973), pp. 385–393.

Table 10–3

Selected Multipliers—Wharton Model

		QUARTERS ELAPSED SINCE CHANGE			
		1	4	12	40
1. Government Expenditures—Nondefense	Y_c	2.33	2.63	2.92	3.72
	Y_r	1.98	2.03	2.07	1.93
	P	1.18	1.30	1.41	1.93
2. Government Expenditures—Defense	Y_c	2.60	2.85	2.86	3.90
	Y_r	2.19	2.10	1.91	2.02
	P	1.19	1.36	1.50	1.93
3. Personal Taxes	Y_c	1.33	1.75	2.36	4.23
	Y_r	1.19	1.35	1.67	2.61
	P	1.12	1.30	1.41	1.62
4. Corporate Taxes	Y_c	0.14	0.30	0.67	1.57
	Y_r	0.11	0.23	0.50	1.11
	P	1.27	1.30	1.34	1.41
5. Exports (or Other Exogenous Private Expenditures)*	Y_c	1.87	3.09	4.34	4.92
	Y_r	1.75	2.69	3.58	3.51
	P	1.07	1.15	1.21	1.40
6. Discount Rates**	Y_c	0.00	1.98	3.23	4.87
	Y_r	0.00	1.66	1.92	2.13
	P	—	1.19	1.68	2.29
7. Free Reserves/Required Reserves**	Y_c	0.00	1.79	2.91	4.37
	Y_r	0.00	1.49	1.73	1.92
	P	—	1.20	1.68	2.28

Note: Y_c = GNP in current dollars, Y_r = GNP in constant dollars, $P = Y_c/Y_r$ = price level effect.
Source: M. K. Evans, *Macroeconomic Activity*, Harper and Row, New York, 1969. Adapted from Tables 20–3 through 20–10, pp. 567–574.

* The effect is described as equivalent regardless of the type of private expenditure increased exogenously. See Evans, p. 575.
** The actual multipliers have been divided by two to make them comparable to the remainder of the table. See Evans, p. 578.

analysis, their numerical significance depends almost entirely upon the extent to which the model faithfully represents the actual economy. On this score the Wharton model rates as high or higher than any other available analytical device in terms of forward predictions (made beyond the period of the data) concerning an entire array of expenditure categories, employment estimates, and price data.[4] The predictive relevance of the Wharton model enhances the faith we may place in these measured values. However, it does not entirely offset the possible effect of stochastic, specification and other errors that may be at work to distort the measured multipliers.[5]

Values appear in Table 10–3 for the effect on both current dollar GNP, denoted as Y_c, and constant dollar GNP, denoted as Y_r, of autonomous changes in the seven variables listed, for the various time periods shown across the top of the table. All changes made in the autonomous variables are in a direction that would produce a positive output effect. Similar negative changes were described as producing similar results and are not shown. For example, an increase in non-defense government expenditures historically produces an increase in current dollar GNP of 2.33 times the increase during the same quarter and 3.72 times the increase after 40 quarters.

Of the governmental effects measured, the strongest same-quarter multiplier associates with defense expenditures. This is explained primarily by the inventory situation peculiar to that industry, in which an increased expenditure usually associates with an immediate addition to work-in-process inventories, thus increasing the GNP. Although not as high as defense (due to the inventory difference) non-defense expenditures are the next most significant in their impact during the initial quarter. However, over more extended periods the difference between the two greatly diminishes as the inventory situation "evens out" in defense. For 12 quarters the two government spending categories produce nearly identical results. However, after 40 quarters, defense expenditures again reveal a slightly more powerful effect.

As expected from conclusions of the earlier simplified graphic model, the immediate impact of personal taxes on aggregate income, being indirect and operating through personal income, is measured to be less than that of government expenditures. However, the eventual impact of personal taxes is seen to be more significant upon real and current dollar income than either form of government expenditure. The powerful long-run impact of personal taxes observed in the table reflects the influence of permanent income and living standard forces. Tax changes become incorporated into disposable income levels, which influence income projections and affect expenditure levels. Then, changes in expenditure levels influence future expenditures by altering standard-of-living goals. The combined result is a powerful expenditure standard-income inertia effect.

The table suggests the "balanced-budget effect" of 1 billion in both

---

[4] See Evans, Chapter 18.

[5] Particularly since we are inferring *ceteris paribus* quantitative magnitudes for economic processes that were measured in a non-*ceteris paribus* context.

new (nondefense) government expenditures and new personal taxes would be $2.33 - 1.33 = 1.0$ times the increase in the quarter of the increase. However, by 12 quarters after the change, the effect has withered to $2.92 - 2.36 = 0.56$ as higher taxes have become more permanently incorporated into consumer buying plans. The 40 quarter result implies the balanced budget effect of offsetting spending-taxing changes eventually completely wears off and in fact becomes slightly negative.

The corporate tax result is particularly interesting and perhaps surprising. As seen, a 1 billion decrease in corporate taxes has a relatively small effect on business fixed investment and consequently a small measured effect on GNP of only 0.14 billion in the same quarter. Subsequent effects show only a slightly greater effect on both current and real output. This indicates that corporate tax increases aimed at cooling off an overexpansive economy are not likely to produce a very great impact on GNP. The reverse effect indicates that corporate tax decreases aimed at stimulating the economy are likely to be ineffective.

The fifth item in Table 10–3, labeled Exports, represents the effects of an exogenous increase in private demand. No difference in impact between any particular form of private demand is measured by the model. This provides a comparison of private sector effects with public sector effects. As seen, the same-quarter impact is greater than the personal tax multiplier but less than government expenditure multipliers. However, by the twelfth quarter and beyond, these effects become the most powerful of all analyzed. This indicates that the influence of demand shifts in the private sector upon business expectations and consumer attitudes (as measured in the Wharton model by private output levels and past consumer expenditures and incomes) are quite powerful. More generally, the long-run impact of a dollar of new spending in the private economy is found to be more significant than the effect of a dollar of expenditures produced through government expenditures of a dollar returned as income through tax decreases. Therefore, public policies directed at encouraging expectational and attitudinal changes that shift private demand functions (thereby producing autonomous private demand shifts) are found to be more stimulating than other governmental alternatives.

The discount rate is an instrument of monetary policy used by the Federal Reserve to influence economic activity. The level of free reserves in the banking system provides a crude indication of the level of monetary tightness in the economy. In terms of their impact on aggregate output, these two monetary measures show the greatest lag, but eventually produce an effect that approximates that of fiscal policy instruments.[6]

---

[6] However, the zero same-quarter effect is forced by the lag structure of the model and should not be specifically attributed to the actual system.

The Wharton model predicts both price levels and real output levels as interdependent parts of the economic model. The difference between current dollar, Y_c, and real dollar, Y_r, results in Table 10–3 represents the inflationary impact of the autonomous changes considered. These have been calculated in the rows of the table labeled P. As seen, the two monetary policy variables (6 and 7) produce the greatest long-run inflationary impact relative to their real output effects. The next most significant long-run price level effect is produced by government expenditures (defense or nondefense) followed by personal tax changes, corporate taxes, and private expenditures, which show the smallest inflationary effect. During the same quarter, corporate taxes surprisingly produce the largest price level effect as producers apparently are quick to adjust product prices to tax changes. In addition, personal tax cuts are somewhat less inflationary than government spending changes in the same quarter. Finally, private demand (exports) involves the smallest price level effect in the same quarter.

Automatic Stabilizers

We have seen earlier that upswings in the level of aggregate output tend automatically to move the governmental budget into a surplus position and that downswings automatically move the budget into a deficit position. An additional reason for this effect in the United States is that tax rates increase as a percentage of income at higher income levels. This characteristic is graphically depicted in Figure 10–7, where the taxing function, and therefore the saving plus taxing function, rises at a rising rate rather than the constant rate assumed earlier. The effect is to enlarge the dependence of tax revenues upon GNP levels, thus producing a similarly enlarged tendency for economic upswings to produce budgetary surpluses or reduce deficits. In Figure 10–7, aggregate equilibrium occurs at Y_0 when G and I are equal to $G + I_0$. At that level, $G > TX$. A shift in I to I_1, raising $G + I$ to $G + I_1$, increases the GNP to Y_1 and moves the budget into a surplus position. This surplus absorbs some of the expansionary pressures related to the increase in I and retards the final resulting equilibrium value.

Looking at the reverse situation, a decrease in GNP (e.g., moving from Y_1 to Y_0) tends to move the budget into a deficit position and thereby lessens the decline in Y that otherwise would occur. Operating in both ways, the tax mechanism tends to smooth out erratic patterns of GNP growth by retarding sharp growth pressures and reducing the effect of similar downward pressures.

The contention that the tax mechanism did too effective a job of retarding growth tendencies formed the crux of the argument for passage of a general tax rate reduction in 1964, during a time when the budget was in

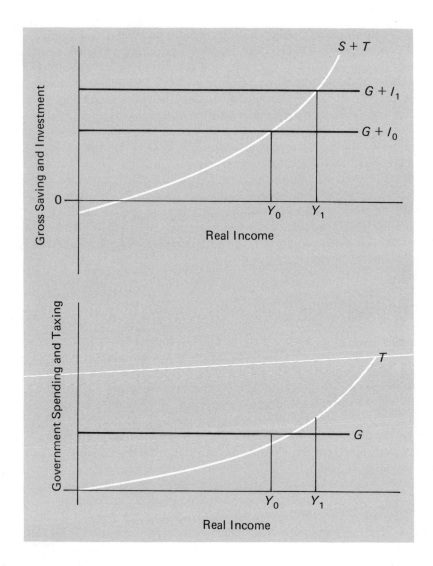

Figure 10–7

Effects of Progressive Taxes

a *deficit* position, with slightly greater than 5.5 percent unemployment. The argument basically was that as the economy drew closer to full employment, the "drag" of higher effective tax rates battered it back. This fiscal drag (as it was so-named) was put forth as the main culprit in preventing the economy from attaining full employment output levels. Figure 10–8 illustrates the approximate situation at that time. At the prevailing 5.5 percent unem-

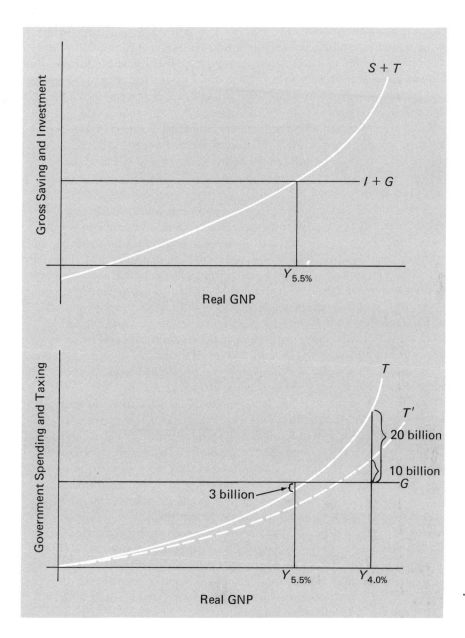

Figure 10–8

Tax Relationships—1964 Tax Cut

ployment ($Y_{5.5\%}$) equilibrium, a small budgetary deficit of about $3 billion was present. However, if the GNP were increased sufficiently to produce approximately full employment at 4 percent unemployed ($Y_{4.0\%}$), the existing tax rate structure would produce a 20 billion budgetary surplus.[7] Advocates of the bill contended that this surplus was an excessive amount of fiscal stabilization and would in fact prevent the economy from realizing full employment. Instead, it was proposed to lower tax rates (such as from T to T'), which would reduce the surplus to 10 billion at $Y_{4.0\%}$. It was argued that this cut would motivate the private economy (particularly business investment) sufficiently to cause an upward shift in investment. Coupled with the increased consumption expenditure associated with reduced personal taxes, Y_e would rise towards $Y_{4.0\%}$, thus reducing and finally eliminating the budgetary deficit.

Upon passage of the 1964 tax act, the consumer and investment sectors of the economy did in fact begin to respond as a vigorous expansion got underway. Indeed, indications are that the federal budget may have moved into a surplus position during 1965 if G would have been maintained at projected levels. However, unanticipated increases in military spending associated with U.S. involvement in Southeast Asia caused G to be increased greatly beyond expectations; thus, the effects predicted by the bill's advocates were not observable. However, with all major categories of private demand expanding briskly and a coincident and continuing sharp rise in G, full employment was shortly attained followed by unprecedented peacetime tightness in labor markets and eventually by unemployment rates of slightly over 3 percent (along, unfortunately, with a period of rapidly rising prices).

In addition to the effect of tax rates, unemployment compensation programs also provide structural economic stabilizers. These payments decrease at higher employment levels and increase as unemployment increases. This effect tends to add to the tax effect on budgetary positions. Perhaps more importantly, it insulates fluctuations in basic consumer purchasing power from fluctuations in GNP. For example, in an economic contraction, loss of purchasing power through layoffs, etc., is offset by higher payments of unemployment compensation. The reverse occurs during expansions. Personal tax withholding has a similar insulating effect since these withholdings increase in a booming economy and decline during contractions. The effect on disposable income of both these flows is to lessen the impact of GNP change on DPI change, which usually causes the rate of growth in DPI to lag behind GNP in expansions and similarly causes the rate of DPI decline to be less than GNP during recessions.[8]

---

[7] The exact figures are not easy to pin down since the bill was discussed over a period of time and the current figures changed.

[8] In effect, the multiplier is greater in contractions and smaller in expansions.

Determinants of the GNP in a Three-Sector Model

This chapter has added the role of government expenditures and taxes to that of private expenditures in determining the GNP. In this three-sector model, we have the broad outlines of an aggregate expenditure model that accounts for all major GNP categories of spending. Figure 10–9 illustrates this model, where $G + I_0$ along with $S + T$ produces equilibrium of Y_{I_0} and so forth for other values of I. In Chapter 8, an important theoretical role was seen for rates of interest and output levels in influencing investment. This role was verified statistically in the empirical models analyzed. In Figure 10–9, the levels of investment expenditures I_0, I_1, and I_2 (1) rise with output increases and (2) can be assumed to associate with various interest rates, say $i_0 > i_1 > i_2$. Thus one determinant of goods market equilibrium we have implicitly assumed known in advance is the interest rate underlying the level of I. Any equilibrium Y (such as Y_{I_1}) is based on a specific interest rate level. If i is determined independently of the GNP, this presents no particular difficulty. However, if the level of GNP significantly affects i, then i must be

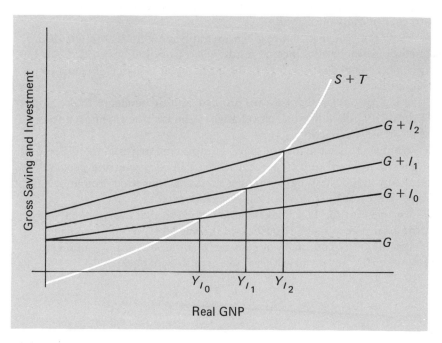

Figure 10–9

Goods Market Equilibrium

determined jointly with GNP as it cannot be known in advance. Many economists believe that GNP does exert an important influence on the value of i. If so, the goods market framework of Figure 10–9 is incomplete without providing also for the determination of i.

Understanding the determination of i requires consideration of the supply of and demand for money, as well as the availability of and demand for loanable funds. These considerations provide the remaining components in a complete model of aggregate demand. It is to this topic that attention turns in the several chapters that follow. But first we complete our picture of markets for goods and services by considering in the next chapter the impact of the international sector on economic activity.

Discussion Questions

1. How would economic equilibrium be affected by a shift in taxes away from lump-sum taxes and toward income taxes?

2. Assume that an increase in government spending is matched entirely by an increase in lump-sum taxes, but that consumers pay the entire tax from savings, maintaining purchases at pretax levels. What is the multiplier effect of this change in spending and taxes?

3. Using the model structure given by Expressions 10–1 through 10–5, what equilibrium level of income results when $C_a = 100$, $I_a = 125$, $G_a = 150$, $TX_a = 60$, $b = 0.9$, and $t = 0.1$? Is the economy at a budgetary surplus or deficit at this equilibrium?

4. Using the data of the previous problem and the model of Expressions 10–1 through 10–5, how much of a change in the tax rate is required to produce a balanced budget?

5. What would be the impact on real output and prices in the U.S. economy over 12 quarters of a 10 percent increase in corporate and personal taxes, according to the Wharton model results? Under what economic conditions would you be most skeptical of such results?

6. Assume that the U.S. tax system is revised so that everyone pays 25 percent of income as taxes, regardless of income level. Would you expect the impact to be expansionary or contractionary upon output and income levels? Why? Do you see any other impacts of this change?

11

The International Sector

In the U.S. and other advanced economies, international trade means both a source of new demand for goods and services and a savings-like leakage of income out of the circular flow of economic activity. The balance of these activities can be an important factor in shaping business conditions and can have an influence on the formulation of domestic economic policy. In this chapter we consider some of the major questions dealing with the impact of international activities on domestic economic conditions, beginning with the impact of international activities on aggregate equilibrium in markets for goods and services.

International Flows and the Domestic Economy

In the three-sector model discussed in the previous chapter, the equilibrium level of real income was found to occur at the point where total public and private saving flows exactly offset total public and private investment flows. Letting S equal private saving, TX equal government taxes, I equal intended private investment, and G equal government spending, and where all magnitudes are real, this equilibrium condition is

$$S + TX = I + G \qquad\qquad (11-1)$$

Imports are the level of foreign-made goods and services purchased by domestic buyers. The basic influence of imports upon aggregate equilibrium

195

is as a savings-like disposition of current income. Rather than income being entirely accounted for as the sum of consumption expenditures, savings, and taxes, we must also add the value of imports, producing the modified identity for the disposition of income:

$$Y = C + S + TX + Z \qquad (11\text{--}2)$$

where Y is aggregate real income and Z is the real value of imports. In Expression 11–2, the total level of domestic consumption and international expenditures is $C + Z$. If imports are added to a formerly closed economy with no effect on domestic expenditure, the level of total domestic and foreign expenditure rises. On the other hand, if the impact of adding imports to a closed economy is only to substitute foreign for domestic goods, the level of domestic expenditure will fall as Z is added such that the total level of foreign and domestic expenditure equals the original domestic expenditure. Neither of these two extremes is likely. Rather, imports undoubtedly substitute somewhat for and add somewhat to the level of domestic expenditures.

Even though imports are expenditures made by domestic consumers, firms, and governments, they affect the domestic economy as if they were saving. This is because import expenditures add to the national income and production levels of other nations, but do not add to the level of domestic production and income. Indeed, if changes in tastes cause a net shift in demand toward imported goods and away from domestic goods, the level of domestic production and income falls exactly as if a shift toward higher saving levels had occurred. It is for this reason that imports are a savings-like leakage to the domestic economy even though they are expenditures by consumers, firms, and governments.

Exports are goods produced domestically that are sold to consumers in other nations. Exports are similar to business investment in that they are essentially a source of income-independent product market demand. Accordingly, exports are a component of intended expenditures that add to the total of consumer spending, C, investment spending, I, and government spending, G, giving the total intended real expenditure as

$$C + I + G + X$$

where X is the level of exports.

In the discussion that follows we assume for simplicity that rates of monetary exchange are fixed and, also for simplicity, we ignore monetary and interest rate effects on the trade balance. Under these conditions, equilibrium occurs where intended spending equals total income, i.e., where

$$C + I + G + X = C + S + TX + Z \qquad (11\text{--}3)$$

or, where

$$I + G + X = S + TX + Z \qquad (11\text{--}4)$$

A comparison of this expression with equilibrium in the three-sector case as given in Expression 11–1 shows that for the four-sector model an additional term is added to both the gross investment and gross saving sides. If exports exceed imports, i.e., $X > Z$, then the nation's balance of trade is said to be in a surplus position. When imports exceed exports, a deficit occurs in the balance of trade. Since $X - Z$ is a net injection into the circular economic flow of new spending, movements toward surplus positions in the balance of trade are expansionary in their economic impact, while movements toward deficit positions are contractionary.

The transactions entering into the calculation of the balance of trade position involve only international purchases and sales of goods and services. In addition to these activities, new investments are made by domestic investors in foreign assets and by foreign investors in domestic assets. Also, other payments such as military expenditures and transfer payments in the form of grants and foreign aid occur. These flows are not product market expenditures but nonetheless involve the transfer of funds among nations. When the net effect of investment and transfers are added to the balance of trade, the balance of payments results. The balance of payments is thus a more inclusive concept than the balance of trade, accounting for the total net flow of claims on the currency of the country by other nations. It is quite normal to find an advanced economy such as the United States running a surplus in its balance of trade and a deficit in its balance of payments, particularly during a time of industrial strength in the domestic economy when domestic producers see important and profitable investment opportunities abroad and are encouraged to pursue these opportunities. While the balance of payments has little directly to do with equilibrium in the economy in terms of Expression 11–4, it is important in the relative strength of currency values between nations, as we shall later see.

Determinants of Imports and Exports

Because imports are the purchase of goods and services by domestic consumers, we expect them to be influenced by current income flows in the same general way that domestic consumption is influenced by current income. Accordingly, imports are usually taken to be a positive (upward sloping) function of income. A second important determinant of imports is the relative price structure of domestic and foreign goods. Clearly, as foreign goods rise in price relative to domestic goods, the demand for domestic goods will rise for all the products and services where domestic and foreign goods are important substitutes. The relative prices of foreign and domestic goods are influenced not only by the selling prices of these goods in the respective nations, but also by the rate of currency exchange. Later in the chapter, we consider this aspect of international trade. For now, we can usefully proceed with the simplifying assumption that relative prices of domestic and foreign goods are unchanged. With this simplification, we may think of the import relationship as being approximately proportional to disposable income, as follows:

$$Z = cY_D \qquad\qquad (11\text{-}5)$$

where Y_D is the level of disposable income.

By similar reasoning, exports may be thought of as largely dependent upon the level of income available in the group of nations that are the domestic nation's trading partners, since domestic exports are imports for foreign nations. For some purposes, it is reasonable to consider foreign income levels as autonomous with respect to domestic income levels. This is particularly appropriate in the case of a country with a small level of imports but not as appropriate for the case of a country with a large level of imports. The reason for this distinction is that domestic imports of a particular country, say country A, add to the income of the foreign nations with which it trades, which influences their level of imports and thus exerts a secondary influence on the level of exports for country A. If a nation's level of imports is small relative to the income levels of its trading partners, this secondary influence will be inconsequential, and exports will be independent of imports for the nation. On the other hand, if a nation's level of imports are an important proportion of the income of its trading partners, then an increase in that nation's imports may add sufficiently to the purchasing power of its trading partners to cause them to increase their international purchases.

Figure 11-1 shows the effects graphically. For the "small country" case, imports rise with domestic real income according to the import function given in Expression 11-5, while exports are constant. For the "big country" case, increasing imports induce increases in exports, imparting an upward slope to the export function and making it in effect also a function of income. For the small country case, an increase in domestic real income from Y_0 to Y_1 increases the level of imports from Z_0 to Z_1. Since exports are constant, the balance of payments moves toward deficit levels by the exact amount of the increase in imports, $Z_1 - Z_0$. In the figure, the increase in income converts an initial trade surplus into a deficit. For the big country case, an increase in domestic real income increases imports along a similar import function from Z_0 to Z_1, but exports also increase from E_0 to E_1. The

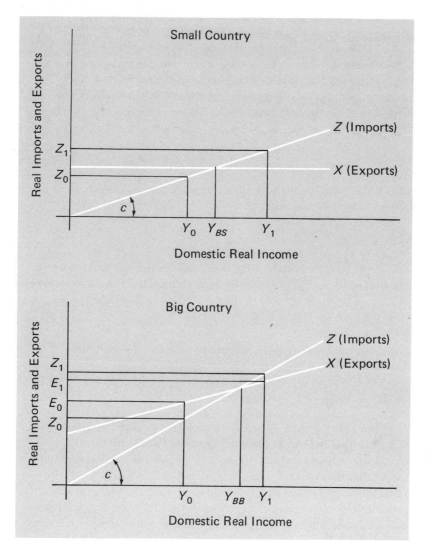

Figure 11–1

Balance of Trade Relationships

impact on the trade position of a domestic income increase is thus less adverse for the big country case than for the small country case, since the position moves toward a deficit by an amount equal to $(Z_1 - Z_0) - (E_1 - E_0)$ rather than $Z_1 - Z_0$. In addition, the income level at which a zero trade balance occurs is increased due to the big country effect, as illustrated in Figure 11–1 by a shift to the right of the zero trade balance point from Y_{BS} for the small country case to Y_{BB} for the big country case.

Equilibrium in the Four-Sector Model

We may now profitably return to the equilibrium statement given by Expression 11–4 and develop from it a statement of the four-sector model for both the small country and big country cases. As in the previous chapter's three-sector model, we assume consumption to be a simple linear function of disposable income:

$$C = C_a + bY_D \tag{11-6}$$

where C_a is the level of autonomous consumption and b is the marginal propensity to consume. Assuming taxes, TX, to be given by

$$TX = TX_a + tY \tag{11-7}$$

where TX_a is the level of autonomous taxes and t is the marginal tax rate, disposable income $(Y - TX)$ is given by subtracting 11–7 from Y as follows:

$$Y_D = Y(1 - t) - TX_a \tag{11-8}$$

Since saving, S, is defined as $Y_D - C$, we can subtract 11–6 from 11–8 to obtain

$$S = Y(1 - t)(1 - b) - TX_a(1 - b) - C_a \tag{11-9}$$

We follow the model of the previous chapter in assuming investment and government spending to be autonomous, i.e., $I = I_a$ and $G = G_a$.

We consider the small country case first. In this case, exports can be considered autonomous, i.e., $X = X_a$. According to Expression 11–4, equilibrium domestic real income occurs where total leakages equal total new injections. We have now given expressions for each leakage, i.e., saving 11–9, taxes 11–7, and imports 11–5, and have defined the values of the new injections I, G, and X as autonomous. We may combine these according to Expression 11–4 and substitute for Y_d in the import expression the right-hand side of 11–8. Thus equilibrium occurs where

$$Y(1 - t)(1 - b) - TX_a(1 - b) - C_a + TX_a + tY + c(1 - t)Y$$
$$- cTX_a = I_a + G_a + X_a$$

Combining terms and solving for Y gives

$$Y = \frac{1}{1 - (b - c)(1 - t)}$$
$$\cdot [I_a + G_a + C_a + X_a - (b - c)TX_a] \tag{11-10}$$

This expression shows that the net effect of the import function is to reduce the multiplier. The after-tax marginal propensity to consume is reduced from $b(1 - t)$ in the case of no imports to $(b - c)(1 - t)$ when imports are included. This is a concrete illustration of the saving-like role of imports in the economy. The higher the value of C, the lower is the after-tax marginal propensity to consume. On the other hand, exports add to the level of autonomous expenditures and are subject to the multiplier similar to investment or government expenditures. While imports rotate the aggregate demand function downward by reducing its slope, exports shift it upward by increasing its intercept.

The large country model differs from the model now developed in that the level of exports are a positive function of the level of imports, as

$$X = X_a + dZ \qquad (11\text{--}11)$$

When this expression is inserted into the model in place of the expression $X = X_a$, the following expression for equilibrium Y results:

$$Y = \frac{1}{1 - (1 - t)[b - c(1 - d)]}$$
$$\cdot [C_a + I_a + G_a + X_a - [b - c(1 - d)]TX_a] \quad (11\text{--}12)$$

Expression 11–12 shows that the big country impact of imports upon exports reduces the leakage effect of imports. The effective big country value of the import leakage is reduced from c in the small country case to $c(1 - d)$ for the big country. Accordingly, the multiplier is increased somewhat by the big country effect over its value for an otherwise equal small country model. Notice in this expression that in the unlikely case that $d = 1$, each dollar in imports generates a matching dollar in exports. This means that no net leakage occurs on account of imports, since their effect is entirely neutralized by the reaction of exports. This is illustrated in Expression 11–12 by the fact that when $d = 1$, c completely disappears from the model.

The four-sector model is illustrated graphically in Figure 11–2. In this figure, the equilibrium level of income is at Y_0 when total injections are given by $G_0 + I + X$. The $G + I + X$ curve is shown with a positive slope, illustrating a big country effect. If government spending is increased from G_0 to G_1, domestic equilibrium income increases to Y_1, and the balance of trade moves from a small surplus position at Y_0 to a deficit at Y_1, as shown in the lower graph.

In our model, a zero balance of trade means the international sector has a neutral effect on domestic real income levels. When $X = Z$, new international expenditures and international saving-like leakages exactly offset each other, leaving equilibrium at the same level as in the three-sector

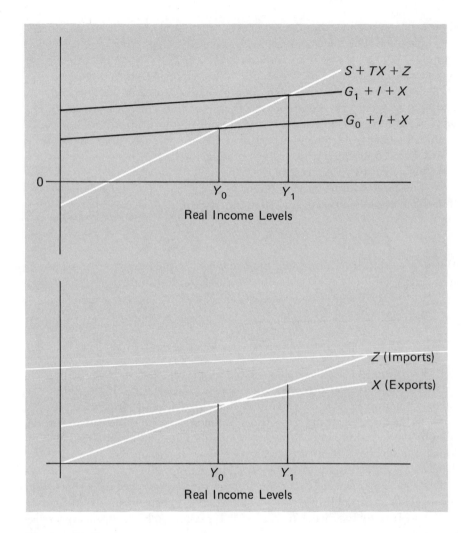

Figure 11–2

Four-sector Model

model. Figure 11–3 illustrates this proposition for the big country case. At income level Y_0, $S + TX = (I + G)_0$, meaning the domestic economy is in equilibrium without considering the effect of international economic activities. Adding imports shifts the gross saving function up to $S + TX + Z$, whereas adding exports shifts the gross investment function up to $(I + G + X)_0$. Equilibrium remains at Y_0, since $S + TX + Z = (I + G + X)_0$. The lower graph in Figure 11–3 shows that the reason for this result is that

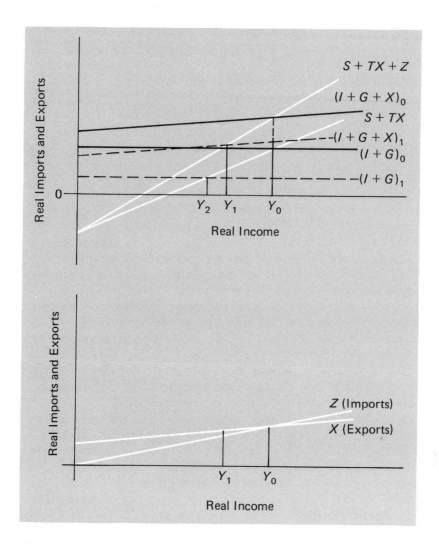

Figure 11–3

Balance of Trade Relationships

the import and export functions are positioned and sloped such that income level Y_0 causes $X = Z$; thus, we are adding the same magnitude to the gross saving function at Y_0 as we are the gross investment function. However, if the level of gross domestic investment should fall, say from $(I + G)_0$ to $(I + G)_1$ in the figure, the picture changes. Equilibrium in the four-sector model now occurs at Y_1 where the lower graph shows that a surplus balance of trade occurs. The effect of this surplus on the domestic economy is to increase it from Y_2 where $S + TX = (I + G)_1$ to Y_1 where $S + TX + Z = (I + G + X)_1$. For positive demand shifts in the private sector that lead to higher equilibrium income levels than Y_0, the effect is reversed, as the resulting deficit in the trade balance has a negative impact on domestic equilibrium.

Exchange Rates and Economic Activity

When merchants and manufacturers of one nation want to buy goods from another nation, they must ordinarily make payment in the currency of the other nation. A U.S. manufacturer who sells a machine tool to a Japanese producer expects to be paid in U.S. dollars, not Japanese yen. This universal practice has long created a need for currencies of various nations to be traded back and forth to facilitate international trade. Accordingly, an increasingly complex system of world monetary exchange has emerged from the period of the eighteenth and nineteenth centuries when nations transported gold bullion across the seas for payment of international obligations. Although physical shipment of gold among nations as international payment was gradually reduced and replaced by use of currencies as gold substitutes, it was not until recently that the role of gold in international transactions was essentially eliminated.

Perhaps the most essential and unchanging function of a system of international monetary exchange is that of accommodating changes in the demand for and supply of individual currencies of various nations in such a way that orderly markets exist in which supply approximately equals demand. Until recently this function has been performed at major international currency exchanges in cities such as London, Paris, and Zurich by the use of a system of fixed exchange rates among currencies.

Under fixed exchange rates, the price of each currency is held constant relative to all other currencies. Fluctuations in the supply of or demand for a currency cause an abundance or scarcity of the currency in the international currency market. Figure 11–4 helps illustrate the point. In this figure, the supply of dollars in an international market, SS, is shown as an upward sloping function of the price of the dollar relative to other currencies, while the demand for dollars, D_0D_0, is shown as a declining function of the dollar's exchange rate. The shapes of these curves reflect the influence of exchange rates upon the international value of a nation's goods and services. As nations pay more for dollars in currency markets, U.S. goods become more expensive for them to buy. Their demand for both U.S. goods and the associated dollars with which to do business declines. Thus, the demand curve for dollars is downward sloping. The supply curve

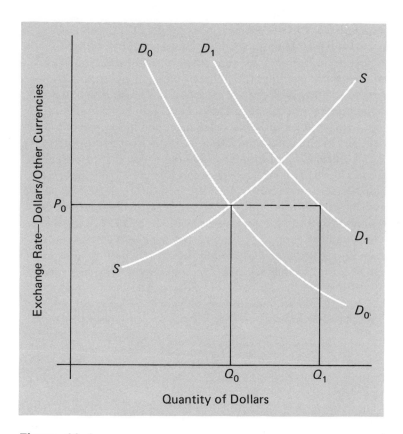

Figure 11–4

Supply and Demand for Currency

reflects the same type of reasoning. An increased price for dollars motivates a shift in demand away from U.S. products and motivates an increased exchange for dollars for other currencies.

In Figure 11–4, an exchange rate of P_0 clears the market by equating demand and supply at a volume of trading equal to Q_0. Suppose that the demand for dollars shifts positively in response to, say, a booming demand for a new type of U.S. produced product. In Figure 11–4, the demand curve shifts out to D_1D_1. If the exchange rate remains fixed, the demand for dollars increases to Q_1 while the supply remains at Q_0. A shortage of dollars exists. For a short while, the difference $Q_1 - Q_0$ could be supplied by trading inventories of dollars at the monetary exchange. But, if the gap persists, under fixed exchange rates the U.S. Treasury would have to sell dollars at P_0 in return for either gold or other currencies. If the shift in demand had instead been negative (back to the left) an excess supply of dollars would appear on the market. If persistent, the United States would be called on to purchase the excess dollars at P_0 for gold or other currencies. An important premise of fixed exchange rates is that excess demand and supply for individual currencies will approximately balance out over time, such that long-term imbalances between currency demand and supply will not appear.

In the world's experience with fixed exchange rates in the post-World War II era, a number of circumstances have arisen where long-run shifts have occurred in the demand and supply of currencies such that persistent imbalances have occurred. The U.S. experience of the latter 1960s and early 1970s is the most vivid case in point. A chronic balance of payments deficit over this period created an oversupply of U.S. dollars in international money markets and a continued repurchase of dollars by the United States. As it became clearer and clearer to speculators that the United States could not continue to repurchase dollars indefinitely due to a dwindling stock of gold, several international monetary crises were experienced in the late 1960s and early 1970s as speculators rushed to exchange dollars for gold or other currencies in anticipation of decrease or devaluation in the price of the dollar. Figure 11–5 illustrates the effect. From an initial equilibrium

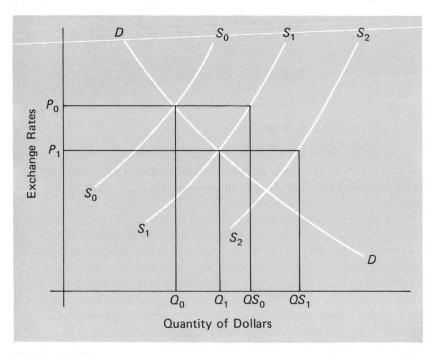

Figure 11–5
Run on the Dollar

position of S_0S_0 with an exchange rate of P_0, the supply of dollars begins
to shift outward, creating an excess supply of dollars. Speculators seize upon
this circumstance, supplying more currency on international currency markets as they shift out of dollars and into gold or other alternatives. The
supply curve for dollars shifts out further, say to S_1S_1, enlarging the oversupply of dollars, given by $(QS_0 - Q_0)$, and creating a crisis environment.
Eventually, the crisis reaches a peak and the dollar is devalued from P_0 to
P_1 to bring its exchange rate in line with current market conditions. Equilibrium is reestablished at P_1Q_1. However, continued deficits in the U.S.
balance of payments, coupled with continued speculative activities, causes
a further shift in the supply of dollars to S_2S_2, which reestablishes an excess
supply condition $(QS_1 - Q_1)$ and sets the stage for a further devaluation.[1]

This pattern eventually proved fatal for the system of fixed exchange
rates. In August 1971, the United States suspended sales and purchases of
gold to other nations. The dollar's rate of exchange was allowed to find its
own level in a system of floating exchange rates. Its value dropped sharply
over the next several months, but then found a satisfactory and reasonably
stable level as dictated by supply and demand.[2] After this period of adjustment, the shifts in exchange rates that have occurred have been gradual,
relatively minor, and made as a by-product of an auction market rather than
in an air of economic and political crisis.

The experience tends to illustrate essential advantages of exchange
rates being set in markets according to supply and demand rather than by
central governments as in the fixed rate system. The predominant advantage
is the removal of the motivation for speculative runs on the dollar, since no
value of the dollar is too low or too high for market equilibrium. A second
powerful advantage of flexible exchange rates is the impact upon the balance of payments that results from fully adjusted exchange rates. When a
deficit in a country's balance of payments increases the supply of its currency on world markets, its exchange rate gradually declines, making the
nation's exports cheaper and its imports more expensive. The result of these
realignments is a narrowing and elimination of the deficit, at which point
the oversupply of currency is eliminated and the exchange rate stabilized.
Over the long-run, flexible exchange rates tend to settle at levels that associate with balanced trade positions.

---

[1] The situation with the U.S. dollar in the 1950s is almost exactly the reverse of this
situation. A persistent balance of payments surplus created a shortage of dollars, leading
to an upward pressure on the dollar's exchange rate and a pattern of net gold purchases
by the U.S. over the period.
[2] The dollar's official rate was de facto devalued by 8 percent in December 1971 and
formally devalued by an additional 10 percent in February 1973.

The Payments Position and the Money Supply

A nation running a surplus in its balance of payments is receiving more of its own currency as payment for goods and services by other nations than it is paying out to buy the currency of other nations for purchase of their goods. Thus, one result of a payment's surplus is a growth in the domestic money supply. Similarly, a deficit in the balance of payments has the effect of decreasing the domestic money supply.[3] As we shall discuss in some detail in later chapters, an increase in the domestic money supply usually lowers domestic interest rates. In turn, a decreased level of domestic interest rates has two effects on the economy. First, as our discussion of investment in Chapter 8 has suggested, the level of investment and therefore aggregate income should rise in response to the fall in interest rates. Given an upward-sloping import function, a larger level of aggregate income resulting from the investment increase should generate a net increase in imports. The induced import increase reduces the surplus position due to the normal tendency for the trade position to move into a deficit position at increased income levels. Thus, the existence of a payments surplus sets into motion a reaction in the domestic economy that tends to reduce the surplus.

The second effect of surplus induced falling domestic interest rates is to motivate money capital to flow into investments abroad. The assumption behind this effect is that some investors will shift their funds from falling interest rate investments domestically to other investment alternatives abroad. An increased outflow of investment capital in response to a surplus induced fall in domestic interest rates increases the supply of dollars on foreign exchange markets, which tends to offset the shortage of dollars on these markets associated with the initial surplus position.

Thus, we find exchange rate, interest rate, and capital flow effects induced by the impact of a balance of payments surplus that tend to counteract and offset the surplus. The effects in reverse will have an identical counteracting influence on a deficit. These induced effects show that a balance of payments surplus or a deficit are disequilibrium positions in that they generate a set of reactive influences. Only when a zero balance of payments exists do the induced effects of the payments position disappear so that the economy is in an equilibrium position.

In this chapter we have added the international sector to the three-

---

[3] The magnitude of this effect depends on the size of the balance of payments relative to the domestic money supply. In the United States, a domestic money supply of 250 billion or better in the early 1970s probably makes the money supply effect small. However, in nations such as Belgium or the Netherlands, the effect of payment position on money supply may be significant, as the value of the payments position is large relative to the domestic money supply.

sector model. We have found the direct effect of this addition to be upon the multiplier and upon the level of autonomous expenditures. We have discussed the role of exchange rates upon the economy and upon the international balance of trade. We have found that monetary repercussions of payments imbalances tend to offset the imbalance. With this exception, our discussion of goods market equilibrium in the two-, three-, and four-sector model has held monetary influences offstage. While this has enabled the formation of an uncluttered understanding of goods market behavior, it also may create an impression that monetary factors do not influence goods market equilibrium. Such an impression is false, for monetary influences on economic activity are important and of increasing interest and concern to economic analysts and policy makers. In the next several chapters, we set about to fomulate the role of monetary markets in overall economic activity and to integrate the impact of monetary variables with goods market variables for the comprehensive determination of goods and money market equilibrium.

Discussion Questions

1.   In the four-sector model presented in this chapter, what is the implication of a large country model in which $c = d$?

2.   Can a nation count on having a positive level of net exports over a continued period of time? Explain.

3.   What do you see as the major advantage of fixed exchange rates over flexible rates? What is the major advantage of flexible rates over fixed rates?

4.   Milton Friedman once said that he was in favor of stable exchange rates, but was opposed to fixed exchange rates because they were less stable than flexible rates. What do you see as the reasoning behind this statement?

5.   The increase in oil prices that occurred worldwide in 1973 and early 1974 created a huge trade surplus for oil exporting nations and moved the trade positions of many oil importing nations toward deficit positions. In the United States, a surplus position was translated into a deficit in a period of only a few months. What should the repercussions of this situation be on both the oil exporting and oil importing nations?

12
Money and Capital Markets—I

In this and the next several chapters, we shall be concerned with exploring the specific way in which money affects general economic activity and is affected by it. Earlier it was seen that a major way in which money influenced the economy was through the influence of money's cost (interest rates) upon private investment. In the United States, this interest rate investment mechanism is a greatly simplified abstraction of the actual processes that bind money and goods markets together. In this chapter, we shall attempt to develop a more detailed analysis of these processes in the United States to help evaluate and interpret the effects of changes in the flows of monetary and expenditure variables.

Money Defined

In the United States, money performs two essential functions in addition to providing a uniform unit of monetary value. Money is (1) the national medium of exchange and (2) a store of value. The medium-of-exchange function indicates that money is a standard reward for productive services, a uniform means of payment for goods and services and a final means for settlement of debt. The store of value function means that money enables rewards from productive labor to be retained across time periods, providing a reserve of purchasing power.

A specific definition of money in the United States should encompass all the financial instruments that serve these two essential functions. There is general agreement among economists that coin and currency in circulation and demand deposits (checking account balances) fall into this category. Federal Reserve Notes are issued by and under the direct control of the Federal Reserve System, which is the central banking authority in the United States. As such, Federal Reserve Notes are often called primary or outside money. Demand deposits are issued by commercial banks, under regulations issued by the Federal Reserve. Thus, their control is shared by the Federal Reserve System and commercial banks. Because of this, this component of money is often referred to as secondary or inside money. As we shall later see, the volume of inside money issued by commercial banks is dependent on the volume of outside money in a less than simple way. The sum of currency and demand deposits is often referred to as the narrow definition of money. A broader definition is occasionally used in empirical work, which in addition includes the level of small denomination time deposits (savings accounts) issued by banks. This version is based on the concept that time deposits, while not capable of functioning as a medium of exchange (they cannot be used for the payment of debt) are in fact so easily convertible into demand deposits that they are "near-money" and can be considered as money for some purposes. Unless otherwise noted, references to money in this chapter imply the more widely used narrow definition.

Supply of Money and Supply of Lending

In discussions of monetary effects upon economic activity, it is increasingly important to distinguish between the total stock of available money and the rate at which funds flow from lenders to borrowers in the nation's capital markets. Historically, changes in the stock of money can not be closely associated with the flow of funds through capital markets without considering other factors. Figure 12–1 shows the relationship between changes in the stock of money and changes in the level of total corporate new long–term debt and equity financing. This figure illustrates the somewhat divergent paths taken by these variables. In fact, about 52 percent of the variation in one associates with the other according to the calculated coefficient of determination. A divergence is particularly evident during times of tight money market conditions of the type indicated by the negative growth in the money supply. The pattern of Figure 12–1 illustrates that changes in the money supply cannot always be counted on to produce changes in the supply of capital on capital markets.

Of the two concepts, the flow of available capital market funds is the more directly related to our overall concern with evaluating the impact of money markets upon economic activity. It is this flow that in part enables

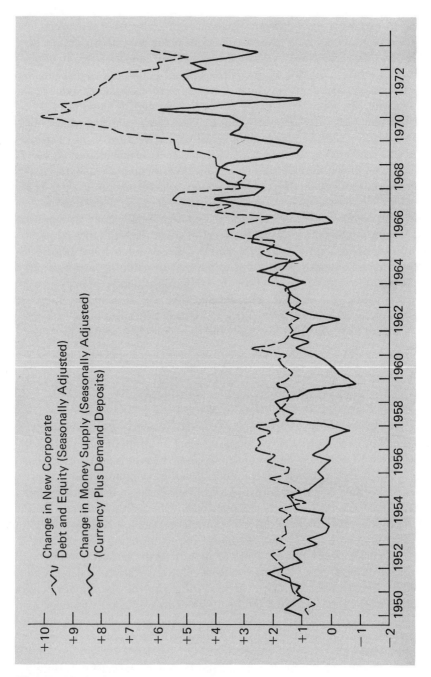

Figure 12–1

Money Supply and Flow of Corporate Capital

anticipated investment expenditures to be translated into actual expenditures. Through capital market channels, investment and aggregate expenditures are affected by monetary factors. Accordingly, our attention is first directed toward a more extensive consideration of capital market funds flow.

Institutional Factors in the Flow of Capital

As a first step in understanding capital market flows, we shall consider the role of the Federal Reserve System in influencing monetary conditions as compared to the role of commercial banks and other savings institutions.

The nation's 12 regional Federal Reserve Banks are the core around which the nation's banking system is organized. They have often been called "banker's banks" since they do not generally deal with the public but with the nation's commercial banks. The nation's monetary statutes require that member commercial banks maintain vault cash plus deposits with the Federal Reserve System in amounts equal to a fractional portion of the outstanding liabilities of the member bank. This provides a minimum standard of bank solvency and enables the Federal Reserve Bank to exercise surveillance and control over member banks' asset-liabilities positions. In addition, the Federal Reserve System issues and is responsible for control of the primary currency in circulation. Table 12–1 shows the consoli-

Table 12–1

Federal Reserve Banks
Consolidated Balance Sheet
(January 30, 1974)

ASSETS	BILLIONS
Gold Certificate Account	11.5
U.S. Government Securities	78.2
Cash Items in Process of Collection	6.8
Commercial Bank Loans and All Other	5.0
Total Assets	101.5
LIABILITIES	
Federal Reserve Notes	61.7
Member Bank Reserve Deposits	28.3
Other Deposits and Liabilities	11.5
Total Liabilities	101.5

Source: Federal Reserve Bulletin, **February 1974.**

dated asset position of the nation's 12 Federal Reserve Banks. The most important asset categories are seen to be gold certificate accounts, U.S. government securities, and cash items in process of collection. The first of these includes the asset value of the nation's stock of gold bullion. The Federal Reserve System is credited with the value of this stock as an asset.

The portfolio of U.S. government securities is an investment by the Federal Reserve in U.S. debt obligations. The Federal Reserve normally pays for purchases of securities by increasing the reserve accounts of the selling commercial banks or by issuing checks drawn against the Federal Reserve. When a check drawn against the Federal Reserve is presented by a commercial bank at their Federal Reserve Bank, the commercial bank's account at the Federal Reserve is increased. Similarly, when the Federal Reserve sells bonds from its portfolio, the payment for the bonds by commercial banks or others reduces the size of the bank's reserve account at the Federal Reserve by the amount of the sale. Thus, the sale or purchase of their own securities by the Federal Reserve brings about a direct change in the reserve account levels of commercial banks. Changes in reserve accounts are the same in their effect on the total money supply as changes in the level of circulating currency, since they are a component of outside money and can be the basis of a further expansion of demand deposits by the banking system.

Thus, through transactions in their bond portfolio, the Federal Reserve has available a means to directly influence the total supply of money. In practice, the System uses transactions in this portfolio to make gradual adjustments in the supply of outside money corresponding to the overall policy of the Federal Reserve System regarding the objective of monetary ease or tightness. For example, if the System decides that a policy of gradually expanding the available money supply is in order, this can be implemented by consistently buying more government securities than are sold over an extended period of weeks or months. Such a policy is called *open market policy* and is one of the major ways in which the Federal Reserve can influence the money supply.

The third major asset category in Table 12–1, Cash Items in Process of Collection, represents the amount of funds tied up in the process of clearing checks throughout the banking system. When banks receive checks drawn upon other banks, these checks are sent to the Federal Reserve, where the account of the recipient bank is increased and the account of the paying bank is reduced. The net effect of these additions and subtractions from each bank's account is determined at the Federal Reserve Bank and the accounts of each bank increased or reduced accordingly. Finally, among the other assets of the Federal Reserve are loans made to member banks to enable these banks to meet their required reserve deposits with the Federal Reserve System. The interest rate on these loans is called the discount rate and is set by the Federal Reserve in accordance with overall Federal Reserve policy. For example, when the System feels it is necessary to engage in restrictive monetary policy, it may raise the discount rate, thus making borrowing of required reserves more costly to member banks and thereby discouraging such borrowing. In recent years the discount rate has been changed rather frequently in conjunction with overall Federal Reserve policy.[1]

As Table 12–1 shows, the liabilities of the Federal Reserve consist principally of member bank deposits and Federal Reserve Notes, with the latter being the largest Federal Reserve liability.

Major decisions as to the management of the assets and liabilities of the Federal Reserve System and as to the policy positions to adopt in the manipulation of the Federal Reserve instruments of policy are made by the board of governors under the leadership of a chairman and by the System's open market committee, which deals with open market policy. The Federal Reserve Board and its chairman are appointed by the President of the United States for 17 year terms. Board of governor appointees are highly insulated from current political pressures by virtue of these long appointments, leading to the opportunity for a highly autonomous policy stance. In practice, the Federal Reserve Board has a reputation of being a highly independent agency from incumbent presidential administrations, occasionally directly conflicting with them in economic policy recommendations and actions.

Table 12–2 contains a consolidated balance sheet for representative large commercial member banks in the Federal Reserve System. As seen, the major asset categories of large commercial banks are loans and investments (over two-thirds of assets). The Federal Funds Sold asset category consists of the volume of reserves that commercial banks loan to other commercial banks, principally for very short-term periods for the purpose of meeting reserve requirements at the Federal Reserve and other short-term liquidity constraints. Similarly, the Federal Funds Purchased liability category consists of the funds borrowed by commerical banks from other banks, also usually for short-term periods to meet liquidity needs. If the data of Table 12–2 included all commercial banks, the Funds Purchased and Funds Sold accounts would balance off exactly since by definition these funds are those traded within the banking system. Cash Items in Process of Collection measures the volume of checks in process of collection from other banks. In addition, the Reserves with Federal Reserve asset category contains the required reserve deposit with the Federal Reserve Bank. Among the liability categories, Demand Deposits (checking accounts) and Time and Saving Deposits accounts are the dominant claims made on commercial bank assets.

[1] The student may wish to verify this by a review of the historical pattern of the discount rate. For this, a recent issue of the *Federal Reserve Bulletin* provides the record.

Table 12–2

Consolidated Balance Sheet
Large Commercial Banks
(*January 30, 1974*)

ASSETS		BILLIONS
Federal Funds Sold		15.6
Loans		266.9
Security Investments		87.1
U.S. Treasury	25.8	
Other Government	47.8	
Corporate and Other	13.5	
Cash Items in Process of Collection		30.1
Reserves with Federal Reserve		24.2
Currency		4.5
Other Assets		33.6
Total		462.0
LIABILITIES		
Demand Deposits		158.0
Time and Saving Deposits		193.3
Federal Funds Purchased		50.6
Borrowing From Federal Reserve		1.3
Borrowing From Others		5.3
Other Liabilities		16.7
Capital Accounts and Reserves		36.8
Total		462.0

Source: Federal Reserve Bulletin, February 1974.

Fractional Reserves and the Financial Multiplier

In accordance with the fractional reserve concept of U.S. banking, the level of demand deposits can be a multiple of available primary currency and Federal Reserve deposits. The mechanics of this expansion involve the ratio of reserves required by the Federal Reserve and the typical method by which loan transactions are made. If more reserves are available in the banking system than are required for the level of demand deposits outstanding (say the actual ratio of reserves to demand deposits is 18 percent compared to a required ratio of 16 percent), then additional demand deposits can be created by commercial banks if they so desire. This is accomplished through the process of extending new loans. New loans are typically extended to borrowers by simply crediting checking accounts, i.e., by banks adding to the liability category Demand Deposits by the same amount they add to the asset category Loans. Through this process, the banking system can expand lending and demand deposits to the limits of the Federal Reserve required reserve ratio. In the same way, the introduction of new primary reserves (outside money) in the banking system can give rise to a multiple expansion of the demand deposit component of the money supply.

To illustrate this process, assume that open market policy results in a net increase in the size of the Federal Reserve bond portfolio by $100 million. The 100 million payment by the Federal Reserve is added to the reserve accounts of commerical banks. If we assume for the moment that nothing else changes, the banking system has a total of 100 million in excess reserves as a result of the open market action. The fact that only fractional reserves must be held against the outstanding level of demand deposits means that the entire banking system can expand reserves by a multiple of the newly acquired 100 million in reserves. If the required reserve ratio is 20 percent, then deposits could be expanded by 500 million before the 100 million in new reserves is entirely absorbed as increased required reserves. The multiple of new reserves by which deposits can be expanded is given by the expression

$$M = \frac{1}{RR}$$

where RR is the required ratio and M is the financial multiplier.

Even though an expansion in deposits of M times an increase in reserves is possible for the entire banking system, it is not possible for an individual bank to achieve this result. If an individual bank finds it has 1 million in excess reserves, it cannot create 5 million in new demand deposits but only 1 million. To see this, consider the way in which the individual bank converts 1 million of excess reserves into earning assets. Assume the bank lends out the 1 million by crediting the checking account of a borrower by this amount. We also assume that the borrower does not want the loan just for the purpose of having a bulging checking account, but almost immediately spends the money for the purpose for which it was borrowed by writing a check against his account at the initiating bank. If this check is cashed at another commercial bank and presented to the Federal Reserve for clearance, the reserve account of the initiating bank is reduced by the 1 million and the reserve account of the bank that received the check increased by 1 million. The initial bank in turn reduces the demand deposit of the borrower by the 1 million. After all these adjustments, the initial bank shows an increase in loans of 1 million, a reduction of reserves of 1 million, and no net change in demand deposits. Thus, the initiating bank has not contributed to any expansion in demand deposits in the course of converting 1 million in excess reserves into a new loan of the same amount.

But this is not the end of the matter, because the bank that received the check now has an increase in reserves of 1 million as a result of the check payment and an increase in 1 million in demand deposits credited to the account of the party that deposited the check. The 1 million increase in demand deposits requires this second bank to increase its reserve account by 20 percent of the new deposit, or $200,000. This leaves the second bank with $800,000 in new excess reserves. If we assume this bank wants to convert excess nonearning assets into earning assets as in the case of the initial bank, we find loans and demand deposits can be safely increased by $800,-000 for the second bank. As in the initial round, the expenditure of the newly created loan by the second bank borrower involves writing a check against the second bank. When this check is fully disposed of, the reserves of the second bank are reduced by $800,000 and the demand deposit of the second bank's borrower is reduced by the $800,000 borrowed and now spent. The net effect on this second bank is an increase in required reserves by $200,000, an increase in loans by $800,000, and an increase in demand deposits of the initial $1 million (the secondary $800,000 having been completely eliminated). Thus, assets and liabilities have both increased by the same $1 million.

The second bank's $800,000 loan touches off a continued effect. Assume the check resulting from its expenditure is deposited in a third bank. This bank must retain 20 percent of the amount, or $160,000, and may loan out the remaining $640,000. If it does this, a new check in this amount is introduced into the banking system, which generates a fourth-round effect of $512,000, and so forth. The amount of the new deposit is reduced by 20 percent on each round, but the process may continue until all the initial increase in reserves has leaked out of the system into required reserves. If we start with an initial amount of new reserves equal to A, the total demand deposits created can be summarized as follows:

$$T = A[1 + (1 - RR) + (1 - RR)^2 + (1 - RR)^3 + \cdots]$$
$$= A\left[\frac{1}{RR}\right]$$

which for our example is

$$T = 1[1 + 0.8 + 0.64 + 0.512 + \cdots] = (1)(5)$$
$$= \$5 \text{ million}$$

Thus, the entire banking system can accomplish what a single bank cannot. Of course, if all the transactions we have discussed took place in a single bank, then no loss of reserves occurs due to the cashing of checks by other banks. In this case, if the bank could fully count on this monopoly position, it could proceed to directly expand its level of demand deposits to the full multiple allowed by the required reserve ratio. Such would be the case under a monopoly banking system operated by a single bank.

The multiplier we have described reflects the maximum possible expansion of demand deposits by the banking system, but it does not imply we should always expect the system to translate an increase in reserves into the maximum amount of monetary expansion. Only if individual banks keep their reserves fully used in earning activities will the maximum effect take place. If banks decide to retain some reserves as excess, then more than RR percent of the initiating reserve will leak out of the system at each round, and the financial multiplier is reduced.

The maximum volume of outside money to which deposit expansion applies is under the control of the Federal Reserve principally through open market policy. The maximum multiplier effect of this outside money can be influenced by the Federal Reserve through changes in the required reserve ratio, RR. Raising or lowering that ratio is a prerogative of the Federal Reserve Board and has the effect of immediately absorbing or releasing required reserves from the system, thus similarly influencing the volume of outstanding demand deposits. If the ratio is increased, commercial banks must either find new reserves to meet the increase or cut back demand deposits by a sufficient multiple of the reserve difference so that original reserves are adequate or engage in some combination of the two programs.

The flow of funds from bank and other lenders to business and other borrowers is facilitated by a structure of financial instruments in the United States. These instruments provide the medium by which money flows from the supply side to the demand side of money and capital markets. We now consider these instruments, beginning with those facilitating short-run money flows and moving to those involved with long-term capital flows.

Money Market Instruments

The U.S. money market is the national arena where lenders and borrowers of short-term funds interact, creating an array of financial instruments and setting the structure of short-term interest rates. Among the financial instruments, the following are major vehicles of finance: (1) federal funds, (2) commercial paper, (3) certificates of deposit, (4) U.S. Treasury bills and other short-term Federal notes, (5) banker's acceptances, and (6) lines of credit and commercial loans. While these instruments all serve the same money market function of a supply-demand medium, they are not identical in their characteristics and they usually support differing rates of interest in recognition of these differences. We now consider the characteristics of each instrument.

Federal Funds

For money market purposes, *federal funds* are so designated because they are funds on deposit by commercial banks at Federal Reserve Banks. When the amount of these deposits exceeds the level required by the Federal Reserve for a particular bank, that bank may lend the excess to other banks by effecting a transfer of Federal Reserve deposit liabilities from its account to that of another bank. In practice, these loans are made on an extremely short-term basis, say 1 or 2 days up to 1 week. Thus, the annualized interest rate on these funds is a measure of very short-term interest rates. It is interesting to note that while the actual interest percentages on loans of such short periods may be small, it still pays bankers to sell these funds whenever any temporary excess of sizable proportions develop. For example, say the interest rate on federal funds is 5 percent. This works out to a daily rate of $5\%/365 = 0.0137$ percent. Thus, the loan of $5 million of excess reserves for 3 days would produce $5 \times 3 \times 0.000137 = 0.002055$ million or $2,055 in income for the lending bank—lucrative income for a few phone call arrangements.

To facilitate the trading of federal funds, a marketplace centered in New York operates with sellers and buyers communicating by means of brokers and cooperating banks. The brokers communicate bid and ask data to the market via telephone and quote market rates for the funds. Besides this market, a large number of city banks also broker federal funds for smaller country banks affiliated with them on a correspondent basis. These banks are known as accommodating banks.

Commercial Paper

Commercial paper refers to short-term notes redeemable at a fixed expiration date, say 30 to 90 days after issue, at a fixed price. They are sold at a discount from the redemption price, thus producing income to the buyer upon expiration. The rate of interest on commercial paper refers to the annualized rate resulting from this discounting process. For example, if 30-day commercial paper is yielding 5 percent, this means the effective 30 day (1 month) interest rate is $5\%/12 = 0.417$ percent. Thus, commercial paper with a redemption value of $1.0 million after 30 days would sell at $1.0/1.00417 = \$995,847$ for a profit of $4,153 to the buyer of the paper.

The dominant borrowers of commercial funds at the present time are consumer finance companies that are in business to lend money to consumers principally for the purchase of automobiles and other large-value consumer durable goods. A considerable proportion of the borrowing in the commercial paper market involves dealers, who buy this paper at a certain discount from the originating seller and then offer it for resale at a smaller discount to banks and other lenders. This inventory function of the dealers provides the seller with an immediate buyer for an issue of new commercial paper and allows the buyer to buy the quantities and types of notes that exactly fit his needs. Larger issues of commercial paper are sometimes placed directly with the final buyer rather than going through the dealer. These direct placements provide a slightly higher return to the buyer.

Certificates of Deposit

Certificates of deposit, often called CDs are typically short-term (30 to 90 day maturity) fixed interest rate notes used regularly by large nonfinancial corporations as a way to earn interest on their short-term excess liquidity. They are usually sold at face or redemption value with a stipulated interest rate. CDs normally arise out of negotiations between bankers and nonbank firms in which the bank offers a rate it feels is reasonable for the short-term use of these funds and the firm asks a rate it believes to be reasonable to part with the funds for a particular period. Some CDs are negotiable in that they may be resold by the bank to other banks. Thus, a 90-day negotiable CD does not necessarily lock the bank into an investment for this period of time. One principal source of CD funds is the seasonal patterns of nonfinancial business. Firms in highly seasonal industries find their revenue inflows and cost outflows are regularly mismatched, creating short-term excess funds in some periods and short-term deficiencies in others. By contrast, banks often aggressively seek CDs to bridge over short-term liquidity deficiencies.

Short-Term U.S. Securities

The U.S. Treasury regularly sells short-term notes of various types. Treasury bills have a maturity of 90 days to 1 year and trade actively in a secondary market. They are perhaps the most liquid of the Treasury instruments. Like commercial paper, they are sold at a discount that varies depending on conditions in the money markets. By contrast, Treasury certificates and Treasury notes are sold at approximately their redemption value like CDs and bear a fixed interest rate. Maturities on certificates vary from several months up to a year while maturities on notes range from a year to 7 years.

Of the available Treasury instruments, Treasury bills are the most important factor in money market conditions. Their short maturity and essentially riskless character make them attractive to banks and other investors as well as to private investors and other nonfinancial investors with short-term liquidity. In addition, there is typically a large volume of these funds outstanding at any point in time, due to the extensive concentration on bills by the Treasury as their predominant instrument of short-term finance. This leads to an active secondary market that normally produces pleasingly nonvolatile prices to buyers and sellers.

New Treasury bills are sold at auction through sealed-bids each week by the Treasury in conjunction with the Federal Reserve. The buyers at this auction include the Federal Reserve itself buying for its own inventory, dealers in these securities, and a number of large commercial banks. Dealers in Treasury bills operate in a way similar to dealers in commercial paper. They buy into their inventory at the prices prevailing at the auction and sell from their inventory to banks and other investors at lesser discounts that yield a dealer profit on the transaction. The large-bank participants in the auction may either function as dealers or hold their bills in their own short-term investment portfolio.

Banker's Acceptances

Banker's acceptances are short-term notes originated by nonfinancial business and sold in an open market for such paper. Payment on these notes is guaranteed by the borrower's bank—thus the term banker's acceptances. They are similar in most respects to commercial paper, except for certain regulations that apply to the accepting banks. The regulations involved have caused banker's acceptances to be less popular among many banks in recent years, and their use has evolved toward the financing of international trade, where they provide certain tax advantages.

Lines of Credit and Commercial Loans

So far we have discussed CDs and U.S. Treasury bills as popular vehicles by which nonfinancial business firms may realize earnings on excess short-term liquidity by entering the supply side of the money market. Seasonal needs are an important reason why nonfinancial business firms are often active on the demand-side of money markets, as a borrower of short-term funds. *Lines of credit* are open-ended agreements between banks and nonbank businesses whereby the borrower may extend his short-term debt as necessary up to a ceiling level. Such agreements also typically contain provisions stipulating a clean-up period each year during which the balance must be reduced to zero. An alternative to lines of credit is a commercial short-term loan of a fixed amount by the bank to the firm, where the terms are worked out to suit both parties. Lines of credit and short-term business loans do not share the property of our earlier described instruments of being a market vehicle. Instead, they are private, negotiated financial arrangements not subject to the leveling influence of a visible public marketplace. Perhaps because of this, the terms of these arrangements vary considerably.

Besides their short-term loans to nonfinancial business, banks active in money markets also regularly lend short-term funds to dealers in government and other securities. These loans are usually callable on demand of either party within arranged time limits and are called call loans to securities dealers.

Structure of Money Market Rates

Our discussion of money market instruments has suggested certain popular customers and market segments for particular instruments, for example, commercial paper is most attractive to consumer finance companies while CDs are widely used by large nonfinancial businesses. However, with the exception of federal funds, which are confined to inside the banking system, each money market instrument is somewhat of a substitute for others. The result of this interrelationship is a structure of money market interest rates that differs somewhat between instruments but which typically moves consistently in response to changes in overall monetary conditions. Market forces of supply and demand establish customary parities among rates on various instruments.

Economists and others often discuss *the* interest rate. Even if we attach the modifier short-term or money market to this concept, it is clear that such a phrase must be a shorthand reference to a structure of rates that move generally in a consistent manner with each other in response to changes in economic conditions. That is the meaning we shall intend in our later discussions of the interest rate. In contrast to money market rates, long-term interest rates generally reflect the price of funds flowing into capital investment channels. We now consider instruments involved in the flow of these funds.

Capital Market Instruments

Capital market instruments are characterized by longer maturities than money market instruments. This is logical. Capital market instruments are to facilitate the flow of more permanent type funds that support the purchase of fixed-type plant and other assets. The most important capital market instruments are (1) bonds, (2) mortgages and term loans, and (3) stocks. We now consider these instruments.

Bonds

Bonds are long-maturity debt obligations with fixed-interest coupons attached that become payable periodically at a fixed interest or coupon rate. The yield to maturity on bonds is affected by the market price of the bond in addition to the coupon rate. If the market price is lower than the redemption price, then a capital gain will accrue to holders of the bonds. This capital gain raises the yield to maturity above the coupon rate. The opposite is true for bonds selling at greater than redemption value—their yield to maturity is less than the coupon rate. The listed prices of bonds are generally per $100 of value, and bonds are generally redeemable at 100. Thus, a market price of 90 for a bond with a coupon of 6 percent maturing in 2 years provides a yield of greater than 6 percent when held to maturity.

Bonds are issued by corporations, by the federal government, and by state and local governments. They are usually not secured by any specific assets of the issuing party. Instead, they are "backed" by the general financial condition of the issuing party. The principal exception is mortgage bonds, which are secured by specific physical assets of the corporation. To aid investors in assessing the risk associated with purchasing an unsecured bond, rating services regularly rate bonds according to their risk character. Perhaps most widely used among such rating schemes is that of Moody's. Moody's rates bonds in each of the categories of industrial, utilities, and municipal (state and local governmental) bonds. The highest rating lowest-risk class is Aaa followed by Aa, A, B, and so forth.

The bond market is characterized by two important segments, newly issued bonds and existing issues. The new issues segment is where newly originated bonds are sold to the investing public, whereas existing bonds are exchanged among buyers and sellers in the secondary market. The interest rates in each segment of the market are maintained in close proximity to the other segment due to the nearly identical investment opportunities provided by each. Thus, it is customary to refer to the bond market rather than to the new-issues or secondary bond markets.

Mortgages and Term Loans

Mortgages are loans secured by a physical asset such as buildings or land. They are typically originated to support the purchase of a home or building and carry maturities from 20 to 30 years. In fact, over half the mortgages written are for the purpose of financing one- to four-family dwelling purchases. Other mortgages support the purchase of apartment buildings and business facilities. Mortgage loans are made by banks, insurance companies, mutual savings banks, and savings and loan associations. The latter two groups specialize in these instruments, channeling lendable funds explicitly into this market. This imparts a local character to the mortgage market that does not characterize other capital market instruments. Since savings and loan and mutual savings firms' lending base is essentially a function of local deposits, they will serve the function of translating these savings flows into mortgage instruments on a local level. In this respect, a mechanism is not present to balance regional differences in mortage market conditions. As a result, it is not unusual at the present time to find substantial differences among regions in mortgage rates and other lending conditions.

In the past, mortgages have been a highly illiquid investment commitment due to the absence of a secondary market in these instruments. For example, while city banks have often found that they could resell mortgages in their correspondent country banks, their ability to move in and out of mortgages has been less than with nearly any other investment vehicle. Recently, mortgage brokers have emerged as the possible beginnings of a secondary market in mortgages where such instruments could be traded in "units" of a fixed redemption value. Such a secondary market could greatly alter the institutional character of mortgages as an investment asset.

Term loans are typically unsecured instruments through which firms regularly borrow funds from banks. They are similar to mortgage loans in that an organized marketplace on a primary or secondary level does not exist for these instruments. Instead, they are originated through private negotiations between borrower and lender. Unlike mortgages, the maturity of term loans to business is usually less than 10 years, often 3 to 5 years in duration. Private corporations usually "shop" for term loans at several banks before deciding upon the lender with whom to do business. This has the effect of leveling the interest rate and other terms for such loans at a given point in time. Accordingly, even in the absence of an organized trading market for term loans, it is usually realistic to talk about a "market term loan" as that loan generally available to a particular type of firm. So, although a result of private negotiations, business term loans are not without their market character.

Stocks

Common stocks are ownership or equity units in corporations. They carry voting rights with respect to direction of the firm and offer no assurances of fixed income to the owner. Preferred stocks carry no such ownership rights and often carry obligations for payment of dividends. Thus, they stand somewhere between the owner status of common stockholders and the lender status of bondholders or holders of term loan instruments.

Newly issued stocks represent a way by which firms may acquire new permanent capital in their firm. A firm whose stock is already outstanding and traded in the secondary market usually may sell additional stock at rates close to existing prices. This is called a secondary offering. Other firms may raise capital by "going public" through initially offering its equity shares to the investing public. Such an initial offering is usually underwritten by a syndicate of brokerages who guarantee the sale of the stock at a negotiated price per share. In return the brokerages receive a fee for their services. The active secondary market in many stocks is an important factor in the flow of newly raised equity capital since the prices set by the forces of supply and demand in this secondary market strongly influence the selling prices of new equity shares and therefore strongly influence the attractiveness of raising capital by these means.

The Term Structure of Interest Rates

The partial substitutability among money market instruments was earlier discussed as a reason for money market rates to move somewhat together over time. Markets for long-term capital share somewhat the same property. To illustrate, the returns on stocks and the returns on bonds tend generally to move up and down together, with the return to stocks somewhat higher but the fluctuation in this return also greater. This pattern is without doubt due to a degree of substitutability between stocks and bonds that motivates investment funds to shift between these two markets when expected returns by investors favor one or the other market.

But what of the substitutability of short-term and long-term investments, i.e., the decision whether to purchase or sell a money market or a capital market instrument? The relationship between market rates of interest on short- and long-term financial instruments is known as the term structure of interest rates. Strictly speaking, the term structure is the interest rate difference on fixed income securities (securities with a finite maturation date) that is due entirely to differences in time to maturity on otherwise identical bonds. Accordingly, the term structure is a concept that applies to individual fixed income securities that are issued in long and short maturities. The concept does not apply to comparisons of bonds or notes with differing risk characteristics, differing legal definitions, or to equity securities that have no maturation date.

If we plot the interest rates (or yields) on homogeneous bonds that differ only by their time to maturity on one axis and the associated maturity on the other axis, the result is often called a *yield curve*. Figure 12–2 shows characteristic shapes for the yield curve as it might appear for a given security at different points in time. The curve *AA* shows a situation where bonds of longer maturities have higher yields. Curve *DD* shows the opposite situation, where short-term bonds have higher market yields than long-term bonds. The curve *BB* shows a situation where yields rise to a peak and decline thereafter with longer maturities. Finally, the curve *CC* shows a situation where investors are indifferent to maturity in their market behavior, since bonds of all maturities trade at the same market yield. For particular

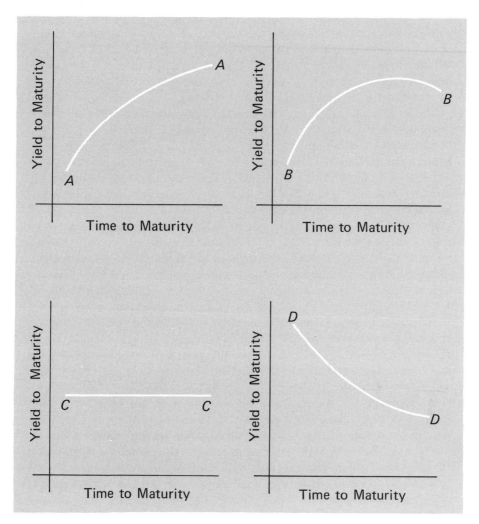

Figure 12–2
Yield Curve Shapes

bonds, it is normal to find some or all of these shapes at different points in time.

The theoretical significance of various shapes is the subject of *term structure theory*, a detailed discussion of which is beyond our objective here.[2] However, this theory basically relies upon differing expectations to explain the differing observed yield curve shapes. Figure 12–3 shows the essential structure involved. Suppose the yield curve is positioned at $r_0 r_0$ initially. Investors revise upward their expectations about the future level of interest rates. As a result, the yield of r_0 percent on bonds of t_l periods to maturity is seen as lower than it is likely to be in the future. If the typical investor expects the yield on bonds of t_l periods to maturity to rise toward r_2, then a net selling pressure will occur for bonds of this maturity. The reason for this is clear. Rising yields on bonds mean falling prices on existing bonds, since the mechanism by which the yield to maturity on existing bonds changes is by a change in the price of the bond. Thus, an investor expectation of rising yields means the investor expects the price of his bond to be lower in the future than it is today. The result of this situation is an increased supply of t_1 maturity bonds. Sellers of new bonds of t_l maturity may also decide to supply the market now instead of later if they share the same expectation. The result is a rise in r toward r_2. If we assume that investors want to maintain their capital invested in bonds, we may reason that they can "hide" in short-term securities until the expected long-term rate adjustments actually come to pass. An increased demand for shorter term securities follows, pushing up their prices and lowering their yields. For example, at maturity t_s, the yield would be reduced from r_0 toward r_1. The result of these adjustments is to push the yield curve up on the long end and down on the short end toward position AA in Figure 12–3. Once the yields have adjusted fully to the levels expected by investors, the selling and buying pressures subside, leaving the yield curve in the altered but stable position shown by AA.

Figure 12–3(b) shows a different possibility. In this figure, rates on intermediate-term bonds such as t_i periods to maturity are expected to rise relative to both short- and long-term bonds. Thus, selling pressures dominate the middle range of the yield curve while excess demand occurs in both the short and long maturity regions. The result of this type of revision in investor expectations creates a humped shape curve from an initial upward rising curve similar to curve shape BB in Figure 12–2. This is in fact a frequently found yield curve shape for U.S. government securities.

These two examples illustrate an important aspect of term structure relationships. The shape of the yield curve contains information about investor expectations regarding future interest rates. When we find the yield curve shifting such that long-term rates fall below short-term rates or vice

---

2 The interested reader may wish to consult older sources on the theory of the term structure such as Irving Fisher, *Theory of Interest,* Kelley, Clifton, N.J., 1930 and John Hicks, *Value and Capital,* 2nd ed., Oxford University Press, New York, 1946; or recent surveys by Charles Nelson, *The Term Structure of Interest Rates,* Basic Books, New York, 1972 or Richard Roll, *The Behavior of Interest Rates,* Basic Books, New York, 1970.

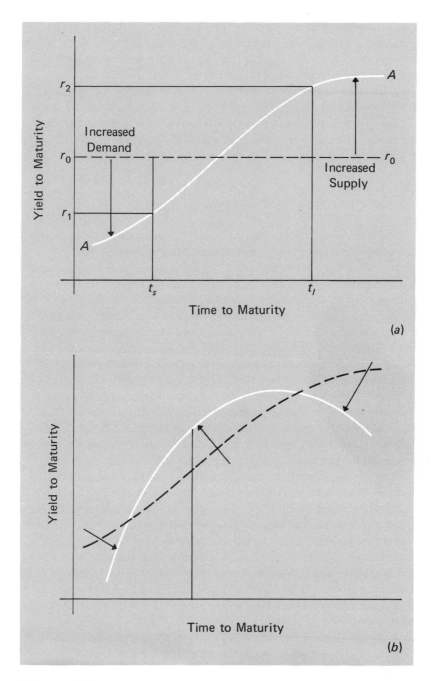

Figure 12–3

Shifts in Yield Curves

versa, we may interpret this as reflecting the changing expectations of the investment community regarding future interest rates.

We have now discussed major capital market instruments and their role in setting the term structure of interest rates. These instruments are the medium through which funds flow from capital market suppliers to capital market demanders. Considering the structure of these flows and the interrelationships among the instruments involved is an important question. It revolves around the channels through which capital market funds flow. We now turn to this question.

Funds Flow Channels in the United States

To better understand the reasons for ups and downs in the flow of new lending, it is helpful to consider the institutional and market mechanisms relating to the flow of capital funds in the United States. Figure 12–4 shows a basic representation of this funds flow mechanism. Consistent with our aggregate expenditures model, GNP is shown in Figure 12–4 as the principal determinant of consumer saving and of business liquid assets, which flow into bank deposits and deposits of savings and loan companies, mutual savings banks, insurance companies, and other savings-type institutions. The continued flow of these funds into banks, through banks to borrowers, and back into banks by recipients of borrowed funds, illustrates the circulation of money in the economy. The speed of this circulation can be referred to as the velocity of money. As the circular path in Figure 12–4 (from GNP to the supply of new debt and other investments and back to GNP) suggests, the funds flowing into banks through these means do not represent a new source of reserves for banks, but rather a repositioning and reuse of existing reserves and a continual shuffling among individual banks of the same basic pool of reserves. Therefore, the total amount of new investment possible by banks is not increased by this flow, but only maintained. Significant hoarding reduces this flow and negatively affects investment. By contrast, net purchases or sales of securities by the Federal Reserve is an insertion or withdrawal of funds to or from this flow, which does alter the total reserves of the banking system and therefore the total size of the pool of investment funds by banks. A second channel is illustrated in Figure 12–4 for direct additions and subtractions of reserves in borrowing from the Federal Reserve or from other sources. Such borrowings by banks produces new reserves, which can support a multiple expansion of the lending pool.

In Figure 12–4, the lending pool is divided into funds available for corporate debt and all other investments. This enables us to focus upon monetary influences on investment. However, it should be recognized that the two-part partitioning is artificial, i.e., that several other major categories of bank investments are grouped into the Other Investments heading.

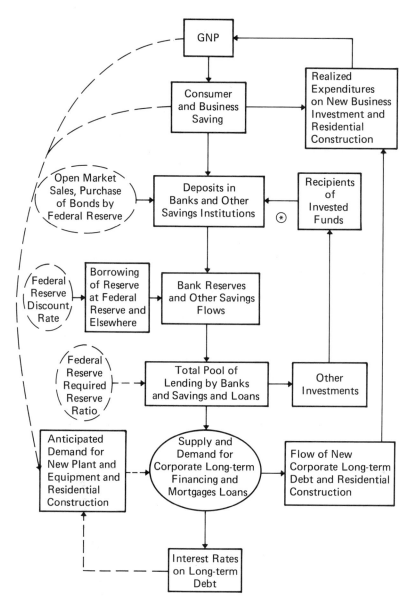

(*) Other savings institutions include savings and loans, mutual savings banks, insurance companies, pension funds, and private accounts.

Note: Round dotted blocks indicate Federal Reserve policy effects; rectangular blocks indicate stock, flow variables; and circular steps indicate decision points. Solid lines indicate fund flows while dotted lines indicate information flows.

Figure 12–4

Flow of Lending

Thus, Figure 12–4 shows two major ways in which the maximum possible lending by banks is altered: (1) by shifts in reserves brought about by Federal Reserve open market policy and (2) by shifts in reserves brought about by bank borrowing from the Federal Reserve and other sources. These influences are only upon the *maximum* possible volume of lending and not necessarily upon the actual level of lending. If banks have more reserves than necessary and decide not to employ them, then alterations in reserve positions through these means will have no effect whatsoever upon lending.

The flow of lending by banks along with anticipated expenditures by firms and others on plant and equipment and residential construction essentially comprise respectively the supply and demand influences in capital markets. As Figure 12–4 illustrates, these influences together can be assumed to jointly determine market rates of interest and the flow of new capital lending via the interplay of supply and demand in the nation's markets for new bonds, stocks, term loans, and mortgages. At the same time, the discussion of Chapter 8 suggests prevailing interest rates, along with profit expectations as influenced by current GNP levels and flows of corporate saving, are likely to importantly influence the demand for new investment. These influences are shown affecting the level of anticipated investment expenditures in Figure 12–4. The final level of new borrowing by corporations supports a portion of investment spending and thus can be expected to strongly influence actually realized expenditures on new capital equipment, facilities, and residential construction along with available flows of consumer and business saving. Finally, these expenditures contribute directly to the final GNP through the goods market multiplier mechanism.

The funds flow mechanism outlined in Figure 12–4 illustrates the considerable role played by the Federal Reserve System in banks' supply of capital. As seen, open market policy affects the level of available reserves through the creation or retirement of claims on Federal Reserve assets that enter banks as new deposits (i.e., Federal Reserve Notes or checks drawn against the Federal Reserve in payment for bonds). Secondly, the Federal Reserve can influence the level of required reserve borrowed by commercial banks by changing the cost of that borrowing (the discount rate) and by exercising more scrutiny and imposing more conditions upon the amount borrowed. This works an indirect effect upon the level of available bank reserves, to the extent that banks react typically to higher discount rates. Raising (or lowering) discount rates has also often been a signal to commercial banks to raise (or lower) their prime and other lending rates to preserve a parity with the discount rate. This may be expected to reduce (or expand) the demand for loans accordingly, which has an influence on the level of bank reserves available.

Finally, changes in the required reserve ratio can be made by the

Federal Reserve. As Figure 12–2 illustrates, such changes operate directly upon the total pool of lendable funds by changing the volume of deposits that must be set aside as required reserves for a given level of deposits. For example, say total available reserves are 15 billion, the level of demand deposits 100 billion, and the required reserve ratio is 15 percent, so that required reserves are just met and the money supply is expanded to $1/0.15 = 6.67$ times the base. If the required ratio is raised to 16 percent, then immediately the available reserves are less than required for 100 billion in demand deposits, and banks must either (a) locate 1 billion in additional reserves or (b) reduce demand deposits sufficiently so that the original 15 billion in reserves represents 16 percent of deposits (15 b$/0.16 = 93.7$ maximum new level of demand deposits), or (c) some combination of the two. At the same time, the multiplier has been reduced to $1/0.16 = 6.25$. Empirically, changes in the required reserve ratio have occurred less frequently than changes in other Federal Reserve policy variables but have had perhaps the most immediate and substantial impact on the economy among the policy alternatives open to the Federal Reserve.

In this chapter we have considered the nature of money and capital market instruments in the United States and their role in facilitating the flow of funds from short- and long-term suppliers to those demanding funds in money and capital markets. We have considered the term structure of interest rates. We have discussed the role of banks in facilitating the transfer of funds from suppliers to demanders. However, in the United States, banks are not the only institution engaged in such activities. In the next chapter, we consider the role played by nonbank financial intermediaries in facilitating the flow of funds through money and capital markets, plus several topics related to an expanded view of the role of financial intermediaries in monetary flows.

Discussion Questions

1. Should time deposits be included in the definition of the money supply? What are the arguments for and against it in your mind?

2. If the Federal Reserve contracts the supply of money, is it necessary for the supply of lending to also contract? Explain as fully as possible.

3. Distinguish between Treasury bills and Treasury notes.

4. What is the distinction between a money market instrument and a capital market instrument? At what maturity do you draw the line between the two?

5. If the yield curve for government securities is flat and then shifts into a downward sloping position such that short-term rates are higher than long-term rates, what does this imply about investor expectations?

6. What is the essential reason for a difference between anticipations and realizations in the markets for plant and equipment and residential construction? When would they be equal?

A Problem in Money Markets

A recent article in *Business Week* (April 6, 1974, pp. 16–17) has discussed the impact of rising interest rates on markets for money and capital. Several interesting observations are contained in this article. Commenting on the nearly 10 percent rate of inflation, one bank executive complained that just to finance the inflation would require an increased level of bank loans, even in the face of an economy that has not yet undergone a full-fledged recovery from a period of weakness. A heavy demand for loans in the first part of 1974 has had an unsettling effect on the nation's markets for both short-term and long-term debt, and the resulting soaring interest rates have drawn money away from the nation's stock markets, according to the views of some.

In commenting on an upward surge in corporate and government bond yields in the same period, an executive for U.S. Trust Company stated "You could see some of the government dealers getting out of the market, this has been such a fast turnaround." With bond rates rising rapidly, the period has produced increasing evidence of some borrowers being rationed out of the market. Over $400 million in corporate bond issues planned for the first quarter of 1974 have been postponed, and bond calendars are still bulging.

The situation in credit markets in early 1974 appears to be bad news to the stock market. Unless rates decline substantially, many brokers are not optimistic about the stock market's chances of a sustained upswing. Says one observer, "If rates stay where they are, it's going to be pretty hard to get the stock market going."

1. How can companies really postpone a bond offering? If they have capital investment or other plans, isn't it really true that they must finance at whatever the market rate may be?

2. What do bond yields have to do with stock prices? Gather some evidence that relates to the relationship between bond and stock yields or prices to use in your answer to this question.

3. If rising prices and rising interest rates are supposed to go together, then stocks should rise as the rate of inflation rises, in order to function as a hedge against inflation. This means that rising interest rates and rising stock prices should go together. Is this reasoning correct? What does the evidence show relative to (a) the performance of stocks during inflation and (b) the performance of stocks during periods of rising interest rates?

13
Money and Capital Markets—II

The previous chapter focused on the role of commercial banks in creating money, financial instruments, and in otherwise facilitating the flow of money capital from the supply side to the demand side of the nation's capital markets. In this chapter, we add to this picture by considering the role of nonbank financial intermediaries in the flow of investment capital. We also consider the impact of intermediation by consumers and other savers on capital markets. We deal with the basic outlines of the portfolio strategies of banks and consider the shifts in bank portfolios that relate to extreme monetary conditions. We begin our discussion by an expansion of the picture of funds flow channels developed in the previous chapter.

Impact of Nonbank Financial Intermediaries

In the United States, there are substantial differences in the functioning of banks as opposed to nonbank financial institutions. Perhaps the most apparent is the authority to create checking account liabilities. This function is reserved for banks in the United States, making them the only financial intermediary that can create money and alter the multiple expansion of outside money by their lending policies. However, other financial institutions such as insurance companies, savings and loans, and mutual savings banks, play an important role in the supply of money capital to business investors by organizing the saving flows of households and making them available on capital markets.

235

We now discuss the nature of a more comprehensive funds flow structure that accommodates the role of nonbank financial intermediaries and other suppliers of corporate capital. To begin, we consider the actual supply, acquisition, and advancement of funds by all parties in U.S. capital markets. Table 13–1 shows a source-use type accounting breakdown for investment funds in the United States. Part A shows the economic sectors acquiring funds in capital markets. Although every major sector to some extent is seen to demand funds, the figure reveals that the two principal acquirers of funds are business firms and households. It is of further interest to consider prin-

Table 13–1

Supply and Demand for Capital in the United States

| A. FUNDS ACQUIRED BY | (BILLIONS OF DOLLARS) | | | | |
	1965	1967	1969	1971	1973
1. U.S. Government	1.7	13.0	−3.6	25.5	9.7
2. State and Local Government	7.6	7.9	8.9	17.0	8.8
3. Nonfinancial Business	29.6	37.9	47.8	48.5	81.3
4. Households	28.8	19.7	31.6	38.3	70.9
5. Foreign	2.6	4.1	3.5	5.7	6.9
Total	70.4	82.6	88.2	135.0	177.6
B. FUNDS ADVANCED BY					
1. U.S. Government	2.8	5.1	2.7	−3.5	18.5
2. Commercial Banks	28.3	36.8	9.4	50.6	85.2
3. Savings Institutions	13.7	16.9	10.3	41.5	35.2
4. Insurance Companies	17.9	20.4	22.3	14.1	24.3
5. Other Finance Companies	−1.4	−1.3	−1.7	5.3	14.3
6. Nonfinancial Business, Households and Other*	9.2	4.7	45.2	27.0	0.1
Total	70.4	82.6	88.2	135.0	177.6
C. FUNDS SUPPLIED BY					
1. Additions to Demand Deposits and Currency	8.0	11.6	5.5	13.0	13.7
2. Additions to Time Deposits	32.6	39.0	−4.0	81.2	76.9
3. Direct Purchases of Financial Instruments by Nonfinancial Institutions and Households	9.2	6.7	52.0	−4.2	33.8
4. Insurance, Pension Funds, Other	20.5	25.5	34.8	45.0	53.2
Total	70.4	82.6	88.2	135.0	177.6

Note: Details may not add to totals due to rounding.
Source: Federal Reserve Bulletin.

* Includes Foreign, State and Local Governments, Security Credit, and Federal Reserve.

cipal uses to which these funds are put by business and household sectors. Refinancing of maturing long-term debt, new fixed business investment, and changes in business working capital constitute the largest uses for the capital raised by the business sector, while new residential construction provides the biggest use of funds raised by the household sector.

Part B of Table 13–1 shows the institutions, firms, and others who advance funds on the supply side of the capital market. As seen, banks, savings and loan, and insurance companies advance the largest portion of the funds in normal years such as 1965 and 1967, whereas households and nonfinancial business also account for a substantial portion of funds advanced in tight money periods such as 1969. Later in the chapter, we shall explore some of the reasons for a shift of this type.

Part C of Table 13–1 shows the primary sources of the funds advanced by the firms, institutions, and agencies listed in Part B of the table. In years such as 1965 and 1967, funds flowing into bank and savings and loan time deposits along with newly acquired insurance and pension funds constituted major primary sources of capital market funds. Additions to currency and demand deposits was also a significant category. This pattern is likely to be interrupted in periods of high interest rates such as 1969 when time deposits actually declined by 4 billion, while direct purchases of bonds by nonfinancial institutions and households jumped dramatically to become the major source of capital funds that year. Thus, the patterns of capital supply and advancement are subject to considerable shifts in response to changes in market conditions, an attribute that affects the institutional channels of capital supply to a considerable degree.

The categories of Table 13–1 illustrate extensive involvement in capital market fund flows by institutions and agencies not included in the funds flow discussion of the previous chapter. In addition, the observed shifts in funds flow among categories suggest possibly important trade-offs among suppliers and advancers of funds that are not suggested by our earlier Figure 12–4. Figure 13–1 deals explicitly with these factors.

Figure 13–1 shows funds flow (solid lines), informational flows (dotted lines), decision trade-offs (oval steps), Federal Reserve action points (dotted oval steps) and other governmental influences (dotted rectangular boxes) upon money market variables. In the figure, aggregate output, measured by the GNP, provides an inflow of money into several key cash flow categories:

(1) corporate cash flow and business liquid assets
(2) available pension and fire and casualty insurance funds
(3) available life insurance funds
(4) household noncontractual saving (which consists of saving less insurance-type saving and other private savings programs such as pension funds)

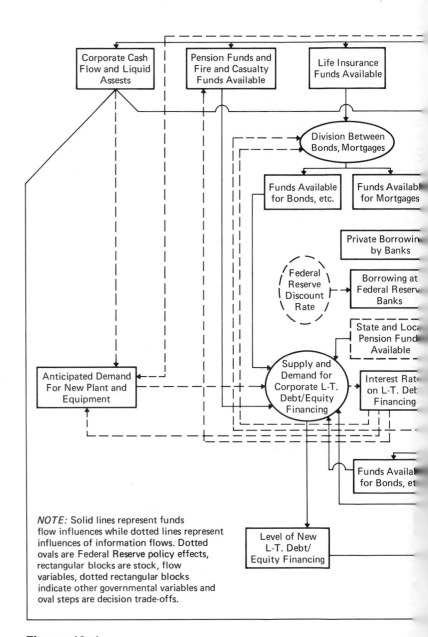

Figure 13–1

Flow of Capital Lending—Second Approximation

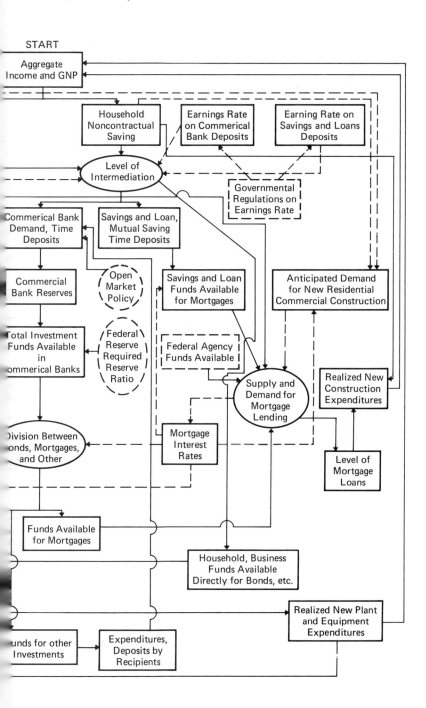

START

Aggregate Income and GNP

Household Noncontractual Saving

Earnings Rate on Commerical Bank Deposits

Earning Rate on Savings and Loans Deposits

Level of Intermediation

Governmental Regulations on Earnings Rate

Commerical Bank Demand, Time Deposits

Savings and Loan, Mutual Saving Time Deposits

Open Market Policy

Savings and Loan Funds Available for Mortgages

Anticipated Demand for New Residential Commercial Construction

Commercial Bank Reserves

Federal Reserve Required Reserve Ratio

Federal Agency Funds Available

Total Investment Funds Available in Commerical Banks

Supply and Demand for Mortgage Lending

Realized New Construction Expenditures

Division Between Bonds, Mortgages, and Other

Mortgage Interest Rates

Level of Mortgage Loans

Funds Available for Mortgages

Household, Business Funds Available Directly for Bonds, etc.

Realized New Plant and Equipment Expenditures

Funds for other Investments

Expenditures, Deposits by Recipients

The figure shows a connection between corporate cash flow and the demand for plant and equipment, which responds to the empirical work discussed in Chapter 8 on the relevance of corporate cash flow in capital investment. As seen in Figure 13–1, flows of new pension and fire and casualty insurance funds in the United States go largely into the purchase of new capital market debt and equity instruments.[1] Therefore, this flow provides a direct source of funds to business capital markets. Life insurance flows, on the other hand, are typically split between purchases of business capital market instruments and purchases of residential mortgages in proportions that vary from year to year. As seen in Figure 13–1, the decision by life insurance companies as to this division logically involves a comparison of prevailing interest rates on corporate debt with interest rates on mortgage loans, along with an assessment of the comparative risks. Since mortgages typically have a less active resale market than corporate securities, they represent more of a fixed commitment. Thus, liquidity objectives of lenders usually require that mortgages yield a somewhat higher rate than bonds in order to successfully compete for available funds. As this spread narrows, more available funds flow into bonds while a larger than normal spread increases flows into mortgages. The outcome of this trade-off procedure results in flows of funds into both corporate securities and mortgage markets.

Impact of Shifts in the Rate of Intermediation

Flows of household noncontractual savings and additions to corporate liquid assets provide continuing circular flows of funds for banks and savings institutions. From the standpoint of households and corporations, the allocation of these flows can be made in several ways, including the following major categories:

(1) to bank time and demand deposits
(2) to savings accounts
(3) for the direct purchase of securities in capital markets

Alternatives (1) and (2) represent choices to utilize the nation's financial intermediaries, who in turn typically are major purchasers of securities and mortgages, while alternative (3) bypasses these intermediaries to participate directly as suppliers of funds in capital markets. There is normally a positive spread between the rates financial intermediaries pay for new funds and the

---

[1] This and the following empirical funds flow conclusions are based upon an analysis of sources and uses of funds for various financial institutions and agencies as presented in *Investment Outlook for 1969*, Banker's Trust Company, New York, 1969.

rates they receive from securities and mortgage investments. This spread is approximately equal to gross profit margin of financial intermediaries, from which expenses are paid and profits possibly earned. When the spread widens, the opportunity cost to household and corporate savers rises, since an increasingly higher rate of return is foregone for the convenience and lower risk of accounts with intermediaries. As a result, these savers typically respond by making higher levels of direct security market investments. As an example, in 1969 the spread between maximum payments on savings accounts and under-1-year time deposits (average) was 3.78 percent as compared to the average from 1964 to 1968 of 1.1 percent. As illustrated in Part B of Table 13–1, the result was a market shift in funds supplied directly to securities markets by households and nonfinancial business firms. This kind of funds flow shift is often referred to as disintermediation.

Disintermediation can have a substantial impact on the pattern of capital market flows and upon the supply and demand for money capital. As Figure 13–1 suggests, banks and savings institutions could head off disintermediation by adjusting rates paid on time and savings deposits so as to maintain a rate spread small enough to retain most of the saving flow. However, such adjustment is not normally possible as the maximum rates (for practical purposes the actual rates) are set by the Federal Reserve and by the Federal Home Loan Bank Board, who apparently have not been concerned with maintaining near normal rate spreads. For these agencies to allow a substantial volume of disintermediation to occur is a de facto tool of restrictive monetary policy.

The principal effect of funds flowing around intermediaries and straight into capital markets is a loss of household time deposits by banks and savings and loans. Demand deposits in banks are not much affected by such a situation since money is not removed from circulation by substantial disintermediation, but only rechanneled. Thus, the primary burden of disintermediation is upon the borrowers from savings and loan associations—almost exclusively buyers of housing and residential builders. Therefore, when disintermediation occurs, it is likely to have a concentrated impact upon housing markets.

Unlike savings and loan firms, commercial banks have a number of options available to offset the impact of an outflow of deposits and reserves. As indicated in Figure 13–1, banks can offset an outflow of reserves by borrowing from two sources: (1) private channels and (2) the Federal Reserve. Private borrowing by banks can take several forms. Among these, the previously discussed federal funds market is a common and often active arena for bank-to-bank borrowing. However, commercial banks can usually look to federal funds for only temporary and relatively small volume loans that can make up temporary reserve deficiencies. Nevertheless, federal funds borrowing tends to activate unused reserves by making them available to banks in need of additional reserves to support an expansion of demand deposits. Of course, when most banks have no excess reserves, this source of borrowed reserves declines sharply in importance.

A second source of borrowed reserves of increased importance recently is Eurodollar borrowings by U.S. banks. The Eurodollar market has traditionally been a European market for borrowing and lending U.S. dollars whose participants are mainly European firms with surpluses and demands for U.S. currency. However, with reserves under great pressure due to restrictive monetary conditions, U.S. banks borrowed substantial amounts in this market in 1969–1970. This lending provided an important source of new reserves for U.S. commercial banks during this period. Besides private borrowing, commercial banks borrow reserves from the Federal Reserve as discussed earlier at the discount rate and according to terms prescribed by the system's Board of Governors.

Along with the required reserve ratio, the level of bank reserves stipulates the maximum level of loanable and investable funds by banks, as shown in Figure 13–1. Banks allocate substantial amounts of these funds to securities and mortgages, engaging in a tradeoff of relative return on investment and risk for these two types of investments as compared to other alternatives. We now consider substantive elements in this tradeoff.

Bank Portfolio Selection and Adjustment

Studies by Tobin, Goldfeld, Meigs, and others have been concerned with analyzing the process by which banks decide on the fraction of their assets that will be held in loans as opposed to more liquid types of assets.[2] This work has led to a theoretical framework for portfolio selection and adjustments, to which our attention now turns.

We begin by outlining five kinds of investment-like financial instruments in the typical commercial bank's asset structure:

(1) Commercial loans to business
(2) Mortgage loans to households
(3) Long-term government and corporate securities
(4) Short-term government bills, notes, and other securities
(5) Vault cash and Federal Reserve deposit

---

[2] See J. Tobin, "Commercial Banks as Creators of Money" in D. Carson (ed.), *Banking and Monetary Studies*, Richard D. Irwin, Inc., Homewood, Ill., 1963; S. M. Goldfeld, *Commercial Bank Behavior and Economic Activity*, North Holland Publishing Company, Amsterdam, 1966; J. A. Meigs, *Free Reserves and the Money Supply*, University of Chicago Press, Chicago, 1962.

The studies cited here have repeatedly characterized loans (1) as having a special priority claim on available investment funds, for reasons generally related to felt obligations of bank managers to serve the business customers. Statistical evidence also bears out this claim as business loans show the highest degree of insulation from changing monetary conditions among all bank assets. In terms of liquidity, business loans are among the least liquid assets held by banks, as only a highly fragmented secondary market is available in which these notes may be resold by banks. This factor in general causes yields on business loans to be higher than yields on short-term notes held by banks, although there are several periods in recent U.S. history in which this pattern does not hold.

While banks often display an obligation to meet the loan demands of their business customers, they do not evidence a similar position regarding household mortgage loans (2). This investment category is usually quite sensitive to conditions of monetary ease or tightness. If investment funds must be cut, new mortgage loans are often an easy way to achieve the reduction. The ease perhaps relates to the typical absence of a continuing lender-borrower relationship in the case of mortgage borrowers such as exists with business accounts. This in turn logically reduces the banks' felt obligation to loan to mortgage borrowers during times of monetary tightness. Secondly, the liquidity of mortgage loans is less than business loans and the maturity longer, both of which increase the market exposure of mortgages compared to commercial loans in the case of rising interest rates. As a result, during periods when interest rates are rising, banks do not prefer to lend mortgage money long-term at fixed rates of return. Mortgage loans typically are 10 to 30 year notes with fixed interest rates and a still fragmentary secondary market.

Category (3), long-term government and corporate securities, is usually viewed as more liquid than (1) or (2) due to an active secondary market. Thus, when banks feel a need for greater liquidity than loans provide while retaining some of the earning power, they find category (3) investments a useful financial vehicle.

Categories (4) and (5) constitute the defensive holdings and cash position of banks. Short-term government securities provide some earnings to banks while offering a high level of liquidity since an active secondary market exists in these instruments and since their fixed value redemption periods are short (90 day Treasury bills are a common example).

In evaluating decisions of banks to shift the composition of their investment portfolio among these five categories, the yields associated with each are of interest in analyzing shifts in bank portfolio composition among higher earning and lower or zero earning categories. Banks are viewed as having desired levels of holdings in each of the five categories toward which they continually adjust their actual holdings. Clearly, the desire of profit-seeking banks is to keep the level of assets tied up in cash and equivalent (category 5) to a minimum consistent with legal requirements and safe management practices. Thus, when the level of reserves in banks rises, say due to open market actions of the Federal Reserve, banks are motivated to decrease their expanded cash and reserve position back to desired levels by increasing their holdings of short- and long-term securities in accordance with the desired holdings of these assets. A similar effect is presumably transmitted to categories (1) and (2) assets as well. This process of portfolio adjustment provides the channel by which expansive Federal Reserve policy impacts upon market interest rates. More available investment funds in the banking system are expected to lead an increased demand for short- and long-term investments and to lower money and capital market rates of interest on these securities as their prices are pushed up by the increased demand. Similarly, a contraction of reserves in the banking system leads to a shortage of investment capital in the banking system and pushes up rates of interest.

The size of banks' defensive position (holdings of categories 4 and 5 assets relative to the total) has been found to be statistically influenced by the spread between interest rates on loans and long-term securities, which we denote by i_l, and the rate on short-term securities, which we call i_s. As our earlier discussion of the term structure (Chapter 12) suggested, the relationship between i_l and i_s reflects the position of the yield curve. As the yield curve becomes more upward sloping, $(i_l - i_s)$ widens, and the opportunity cost of holding assets in categories 4 and 5 increases. As a result, desired holdings in these categories decrease, and banks tend to attempt to reduce their holdings as much as possible consistent with their reserve requirements. The opposite effect is expected if the gap between i_l and i_s narrows.

The discount rate (i_d) is found to exert an influence upon the defensive holdings of banks. When i_d is high relative to short-term security rates, i_s, the explicit cost of borrowing funds for use as required reserves outweighs the opportunity cost of obtaining those funds by liquidating short-term assets. Thus, under such circumstances, we would expect to see banks' holdings of category (4) assets reduced when i_d is in the neighborhood of i_s or when $i_d < i_s$, we would similarly expect greater levels of borrowing of needed reserves and less of a reduction in short-term securities.

Bank Reactions to Tight Money

The priority position business loans are found to occupy in bank portfolio decisions indicates that during times when total usable reserves available to banks are declining, portfolio adjustments by banks will be concentrated as much as possible on the remaining investment categories (2) to (5), while efforts will be made to maintain the level of loans largely intact. Declines in usable reserves of banks occur when the supply of outside money is being contracted by the Federal Reserve or when the Federal Reserve increases the ratio of required reserves.

An initial response by banks to the loss of reserves accompanying a reduction in outside money is to liquidate short-term assets (4). While this adds cash to the accounts of an individual bank, it does not affect reserves of the whole banking system. The same stock of outside money is only repositioned among buying and selling banks. However, an increased inclination to sell short-term securities by most banks can put selling pressures on money markets and drive down prices of short-term securities. Since the short-term interest rate rises with falling security prices and vice versa, the result of such portfolio adjustments is to raise short-term interest rates. Thus, we can expect an initial response of the banking sector to a deficiency of usable reserves to be little if any decline in lending, but an increase in short-term money market rates. This increase lowers the differential between loan returns and security returns, and eventually it reaches an equilibrium in which the pressing lending obligations of banks are met and at the same time the short-term interest rate has risen to the point where further selling pressures by banks subside.

A second response by banks to reserve deficiencies is to sell long-term securities (category 3). The implications of this alternative are similar to those of short-term securities in that such sales have no immediate impact on reserves throughout the banking system, but lead to higher long-term interest rates. This response by banks is perhaps motivated by a sharply narrowed or negative gap between the return on short-term and the return on long-term securities resulting from initial adjustments in the short-term portfolio. Instances where short-term rates rise above long-term rates are not entirely uncommon during periods of bank reserve contraction. In this extreme case, a bank's current earnings can be increased by selling long-term bonds and buying short-term bonds. This type of motivation, along with a continuing pattern by banks of trying to preserve the level of loans from the effects of declining reserves, provide the motivation for the secondary reaction of selling longer term securities.

Reducing new mortgage loans (category 2) is an actively pursued alternative in response to reserve deficiencies. This can enable the flow of payback funds (i.e., monthly payments) to be a net source of liquidity where this flow is greater than new mortgages. In addition, it is possible for banks to sell existing mortgages to other banks and to nonbank financial institutions and in this way to individually become more liquid.

Thus far, our discussion of portfolio shifts has indicated that individual banks have several channels through which they may postpone the effects of reserve deficiencies upon business loans. At the same time, it is clear that portfolio adjustments cannot of themselves generate new primary reserves.

Thus, from the standpoint of the entire banking system, reserve deficiencies will not be affected by portfolio adjustments, although interest rates on short-term and long-term notes can be expected to respond to the shifts in supply and demand accompanying portfolio shifts.

From the standpoint of the entire banking system, reserve deficiencies can ultimately only be eliminated by (1) Federal Reserve purchases of securities, which place more outside money in the economy, (2) borrowing at the Federal Reserve, (3) changing the reserve requirements, or (4) reducing loans and thus demand deposit levels such that a smaller volume of reserves is required. Of these, the Federal Reserve is directly involved in all but the last avenue, and thus the Federal Reserve ultimately is in a position of control. However, observation of banks during periods of tight money indicates that bankers faced with reserve deficiencies who are reluctant to reduce loans find in the alternatives and avenues now discussed important vehicles by which to ride out periods of monetary tightness, so long as these periods do not become too lengthy. In extended periods of monetary tightness accompanied by a relentless Federal Reserve System, banks have no options except to reduce business loans and raise interest rates.

Flows of Capital for Investment— An Expanded View

The general structure of bank portfolios at any point in time produces a flow of available funds into both corporate security and mortgage markets by these institutions. With our earlier discussion of nonbank lending sources, this gives as major private sources of capital to new corporate securities markets:

(1) Life insurance funds
(2) Pension funds and fire and casualty insurance funds
(3) Commercial bank funds
(4) Funds advanced directly by households, corporations

as depicted in Figure 13–1. In addition, state and local pension funds provide a fifth source of capital, which, while small, is of growing importance in recent years. This flow of money capital, along with anticipated corporate demand for investment, outlines the major ingredients in the market for securities. These supply and demand factors continually interact, producing a prevailing market rate of return on securities and a corresponding flow of actual borrowing. The market interest rate can be thought of as a simultaneous product of supply and demand influences and, as indicated earlier, can be expected to influence subsequent demand for new plant and equipment as well as decision trade-offs by life insurance firms, banks, households, and others to supply more or less funds. Thus, rates of return in securities markets are affected by and affect sources of demand and supply of these funds.

Figure 13–1 does not specifically show the market for government securities, in the interest of simplicity. However, the same principal suppliers of corporate capital also typically supply government capital. Accordingly, rates on government securities tend to follow closely rates on corporate securities, once a rate difference is taken into consideration to allow for the different risk character of each type security. Although risks on government securities are generally considered less than the risk on corporate debt, both types of securities share the same general market and compete for some of the same available funds. In the United States, observation tends to verify this relationship. When demand for corporate capital is heavy, pressure is put on government securities and vice versa.

In addition, Figure 13–1 does not show the influence of secondary markets for corporate or government bonds or common stocks. In these markets, existing holders of securities may sell securities and investors may buy existing previously issued issues. The same investors who trade new securities also often trade in these secondary markets. As such, these secondary markets provide a buffer for interest rates and yields in primary securities markets. As new securities issues come to market, they are offered at yields that closely correspond to rates in secondary markets. It is safe to say that if this were not so they would soon be pushed by investors down to market rates if they were higher or go unsold if they were lower. At the same time, the volume of new issues diverts funds from secondary markets and affects yields in secondary markets.

In the interrelated market for mortgage loans, both banks and life insurance companies are typically significant sources of supply of these funds, to the extent that available funds in these institutions are diverted from securities investments. According to their basic charters, savings and loan associations and mutual savings banks devote a great majority of their assets to mortgage loans and are a principal factor in mortgage markets. Unlike banks, savings institutions by law cannot engage in creation of demand deposits. The primary source of new lendable funds by these institutions is the flow of new savings deposits. Without adequate new deposits, savings institutions have relatively few options (as compared with banks) to preserve their lending power, although they can engage in some borrowing from the Federal Home Loan Bank Board in a manner similar to that of commercial bank borrowing at the Federal Reserve. Thus, the level of intermediation becomes a crucial factor in the supply of mortgage funds by savings institutions. In addition, the division of funds between bank time deposits and savings deposits is an equally crucial ingredient in mortgage market conditions.[3]

As Figure 13-1 illustrates, the interplay of these major sources of supply along with the anticipated demand for new residential construction can be expected to largely determine mortgage rates and the volume of mortgage lending. At the same time, mortgage rates can be expected to influence the proportions of bank and life insurance funds supplied to mortgage markets as opposed to other investments. As mortgage rates rise relative to bonds and other investment alternatives, banks and life insurance companies can be expected to increase their supply of mortgage money and can be expected to reduce their supply when relative rates are falling.

The fund flows and information flows shown in Figure 13-1 combine to produce security yields, mortgage rates, and flows of new security and mortgage lending and in this way ultimately influence expenditures on new plant and equipment and residential construction. As illustrated in Figure 13-1, this impact on expenditures (and GNP) provides an important linkage between money market variables and aggregate output and expenditures.

However, the connections we have seen between aggregate expenditures and flows of funds into mortgage and security markets further indicates the linkage runs both ways, i.e., that plant and equipment and residential construction expenditures influence security yields, mortgage rates, and flows of lending in these two markets and at the same time are influenced by these yields, rates, and flows. In other words, the market yield on bonds and mortgages and the rate of interest on commercial loans is influenced by the underlying demand for investment goods and housing, as well as by the flows of money capital into the supply side of these two markets.

In addition, Figure 13-1 also suggests the operation of a mechanism that maintains a balance between mortgage rates and bond rates. The essential ingredient in this mechanism is the customary allocation of funds by banks and life insurance companies into both investment categories. When bond prices rise relative to mortgage rates, more funds usually flow into bond investments by these institutions. This shift tends to raise mortgage rates as the funds are diverted away and at the same time lowers yields on bonds as a result of the buying pressures in bond markets. The reverse pattern generally applies to increases in mortgage rates relative to bond rates. However, this market balancing mechanism operates only imperfectly due to stickiness in mortgage rates in responding to market forces, particularly when rates are

---

[3] This split is affected by relative earning rates on funds deposited in both institutions. However, the spread between the two rates is largely set by control of the maximums by regulation. In practice, the party has not varied greatly on savings accounts. However, on time deposits, particularly of the variety associated with corporations, the parties have been subject to greater fluctuation and have been a factor in major shifts of deposits by corporations between banks and savings institutions.

rising. In the case of rising mortgage rates, the usual pattern is that mortgage rates lag behind their balanced market value due to the role of government insured loans through the FHA and VA loan programs. Rates on these loans typically move reluctantly and belatedly in response to changes in bond rates, so that the bond rate tends to move toward the mortgage rate. Since the mortgage rate is slow to adjust, the result is a rapid withdrawal of funds from mortgage markets by life insurance companies and banks during periods when bond yields are rising rapidly. This pattern has often created crisis-like conditions in markets for mortgages, while money continues to flow into bond markets in search of the high market yields available there. The final consequence is an associated decline in new construction expenditures, particularly for residential construction.

Some Illustrative Applications

The analytical description of U.S. capital markets now constructed can be applied to make inferences about the general effects upon interest rates and lending flows of changes in various initiating variables. For example:

(1) *If* a permanent rise in government expenditures, financed by new government securities, causes a general increase in GNP, employment, and incomes; *Then* corporate and personal savings flows will rise, along with insurance and pension fund receipts. A proportion of this flow will be deposited in financial intermediaries. The remainder may either flow directly to capital markets or leak to other uses.

The higher flow of new deposits in banks resulting from this GNP and saving increase places pressures on required reserves of banks, which need to be higher due to the higher deposits. If excess reserves are available in the banking system, they will be absorbed into required deposits. However, if no excess reserves are available (and the Federal Reserve was not at the same time supplying additional reserves through open market policy), banks would be required to borrow additional reserves from the Federal Reserve or elsewhere. A tightening in money market conditions occurs. This trend is heightened by the initial financing of the government expenditure, which represents a new increase in the demand for money and contributes to a bidding up of interest rates in securities markets.

The result of higher general incomes is expected to be some increase in residential construction according to the discussion of Chapter 9. In addition, the operation of an investment accelerator such as that discussed in Chapter 8 is a higher level of plant and equipment demand. For both these reasons, the demand function for new money capital shifts positively. We illustrate this situation graphically in Figure 13–2, where the demand function for money capital by all involved sectors is shown as a downward

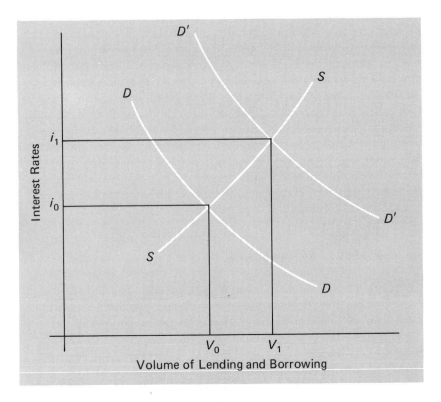

Figure 13–2

Supply and Demand for Money Capital

sloping function of the market rate of interest. In the figure, the effect of the induced new construction and plant and equipment demand is to shift the demand for capital curve from an initial position at DD to the new position $D'D'$. At the same time, the banking system can be expected to react to the increased demand by mustering new reserves and more efficiently using their existing reserves by the methods discussed earlier in the chapter.

As a result of these reactions, the level of usable reserves might be expected to increase and, along with it, the capacity of the banking system to supply money capital to bond and mortgage markets. In addition, rising interest rates may motivate some additional consumer saving, as discussed in Chapter 4. These combined effects are illustrated in Figure 13–2 by an upward sloping supply of capital curve, SS. The result of the shift in demand is thus an increase in interest rates, which rise from i_0 to i_1, and an increased volume of lending, as banks and other suppliers of capital channel more money to capital markets in pursuit of the rising rates. Notice that this increased lending volume can occur even with the assumption of no Federal

Reserve additions to available bank reserves if banks either (a) have excess reserves available or (b) borrow additional reserves. However, if neither of these avenues is employed, then the increased volume of new lending will depend upon Federal Reserve policy, and upon changes in consumer spending behavior.

(2) *If* some exogenous event causes the aggregate consumption function to shift outward so that consumers begin to spend more on consumer goods; *Then,* the GNP will increase via the multiplier effect. At the same time, the shift may positively affect business expectations, so that the demand for new plant and equipment increases and, along with it, the total demand for new private money capital. The result is a rightward shift in the demand for capital function in exactly the same way as in the previous example and as shown in Figure 13–2.

(3) *If* Federal Reserve policy becomes highly restrictive, resulting in some combination of a rise in the discount rate, an increase in reserve requirements, and an open market policy of net bond sales; *Then,* bank reserves will be drained away and will be inadequate to meet the required ratio of deposits. Banks will be induced by this situation to borrow privately or from the Federal Reserve to replenish their reserve position, or alternatively, to reduce their level of deposits and new lending. If they are successful in replenishing reserves through borrowing, then little effect on the supply of capital will occur. If such measures are insufficient, then banks will be forced to reduce their supply of new business capital and mortgage loans. Given a constant level of demand for new money capital, this pattern indicates a rise in interest rates and a reduction in the volume of lending, as illustrated in Figure 13–3. In this figure, the impact of the decline in reserves results in a backward shift in the supply of money capital function from an initial position SS to the new position $S'S'$. This rations some investment out of the market, as depicted by the decline of new money capital lending and borrowing from V_0 to V_1, while the interest rate rises from i_0 to i_1.

If such a rise in interest rates is significant, it may lead banks to other sources of borrowing formerly too expensive to pursue, e.g., Eurodollars, which would then lessen the decline in the volume of lending that otherwise would have occurred by shifting the supply curve back to the right. As both bond and mortgage interest rates increase, mortgage rates rise toward government insured mortgage maximums. As these maximums are reached, the gap between mortgage rates and bond yields falls below market equilibrium levels. As this equilibrium is disrupted in favor of bonds, the supply of mortgage funds can be expected to fall below the demand for these funds at the maximum allowable rates. This creates a gap of demand over supply evidenced by unavailability of money at existing rates of interest and leads to rationing of available funds by suppliers. The increased allocation of capital funds by banks to securities resulting from this shift can at the same time be

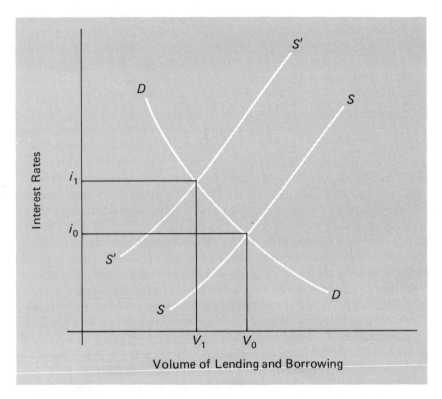

Figure 13–3

Restrictive Monetary Policy

expected to reduce yields on securities, somewhat buffering the initial effect of the shift by lowering bond yields at the same time mortgage rates are rising to maximums, thus moving rates toward normal parities between bonds and mortgages. Subsequently, the reduced flow of mortgage lending can be expected to lower new residential construction.

We have considered nonbank institutional factors in the operation of capital markets in the United States. This led to a more explicit consideration of the channels through which capital moves from lenders to borrowers than that undertaken in Chapter 12. The role of commercial banks' portfolio adjustments in these flows was considered. Finally, illustrations of the application of the resulting funds flow structure were given. In this discussion, our concern has been more with describing persistent characteristics of U.S. capital markets than with building logical theories of monetary behavior. In the next chapter we shift this focus. Economists have developed logical constructs aimed at explaining interest rates and other capital market variables. These models greatly abstract from the factors in capital market behavior in order to focus on the logical implications of certain broad behavioral assumptions about monetary behavior. These theoretical constructs offer insights useful in our analysis of monetary conditions. They are the topic of our next chapter.

Discussion Questions

1. Who are the major nonbank financial intermediaries? What differences would occur if these intermediaries had the power to issue checks?

2. Should credit cards be counted in the money supply? In what ways are they money? How are they unlike money?

3. What if a law were passed that required banks to supply only bond markets and prohibited life insurance companies from investment in mortgages, so that they could not "crowd in on the act" of savings and loan institutions? What would be the impact of such a law?

4. According to the patterns of financial intermediation discussed in this chapter, what is the major impact on interest rates and money capital markets of a general income tax increase?

5. Even though the role of secondary markets in stocks has not been discussed explicitly in the chapter, what do you suppose would be the effect on interest rates of a substantial bullish (optimistic) shift in attitude on the part of investors? Explain as fully as possible.

6. What does the discussion suggest would be the impact of a "fair home-owners law" that would prohibit mortgage interest rates from rising above 6 percent? Explain.

14
Monetary Theories

The analysis of funds flow channels in the previous chapters leads to conclusions about monetary activity only when we apply assumptions about the behavior of banks, insurance companies, and other major factors in these channels. We have shown major decision points and illustrated information flows interest rates, etc., pertinent to these decisions. We have illustrated the use of this analysis by assuming logical responses by banks and others at specific decision points in the funds flow channels. But we have not proposed general statements about the *behavior* of these banks and other institutions, i.e., we have not proposed general propositions about how these decisions will be made. Such statements and general propositions are the fabric of monetary theory, to which our attention now turns.

We shall first consider the neo-Keynesian liquidity preference model. This model is concerned with the evaluation of interest rate and national income levels consistent with supply-demand equilibrium in money markets. The involvement of national income levels in the explanation of monetary equilibrium positions means the liquidity preference model does not stand alone as a theory of monetary behavior but is instead intertwined with an explanatory model of national income.

By contrast, the second model we shall consider, the quantity theory model, is a complete theory of economic activity that explains national income in the context of a model of monetary behavior. As such, it may be mislabeling to call this model a theory of monetary behavior. Rather it is a monetary theory of economic behavior. We first take up the liquidity preference approach.

Liquidity Preference Theory

The funds flow mechanism of the previous two chapters emphasized the supply and demand factors brought to bear on capital markets. This mechanism was relied upon to explain the movement of interest rates and the volume of lending activity. It was assumed that interest rates on capital market instruments are established in a manner similar to prices in any market mechanism approaching competition, i.e., that these interest rates are the price of capital that along with lending volume are the joint products of a myriad of supply and demand variables.

A second way to consider the impact of money on the economy is by focusing explicitly on the propensity of the economy to hold the stock of money available without direct reference to capital markets. The general approach is called liquidity preference analysis. In this framework, the entire structure of interest rates is seen as essentially a product of the interaction between those who seek to hold inventories of money *in contrast to other purchasing power* as compared to the total amount of money available. Whereas our earlier analysis focused on money market rates, bond yields, and mortgage rates, liquidity preference models normally summarize the entire money and capital market interest rate structure by reference to "the" interest rate. This simplification enables an uncluttered analysis of the basic factors in the supply and demand influences upon money holdings. However, we should keep in mind that impacts on the structure of interest rates are not necessarily unchanged when "the" interest rate is rising or falling as a result of liquidity preference model considerations. They are merely masked from view by the shorthand reference to a single interest rate. Finally, the analysis we shall consider is meant to be in constant dollar terms throughout, in which the price is fixed and invariant. In later chapters, we shall explore the implications of price level changes on the demand and supply of money.

While we may safely assume the demand for purchasing power by most consumers to be sufficiently large so as to be considered infinite, the demand to hold dollar balances is clearly limited. Holding wealth in dollar balances is only one alternative way of configuring an asset portfolio and not a profitable way at that, since money balances normally earn little if any interest. Therefore, it is of interest to consider the factors motivating consumers and business firms to hold inventories of cash rather than inventories of earning assets. In this regard, two general categories of demand for money balances are postulated in liquidity preference theory. The first deals with the routine transactional requirements of the economy. The second stipulates an investment oriented speculative demand for money holdings.

Transactions and Precautionary Demand

The first category of demand represents the need for money by all economic units to conduct transactions and provide for unexpected occurrences. This demand is evidenced by the level of currency and demand deposits that consumers, business firms, and others want to maintain to provide a buffer against receipts and dispersal of income and to provide for emergencies. As incomes and paychecks increase, dispersals for consumption and other spending also increase. This increase in both incomes and consumption can be expected to result in a higher demand to hold money in the form of currency and demand deposits. Similarly, a decrease in income and consumption results in a decreased demand for transactional balances. Precautionary money balances are held to provide security against possible emergencies. These balances can also be expected to grow along with incomes and consumption. As higher standards of living are achieved, the money balances required to guard against a sudden drop in the standard of living also grow.

In addition to income levels, other influences on the level of transactionary and precautionary balances in the economy include:

(1) Frequency of typical pay period. As income earners are paid more frequently, they have less of a need for buffers between income and expenses and less of a need to maintain a precautionary reserve to tide them over until the next paycheck. The transactionary/precautionary demand for money could be expected to drop for a given income level under such circumstances. The opposite is true for less frequent pay periods.

(2) Extent of contingencies commonly insured against. As more fire, medical, dental, accident, theft, etc., loss contingencies are dealt with through insurance programs, the economy's need for precautionary balances declines for a given income level.

(3) Extent of once-a-month payment plans. As retailers and banks engage in multipurpose credit cards with once-a-month billing and payment schedules, to the extent these coordinate with pay periods the need for transactionary balances is reduced for a given income level. Essentially, the liabilities accrue without drawing down demand deposit levels and can be liquidated upon receipt of a monthly check.

In our discussion of the liquidity preference model, we focus attention upon other influences on transactions/precautionary demand besides the three types now listed as passive factors. Accordingly, we proceed with the simplifying assumption that the transactionary/precautionary demand for money is proportionate to income in the absence of changes in such determinants. This assumption produces the transactions demand function shown graphically in Figure 14–1. In this figure, the slope of the function shows the proportionality factor. When the slope is given by a_0, a level of income of Y_0 associates with a transactionary/precautionary demand for money of TD_0. If an underlying determinant of transactions demand (such as the frequency of pay period) changes, the value of the proportionality factor (a) changes, and the function rotates about the origin. For example, assume the frequency of pay period is lowered by a new federal law to 1 week. This lowers the transactions demand at all income levels and rotates the function from position A to position B, where the new slope is a_1. At this position, the same level of income associates with the smaller level of transactions demand TD_1.

Speculative Demand

A second demand for money holdings, entitled *speculative demand*, relates to money held in cash and demand deposits in the expectation that

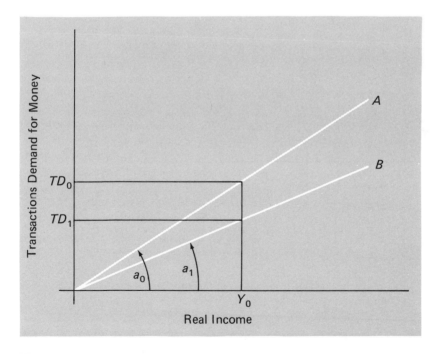

Figure 14–1

Transactions Demand for Money Balances

future yields on securities investment will be higher than present yields. Holders of money balances for this reason feel that present yields on stocks and bonds are too low (compared to an expectation of normal yields) and will rise in the future. This is equivalent to the feeling that stock and bond prices are too high given present dividends and interest rates and are likely to fall in the future. This attitude reflects the economy's preference for liquidity as opposed to nonliquid financial investments. Thus, during times when security yields are widely considered higher than normal, we may expect the volume of funds held in such speculative accounts to be low. Similarly, when security yields are widely considered lower than normal, the volume of funds held in speculative accounts can be expected to be high. Speculative demand is therefore presumed to be primarily responsive to security market yields relative to the prevailing judgment of what constitutes normal yields. Figure 14–2 shows this situation graphically. The function LL shows the economy's speculative demand for money as a downward sloping

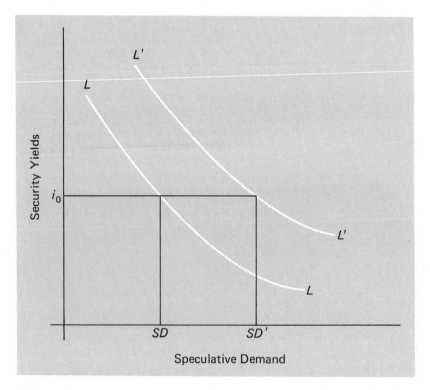

Figure 14–2
Speculative Demand for Money

function of security yields. A securities yield of i_0 produces a speculative demand for SD dollars in speculative money holdings. Higher yields will draw a portion of these dollars out of money holdings and into securities markets while lower yields cause speculative cash holdings to be increased.

The position of the speculative demand function reflects basic expectations of households and institutions regarding normal security yields and expected future yields. If a general wave of economic pessimism occurs in the economy, security prices are expected to drop, raising yields. This expectation of higher yields causes more funds to be held in speculative balances. The situation is graphically depicted in Figure 14–2 by a shift from LL to $L'L'$ (a greater speculative demand) where the volume of money demanded for speculative purposes rises from SD to SD'.

Equilibrium

While separation of the total demand for money into transactions and speculative categories is useful for purposes of discussion, such a separation in the minds of households and other economic units is likely to be ill-defined, since a single pool of cash holdings and demand deposits typically serves both purposes. In the liquidity preference model, these demands are added together, forming a total demand for money (DM) function:

$$DM = TD + SD$$

If we focus on income, Y, as the primary determinant of transactions demand and interest rates, i, as the primary determinant of speculative demand, we have

$$TD = f_1(Y) \qquad\qquad (14\text{--}1)$$

and

$$SD = f_2(i) \qquad\qquad (14\text{--}2)$$

which gives

$$DM = f_3(Y, i) \qquad\qquad (14\text{--}3)$$

Expression 14–3 shows that either increases in income or decreases in interest rates, or both, can be expected to increase the total demand for money. Income declines or interest rate increases similarly decrease the demand for money. Monetary equilibrium occurs where the total demand for money is brought into equality with the supply of money. For the present, the supply of money, SM, is assumed autonomous, determined by Federal Reserve policy, and equal to SM_0. Later, we shall alter this assumption. Equilibrium occurs where

$$SM_0 = f_3(Y, i) \qquad\qquad (14\text{-}4)$$

With the supply of money autonomous, Expression 14–4 shows that adjustments in the determinants of the demand for money must be relied upon to produce monetary equilibrium.

To illustrate, consider the effect of an increase in the supply of money, from SM_0 to SM_1. An excess supply of money now exists for the present demand. Some combination of a decrease in interest rate and an increase in income must occur to restore equilibrium, each of which increases the demand for money balances and reduces the excess supply condition. The availability of the additional funds $(SM_1 - SM_0)$ on capital markets provides a direct motivation for the decline in interest rates. In turn, declining interest rates motivate higher levels of investment spending that lead to the general increase in Y. This pattern continues until equilibrium is restored.

As a further illustration, assume the supply of money is constant, but that an increase in Y occurs. More money is now demanded for transactions balances to support the higher income level. With a fixed supply, interest rates must rise to free money balances from speculative accounts. Equilibrium is restored at sufficiently higher interest rates that the demand for money is again in balance with the supply.

Variants on the Liquidity Preference Model

There is little disagreement among economists on the plausibility of the assumption of a transactions demand for money balances. But there is substantial disagreement as to the viability of the idea that speculative money balances are a stable and systematic function of the interest rate. Several economists have argued that the availability of highly liquid interest bearing near monies such as savings and loan accounts, time deposits, certificates of deposit, and U.S. Treasury bills cause virtually all speculative accounts to be held in nonmoney rather than money forms.[1] If this is indeed the case,

---

1 The most prominent sponsors of the general idea are Professors Gurley and Shaw. See J. G. Gurley and E. S. Shaw, *Money in a Theory of Finance*, The Brookings Institution, Washington, D.C., 1960; or "Financial Aspects of Economic Development" by the same authors in the *American Economic Review*, 45 (1955), pp. 515–538. An excellent article reviewing the Gurley-Shaw hypothesis is by L. S. Ritter, "The Role of Money in Keynesian Theory" in D. Carson (ed.), *Banking and Monetary Studies*, Richard D. Irwin, Inc., Homewood, Ill., 1963, pp. 134–150.

then more money cannot be enticed into circulation by higher interest rates or absorbed into speculative balances by lower interest rates, as implied by the speculative demand for money function. Instead, the impact of higher interest rates is to motivate a shift in speculative holdings away from the nearest money financial instruments that presumably bear the lowest interest rate to less liquid and higher yielding financial instruments. We can think of this response as a shift in demand for speculative balances from money market to capital market instruments. Such a shift has an impact on the term structure of interest rates, but it releases no formerly speculative money holdings into the circular flow of monetary activity in and of itself.

The logic of the near monies argument is not at all strained when applied to the type of financial system outlined in the previous two chapters. Investors in the United States who are waiting on the sidelines for a better investment opportunity in the future need not settle for zero interest on their investment funds by holding them as money balances. Time deposits and extremely short maturity Treasury bills purchased in the secondary market are but two ways U.S. investors can provide an earning repository for speculative assets that is as good as cash for all practical purposes. Thus, fluctuations in money balances due to the influence of interest rate fluctuations on speculative motives may be close to zero in a nation with the complex and sophisticated financial intermediaries of the United States. If so, the important line of inquiry is whether the demand for money is in reality not an important function of the rate of interest, but instead only a function of the level of real income.

In response to this question, an argument has been advanced that the demand for money is a negative function of the rate of interest, even in the absence of any speculative demand for money. The plausibility of this argument is important in our overall understanding and evaluation of the liquidity preference structure, because it relates to whether or not it is reasonable to retain the central conclusions of the liquidity preference model without necessarily retaining the speculative demand for money function.

Interest Rates and Transactions Demand

An alternative line of reasoning associated with William J. Baumol and James Tobin relative to interest rates and the demand for money is concerned with the economic logic of the decision to move out of cash holdings and into short-term near money assets.[2] Basically, the contention is that the

2 See W. J. Baumol "The Transactions Demand for Cash: An Inventory Theoretic Approach," *Quarterly Journal of Economics*, 66 (1952), pp. 545–556; and J. Tobin "The Interest Elasticity of the Transactions Demand for Cash," *Review of Economics and Statistics*, 38 (1956), pp. 241–247.

holding period of transactions balances may be of sufficient length that a portion of funds required for transactions purposes can be loaned out short-term by the purchase of short-term money market instruments. Then, as transactions demands require, the money market instruments are liquidated. In the meanwhile, nonearning cash balances are reduced while interest is earned on the security holdings. The ability to find temporary outlets for transactions balances depends upon the availability of notes that have a wide variety of maturities such that the investment will mature when the cash is needed. Such an outlet is available in U.S. money markets through the vehicle of Treasury bills. It is usually possible to buy Treasury bills of 2, 3, or 4 days to maturity or with maturities up to 180 days. Thus, the channel by which transactions balances can be converted temporarily into earning assets is readily available in U.S. money markets, giving life to the possibility that some transactions balances may be used for this purpose.

The structure of cash and short-term bond holdings is shown in Figure 14–3. The upper part shows the transactionary balances of a firm or household that receives revenues of Y dollars every P periods of time. Thus, upon receipt of Y dollars at time zero, cash balances are equal to Y. The continual

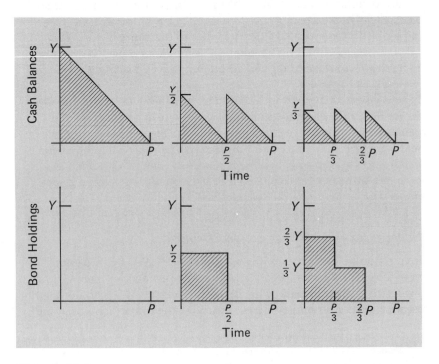

Figure 14–3

Cash Holdings and Bond Holdings

dispersal of Y as expenditures and as payments to claimants reduces the cash balances steadily until at the end of P time periods, the cash balance is zero and the stage is set for another receipt of Y dollars. The cycle is repeated each P period, giving the transactions balance a sawtooth pattern that has an average balance of $Y/2$ dollars if the expenditure pattern is linear. The upper left-hand graph in Figure 14–3 shows the situation where no transactions balances are converted into bonds over the P period. Thus, bond holdings are nonexistent, as shown in the lower left-hand panel. However, if half the initial transactions balance $(Y/2)$ is used to purchase short-term bonds having a maturity of $P/2$ periods, then the situation is as shown in the middle graphs in Figure 14–3. The bonds mature halfway through the transactions period, providing the needed transactions cash at the point where it becomes needed. The result is a level of cash holdings that is reduced from $Y/2$ in the nobond case to $(Y/2)/2 = Y/4$ in the case of one bond purchase and sale. (Bonds in the amount $Y/2$ are held for $P/2$ periods, for an average holding of $Y/4$ bonds for the entire P period.) In this case, the transactions balance is apportioned one-half to cash and one-half to bonds on the average over the period, i.e., the combined area under the cash balances curve is equal to the area under the bond holdings curve. If two-thirds of the initial transactions balances are converted to securities, the picture is as shown in the right-hand graphs of Figure 14–3. Half the bonds purchased carry maturities of $P/3$, while the other half carry maturities of $(2/3)P$. Thus, at $P/3$, the first half of the bond purchases mature, providing cash balances sufficient to carry through until time $(2/3)P$. At this point, the remaining bonds mature, providing liquidity for transactions until P. As seen in the figure, the cash balances are even lower than in the middle graph and the bond holdings higher on the average. In fact, the average cash holding is now one-half the average bond holding.

The pattern in Figure 14–3 raises the question, why not convert the entire initial transactions cash balance into a portfolio of bonds having maturities of one, two, three, and so forth periods up to $P - 1$ periods, such that a continual stream of maturing bonds becomes available that exactly matches the stream of transactions demand for cash? If this were done, cash balances are kept at zero (except for the instant of payment), and the average holdings of bonds is maximized at a value equal to the total level of transactions demand, $Y/2$. The problem with this solution is that transacting in short-term bonds involves a commission rate that is based on the dollar amount of the transaction and not on the length of time over which it is held. Thus, buying and selling a bond over a period as short as 1 day would not be profitable because the essentially fixed cost of the transaction outweighs the 1-day's interest return for all reasonable interest rate levels. However, at some minimum holding period, the rate of interest outweighs the fixed transactions cost, making the bond purchase a profitable undertaking.

We can examine these ideas more concretely by developing a specific expression for the cost of transacting and the revenues available from holding bonds. If we denote the number of transactions by n, and the cost per transaction by c, then the total cost of transacting, C, is given by

$$C = n \cdot c \qquad (14\text{--}5)$$

The revenues from bond holdings are also dependent upon the number of transactions, which influence directly the average bond holdings for a given Y. Inspection of the pattern of Figure 14–3 reveals that the initial level of bond holdings can be given as a direct function of the number of transactions. When two transactions are made, as in the middle graph (one buy and one sell), the initial level of bond holdings is $(1/2)Y$. When $n = 3$ as in the right-hand graph (one buy and two sells), the initial level of bond holdings is $(2/3)Y$. In general, the initial level of bond holdings is $[n - 1/n]Y$. Since the final level of bond holdings is zero, the average level of bond holdings is equal to one-half the initial level, or $[n - 1/2n]Y$. When we multiply this average level of bond holdings by the interest rate, i, the total revenue from transacting, R, results:

$$R = \left[\frac{n - 1}{2n} \right] iY \qquad (14\text{--}6)$$

We can find the optimal number of transactions and the associated optimal level of bond holdings and cash holdings by subtracting Expression 14–5 from 14–6 to obtain an expression for net profits, $R - C$, and then maximizing it with respect to the value of n.[3] For our discussion, it suffices to recognize that the costs involved in transacting in bonds are a linear function of the number of transactions while the revenues are a nonlinear function of both the number of transactions and the rate of interest. The comparison is shown in Figure 14–4. Revenues rise according to curve R in (a), approaching the value $iY/2$ as the number of transactions becomes large and the level of bond holdings approaches the total average transactions cash balance given by $Y/2$. For a small n, the comparison between $n - 1$ and n in Expression 14–6 causes revenues to rise rapidly, while for large n, $n - 1$ more

---

[3] The value that results from this procedure is equal to

$$n^* = \sqrt{\frac{iY}{2c}}$$

which shows that the number of transactions is a direct but nonlinear function of both Y and i and an inverse nonlinear function of c.

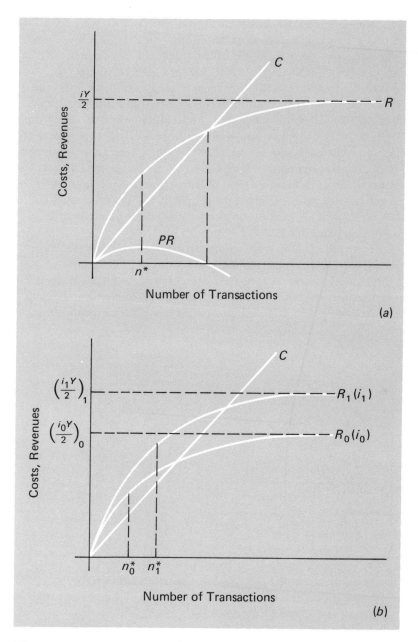

Figure 14–4

Effect of Interest Rates on Transaction Demand

nearly equals n, and the curve rises more slowly. Costs rise linearly according to C, with a slope of c. The level of profits is given by the difference between the two curves, shown as PR in Figure 14–4(a). For the curves shown, the profit is maximized for n^* transactions.

For our purposes, a crucial aspect of this analysis is the response of bondholders to changes in the interest rate. Figure 14–4(b) illustrates the discussion. If the interest rate should rise from i_0 to i_1, its role in Expression 14–6 shows that the revenue function shifts up as shown in the figure from $R_0(i_0)$ to $R_1(i_1)$. This shift shows the higher profitability now attainable from holding bonds. As a result, the average number of transactions that associates with maximum profits rises from n^*_0 to n^*_1, reflecting a larger average level of bond holdings and a smaller average holding of cash balances. Thus, an increase in interest rates reduces the level of transactionary cash holdings. The higher the interest rate, the larger the proportion of transactionary balances that can be profitably held in short-term bonds and the smaller the transactionary cash balances.

The interest rate effect on transactions demand is summarized in Figure 14–5, where we return to our initial representation of transactions demand as a function of income. Although the level of transactions balances rises with income, we now have seen it may decline with higher interest rates and increase for lower rates. At an initial interest rate of i_0, an income level

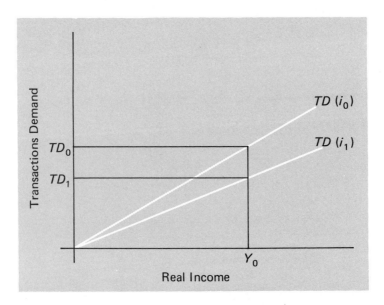

Figure 14–5

Shift in Transaction Demand

of Y_0 produces a level of transactionary demand of TD_0. However, if the interest rate should rise to i_1, the transactions demand function rotates from $TD(i_0)$ down to $TD(i_1)$, lowering the level of demand at the same income level Y_0 to an amount TD_1. Thus, in this scheme, we find a logical reason to expect interest rates to exert an effect on the demand for money apart from the operation of a speculative demand for money function. In addition, the increasing sophistication of corporate financial managers and the growing levels of transactions balances available to large corporations make the application of highly rationalized rules of behavior such as we have outlined in no way lacking in plausibility.

Several more recent studies of the demand for money have emphasized the possible role of wealth position in the demand for money balances.[4] The general logic of this position is that the size of the total holdings of assets by households and firms determines the levels of each type of wealth component in the asset portfolio. Thus, if total wealth is doubled, the cash balances will be enlarged along with security holdings and other assets. In this way, wealth is seen as an argument in the demand for money function in addition to interest rates and income levels. The function that results from this addition is

$$DM = f(i, Y, W) \qquad\qquad (14\text{--}7)$$

where W is the real wealth position of the economy. This function does not require that interest rates influence the demand for money in any particular way. The Baumol-Tobin approach is as sound a rationale for the inclusion of i in Expression 14–7 as is the speculative demand function. Thus, this expression is a highly general and well accepted representation of the money demand function in modern liquidity preference theory.

The Supply of Money and Interest Rates

In our introduction to liquidity preference analysis, we took the supply of money to be fixed and a product of Federal Reserve policy. When we recall the array of options discussed in the preceding two chapters available to banks to expand the money supply and the role played by nonbank financial intermediaries in supplying capital markets, it is clear that this is a simplification that is not totally realistic when applied to money and capital markets in the United States. In particular, banks can engage in a number of borrowing programs designed to increase their reserve position during times when they find it desirable to expand deposits. First, they may have excess reserves that can lead to an expansion of the money supply by creation of additional

[4] For an interesting exposition, see J. Tobin, "A Dynamic Aggregative Model" *Journal of Political Economy* 63 (1955), pp. 103–115.

demand deposits. Secondly, if banks are fully loaned up, they may be able to borrow deposits in the Eurodollar market, which enter the banking system as new reserves and can support an increase in the money supply. Third, banks can borrow reserves from the Federal Reserve. Fourth, banks can implement programs to make more efficient use of their existing reserve, such as vault cash management and check clearing management programs.

By some combination of these means, banks may be able to increase the level of demand deposit or inside money when it is in their interest to do so, even with no new reserves being added to the system by the Federal Reserve System. Furthermore, it is usually more profitable for banks to seek such means to acquire new reserves when interest rates are high than when they are low. Under these circumstances, the supply of money will be an upward sloping function of the interest rate as well as a function of the total reserves available to the banking system. The resulting money supply function is

$$SM = g(i, RF) \qquad\qquad (14\text{--}8)$$

where $RF =$ the total reserves in the banking system. However, the avenues we have suggested as the basis for this interest rate relationship are not inexhaustible. Indeed, they are basically temporary means by which banks can increase or maintain reserves in the face of contrary market pressures. When these avenues are substantially exhausted, we should not expect Expression 14–8 to continue to characterize the pattern of the supply of money, but instead should expect to find the total supply of money to be a function of only RF, the level of total reserves controlled by the Federal Reserve.

Monetary Equilibrium in the Expanded Model

Figure 14–6 shows monetary equilibrium in the case of the demand for and supply of money functions given by Expressions 14–7 and 14–8. When the reserve position is at RF_0 and the income level is Y_0, the demand and supply for money equate at an interest rate of i_0 where M_0 money balances are both demanded and supplied. If income rises to Y_1, the transactions demand for cash increases, shifting the curve to the right from DM_0 to DM_1 as shown in the figure. Interest rates begin to rise. This rise in interest rates brings some additional supply of money into the circular flow, as interest rates climb along the upward sloping supply of money function, SM_0. Equilibrium is reestablished at interest rate i_1. Notice that the rise in interest rates is not as steep as it would have been with no banking system ability to expand the money supply. Under this latter condition, interest rates would have risen to i_2 along a perfectly vertical supply function. Notice also that the supply curve is assumed to become vertical past a certain interest rate at which point all accessible bank reserves are actively employed.

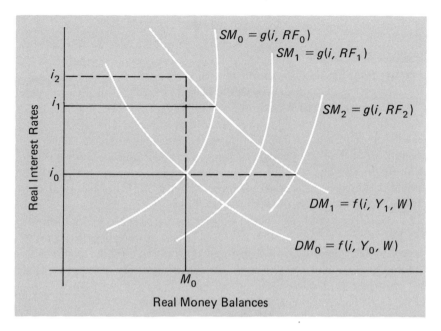

Figure 14–6
Monetary Equilibrium

An increase in the supply of bank reserves by the Federal Reserve, from RF_0 to RF_1, shifts the supply curve for money out, from SM_0 to SM_1, which reduces interest rates as shown in the figure. In fact, if the Federal Reserve responded to an increase in Y from Y_0 to Y_1 with a policy of supplying sufficient reserves to the banking system to maintain stable interest rates, then they would expand reserves to RF_2, where the shift in the supply curve to SM_2 exactly offsets the shift in demand and leaves the equilibrium level of interest rates unaffected.

The expanded model shown in Figure 14–6 allows the effects of several indirect influences upon monetary equilibrium to be evaluated. For example, consider the impact on equilibrium of an across-the-board decrease in the commissions on the purchase and sale of short-term bonds. As a result of this change, the value of c in Expression 14–5 would decline, rotating the cost function for bond transactions downward and increasing the average size of the optimal bond portfolio. As the average bond holding rises, the average level of transactions balances declines for each and every interest rate. As a result, the total demand for money function shifts back to the left, lowering interest rates and increasing security prices.

Next, consider the effect of a revision in the law that allows savings and loan associations to issue check-like script intended for use as locally circulating money. Account holders would be able to earn interest on their deposit and at the same time write quasi-checks on it. One effect of this circumstance would be to lower the value of c as in the previous example, as some money holdings used for local payment are transferred to the interest bearing alternative. Another effect would be to increase the supply of money function, as savings and loan associations can now join banks in issuing more quasi-money during times of high or rising interest rates. The effect of a decreased demand for money and an increased supply of money is shown in Figure 14–7 to be a decline in interest rates. The effect on transactions demand shifts the demand for money function from DM_0 to DM_1 while the effect of the additional quasi-inside money shifts the supply of money function from SM_0 to SM_1. The interest rate is reduced from i_0 to i_1.

The liquidity preference model is not a theory of aggregate economic activity because it does not explain the level of output and income in the real sector of the economy. In fact, it requires the level of real income to determine the demand for money and thus the interest rate in the monetary

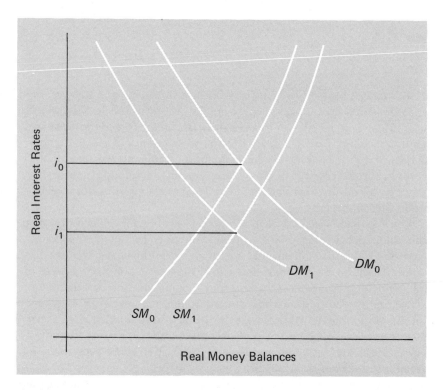

Figure 14–7
Impact of Saving and Loan Script

sector. Since our earlier discussion of investment demand in Chapter 8 has shown the interest rate to be an important determinant of investment demand and, via the multiplier, total income, it is clear that the determination of Y requires the determination of the interest rate. Accordingly, our discussion has indicated a circular dependence of Y and i upon each other. The solution of this problem and the joining of the real goods and money market models is the subject of the next chapter. However, we need not confront these complexities in order to consider a monetary model that does explain the level of income. The quantity theory provides such a model.

The Quantity Theory

The essential ingredients of the quantity theory of money date back to classical economics and the identity of exchange. That identity is an accounting proposition as follows:

$$(SM)(V) = (P)(Y_r) \qquad\qquad (14\text{--}9)$$

where SM is the supply of money as before; V is the income velocity of money, i.e., the number of times a dollar is earned as income in a period of time; P is the general level of prices; and Y_r is the level of real income/output in the economy. The left-hand side of Expression 14–9 measures total nominal income to be the product of the supply of money and the number of times this stock of money turns over as income. The right-hand side of Expression 14–9 shows nominal income as the product of real income and an index of general prices. The two sides of the identity are quite clearly alternative ways of looking at the same level of nominal income and must be equal by definition.

Expression 14–9 proposes no behavioral propositions about the workings of the economy. However, if key assumptions are made about patterns of fluctuation in one or more of the four variables involved, the identity then begins to yield predictions about resulting aggregate behavior of the economy and becomes a simple economic model. The older quantity theory made two such assumptions:

(1) that the income velocity of money, V, is likely to be approximately stable over short-run periods, since it is seen as largely resulting from patterns of household money holdings, pay periods, and other factors of a largely fixed institutional nature.

(2) that inherent technological forces in the economy are the root determinants of real output, normally causing the level of real output, Y_r, to reach an equilibrium that is independent of SM, V, or P. Therefore, Y_r can be assumed to be approximately fixed relative to these other variables.

These two assumptions transform the identity of 14–9 into a simple monetary model of price behavior, which is often referred to as the crude quantity theory. With V and Y_r assumed essentially exogenous, changes in the money supply produce proportional changes in price levels. That is, if we fix the values of V and Y_r in 14–9, then changes in SM and changes in P must correspond in order to preserve the accounting identity. The outcome is unambiguous. Increases in the money supply cause the prices on goods and services to be bid up, whereas decreases in the money supply produce lower prices. A stable money supply means stable prices. Quite clearly, the crude quantity theory implies a powerful role for monetary policy in influencing general price levels.

The second assumption of the crude quantity theory, that real income is independent of the money supply, prices, and velocity, has been found to be unappealing to many economists, both on intuitive and empirical grounds. If it is dropped, the quantity theory is revised but not done away with altogether. If we retain the first assumption of the crude quantity theory, the identity of 14–9 becomes a simple monetary theory of nominal income rather than prices. In this revised version, the remaining assumption of an approximately constant velocity of money leads to the conclusion that changes in the money supply produce proportionate changes in $(P)(Y_r)$, which is the level of nominal income. Thus, the revised quantity theory states that the ultimate and primary determinant of the level of nominal GNP is the money supply. This conclusion suggests that in a world that follows the revised quantity theory, monetary policy will have pivotal and potent effects upon the nominal GNP and that other phenomena such as consumer saving ratios, business expectations, government spending, and tax changes are not likely to have much of an ultimate effect on nominal GNP except to perhaps influence its composition. The boldness and simplicity of such a conclusion and the resulting policy prescriptions make the applicability of the quantity theory assumptions to the U.S. economy a provocative if not readily answerable question.

The empirical validity of the conclusions of the revised quantity theory rests upon two assumptions about aggregate economic behavior. As already indicated, the first is that the income velocity of money is approximately constant for short-run periods. Since

$$(SM)(V) = (P)(Y_r) = \text{GNP}$$

and

$$V = \text{GNP}/SM \qquad\qquad (14\text{--}10)$$

this is equivalent to the assumption that the ratio of nominal GNP to the money supply is approximately constant over time. The second crucial assumption is that the direction of association runs from the money supply to the GNP and not the other way.

Both these questions are difficult to answer by reference to simple his torical data. However, some impressions on the constancy of the velocity of money over time can be gained by inspecting its recent pattern in the United States. Figure 14–8 shows the quarterly movement in velocity as defined by

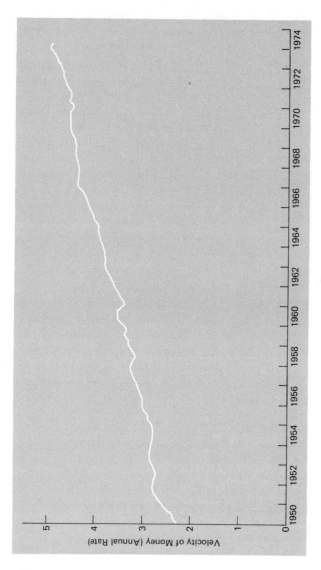

Figure 14–8

Velocity of Money

Expression 14–10. As this figure shows, the velocity has been in somewhat of an upward trend over the period 1950–1973 and has shown rather mild appearing deviations from this trend in general. However, we should take the appearance of Figure 14–8 with a grain of salt. For a money supply of 250 billion and a velocity of 4.5 (both approximately representatives of early 1970s data), an increase of only 0.1 in velocity to a value of 4.6 raises the associated GNP from 1,125 billion to 1,150 billion, an increase of 25 billion. Thus, entirely normal fluctuations in velocity may associate with noticeable and consequential fluctuations in nominal income over the short-run. At the same time, if we take a long-run view of the pattern of velocity in Figure 14–8, the deviations from the trend are not substantial when balanced over periods of several years in length. Accordingly, a substantial pattern of stability is suggested over long-run periods.

Milton Friedman, a contemporary proponent of the conclusions of the revised quantity theory, and a coworker, Anna Schwartz, have presented and commented upon a large amount of historical data bearing on the relevance of the revised quantity theory's assumptions using annual data in the United States from the period 1867–1960.[5] In this analysis, the authors take an extremely long-run view of the question, focusing on movements over 5 and 10 year periods and giving little attention to the short-run patterns of velocity over the period.

On the stability of the velocity of money, Friedman and Schwartz reported that the only substantial fluctuations about the trend over this long time period were associated with depressions of a severe nature or extreme price fluctuations. In general, they concluded that velocity had shown a systematic and stable pattern of variation about its long-run trend.[6] On the associated relationship between movements in the money supply and movements in aggregate business activity, the authors reported similar conclusions. They reported on having found a largely stable relationship, with disruptions associated primarily with severe business fluctuations.[7]

On the second assumption about the direction of effect between money and economic activity, their conclusion is

> The close relation between changes in the stock of money and changes in other economic variables, alone, tells nothing about the origin of either or the direction of influence. The monetary changes might be dancing to the tune called by independently originating changes in the other economic variables; the changes in income and prices might be dancing to the tune called by independently originating monetary changes; the two might be mutually

[5] See M. Friedman and A. Schwartz, *A Monetary History of the United States, 1867–1960,* Princeton University Press, Princeton, N.J., 1963.
[6] See Friedman and Schwartz, pp. 681–682.
[7] Friedman and Schwartz, p. 682.

interacting, each having some element of independence; or both might be dancing to the common tune of still a third set of influences. A great merit of the examination of a wide range of qualitative evidence, so essential in a monetary history, is that it provides a basis for discriminating between these possible explanations of the observed statistical covariation. We can go beyond the numbers alone and, at least on some occasions, discern the antecedent circumstances whence arose the particular movements that become so anonymous when we feed the statistics into the computer.

One thing is abundantly clear from our narrative. Monetary changes have in fact often been independent, in the sense that they have often not been an immediate or necessary consequence of contemporaneous changes in business conditions." [8]

In support of this conclusion of independence in monetary variables, Friedman and Schwartz's narrative discusses the specific social, political, and economic circumstances existing at the time of all major cyclical changes in money and in economic activity. In these circumstances, the authors saw evidence suggesting that money initiated the major economic cycles of the post-Civil War U.S. economy. Therefore, they affirmed the appropriateness of the second major assumption of quantity theory.

The case presented by Friedman and Schwartz in 1963 for the empirical significance of a quantity theory-type role of the money supply in influencing economic activity has evoked considerable reaction of both a positive and negative nature. On the positive side, Friedman initiated a new school of monetarists who essentially hold the view that fluctuations in the money supply are the essential, perhaps even the exclusive, exogenous factor in aggregate economic fluctuations. On the negative side, the conclusiveness of Friedman's evidence regarding the reasonableness of the quantity theory has been questioned on several counts. A principal line of objection is that the statistical association observed between money supply and economic activity only represents the joint movement of two truly endogenous variables —the GNP and the money supply. In other words, this comment rejects the arguments of Friedman and Schwartz that money supply changes typically occur independently of GNP change and initiate changes in the economy. Rather, proponents suggest that changes in the demand deposit portion of the money supply occur concurrently and more or less routinely as bank lending (typically facilitated by demand deposit creation) adjusts to changing levels of general economic activity and demand for money capital. This view holds that money supply changes and GNP changes are measures of two facets of the same underlying economic forces.[9] However,

[8] Friedman and Schwartz, p. 686.

[9] An illustrative study that presents evidence on the endogenous nature of the money supply in the United States is by Patrick Hendershott, *The Neutralized Money Stock*, Richard D. Irwin, Inc., Homewood, Ill., 1968.

conclusive proof of the exogenous or endogenous nature of an economic variable is nearly impossible to quantitatively establish, so that understandably the empirical evidence that has appeared bearing on the endogenous nature of the money supply has evoked a stream of counterclaims. Research into effects of the money supply has also taken the direction of evaluating the extent to which Keynesian type autonomous expenditures affect GNP through the multiplier as opposed to Friedman type money supply measures through the quantity theory framework. This research has been fraught with measurement problems and has not produced clear results. Other research aimed at comparing the relative stability over time of the velocity of money as compared to the Keynesian multiplier has attempted to establish the strengths of one or the other as a guide to application of economic policy. This work has also produced somewhat inconclusive results.

Interest Rates and the Quantity Theory

The revised quantity theory offers an explanation of nominal income determination that does not depend on the interest rate. In contrast, in the Keynesian model the interest rate is jointly determined with the level of income due to the impact of rates on the level of investment. A falling interest rate brings about higher levels of investment while a rising rate produces lower investment, with the level of consumer spending essentially unchanged. Investment in the quantity theory is assumed to be the same downward sloping function of the interest rate that characterizes the Keynesian model. However, consumer spending in the quantity theory is assumed to depend in an important way upon the rate of interest as well as upon income levels, due to the role of interest rates in motivating greater saving as discussed in Chapter 6. Higher interest rates draw out more saving by consumers while lower rates produce less saving and more consumption. The effect of interest rates on consumer spending in the quantity theory provides an offset to the effect of interest rates on investment. The result of this combined effect is that interest rates govern the composition of income into consumption and investment, but not the total level of income. Furthermore, interest rates are determined by the interaction of real income levels and saving and investment preferences in the economy. More specifically, a condition of greater (lesser) demand for investment funds than the available saving flow creates upward (downward) pressures on the interest rate.

Figure 14–9 depicts the situation for the case where the income level is held constant. In this figure, the supply of saving curve, S_0, is similar in concept to the marginal cost of capital (MCC) curve developed in Chapter

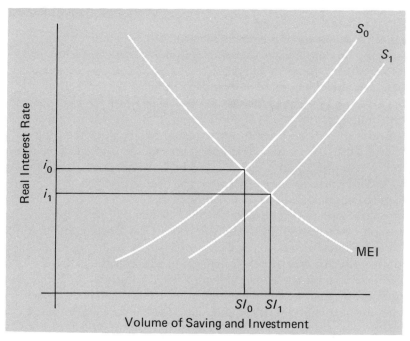

Figure 14–9

Interest Rates in the Quantity Theory

8. The MCC curve was seen to be a function of interest rates, through the effect of interest rates on the weighted average cost of capital. Given this interpretation of the S_0 curve in Figure 14–9, investment is assumed to be driven to equality with the interest rate in the same manner as in the case of the earlier more specific MCC function. The S_0 function represents total consumer, business, and other saving. On the part of business, internally generated cash flow represents saving that normally is allocated to new investment. In fact, Chapter 8 has shown that corporate saving usually amounts to about 80 percent of total new investment capital raised. For consumers, saving is simply nonconsumer spending. Thus, a normal composition of the equilibrium level of new capital, denoted as SI_0 in Figure 14–9, is roughly equal to 80 percent business saving and 20 percent consumer saving.[10] The

[10] Two more possible types of saving can be envisioned. The first is by governments. When a government surplus is incurred, the government is a net saver and funds are supplied to capital markets. The second type of saving is due to the international sector. When a deficit is incurred in the balance of payments, saving flows to the international sector can be made available to U.S. capital markets by Eurodollar borrowing. In our analysis, we focus on the business and consumer sectors as major suppliers of funds and treat the impact of government deficits and surpluses as positive or negative investment demand that adds or subtracts a constant amount from the investment demand function shown in Figure 14–9.

demand for investment funds is equal to the demand for new investment goods, assuming they must be purchased in capital goods markets. Our discussion of investment theory in Chapter 8 led to the development of the MEI function as a representation of investment demand. Accordingly, the interest i_0 in Figure 14–9 shows the rate of interest at which the demand for investment funds given by the MEI and the supply of investment funds given by S_0, are equal. If the interest rate were higher than i_0, more saving would be drawn into the capital markets than the amount demanded for investment. The excess supply of funds would lower the rate toward i_0. If the rate were lower than i_0, more funds would be demanded by the business sector than supplied, leading to a bidding up of the interest rate.

The crucial aspect of the equilibrium interest rate i_0 is that it exactly balances saving flows against investment demands. If the behavior of either consumers or business investors changes, the interest rate in the classical model adjusts in such a way that the composition of spending is altered while total income remains the same. Figure 14–9 illustrates this effect. Assume that consumers increase their propensity to save, similarly reducing their propensity to consume. The consumption function shifts down, while the saving function shifts up from position S_0 to S_1 in Figure 14–9. An excess supply of funds is now present in capital markets, reducing the interest rate to i_1. At this lower interest rate, an increased level of investment funds is generated and an increased level of investment undertaken from SI_0 to SI_1. The higher saving flow means an exactly offsetting lower level of consumption since income is fixed. Thus, the result of an increased tendency to save is a decreased level of consumption spending and an increased level of investment in exactly offsetting amounts. Similarly, if the investment demand function shifted outward, the resulting increase in the interest rate would draw out additional savings and reduce consumption, both of which accommodate the increased demand for investment goods.

An important distinction between the Keynesian and quantity theories of the interest rate is whether the interest rate is primarily the product of real market or monetary market influences. In liquidity preference theory, the interest rate is determined as a result of the demand to hold money balances and the supply of money balances. This model evolves from the monetary sector by relying upon preferences for money holdings to explain interest rates. In this sense, the liquidity preference model is a monetary explanation of interest rates. The quantity theory explanation of interest rates relies upon the demand and supply of money capital to explain rates. The supply function reflects consumption and saving propensities, whereas the demand function is based on the preference to invest (MEI). Both these functions are real market behavioral functions. The two approaches are therefore rooted in different sectors of the economy. We shall explore implications of this distinction in more detail in later chapters.

The quantity theory now outlined is a highly simplified representation of the work of modern monetarist economists. We shall consider a further influence of monetarist ideas upon the basic macroeconomic model in the next several chapters when we consider complete macroeconomic models. At this point, we only note that the work of the new monetarists has produced an increased awareness among economists of the importance of money in affecting economic activity. Reliance on the interest rate effect upon investment expenditures to summarize the entire influence of monetary variables upon the aggregate goods market is becoming an increasingly deficient approach in integrating goods and money markets. As the funds flow analysis of the previous two chapters suggests, the impact of monetary flows upon economic activity is considerably more complicated than either the Keynesian liquidity preference mechanism can summarize through the interest rate or the quantity theory can summarize through the supply of money.

With the analysis of monetary models in this chapter, we have considered the essential ingredients in a complete macroeconomic model. In the next chapter we shall consider a complete macroeconomic model that incorporates both real and monetary sectors.

Discussion Questions

1. Describe in your own words the meaning of a positive shift in liquidity preference. What examples can you give of reasons why such a shift might occur?

2. Both the speculative demand for money function and the Baumol-Tobin model provide reasons why the interest rate is an important argument in the demand for money function. How does the role of each in the demand for money function differ? Explain.

3. Suppose the money supply is fixed and ceilings are in effect on interest rates at their present levels. Also suppose that supply equals demand for money balances. Now assume an increase in income occurs due to an increase in private demand. What would be the reaction in the monetary sphere? How would monetary equilibrium be reestablished?

4. Describe the mechanism in the quantity theory that causes the level of nominal income to be independent of the interest rate.

5. Summarize the differences in interest rate determination between the liquidity preference model and the quantity theory model. In each case, hold the level of income constant.

15

The Complete Macroeconomic Model

In this chapter, we assemble the results of the separate analyses of product market expenditures undertaken in Chapters 5–11 with the results of our analysis of monetary markets and activity undertaken in Chapters 12–14 to form a combined product and monetary market model of the economy. In this undertaking, we keep our discussion manageable by focusing on only the primary goods and money market variables considered earlier, omitting from explicit inclusion many of the factors brought out in our detailed discussions of each goods and monetary segment. This enables our analysis to proceed with a minimum of complications and introduces little loss in generality.

To begin, we recall that equilibrium in the economy's "real" markets (i.e., its markets for goods and services) has been described as a condition where the level of new income independent (autonomous) expenditures is sufficient to offset leakages of current income into savings. We now consider further this investment saving mechanism.

Investment Saving Equilibrium

The two principal sources of autonomous expenditures considered in our earlier three-sector model (Chapter 10) are private investment, I, and government spending, G, while the two sources of leakage are private saving, S, and government taxes, T. This gives the equilibrium condition

$$I + G = S + T \qquad (15\text{--}1)$$

For present purposes, we assume that investment expenditures are determined only by long-run profit expectations and by the impact of market interest rates on the marginal cost of funds. We assume for simplicity that long-run profit expectations are largely invariant with current conditions so that expectations are a factor in positioning the investment function but are not a variable in it for short-run analysis. This gives the investment demand function simply as

$$I = f(i) \qquad\qquad (15\text{--}2)$$

where i is the market interest rate.

This relationship is shown graphically in Figure 15–1 as the MEI function defined in Chapter 8. In Figure 15–1, all influences on investment beside the interest rate provide reasons for shifts in the function while changes in interest rates cause movements along the function. To illustrate, an upgrading by corporations of their projected business outlook shifts the curve in Figure 15–1 from MEI_0 to MEI_1, increasing the level of investment that associates with a given interest rate. We can incorporate an out-

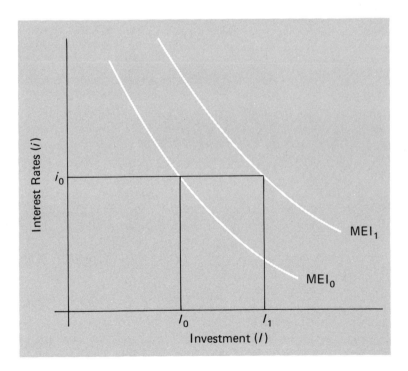

Figure 15–1
Investment Function

put accelerator effect into this scheme by recognizing that each position of the MEI associates with a particular income level. An increase in Y, say from Y_0 to Y_1, then shifts the MEI outward identically as in the case of the shift from MEI_0 to MEI_1 shown in Figure 15–1.

Government expenditures are assumed to be determined independently of income or other current variables, thereby assuming a strictly autonomous role in income determination. For convenience, government expenditures can be added as a constant to the investment demand function, MEI, giving the $I + G$ function shown in Figure 15–2. In fact, the $I + G$ schedule of Figure 15–2 is often interpreted as a single gross investment (public and private) schedule for purposes of broad economic analysis.

In Chapters 6 and 7, income was seen as a fundamental influence on consumer expenditures. At this point, we focus on income as *the* dominant variable in consumption, C, which yields the following simplified function

$$C = g(Y) \tag{15-3}$$

Since consumer saving, S_c, is defined as

$$S_c = Y - C$$

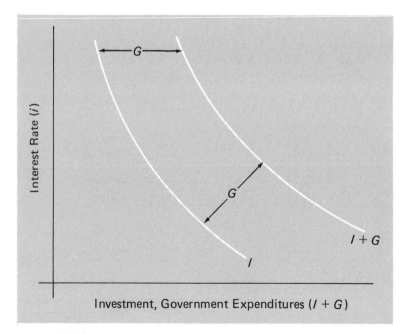

Figure 15–2
I + G Schedule

combining with Expression 15–3 gives

$$S_c = Y - g(Y) = h(Y) \qquad\qquad (15\text{–}4)$$

where the g and h notations mean unspecified but different functions of Y. Expression 15–4 illustrates that if consumption is a function of income, so is saving according to our definition. A representation of this saving function is depicted graphically in Figure 15–3. As seen, assuming a positive level of consumption expenditures at zero income implies that low (or zero) income levels will result in consumption expenditures that exceed income and, therefore, negative saving. At Y_0 in Figure 15–3, $C = Y$ so that $S_c = 0$. Beyond Y_0, positive levels of consumer saving occur.

Two other forms of saving flows can also be assumed to be sensitive to income levels. The first, business saving, consists of net retained earnings plus depreciation of business. Corporate sales and profits grow along with aggregate income, thus producing increased flows of corporate saving. To obtain a simple representation of this flow, we assume

$$S_b = j(Y) \qquad\qquad (15\text{–}5)$$

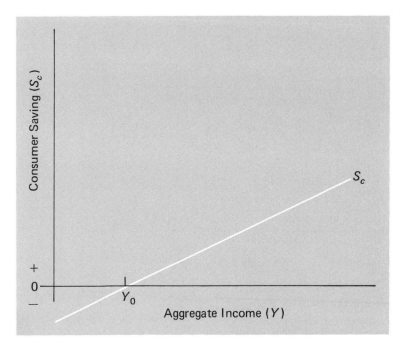

Figure 15–3

Aggregate Saving

As with consumer saving, we assume that very low levels of aggregate income will result in negative net retained earnings (after-tax, after-dividend losses), which could produce negative business saving. Thus, Expression 15–5 can be expected to have a similar shape to the S_c function depicted in Figure 15–3. Thus total private saving, S, is given by

$$S = S_c + S_b = j(Y) \qquad (15\text{–}6)$$

The final saving-type flow occurs by tax withdrawals. Considering both income and nonincome taxes and transfer payments (considered a negative tax), the level of taxes, T, after subtracting transfers), can be expressed as

$$T = k(Y) \qquad (15\text{–}7)$$

where nonincome taxes produce a positive intercept in this expression.

Taken together, the S and T flows constitute total leakages from the economy. They are added together forming an $S + T$ function in Figure

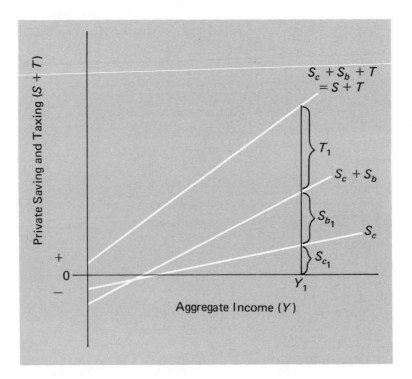

Figure 15–4
Saving and Taxing Flows

15–4. As seen, business saving can be expected to provide a negative addition to saving at extremely low income levels and a positive addition at high levels. On the other hand, net taxes can be expected to add positively to saving at all income levels, increasing as income increases. The composition of total $S + T$ flows can be seen by the vertical line drawn at Y_1, which shows S_{c_1} personal saving flow, S_{b_1} business saving flow, and T_1 tax flow.

The $I + G$ and $S + T$ functions now developed enable a statement of equilibrium in markets for goods and services. We may summarize the discussion this far by (15–8) and (15–9).

$$[I + G] = l(i) \qquad\qquad (15\text{–}8)$$

$$[S + T] = m(Y) \qquad\qquad (15\text{–}9)$$

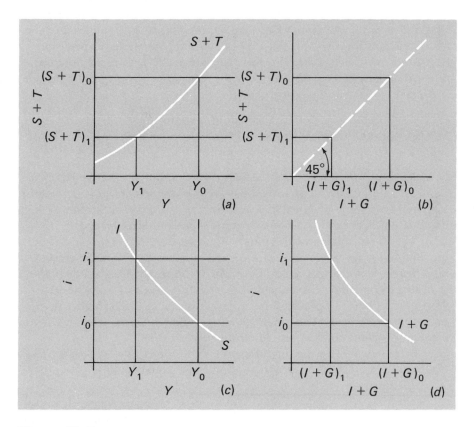

Figure 15–5

Investment-Saving Equilibrium

This means that selection of equalizing values of $I + G$ and $S + T$ involves both the interest rate and the level of aggregate income.

$$IS = n(i, Y) \qquad\qquad (15\text{--}10)$$

where IS means gross investment-gross saving equilibrium in markets for goods and services. This is shown graphically in Figure 15–5. Part (a) shows Expression 15–9, the $S + T$ function. Part (d) shows the $I + G$ function of Expression 15–8. The 45° line in part (b) is a simple way to graphically equate flows of $I + G$ with flows of $S + T$ or vice versa. $I + G$ values projected against a 45° line produce equal $S + T$ values, thereby producing equilibrium combinations of $I + G$ and $S + T$. The IS curve in part (c) depicts Expression 15–10. It contains interest rate-income combinations that each produce equal flows of $I + G$ and $S + T$. The IS curve is thus a locus of investment-saving equilibrium positions. To see this better, consider aggregate income level Y_0 in Figure 15–5. In part (a), Y_0 is seen to associate with a flow of private saving and taxes equal to $(S + T)_0$. In part (b), the associated equilibrating value of investment and government expenditures, $(I + G)_0$, is identified. Part (d) shows that, for $(I + G)_0$ to occur, interest rates would have to be i_0. Thus, the point on the IS curve in part (c) where $i = i_0$ and $Y = Y_0$ has the property that

(1) i_0 will associate with $(I + G)_0$ in gross investment
(2) Y_0 will result in gross leakages of $(S + T)_0$
(3) $(S + T)_0 = (I + G)_0$ producing equilibrium in goods markets

Other IS equilibrium points can be identified in a similar manner. For example, if interest rate i_1 prevails, then gross investment of $(I + G)_1$ results. This will be offset by an equal flow of saving, $(S + T)_1$ only at income Y_1. Thus, i_1 and Y_1 are consistent with investment-saving equilibrium.

The IS equilibrium curve slopes downward with increasing Y, implying that higher levels of equilibrium Y can only occur at lower interest rates, if no other changes occur. This conclusion results from the hypothesis that larger saving flows accompany higher income levels. These larger flows must be offset by greater flows of new investment for the higher income to be sustained. With other investment determinants unchanged, this higher investment flow requires lower interest rates.

Because it reflects the interaction of Expressions 15–8 and 15–9, the IS curve contains all the influences that affect those expressions.

To illustrate

1. An increase in government spending, by shifting the $I + G$ function to the right, shifts the IS function to the right.
2. An increase in personal taxes, which shifts the $S + T$ function up (assume a nonincome tax), shifts the IS curve back to the left.

3. A wave of consumer optimism, which decreases private saving as consumption expenditures increase, shifts the $S + T$ curve down. This shifts the IS curve out to the right.

4. A general feeling on the part of business that profit margins are going to be under heavy pressure in the upcoming time period lowers evaluations of return on new investment projects. New investment falls at existing interest rates. The $I + G$ curve shifts back to the left. Similarly, the IS curve shifts back to the left.

These illustrations make it clear that the IS curve summarizes a great deal of the substantive framework of our aggregate model. So much so that much of the usefulness of the IS framework for drawing general qualitative conclusions depends upon the perception of the user as to where behavioral and other shifts fit and, therefore, how they are translated into IS shifts. If anything, the apparent simplicity of the IS framework heightens rather than diminishes the need for understanding the underlying relationships.

The IS curve leaves us without an answer to the question, "What is equilibrium Y?" unless we already know i. In Chapter 14, the Keynesian liquidity preference model produced the conclusion that Y could be expected to exert an influence on i through the impact of Y upon the transactions demand for money. This indicates we cannot know i without knowing Y, i.e., i and Y are jointly determined. Thus, to complete our model, we need to develop a specific formulation of interest rate-income relationships underlying the supply and demand for money.

Monetary Equilibrium

The liquidity preference model discussed in Chapter 14 emphasized three crucial relationships, (1) the supply (stock) of money, (2) a pure transactions demand for money, and (3) an interest rate sensitive demand for money.

The supply of money, SM, is for now considered a product of Federal Reserve action and is thus taken as essentially autonomous at SM_0, giving

$$SM = SM_0 \qquad\qquad (15\text{--}11)$$

The transactions demand for money balances, TD, was seen in Chapter 14 to be principally determined by aggregate income levels, as

$$TD = p(Y) \qquad\qquad (15\text{--}12)$$

For now, we use the speculative demand function to incorporate the role of interest rates in the demand for money. Later, we shall explore the consequences of altering this assumption. The speculative demand for money,

SD, was earlier described as primarily a function of the interest rate

$$SD = q(i) \qquad\qquad (15\text{–}13)$$

These two expressions indicate that the total demand for money holdings, *DM*, is a joint product of income levels and interest rates. Equilibrium in money markets has been described as the condition where the level of income and interest rates equate the demand for money with the supply. We can describe money market equilibrium, *LM*, as

$$LM = r(Y, i) \qquad\qquad (15\text{–}14)$$

This expression can be examined in more detail by reference to the graphic model in Figure 15–6, which incorporates Expressions 15–11 through 15–14. In Figure 15–6(*a*), the transactions demand is shown rising in proportion to income increases. In (*d*), the speculative demand for money balances is shown as an inverse function of interest rates, according to our earlier discussion. The 45° line in Figure 15–6(*b*) incorporates the assumptions of (1) a fixed money supply and (2) an equilibrium condition in money markets where $SM = DM$. The first of these assumptions is represented by the fixed value marked off on both horizontal and vertical axes (labeled SM_0). If *SM* were not fixed, as discussed in Chapter 14, then it would be shown as a function of interest rates and denoted as $SM(i_0)$, $SM(i_1)$, and so forth. The equilibrium condition is illustrated by the 45° line due to the projection of transactionary and speculative demands on vertical and horizontal axes. For a given transactionary demand, say TD_0, projection to the 45° line produces a value of speculative demand, SD_0, which just absorbs the remainder of *SM*, and illustrates a monetary condition where demand equals supply, i.e., the condition $TD_0 + SD_0 = DM_0 = SM_0$. The mechanics of this process can be seen by noting that the length of the line segment $0\text{–}TD_0$ in (*b*) is the same as the length $SD_0\text{–}B$. Since the line is 45°, this distance $SD_0\text{–}B$ is equal to the distance $SD_0\text{–}MS_0$. This leaves $0\text{–}SD_0$ as the resulting speculative demand, which, when added to TD_0 just equals MS_0.

Combining the relationships in (*a*), (*b*), and (*d*) enables construction of the *LM* function in (*c*). For example, income level Y_0 produces a transactions demand for money holdings TD_0 in (*a*). Given this demand and the constant supply of money, SM_0, Figure 15–6(*b*) illustrates that $SD_0 = (SM_0 - TD_0)$ is available for speculative money holdings. The liquidity preference function in (*d*) indicates that holdings of SD_0 in speculative accounts is consistent with an interest rate of i_0. Thus, the income and interest rate combination Y_0, i_0 produces a level of transactionary and speculative demand for money holdings that just exhausts the stock of money and produces money market equilibrium. If aggregate income is increased, say to Y_1, then more money is required for transactionary purposes ($\Delta TD = TD_1 - TD_0$). With a constant money supply, this increment of funds will

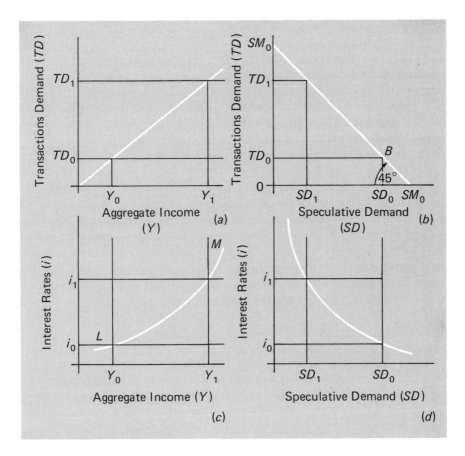

Figure 15-6

Money Market Equilibrium

have to come from speculative balances, which will be reduced by ΔTD through rising interest rates. Thus, a second combination wherein the total demand for money holdings equals the supply is Y_1, i_1. The LM function in (c) represents a locus of possible income interest rate combinations that produce monetary equilibrium.

The positive slope of the LM function illustrates that higher interest rates can be expected to accompany higher income/output levels in the economy if the money supply is kept constant. This is a result of the higher transactionary demand that accompanies higher income levels, which can only be brought into circulation through higher interest rates.

Changes in either the money supply, the determinants of transactions money demand, or the determinants of speculative money demand will alter the position of the LM function. For example

1. If the money supply increases (shifting the 45° line in Figure 15-6(b) to the right), either (a) a higher level of aggregate income can be supported

by a given interest rate, or (b) a given income level associates with a lower interest rate. The *LM* curve shifts down to the right.

2. A trend toward more credit card purchases reduces the need for transactionary balances. The slope of the transactionary demand function in Figure 15–6(*a*) is reduced. This produces additional money available for speculative balances, which reduces interest rates. The *LM* function shifts down to the right.

3. A general wave of bearish pessimism in the economy causes holders of speculative money balances to feel "normal" expected yields on securities are rising (normal expected prices of securities are falling). Thus, existing yields on securities are increasingly viewed as low (prices too high) resulting in an attempt to build liquidity balances. In Figure 15–6(*d*), the result would be a shift in the liquidity preference function out to the right, as more money would be sought for speculative cash holdings. As a result, the *LM* function would shift back to the left.

General Equilibrium

Both real market and monetary equilibria have now been described as functions of interest rates and income levels. As Figure 15–7 illustrates,

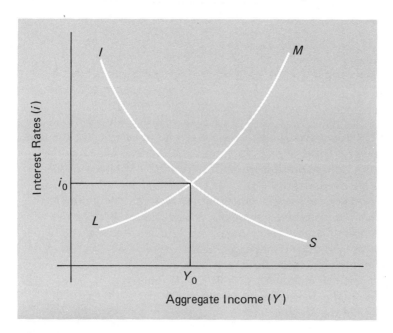

Figure 15–7

General Equilibrium

their interplay produces a unique interest and income rate level, i_0 and Y_0, consistent with equilibrium and stability in both markets. This combination produces equal flows of gross saving and investment in the economy's real markets while at the same time producing demands for money holdings equal to the supply in the economy's monetary markets.

The *IS–LM* framework provides a tool for analyzing the overall economic impact of changes originating in either monetary or goods markets. For example, consider an increase in new plant and equipment expenditures touched off by an upgrading in the business outlook. As illustrated in Figure 15–8(a), the impact is an outward shift in the *IS* function to *I'S'*. Aggregate income is increased toward Y_2. However, as income is increased the increased transactionary demand for money begins to drive up interest rates and reduce the increase in *Y*. In Figure 15–8(a), this process produces a new equilibrium at i_1 and Y_1, involving both a higher income level and a higher level of interest rates.

As shown in the figure by the dotted lines, the maximum multiplier effect associated with the shift to *I'S'* occurs only if i_0 remains constant. However, with increased transactions demand, preserving interest rates at i_0 requires an increase in the money supply (or a decrease in liquidity preference) sufficient to provide for the increased transactions. In the illustration, a money supply increase sufficient to shift the *LM* function to *L'M'* would be required to keep *i* from rising. This monetary expansion is thereby required to produce the full multiplier effect of the initial shift (from Y_0 to Y_2). Thus, when goods and money markets are viewed together, the value of the effective goods market multiplier is seen to depend on monetary changes. Indeed, the impact of a shift in the *IS* function similar to that shown in Figure 15–8(a) could conceivably even be totally nullified by counteracting monetary changes (such as decreasing the money supply), which would shift the *LM* function back to the left.

As a second illustration of the use of *IS–LM* analysis, consider the effect of a continued Federal Reserve policy of net open market sales of securities, which extract reserves from the economy and contract the stock of available money. As Figure 15–8(b) shows, the impact is a leftward shift in the *LM* function to *L'M'*. This puts pressure on existing cash holdings and drives up rates of interest. Increased interest rates motivate a cutback in investment expenditures, which in turn reduces aggregate income. As illustrated by the new equilibrium i_1 and Y_1, the result is higher interest rates and lower income levels.

The effects of governmental fiscal and monetary policy are rather neatly differentiated in the *IS–LM* framework. Fiscal policy actions such as tax changes, transfer payment changes, or changes in government expenditures, all affect general economic conditions through the *IS* mechanism, which transmits effects to the monetary sector. Monetary policy actions such as open market policy, reserve requirement changes, or discount rate

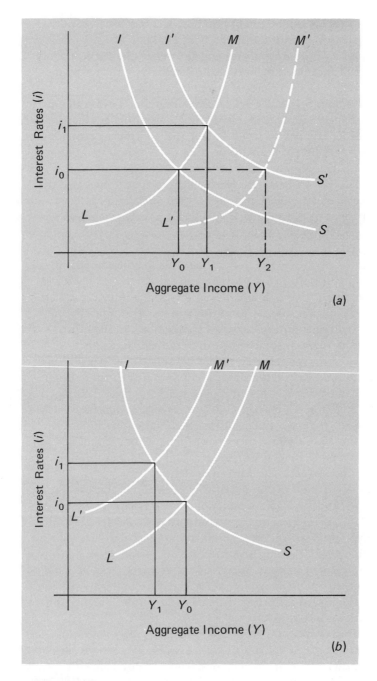

Figure 15–8
Shifts-General Equilibrium

changes, affect the economy through the *LM* mechanism, which transmits effects to real markets. Ultimately, either fiscal or monetary policy actions by governments that shift the *IS* or *LM* curves have an impact on both interest rates and levels of aggregate income/output. Therefore, we cannot assume that monetary policy changes will affect only money markets and fiscal policy will only affect production of goods and aggregate incomes.

The Quantity Theory and Keynesian Regions

The extent to which monetary and fiscal actions are alternative policy tools in their aggregate economic effects depends upon the tightness or looseness of money market conditions and the level of interest rates. To better understand this statement, we need to take a closer look at the extreme ranges of the *LM* function. In Figure 15–9, the probable appearance of

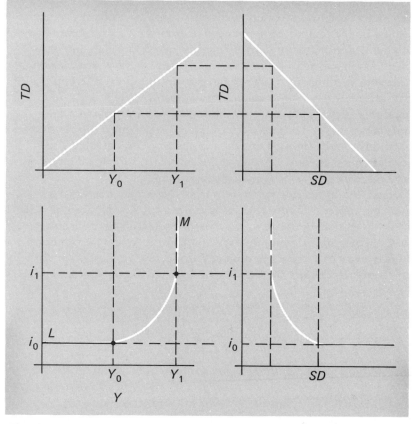

Figure 15–9
Keynesian and Quantity Theory Ranges

the *LM* function is shown in extreme regions of very high interest rates and very low interest rates. Below some very low interest rate, i_0, the economy's liquidity preference may be expected to become nearly absolute, producing a flat *LM* function. In this region, further additions to money holdings will have no effect on interest rates. Yields are so low on financial instruments that holders of cash balances ignore these rates, preferring nearly complete liquidity. Prevailing interest rates are so low that they do not provide a minimum reward for the risk and/or inconvenience of investing temporary idle balances. The flat portion of the liquidity preference function is similarly imparted to the *LM* function. At interest rate i_θ, the mechanism that translates money supply increases into interest rate decreases breaks down, as additions to the stock of money flow into idle balances with little economic impact. Keynes called this phenomenon the liquidity trap. We shall refer to it as the Keynesian region of interest rates.

At extremely high interest rates, say above i_1 in Figure 15–9, yields on financial instruments are so high that most cash holdings have been driven to minimum levels. Only extremely pessimistic speculative holdings remain, which would not be committed to financial instruments at any interest rate. Thus, above i_1, money holdings are no longer reduced by higher interest rates. The *LM* curve takes on a similar vertical shape. This vertical region is characterized by an insensitivity of aggregate output to the interest rate. Aggregate output levels are influenced only by factors changing the *LM* curve such as changes in the supply of money. In fact, above i_1, changes in the supply of money can be expected to produce proportional output changes (as the *LM* shifts to the right). This result is similar to that of the revised quantity theory discussed in Chapter 14. Accordingly, we label the region of interest rates above i_1 as the quantity theory range.

The extreme interest rate conditions we have now identified as Keynesian and quantity theory regions have practical significance only when investment-savings relationships in markets for goods and services actually produce those extreme interest rates. We now consider economic conditions that we may expect to cause the economy to operate in Keynesian and quantity theory regions and the significance attached to these conditions.

Operating in the Keynesian Region

Interest rates may be pushed to extraordinarily low levels by

(1) a collapse in new investment, government, and/or consumption expenditures such that a sharp decrease in the transactions demand for money holdings occurs, thus producing excess money balances.

(2) a sharp and continued increase in the money supply, which produces excess speculative balances.

(3) some combination of the two.

As illustrated by the *IS–LM* framework in Figure 15–10, any of these conditions would cause the *LM* curve to shift to the right relative to the *IS* curve. If such a shift were sufficiently pronounced, it would produce equilibrium in the lower left-hand portion of the *LM* curve. In the United States, the Great Depression of the 1930s produced a sharp collapse in business investment coupled with a sharp contraction in aggregate income and consumer expenditures. The latter portion of the period, from 1935 to 1941, was also characterized by a substantial rate of increase in the money supply. These relationships are shown in Table 15–1. Both short-term and long-term market rates of interest are shown for government and private debt instruments. While long-term rates represent the effective cost of new public and private debt, short-term rates better reflect current supply-demand conditions in money markets.

As Table 15–1 shows, the money supply jumped rather sharply from slightly under 20 billion in 1933 to close to 30 billion in 1936. During this

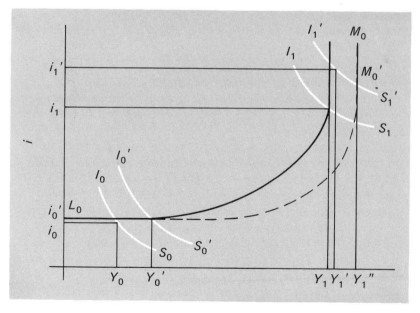

Figure 15–10

Policy Effects in Extreme Ranges of LM Curve

Table 15–1

Security Yields and Money Supply   1931–1941

| Year | SHORT-TERM YIELDS | | LONG-TERM YIELDS | | MONEY SUPPLY |
	3 Month U.S. Treasury Notes	*Prime 4–6 Month Commercial Paper*	*3–5 Year Government Bonds*	*Corporate Bonds Moody's Aaa*	*Currency Plus Demand Deposits (Billions)*
1931	1.40%	2.64%	n.a.	4.58%	23.6*
1932	0.88	2.73	n.a.	5.01	20.6
1933	0.52	1.73	2.66%	4.49	19.6
1934	0.26	1.02	2.12	4.00	21.5
1935	0.14	0.75	1.29	3.60	25.5
1936	0.14	0.75	1.11	3.24	29.2
1937	0.45	0.94	1.40	3.26	30.3
1938	0.05	0.81	0.83	3.19	30.0
1939	0.02	0.59	0.59	3.01	33.6
1940	0.01	0.56	0.50	2.84	39.0
1941	0.10	0.53	0.73	2.77	45.8

* Data are yearly averages of monthly data.

Source: For yields; *Economic Report of the President, 1970.* For money supply; M. Friedman and A. Schwartz, *A Monetary History of the United States*, Princeton University Press, Princeton, N.J., 1963, Appendix A: Table A–1.

period, short-term interest rates dropped from about 1/2 percent to slightly less than 1/6 percent on government short-term issues and from about 1 3/4 percent to 3/4 percent on private short-term issues. Long-term governments fell from 2 2/3 percent to about 1 1/10 percent while corporate bonds fell from about 4 1/2 percent to 3 1/4 percent. By 1938, the subsequent expansion in the money supply coupled with continued weakness in the economy's markets for goods and services quite possibly brought the economy to the proximity of the Keynesian region. For between 1938 and 1941, the money supply was expanded from 30 billion to over 45 billion, a 50 percent advance. Yet, short-term government yields stood in 1941 at somewhat higher levels than their incredible 0.05 percent of 1938. While private short-term notes fell from 0.81 percent to 0.53 percent, the decline in 3–5 year governments was only minor, from 0.83 percent to 0.73 percent as was the drop in yields on corporate bonds from 3.19 percent to 2.77 percent. While crude (we have taken no account of goods market influences on interest rates), the evidence of Table 15–1 is indicative of conditions associated with the Keynesian range, and it suggests that, practically speaking, we may anticipate operation of the economy in this range primarily during major economic contractions that are accompanied by significant expansions in the money supply. It is hard to conceive of U.S. monetary authorities expanding the money supply sufficiently under other than severe recessionary conditions to reach the Keynesian range and equally difficult to see how recessionary or depressionary conditions alone could move the economy into the Keynesian range without monetary expansion.

The impact of fiscal and monetary policy upon the economy is importantly affected by whether or not the economy is in the Keynesian range, as illustrated by the *IS–LM* model in Figure 15–10. In that figure, if the *IS* function is positioned at I_0S_0, an increase in government expenditures or a decrease in taxes that shifts the *IS* curve to $I_0'S_0'$ will have an expansionary effect on the economy without increasing interest rates, as additional transactionary funds will be drawn from saturated speculative balances. In contrast, money supply expansions in the Keynesian range, which shift the *LM* curve from L_0M_0 to L_0M_0', fall into speculative cash balances with little effect on either aggregate income or interest rates. Thus, if the economy is in the Keynesian range, fiscal policy can be expected to be quite effective in bringing about aggregate output and income increases, while monetary policy can be expected to be largely ineffective in increasing aggregate income.

Operating in the Quantity Theory Region

The quantity theory region is characterized by extremely tight monetary conditions and abnormally high interest rates. As this region is approached, speculative money holdings are reduced to minimum levels, as remaining holders of speculative balances no longer respond to changes in interest rates.

For the economy to operate in this range, money must be extremely scarce relative to the level of economic activity. This can logically come about through some combination of (1) a contraction in the stock of money and (2) an expansion in aggregate income/output, which increases demands for transactionary balances. In the United States, extreme tightness in monetary conditions, coupled with expansionary conditions in goods markets, has generally occurred when the economy was operating at over-full employment conditions. Stringent monetary conditions have usually been produced to deal with a superheated economy. Therefore, for practical purposes, the quantity theory range has probably been most closely approximated in a fully utilized, rapidly growing economy (usually accompanied by high inflation) in which monetary authorities are following highly restrictive policies. The first three quarters of 1969 in the United States offer a recent example suggestive of the approximate conditions we have outlined. Monetary policy had been following a strategy of measured tightness over the previous year or so, which had drained reserves from banks and produced net free reserves by banks of −480 million in January 1969 (net borrowed reserves) as compared with +144 million a year earlier. As 1969 opened, little slack remained in the financial system. Then, with current dollar GNP rising by 5.6 percent in the first three quarters of the year, the money supply was allowed to grow by only 2.6 percent, from 198.1 billion in January to 203.2 billion in October. Table 15–2 shows the effects on short-term and long-term interest rates before, during, and after this period. As seen, both short-term and long-term rates on government and private debt rose sharply from January to October of 1969. As the fourth quarter of that year opened, the continued high interest rates and restricted money supply choked off further real growth in the GNP, although inflation caused the current dollar amount to inch ahead.

Returning to the *IS–LM* diagram of Figure 15–10, the type of situation we have described is illustrated by the upper right-hand portion of the curve. With *IS* at I_1S_1, aggregate income of Y_1 and interest rate of i_1 results. If demand increases in goods markets, either through private or governmental expenditure increases, the increase is largely choked off by monetary limitations.

Additional money cannot be drawn from speculative balances as they are at minimum levels and have become insensitive to prevailing interest rates. Thus, in the quantity theory region, growth in aggregate income is

Table 15–2

Security Yields and Money Supply   1968–1970

		3 MONTH TREASURY BILLS	PRIME COMMERCIAL PAPER—4–6 MONTHS	U.S. GOVERNMENT SECURITIES— 3–5 YEAR	CORPORATE BONDS— MOODY'S Aaa	CURRENCY DEMAND DEPOSITS (BILLIONS)
1968	Jan	5.08%	5.60%	5.53%	6.17	183.6
	Apr	5.37	5.81	5.69	6.21	186.6
	July	5.38	6.19	5.44	6.24	191.6
	Oct	5.33	5.80	5.42	6.09	194.3
1969	Jan	6.18	6.53	6.04	6.59	198.1
	Apr	6.15	7.04	6.15	6.89	201.0
	July	7.00	8.65	7.02	7.08	203.1
	Oct	7.04	8.57	7.47	7.33	203.2
1970	Jan	7.91	8.78	8.14	7.91	205.2
	Apr	6.48	8.06	7.49	7.83	208.3
	July	6.47	8.29	7.58	8.44	210.6
	Oct	5.93	6.85	7.06	8.03	213.0

effectively constrained by the supply of money. Increases in the money supply shift the *LM* curve down to the right and produce a nearly proportional effect upon output.

When the economy approaches the quantity theory region, fiscal policy has little effect on output while monetary policy has a large effect. As illustrated in Figure 15–10 by the shift from I_1S_1 to $I_1'S_1'$ or vice versa, either expansionary or (more likely) contractionary fiscal policy is absorbed by the monetary limitations of the fixed money supply. Expansionary (or contractionary) monetary policy that shifts the *LM* curve to L_0M_0' (or from L_0M_0' to L_0M_0) has a large output effect. This result is just the opposite of that obtained when the economy is in the Keynesian range, and it suggests that when dealing with a high interest rate overheated economy in the quantity theory range, contradictory fiscal policy can be expected basically to reduce interest rates while contractionary monetary policy can be expected to reduce output levels.

The *IS–LM* Model with No Speculative Demand

The model now developed jointly explains the interest rate, the level of income, and the levels of consumption and investment under the assumptions that a speculative demand for money function is present and that the supply of money is constant and given by the Federal Reserve. We now consider the implications for the conclusions of the *IS–LM* model of one or both of these assumptions being altered. We consider three cases: (1) the money supply is fixed and no interest rate sensitive demand for money exists; (2) the money supply is a function of the interest rate, and no interest rate sensitive demand for money exists; and (3) the money supply is fixed, no speculative demand for money exists, but the transactions demand is sensitive to the interest rate.

Case 1—Interest Rates Don't Count

In the case where the money supply is fixed in an absolute way by the Federal Reserve (say through 100 percent reserve requirements so that outside money equals total money), the occurrence of higher interest rates cannot draw forth more efficient or more complete use of reserves in the banking system. This is the circumstance we have dealt with so far in this chapter. In addition, if the demand for money is not sensitive to the interest rate due to the breakdown of a systematic speculative demand for money function, then the demand for money is given entirely by the transactions demand, while the supply of money is fixed. Fluctuations in interest rates have no impact on the demand for money or upon monetary equilibrium in the absence of income changes.

Figure 15–11 shows the effect of this condition on the *IS–LM* scheme. Part (*b*) shows the absence of a speculative demand function. The entire demand for money flows into transactions balances. Thus, at a money supply of SM_0, the income level Y_0 is the point where all money balances are absorbed into transactions accounts. It is the only equilibrium income level possible. The *LM* curve is vertical, exactly as in the case of the classical range. The consequences of a vertical *LM* function are identical to operating in the classical range, as illustrated in (*a*). A shift in the *IS* from its original position at I_0S_0 to I^*S^* due to an increased demand for goods and services in the real sector does not draw forth additional real output/income in the absence of an accompanying increase in the money supply. Interest rates rise to i^*, motivating a reduction in investment to accommodate the additional demand, but bringing about no change in the total level of Y. By contrast, if the money supply is increased, from SM_0 to SM_1, the rightward shift in the *LM* function results in an increase in real income from Y_0 to Y_1, while reducing interest rates from i_0 to i_1. Monetary expansion or contraction exclusively determines real output, while shifts in public or private demand that shift the *IS* curve only impact upon interest rates—the same results given by the quantity theory in the previous chaper. Thus, under the conditions describing Case 1, the *IS–LM* model and the quantity theory are virtually identical. This result has important implications, because it shows that differences in the conclusions flowing from the Keynesian and Quantity Theory Models appear because of the interest rate sensitivity of the demand for money. If the demand for money is not sensitive to the interest rate, macroeconomic predictions are virtually unaffected by choice of either Keynesian or Quantity Theory models.

Case 2—Nonvertical LM Due to Banks

We now consider the case where no speculative demand for money exists, but where the supply of money is at least to some degree responsive to the interest rate. This latter possibility was discussed in the previous chapter as being a result of the premise that banks can find ways to muster more reserves and make more efficient use of existing reserves when higher interest rates occur than when rates are lower. The result is an upward sloping supply of money function for a given level of outside money.

Figure 15–12 shows the effect of this case on the *LM* function and on general equilibrium. In (*b*), we again have no speculative demand for money function. However, the money supply increases with increasing interest rates up to the point where the banking system is fully and efficiently using all reserves. Thus, for interest rate i_0, the supply of money is given by SM_0,

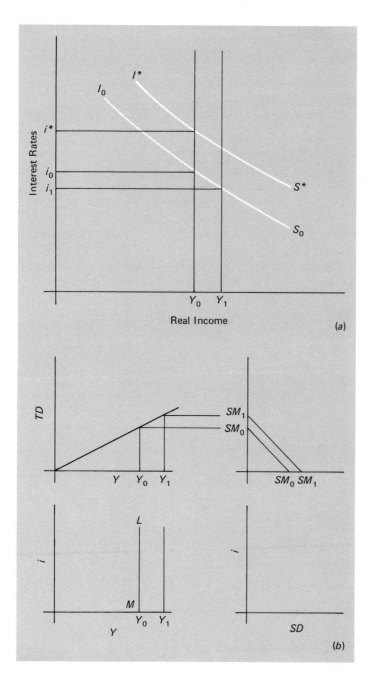

Figure 15–11

No Speculative Demand

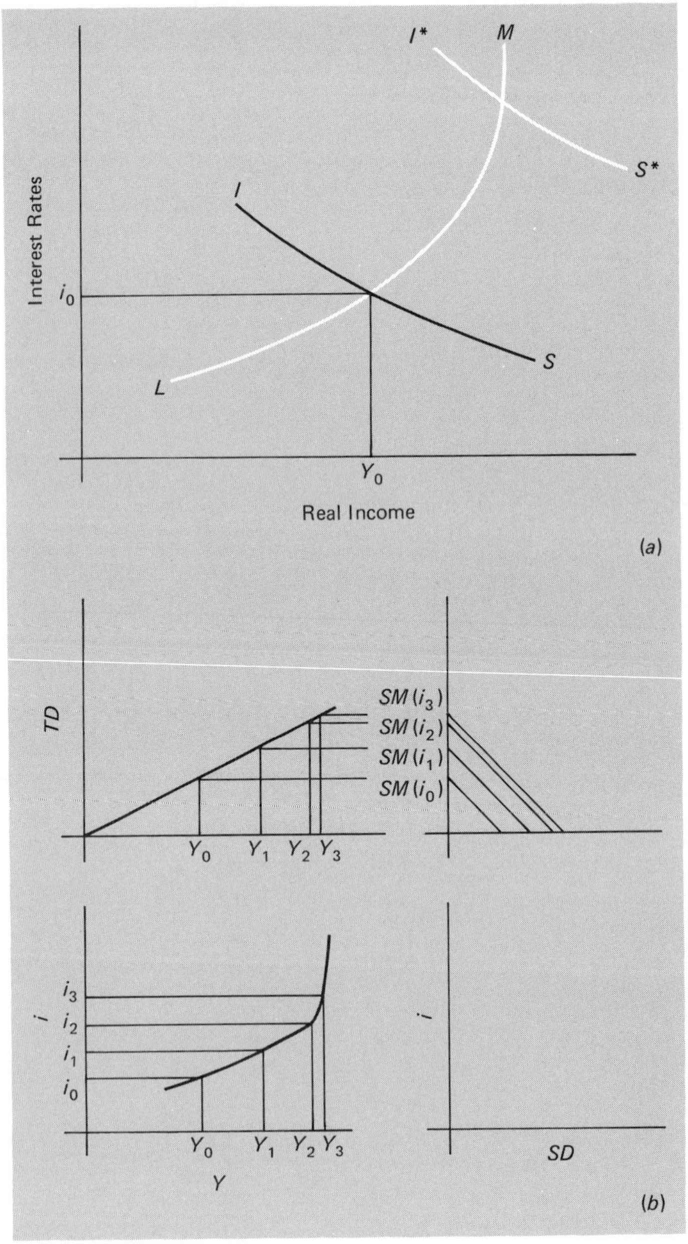

Figure 15–12

Supply of Money Sensitive to Interest Rates

while for the higher interest rate i_1, SM equals SM_1. With no speculative balances, the entire money supply is absorbed into transactions balances; however, now higher interest rates increase the available money supply. The result is seen as an upward sloping LM function much as in the case of the existence of a speculative demand for money function. The LM function becomes perfectly vertical at the point where the banking system cannot further expand upon the available outside money. If equilibrium occurs at this point, as with $I*S*$, Case 2 collapses into Case 1, as the quantity theory region conclusions reappear. If general equilibrium occurs in the nonvertical region of the LM function, such as at interest rate i_0 and income Y_0, the normal IS–LM conclusions hold, even in the absence of a speculative demand for money. Changes in income can result from either the monetary or the real sector of the economy, with positive shifts in the real sector producing increases in both income and interest rates and positive shifts in the monetary sector producing increases in income and lower interest rates.

Case 3—Nonvertical LM Due to Transactions Demand

We now return to the assumption that the money supply is fixed (we assume no speculative demand) but we assume the transactions demand for money balances is sensitive to the rate of interest. The interest rate sensitivity of transactions demand was discussed in the previous chapter as being the result of the availability of highly liquid near-money financial instruments at low transactions costs. Thus, higher interest rates make the holding of larger bond portfolios in lieu of cash profitable while lower interest rates motivate proportionately larger money balances. The impact of this case on the LM function is shown in Figure 15–13. With a fixed money supply and no speculative demand function, an interest rate of i_0 causes monetary equilibrium at Y_0, where transactions demand absorbs the money supply. An increase in interest rates to i_1 rotates the transactions demand function downward to $TD(i_1)$, releasing additional funds. Monetary equilibrium is reestablished at the higher income level Y_1. A further increase in interest rates to i_2 produces the further downward rotation in TD to $TD(i_2)$. The result is an upward sloping LM function and the applicability of the conclusions of the normal IS–LM model, as in Case 2.

If the assumptions of Case 2 and Case 3 are combined, we continue to have an upward sloping LM function with no speculative demand, due to the combination of reasons that the supply of money responds to the interest rate positively and the transactions demand responds to the interest rate negatively.

The last two cases now discussed illustrate that the shape of the LM function, and the conclusions that derive from it, do not depend upon a

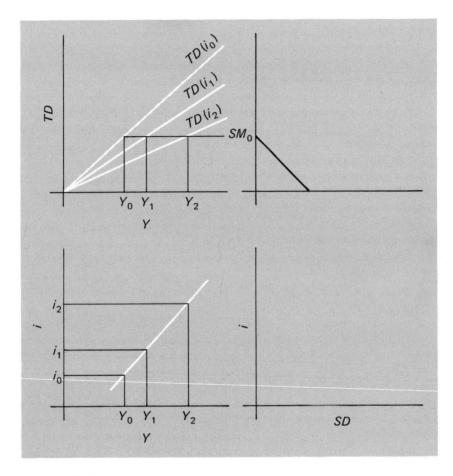

Figure 15–13

Transaction Demand Sensitive to Interest Rates

systematic speculative demand function. Two other (perhaps more readily
apparent) channels have been discussed by which the demand for money is
sensitive to the interest rate and that lead to the same *LM* function result.
In our later discussion of the *IS–LM* framework, it is not always necessary
to delineate which of the channels we assume provides an interest rate sensitivity to the demand for money balances, and we shall not do so. However,
we will in general ignore Case 1 in which no interest rate sensitivity of the
demand for money exists, retaining some version of the liquidity preference
model in which the demand for money is influenced by the rate of interest
as well as the level of income. This choice reflects the broad body of statistical results obtained over the last several decades that show the demand for

money to depend systematically upon the rate of interest. The only important exception to this pattern is the work of Milton Friedman, as discussed in Chapter 14, in which the demand for money is seen to be influenced principally by income levels, such that the quantity theory (Case 1) conclusions prevail.

In this and the previous chapter, we have assumed prices to be fixed, we have ignored labor market conditions, and we have implicitly dealt with all magnitudes in real terms. While this has allowed the essentials of the *IS–LM* framework to emerge simply, it has also hidden from view the related roles of price movements and labor market conditions in influencing economic activity. In the next chapter, we give explicit consideration to the role of prices in the *IS–LM* model and to the related role of labor market equilibrium in influencing product and money market equilibria. This leads to an important distinction between the macroeconomics of the fully employed and the nonfully employed economy.

Discussion Questions

1. Use the *IS–LM* model to identify the impact upon total income, consumption, investment, and interest rates of an increasing tendency toward thrift on the part of consumers.

2. Assume a lump-sum tax system and a balanced budget increase in both spending and taxes of an equal amount. Show the effect on incomes, interest rates, consumption, and investment.

3. Can you think of any circumstance where the U.S. economy might go from equilibrium in the Keynesian range of the *LM* function to equilibrium in the quantity theory region without experiencing operation in the intermediate range?

4. "Monetary policy cannot help the economy recover from a severe recession because it is like pushing on a rope. You can make money available but you cannot assure that it will get spent and create jobs." Use the *IS–LM* framework to comment on this statement.

5. List factors that will shift the *LM* function but not the *IS* function. Now list factors that will shift the *IS* but not the *LM*. Can you think of a factor that shifts both?

16

Prices and Employment

The analysis of goods and money market activity in the previous chapter was based on the view of prices as a fixed datum not influenced by the level of income or the interest rate. That assumption masks some important macroeconomic conclusions about the working of the economy. In this chapter, we relax this assumption in favor of a further development of the model that explicitly incorporates the role of prices. In doing this, we find that prices and employment are importantly related, such that the role of prices and the role of employment go hand in hand. Our discussion of prices and employment leads to a distinction between the operation of the economy in full employment conditions and its operation at under full-employment. We first take up the question of the structural role of prices in the *IS–LM* model.

Prices in the *IS–LM* Model

In the discussion of the previous chapters, the assumption that prices are essentially constant resulted in no important distinction between real and nominal quantities. We now make explicit distinctions for the components in the *IS–LM* model. To do this simply, we denote nominal magnitudes by large letters and real magnitudes by small letters, where in general the real magnitude is equal to the nominal magnitude divided by the price level. For example, real consumption expenditures, c, are equal to nominal consumption, C, divided by prices, P.

Considering real markets first, we may stipulate both the consumption and investment functions to be expressed in real terms, that is

$$c = c(y) \tag{16-1}$$

$$x = x(i) \tag{16-2}$$

where real investment is defined as x rather than i, (to avoid confusion with the interest rate), where y is real income, and where i is the interest rate.[1] These two functions assume that both consumers and investors are not fooled in their product market demand by price changes in consumer and investment goods. For example, consumers are not pursuaded by increases in their nominal income equal to price increases to enlarge their level of real purchases. Thus, if consumer incomes rise by 5 percent, but prices are also rising by 5 percent, y remains constant. Given Expression 16–1, we should expect consumer purchases to increase by 5 percent in nominal terms so as to remain constant in real terms. Expression 16–1 indicates that real income changes are the primary motivation for changes in real consumption.

A similar interpretation applies to Expression 16–2. Investors will change their level of intended investment only by the rate of change in the price level at constant interest rates. Changes in real investment require changes in the rate of interest. These two expressions indicate that the investment-saving equilibrium and the *IS* curve may be entirely expressed in real terms, as

$$IS = f(i, y) \tag{16-3}$$

Accordingly, changes in prices will not affect the position of the *IS* curve, as prices do not explicitly enter into the calculation of the saving-investment equilibrium represented by this curve.

For the monetary sector, the situation is not quite as straightforward. To translate the nominal demand for money function,

$$DM = L(i, Y) \tag{16-4}$$

into its real counterpart

$$dm = l(i, y) \tag{16-5}$$

where $dm = DM/P$ requires the condition that holders of money balances

[1] In a three-sector model, we also assume that government spending can be put on a similar basis.

are not influenced in their behavior by price expectations. In other words, we assume transactors do not hold money balances because of expectations that the price level tomorrow will be different than the price level today. The demand for money balances in Expression 16–5 is instead assumed to be purely for the purposes of present price transactions, given the prevailing interest rate and income level.[2]

In considering the supply of money, we focus on the simplest model

$$SM = SM_0 \qquad\qquad (16\text{–}6)$$

in which the supply is assumed given by the Federal Reserve. However, we could as well consider a money supply function that rises with the interest rate with no change in the results. In either case, we assume the Federal Reserve controls the nominal (not real) supply of outside money by its management of bank reserves, and that it does not endeavor to continually adjust the supply of available outside money so as to maintain the real money supply at any target level. Similarly, we assume that the response by the Federal Reserve to changes in the demand for money is the same whether the increase in demand is due to an increase in the demand for real balances or due to an increase in prices. This situation means that the real supply of money, sm, given by

$$sm = \frac{SM_0}{P} \qquad\qquad (16\text{–}7)$$

is not meaningful as a representation of a completely autonomous variable. Accordingly, we continue to view the nominal money supply, SM, as autonomous according to Expression 16–6 while considering P as endogenous.

Under this condition, monetary equilibrium in the real model occurs where the real money supply, sm, equals the real demand, dm, that is, where

$$\frac{SM_0}{P} = l(i, y) \qquad\qquad (16\text{–}8)$$

Expression 16–8 shows that monetary equilibrium in the real model now explicitly involves the price level in addition to i and y. The revised LM function is

$$LM = g(i, y, P) \qquad\qquad (16\text{–}9)$$

---

[2] If price expectations are a factor, we require an additional term in Expression 16–5 to account for the money holdings associated with the expected change in prices.

Prices enter this revised *LM* framework by shifting the real money supply in the manner indicated by Expression 16–8. Price increases reduce the real money supply while decreases in prices increase the real money supply. Thus, we need to know the level of prices in order to establish the position of the *LM* function. Figure 16–1 shows the effect. At price level P_0, the *LM* curve is in position $LM(P_0)$ and equilibrium occurs at y_0 and i_0. If prices rise to P_1, the decrease in the real money supply shifts the *LM* back to $LM(P_1)$, increasing the interest rate and lowering the level of real income. A further increase in prices to P_2 shifts the *LM* further to the left, reducing real income further and raising the interest rate further.

With the introduction of prices into the *IS–LM* model, we now find that the determination of product and money market equilibrium is incomplete, for without the level of prices we cannot determine y and i. We have three dependent variables, y, i, and P, and only two equations, Expressions 16–3 and 16–9. What is needed is an additional behavioral statement that

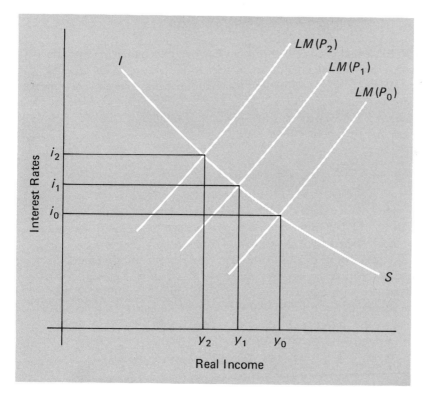

Figure 16–1
Prices and the IS-LM Model

ties prices together with the determinants of product and money market equilibrium. Such an additional statement derives from the labor market where the real wage is determined. We now consider this market.

Price and Employment Determination

In Chapter 4, the decision by producers to supply product markets was assumed to be based on profit maximizing criteria. In particular, we assumed that production by the typical firm is pushed to the point where the marginal cost of production is driven to equality with the marginal revenue. For simplicity, we assumed competitive markets and took marginal revenue to be equal to the price.[3] For the present discussion, it is useful to restate this same profit maximizing criterion in terms of the marginal product and cost of labor rather than the equality of marginal costs and revenues. We start with the earlier stated profit maximizing condition

$$P = MC \qquad (16\text{--}10)$$

where MC is the marginal cost of production, i.e., the change in costs associated with a small change in output. We focus on the case where labor is the only variable cost of production, by virtue of being the only productive input that varies in the short-run. Other inputs, such as capital services, are considered fixed over the short-run period to which our analysis applies. In this case, marginal cost is given by

$$MC = \frac{(W)(\Delta L)}{\Delta Q} = \frac{W}{\Delta Q / \Delta L} \qquad (16\text{--}11)$$

where W is the money wage rate, Q is the level of output in units, and L is the quantity of labor input in man-hours. In Expression 16–11, we assume wages are not affected by changes in the firm's production levels. Thus, changes in costs must be due to variation in the variable input, labor. Thus, the change in the quantity of labor, ΔL, times the wage rate gives the change in cost associated with ΔQ. The denominator of this expression $(\Delta Q / \Delta L)$ shows the change in output that results from a small change in labor input. This is called the *marginal product of labor*, which we denote as MPL. Thus, we can rewrite Expression 16–11 as

$$MC = \frac{W}{\text{MPL}} \qquad (16\text{--}12)$$

[3] The reader unfamiliar with the meaning of competitive markets may wish to consult a text on price theory, such as R. Leftwich, *The Price System and Resource Allocation*, 5th ed., Dryden Press, Hinsdale, Ill., 1973.

According to Expression 16–10, for profit maximizing production, this ratio of wages to marginal product of labor equals the price

$$P = \frac{W}{\text{MPL}} \qquad\qquad (16\text{--}13)$$

or, rearranging

$$\frac{W}{P} = \text{MPL} \qquad\qquad (16\text{--}14)$$

Expression 16–14 shows that at profit maximization the real wage cost (measured in terms of units of output by being divided by the price), is driven to equality with the marginal productivity of labor, also measured in terms of units of output. To illustrate, suppose a firm makes beer. The price per unit of beer is $5.00 while the hourly wage rate is $4.00. The real wage for this firm is $5/4 = 1.25$ units of beer per labor hour. The firm has to give up the equivalent of 1.25 units of its own output at current market prices and wage rates to acquire 1 hour of labor. Also, suppose that an additional hour of labor can produce two units of output, i.e., the MPL = 2. In this case, the additional unit of labor should be hired, since it is more productive than its cost, both measured in physical terms. In fact, additional labor hours should be hired until the marginal product is lowered to the level of the real wage, i.e., until the profit maximizing expression given by 16–14 is satisfied. At this point, all profitable labor units have been employed.

The marginal product of labor is normally thought to decline as more labor is employed, due to the rising marginal inefficiency of adding more and more man-hours of labor to a fixed base of plant and equipment. Thus, we can state

$$\text{MPL} = M(N) \qquad\qquad (16\text{--}15)$$

where N is the level of labor employment.[4] Expression 16–14 shows that the profit maximizing level of labor employment (which we denote as N_d to indicate this is the effective demand for labor by the profit maximizing firm)

---

[4] A more complete statement of this function is

$$\text{MPL} = M(N,K)$$

where K is the flow of services from the current capital stock. Since we assume K is fixed, the function simplifies to 16–15. However, an increase in K should increase the MPL. More specifically, the MPL is the derivative of the production function, which connects inputs to output. Since K is an input to the production function, it should appear as a fixed constant in the MPL expression.

is a function of the real wage, because by combining Expressions 16–14 and 16–15, we obtain

$$\frac{W}{P} = M(N_d) \qquad (16\text{–}16)$$

If we normalize this expression on the profit maximizing demand for labor, we obtain

$$N_d = m\left(\frac{W}{P}\right) \qquad (16\text{–}17)$$

Because the MPL declines with increased employment, increases in the real wage reduce employment by causing marginal labor units to become unprofitable. Cutbacks in output and employment reduce marginal labor inefficiency, raises the MPL, and thus restores equilibrium at lower employment levels. Similarly, decreases in the real wage motivate higher profit maximizing levels of production and increases in employment. Figure 16–2 shows the expected pattern. The MPL function falls off slowly at low levels of employment and more rapidly as higher levels of employment are reached.[5] When the real wage rate is $(W/P)_0$, the firm maximizes profits by the employment of N_0 units of labor, at which point the MPL equals the real wage. Hiring additional labor is not profitable at this real wage, since it involves selling output for less marginal revenue than the marginal labor cost. In order to expand employment to N_1 in the profit maximizing firm, it is necessary to have the lower real wage given by $(W/P)_1$. This lower real wage entices the firm to hire additional labor and expand output accordingly.

The demand for labor function given by Expression 16–17 has now been discussed from the perspective of a profit maximizing firm. If such a firm is typical of a large proportion of firms in the economy, we may usefully apply its logic at the level of the entire economy. In our further discussion we take this approach, defining the demand for labor in general to be a function of the prevailing real wage.

While a given firm may be able to hire as much or as little labor as it wishes at the prevailing wage, attempts by all firms to increase labor use at the prevailing wage rate may not succeed. Expansion in the total level of

[5] In Chapter 4 we discussed the case where marginal costs remain substantially constant over a wide range of output, rising rapidly as full employment is approached. Expression 16–12 shows that this translates into an MPL function that is similarly flat over an initial range and which falls sharply at full employment. This is the general shape shown in Figure 16–2 and subsequent figures.

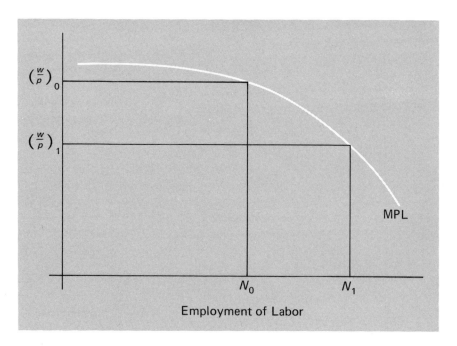

Figure 16–2

Employment Determination

employment may not be possible without an increase in the real wage. At the base of this suggestion is the premise that on an economy-wide basis, the size of the total labor force is an upward sloping function of the real wage. In Chapter 3, the labor force was seen to be influenced by decisions of individuals to seek or not to seek jobs. As more individuals decide to seek employment, the labor force increases. As a general rule, we should expect to find more new job seekers entering the labor force as the real wage increases and a decline in new job seekers as the real wage declines. To illustrate this effect, consider an office worker with family responsibilities. Working outside the home is an alternative to working at family duties within the home. If the money wage available to the potential job seeker is constant, but general prices are rising, including the prices of clothing, babysitting service, transportation, cleaning service, and so forth, then the net gain from work outside the home declines along with the decline in real wage associated with the general price rise. As a result, some reduction in job seeking by individuals in this circumstance may be expected. The upward sloping supply of labor function that results from this reasoning is shown in Figure 16–3, along with the demand for labor function represented by the MPL.

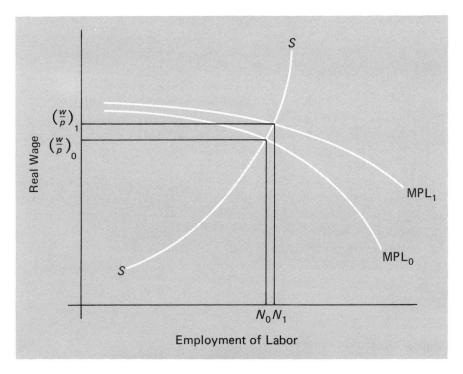

Figure 16–3

Labor Market Equilibrium

With the demand for labor function in the position MPL_0 and the supply of labor function given by SS, the employment level N_0 and the real wage $(W/P)_0$ provide a balance between the supply of and demand for labor. At this real wage, the labor force is enlarged to just the level of employment demand by firms, leading to full employment of the labor force. Real wage levels higher than $(W/P)_0$ will produce a larger labor force while reducing the level of demand for labor. Unemployment will exist, since all those seeking jobs at the prevailing wage cannot find employment. Similarly, for real wage levels lower than $(W/P)_0$ the demand for labor exceeds the supply and a labor shortage exists.

In a world characterized by flexible wages that are set strictly in accordance with market conditions of supply and demand, the only real wage level and employment level that can be maintained are $(W/P)_0$ and N_0. A higher real wage and the resulting unemployment leads to competition among workers for available jobs and to a resulting bidding down of the money wage rate. With a fall in the money wage rate comes a fall in the real wage back toward the equilibrium level. A lower real wage and the resulting labor shortage leads to competition among firms for the available labor and to a bidding up of the money and real wage rate toward $(W/P)_0$. In such a world of free labor market conditions, the supply and demand curves for labor determine the level of employment in the economy.

Where the level of employment is determined by the supply and demand for labor, changes in the level of employment occur as a result of shifts in either the supply or demand for labor functions and not because of changes occurring in product markets. To illustrate, if firms in general increase their stock of plant and equipment as a result of new investment, the result is to shift upward the MPL function, as shown in Figure 16–3 by the shift from MPL_0 to MPL_1. The increased capital base has made labor more productive. At the initial real wage of $(W/P)_0$, the demand for labor now exceeds the supply. The result is an expansion in the level of employment from N_0 to N_1 and an increase in the equilibrium real wage to $(W/P)_1$.[6] However, what if an increase in private demand (say in consumer expenditures) occurs at a point where the labor market is initially in equilibrium? Will this result in an increase in employment? Under our present conditions, the answer is no. In the next section, we explore the reason why.

Output and Employment with Flexible Wages

We continue to consider the case where wages are set according to market conditions of supply and demand and are flexible both upward and downward. We also assume the same flexibility applies to prices. As indicated in the previous section, under such conditions the level of employment is determined completely by the interaction of the supply and demand for labor. However, the decision by firms to employ a certain quantity of labor is equivalent to the decision to produce an associated volume of real output/income, under our assumed conditions that the level of plant and equipment is constant. To see this, we need only consider the production function for a firm, an industry, or an economy, which is defined as the relationship between the quantity of labor, plant and equipment, and other inputs employed in production and the resulting level of output.

We define an economy-wide production function as follows

$$y = p(N, K) \qquad\qquad (16\text{--}18)$$

---

[6] Since a growing economy is generally characterized by a growing capital stock, the MPL curve should undergo a continual outward shift and lead to a rising level of real wages and employment over time.

where y is the level of real income and output and K is the flow of services from the nation's stock of plant and equipment (which we assume to be constant in our short-run framework along with the stock of capital equipment). Clearly, with K constant, y is completely determined by the quantity of N employed. The situation is depicted in Figure 16–4. Part (a) shows the determination of the equilibrium level of employment (N_0) and the real wage. Part (b) shows the determination of the real output level, y_0, that is consistent with the equilibrium level of employment. Thus, the determination of employment levels leads directly to the determination of the equilibrium level of real output.

Figure 16–4 also shows that the equilibrium level of both employment and output will occur at a full employment (or market clearing) point. At N_0 in this figure, the demand for labor equals the available labor force. The real income level y_0 is thus a full employment level of production and one that represents profit maximizing production decisions by firms. Thus, our analysis indicates that under our present assumptions of flexible wages, the economy tends toward full employment equilibrium conditions. To see this tendency, consider the case where the level of demand for real output exceeds the full employment equilibrium level. Two effects are pertinent in this case. First, producers are unwilling to reduce their profits by expanding output further at the current price into a region of production where the real wage exceeds the MPL. Second, demanders of real output are motivated to bid against each other for the constant level of real output. The result is an increase in prices. As prices rise, the real wage falls, thus increasing the demand for labor, but causing a contraction in the labor force and creating a temporary shortage of labor. This emerging labor shortage causes an increase in money wages, which continues until the former real wage level is restored. Real income thus returns to its original level at full employment. The increase in demand has succeeded only in increasing prices and wages, but not real output.

Consider the opposite case of a decrease in the demand for real output (say by consumers) below the equilibrium level of y. In this case, the level of aggregate production exceeds the demand. Inventories increase beyond intended levels. Downward pressures upon prices appear and prices begin to fall as producers move to pare their excessive inventory positions. But falling prices increase the real wage for a given money wage rate. As the real wage rate begins to rise, the current level of production becomes too large for profit maximization and production levels begin to decline. As this occurs, laborers are laid off as the level of employment is reduced. In addition, the increase in the real wage may draw forth additional new members into the labor force. Unemployment emerges. This condition places downward pressures on money wages, which begin to fall. The fall in money wages reverses the initial effect, lowering the real wage, motivating an increase in employment, and bringing about some reduction in the labor force.

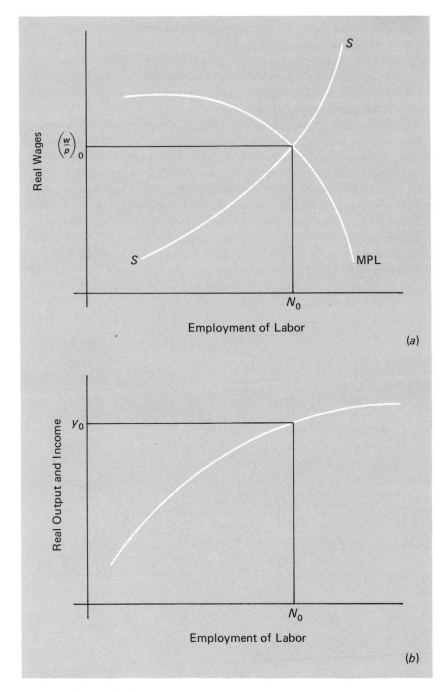

Figure 16–4
Real Output Determination

Equilibrium is reestablished at the initial full employment level, where the supply of labor again equals the demand at the initial real wage. However, at this point, both money wages and prices are lower. The effect of a decrease in demand has only been to lower prices and wages. It has not influenced the level of real output or the final level of employment, although both dipped during the adjustment period.

These two examples of positive and negative demand shifts indicate that demand does not determine the level of real output in the case of flexibility in prices and wages. *Indeed, it is the other way around.* The level of supply is set at a volume of output that maximizes profits of producers and clears the labor market. Fluctuations in product market demand impact on the price and wage level but have no permanent effect on the real income level in the world represented by our present model.

Earlier in this chapter, the addition of prices to the *IS–LM* model resulted in an indeterminant system. The present discussion provides one way of making the *IS–LM* scheme determinant, for the case of flexible wages and prices. Figure 16–5 illustrates the complete *IS–LM* model with the labor

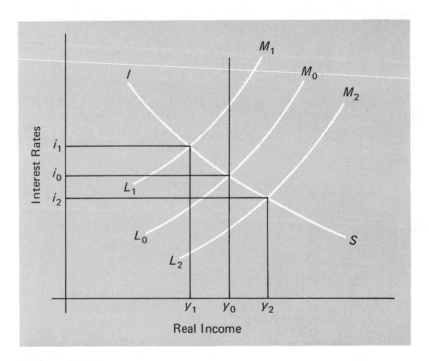

Figure 16–5
Complete IS-LM Scheme

market effect added. Consistent with our earlier discussion, the equilibrium level of y is determined outside the IS–LM scheme. It is shown as the vertical line at $y = y_0$. Consider first the situation created by an intersection of the IS curve with $L_1 M_1$. In this case, product market and money market equilibrium occurs at real income level y_1 and interest rate i_1. There is less product market demand at the intersection of IS with $L_1 M_1$ than the level of profit maximizing production and employment. As we have seen, with flexible wages and prices, this is an unstable situation. Prices fall, and money wages are reduced due to unemployed laborers in the work force. The fall in prices associated with the $y_0 - y_1$ gap now works an effect upon the LM function. Expression 16–9 earlier showed that the position of the LM function is affected by the price level. As the level of prices falls, the real money supply is increased for a given nominal money supply. The increased real money supply causes the LM curve to shift to the right. Falling prices continue as long as any positive gap between aggregate production at y_0 and aggregate demand at y_1 exists. The LM curve accordingly continues to shift to the right, and as this occurs, the product and money market equilibrium level of demand increases toward the equilibrium level of production. When prices have fallen such that the LM has reached position $L_0 M_0$, aggregate demand has increased to the level of full employment production, the real wage is at the full employment level, and wages and prices are reduced from their levels at real income y_1. Real income y_0 thus produces equilibrium in product markets, money markets, and labor markets.

Consider now the situation represented in Figure 16–5 by the intersection of IS with $L_2 M_2$. In this case, the level of product market and money market equilibrium demand is greater than the level of full employment production. The excess demand puts pressures upon prices, which rise as a result. The price rise continues as long as the equilibrium level of demand y_2 exceeds the equilibrium level of production, y_0. The price increase works the opposite effect on the LM curve as on the previously discussed price decrease. Increased prices lower the real money supply, shifting the LM curve to the left. The pattern continues until the LM has shifted back to the position $L_0 M_0$, where equilibrium aggregate demand equals equilibrium supply. Prices have increased along with wages, such that the real wage settles at the full employment level.

The level of interest rates resulting from our analysis in Figure 16–5 provides an alternative way to view the situation of joint equilibrium now discussed. In our expanded model, we continue to view the equilibrium interest rate as being set by the intersection of the IS and LM functions jointly with the equilibrium level of aggregate demand. However, the impact of the equilibrium level of real income and output on the position of the LM curve means that stable interest rates require labor market equilibrium as well as product and money market equilibria. To illustrate, in

Figure 16–5, each of the interest rates i_0, i_1, and i_2 produce an equilibrium in the demand and supply of real money balances. However, interest rate i_1 is too high to be consistent with the full employment level of production, since it associates with an insufficient amount of investment spending to sustain y_0 in output. Accordingly, the decline in prices that occurs at interest rate i_1 increases the real money supply, which lowers the equilibrium rate of interest and motivates an increase in investment. Similarly, interest rate i_2 is too low for full equilibrium, as it associates with an excessive level of investment for the full employment level of supply and produces an increase in prices which in turn shifts the *LM* curve back and increases interest rates. The interest rate i_0 is unique in being consistent with full equilibrium conditions in all markets. We define this unique rate of interest as the *full equilibrium rate.*[7]

In Chapter 14 a distinction was made between the interest rate as a real versus a monetary product. Reference to Figure 16–5 shows that the full equilibrium interest rate under flexible wages and prices is distinctly a real phenomenon. The full equilibrium rate changes only when a change occurs in either the *IS* curve or in the equilibrium level of production, y_0. Since *IS* shifts are motivated by changes in either the investment or con-sumption function, and shifts in real output are motivated by shifts in either the supply of labor function or the marginal product of labor func-tion, it is clear that lasting influences on interest rates are all of the real variety when wages and prices are fully flexible. Temporary changes in interest rates can be brought about by monetary changes that shift the *LM* function. However, the reaction of the price level to such changes will re-turn the interest rate to the full equilibrium level upon full adjustment. Thus, monetary shifts have no lasting effect upon the full equilibrium in-terest rate.

Our discussion of the *IS–LM* scheme with the labor market and prices added shows that the case of flexible wages and prices leads to joint equi-librium in labor, product, and money markets as the only stable position for real income and interest rates. When aggregate demand departs from the level of full employment production, prices and wages change. The result is a reaction in the monetary sector, returning the economy to the full employment equilibrium position.

In reaching this conclusion, we have assumed that the *LM* function is not horizontal, i.e., that we are not in the Keynesian (or liquidity trap) re-gion. If the equilibrium level of product market demand (described by the intersection of the *IS* and *LM*) occurs at such a low level of income that the interest rate is no longer sensitive to fluctuations in the real money supply,

---

[7] This interest rate is also labeled the natural rate by some writers in economics. Our use of the term full equilibrium rate is intended to convey more of the significance of the rate. To some, the term "natural" implies roots and blossoms.

then shifts in the *LM* curve due to changes in the real money supply will not raise the economy to full employment. In this case, the full equilibrium interest rate is too low to be consistent with the minimum market interest rate that suppliers and demanders of money will allow, and monetary re-actions will not return an economy with deficient demand to the full employment level.

Although operation in the liquidity trap provides a plausible excep-tion to the pattern of behavior we have outlined in this section, the instances where the U.S. economy has approximated operation in the liquidity trap region are rare, probably limited to the Great Depression of the 1930s. A much more viable exception to the automatic adjustment of the economy toward full employment is found in the typical unwillingness of the labor market to accept downward changes in the money wage rate. When we alter the assumption of fully flexible money wages, we find the results of this sec-tion are altered considerably. In the next section, we consider how.

Downward Rigid Wages—The U.S. Case

In the presentday United States, there is little evidence that money wage rates will fall in response to declines in employment. Unionized laborers in particular have consistently opted for stability in the money wage rate as the preferred alternative to higher (if not full) employment levels during periods of declining output and employment demand. Thus, in the United States the earlier assumption of downward flexible wages is not a reasonable representation of behavior by individuals and unions. Wage levels, once attained, do not in general tend to fall in U.S. labor markets. On the other hand, wages give every appearance of adjusting upward toward market levels when warranted, although the existence of union contracts tends to slow this process and possibly create lags in the response of money wages to upward movements. According to this view, we trace through the implica-tions of an alternative assumption about wages that seems more applicable to the U.S. economy—that wages are upwardly flexible but downwardly rigid.

We now consider the impact of this altered assumption on the com-plete *IS–LM* model, including labor markets. In Figure 16–6, the labor market is shown in (*a*), the production function in (*b*) and the *IS–LM* curves in (*c*). Part (*a*) shows the full employment level of employment to be N_0 at a real wage of $(W/P)_0$. Part (*b*) shows this level of employment results in a y_0 level of real income, which is shown as the vertical line in (*c*). Thus, the full equilibrium interest rate is i_0. Suppose that originally the position of the *LM* function is at L_0M_0, the full equilibrium condition. Prices and

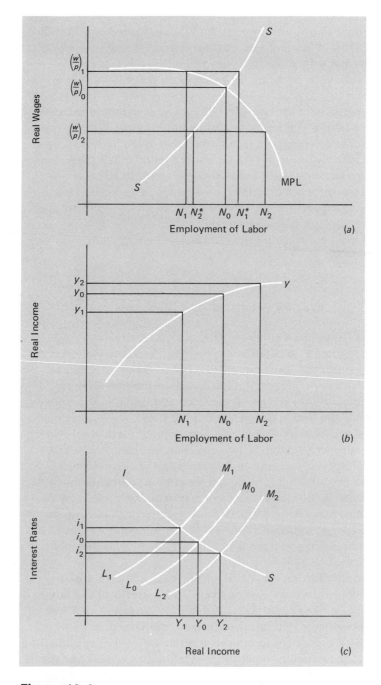

Figure 16–6

Equilibrium with Downward Rigid Wages and Prices

wages are stable, and the market interest rate is at the full equilibrium level. Now, assume the nominal money supply is contracted, producing a leftward shift in the LM curve to L_1M_1. Interest rates rise and the level of real output produced exceeds the declining level of real aggregate demand. Inventories mount, resulting in some cutbacks in both output levels and prices by producers. As prices are reduced due to the weak markets, the real wage rises, reducing the demand for labor by firms. In addition, the price cuts increase the real money supply somewhat, buffering against the leftward shift in the LM function. The level of employment declines from N_0 toward N_1 as the real wage rises toward $(W/P)_1$. At $(W/P)_1$, the demand for labor is at N_1 while the labor force is N_1^*. Unemployment is equal to $(N_1^* - N_1)$, and downward pressures are placed on money wage rates. But, their downward rigidity does not allow them to fall. Real wages remain too high for full employment of the labor force given the current reduced level of product market demand. As a result, output must adjust to the reduced level of demand in order to balance the level of production with the equilibrium demand. When the level of output contracts to y_1, production will be balanced with demand, inventories will stabilize, and prices will stop falling.[8] Accordingly, the rate of unemployment that associates with the equilibrium level of demand, y_1, will persist until a change in the level of demand occurs. As long as output is less than full employment, a shift in either the IS or LM curve that changes the level of equilibrium demand in product and money markets will result in an adjustment in production. At less than full employment, changes in demand will draw forth similar changes in production. Decreases in demand will weaken prices, increase the real wage, and cause output cutbacks, while increases in demand will cause increases in prices and output. If the MPL curve has the initial flat shape shown in Figure 16–6(a), then at high rates of unemployment, changes in demand will result in nearly proportional changes in output and small changes in price; whereas as full employment is approached, changes in demand will call forth larger changes in price and smaller changes in output. This is precisely the conclusion reached in our provisional model of supply in Chapter 4. We now see the full rationale for this premise—that it deals with the profit maximizing response of producers to demand shifts during times of less than full employment with downwardly rigid wages.

The role of interest rates in the under full employment, rigid wage case is similarly revised from the flexible case. Since the level of production adjusts to the level of demand, the intersection of the $IS–LM$ curves determines the interest rate. Thus, unlike the flexible wage case with a single (i_0) full equilibrium interest rate, other interest rates such as i, can be con-

---

[8] We are taking y_1 to be the equilibrium level of demand once the real money supply effect has shifted the LM curve to its new position.

sistent with a stable under full employment equilibrium in the present case. In addition, shifts in the monetary sector that shift the LM curve alter the equilibrium rate in the present case, whereas these influences have only a transitory influence on rates in the flexible case. Thus, the interest rate in the case of downwardly rigid wages is influenced by both monetary and real factors, as long as real output is below the full employment level.

If the LM curve intersects the IS curve to the right of the full employment level, the result is quite different from a leftward shift, and in fact is the same as for fully flexible wages. To verify this, suppose the LM shifts to the right to L_2M_2, leading to a demand for the greater than full employment level of real outut, y_2. With demand greater than production and falling inventory levels, prices begin to rise. This lowers the real wage and increases the demand for labor toward N_2. As the real wage falls toward $(W/P)_2$, a shortage of labor appears, given by $(N_2 - N_2^*)$. The money wage rate, flexible in the upward direction, begins to rise as a result, thus reversing the initial falling real wage. In addition, the rise in prices reduces the real money supply and begins to shift the LM curve back to the left. The labor shortage is reduced by this leftward shift. However, as long as a labor shortage exists, wages continue to rise. Similarly, as long as the level of demand exceeds the supply, prices rise. The excess demand and the labor shortage are both eliminated only when the LM curve shifts back to L_0M_0, giving the full employment level of real output, y_0, and resulting in real wages that are at the full employment level, along with higher money wages and prices than before the shift.

Our consideration of the case of downwardly rigid wages has produced some rather sharp contrasts in results when compared to the case of entirely flexible wages. We have seen that an under full employment equilibrium position can be maintained in the rigid wage case but not in the flexible case. We have seen both cases to be identical in the response to excess demand conditions when the economy is at full employment. However, perhaps the most striking result is that the impetus for changes in production and employment levels shifts from producers to demanders when wages are downwardly rigid and the level of demand moves below the full employment level of supply. When wages are flexible, profit maximizing producers in the economy are motivated to adjust prices and money wages in order to maintain the employment level where the supply and demand for labor are equal. Any other employment level cannot be maintained as it precipitates continued adjustments in wages and prices. When wages are downwardly rigid, profit maximizing producers cannot adjust in this way and so adjust their level of output instead in accordance with changes in demand. Thus, the assumption of downward rigid wages transforms a "supply calls the tune" economy into a "demand calls the tune" economy as long as under-full employment conditions exist.

Although the case of downward rigid wages is a special case of our general model, it is an important case for our purposes since it approximately represents the economy of the United States. In the next two sections we consider the operation of the rigid wage *IS–LM* model under conditions of both full employment and less than full employment.

The Influence of Monetary Policy on the Rigid Wage Economy

In this section we discuss the behavior of the economy in response to monetary policy actions under conditions of downwardly rigid wages. We begin by considering the impact of monetary expansion on the fully employed economy. Figure 16–7 shows the economy in a full equilibrium position at real income y_0 and interest rate i_0. Assume now that the Federal Reserve increases the money supply in an attempt to lower the interest rate below the full equilibrium level i_0. The increase in the nominal money supply

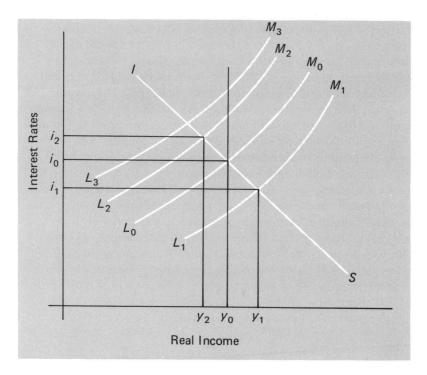

Figure 16–7

Monetary Policy and Full Employment

shifts the LM from L_0M_0 to L_1M_1, which begins to lower the interest rate toward i_1 and increases the level of aggregate demand above the full employment level of supply to y_1. Prices and money wages begin to rise. With the rise in prices, the real money supply begins to contract back toward its original position, finally stabilizing at the original position L_0M_0. The net effect of the increase in the money supply has curiously not been to lower interest rates, except temporarily. After the adjustment of the LM function, rates have returned to their original levels. So has real income and the equilibrium real wage, which are unaffected by the money supply increase after complete adjustment. The only impact has been to increase prices and wages. Interestingly, these latter results are the same as predicted by the quantity theory, as discussed in Chapter 14.

A contractionary monetary policy at full employment is quite a different story. Suppose that the Federal Reserve contracts the money supply such that the LM curve initially shifts back to the left from L_0M_0 to L_3M_3. The result of this shift is to increase the interest rate and reduce the level of equilibrium demand below full employment levels. The fall in demand in turn motivates some fall in prices, which in turn begins to shift the LM curve back to the right. The rigid money wage remains constant. The LM curve stabilizes at L_2M_2, where the reduced level of production has been brought into balance with demand at y_2 of real output. The result of the contractionary monetary policy from an initial position of full employment is to create unemployment, lower prices, increase the real wage, and bring about an increase in equilibrium interest rates from i_0 to i_2. Thus, while an expansionary monetary policy at full employment cannot have a lasting effect on interest rates, a contractionary monetary policy from the same starting point can influence interest rates. In addition, contractionary policy affects the level of real income and employment, unlike expansionary policy. Both policies have an influence on the level of prices.

If monetary expansion is undertaken from an initial position of less than full employment in the rigid wage economy, the results are symmetrical with those just discussed in connection with contractionary policy. If we are in an initial position at L_2M_2 with unemployment conditions existing, an expansionary monetary policy that shifts the LM to L_0M_0 will succeed in increasing real output (from y_2 to y_0) and lowering the interest rate (from i_2 to i_0). Prices increase somewhat as firms react to the increasing level of demand. The pattern continues until full employment is reached, where the response reverts to the flexible wage case initially discussed.

Fiscal Policy in the Rigid Wage Economy

In Figure 16–8, we consider the effect of fiscal policy on the fully employed economy. In Figure 16–8(a), we start from a full employment equilibrium

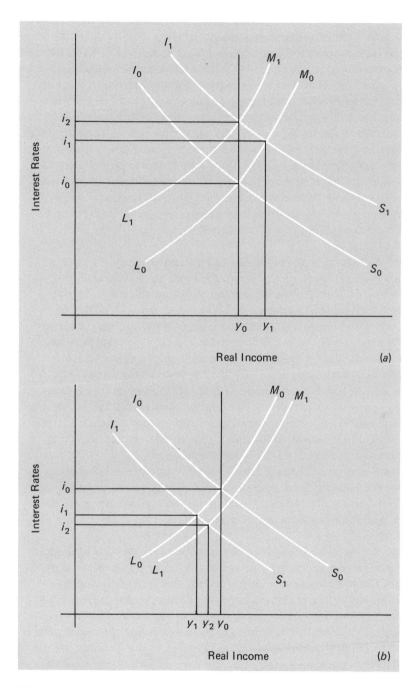

Figure 16–8

Fiscal Policy at Full Employment

at y_0 and i_0. Now consider an increase in the level of government spending, paid for without increasing the money supply or taxes. The initial effect is to shift the IS curve outward from I_0S_0 to I_1S_1. The level of demand initially increases from y_0 to y_1, while the increase in intended expenditures raises the interest rate from i_0 to i_1. The excess demand in product markets over the level of full employment supply now causes prices to increase, which in turn lowers the real wage, increases the demand for labor, and creates a shortage in labor markets. At the same time, the increase in prices associated with the excess demand reduces the real money supply and shifts the LM curve to the left toward L_1M_1. The factors motivating the price increase continue until the LM curve has shifted completely to L_1M_1, where real income has returned to its original level along with the real wage. The net result of the full employment increase in government spending is an unchanged level of real output and income, higher prices, higher interest rates, and higher wages.

Figure 16–8(b) shows the effect of a lump-sum (for simplicity) tax increase imposed on a fully employed economy. From an initial full equilibrium position of y_0 and i_0, the imposition of the tax shifts the IS curve from I_0S_0 to I_1S_1. This shift reduces the total level of demand below full employment production levels, creates inventory buildups, and leads to price cuts by producers in an attempt to balance production and sales. As before, the price decline increases the real money supply, which shifts the LM curve rightward to L_1M_1. This shift further reduces the interest rate. By the time output level y_2 is reached, the level of production is in balance with the level of demand, prices stabilize, and no further shift in the LM curve occurs. The results of the tax increase at full employment are thus a reduced level of real output and income, a lower interest rate, a lower level of prices, and a lower level of money wages.

By now the result of the application of fiscal policy to the under full employment economy is probably clear. Increases in government spending in this circumstance lead to an expansion in output, an increase in prices, an increase in interest rates, and a fall in real wages. The result of a tax cut is similar.[9]

In this chapter, we have added the role of prices to the IS–LM model and found it necessary to develop a model of the employment sector to regain a solution to the IS–LM scheme in this case. We have explored the flexible and rigid wage cases and traced through the response of the economy to monetary and fiscal policy using the expanded model. Our analysis has been basically theoretical, following to their conclusion the implication of a structure of logical assumptions about behavior in the economy. In the next chapter, we consider a few representative empirical models of the

[9] It may be worthwhile for the student to trace these effects through the IS–LM structure.

entire economy that have evolved from a primary interest in the subject of macroeconomic forecasting. We shall compare the forecasting record of representative empirical models as well.

Discussion Questions

1. Explain in your own words the reason for the conclusion that an economy with flexible wages and prices would evolve toward a full employment equilibrium.

2. Do you think the U.S. economy at the present point in time approximately conforms to the sticky or rigid wage model presented in the chapter? Explain, using such statistical and logical arguments as are appropriate.

3. How would the results of the rigid wage *IS–LM* model be changed (if at all) if wages were also sticky in the upward direction, varying only at the time of contract renegotiation by labor unions?

4. How would the results of the rigid wage *IS–LM* model be influenced by adding the stipulation that prices are also downward rigid? Do you think there is any evidence that prices in the United States are downward rigid? Explain and demonstrate.

5. Who "calls the tune" in the U.S. economy—producers or product market demanders—insofar as fluctuations in production levels are concerned?

6. Trace the effect through the rigid wage model of this chapter of a taste-related independent increase in the demand for automobiles by consumers, starting from an initial position of full employment. Will consumption increase as a result? Explain fully.

7. Suppose that the full equilibrium interest rate is 11 percent and the present market interest rate is 7.5 percent. What conclusions can you draw from this? What policy actions should be taken? Why?

8. Outline the circumstance that could lead to an important monetary role in the setting of the equilibrium interest rate.

17

Empirical Macroeconomic Models

Beginning in the early 1950s in the United States, economists began to experiment with multiequation statistical models of the U.S. economy designed basically to predict the short-term progress of the GNP and its major components. They were labeled *econometric models* to reflect the blend of statistical method and economic theory required in their construction. The initial U.S. econometric models were largely inspired by Keynesian theory and, accordingly, gave extensive attention to demand for categories of goods and services in the nation's product markets. The impact of monetary variables upon product market demand and upon overall economic equilibrium was not an important part of the early U.S. models. In the early 1960s, substantial modifications in the Keynesian heritage of U.S. econometric models began to appear, as economists began to give more attention to the explanatory role of monetary variables in product market equilibrium. In the latter 1960s, this trend was greatly extended by the appearance of a model developed by the Federal Reserve Bank of St. Louis along the lines of the quantity theory that emphasizes a direct role for the money supply in explaining fluctuations in the GNP over the near-term.

In this chapter, we consider the composition of a representative sampling of U.S. econometric models. To reflect the essential composition of Keynesian models, we shall assemble the empirical models of the consumer, investment, and monetary sectors developed and discussed in Chapters 7, 8, 9, and 12 into a representative neo-Keynesian model. To represent neo-Keynesian monetarist oriented models, we shall consider a model developed jointly by the Federal Reserve Board and the Massachusetts Institute of

Technology, known as the FRB–MIT model. Finally, we consider the St. Louis Federal Reserve model as representative of an empirical quantity theory oriented model.

In our discussion of these three approaches, we focus on the types of variables each uses to explain fluctuations in the GNP and other product market variables and on the way each model uses the variables. This enables a relatively uncluttered comparison of the different variables and structures relied upon to predict the GNP under the various approaches. The general tendency of econometric model-builders is to utilize theory wherever it has practical explanatory power. Thus, the extent to which we find elements of the theoretical product market and monetary model of the previous several chapters incorporated into econometric model structures gives an indication of the statistical importance of the theoretical ideas in the practical task of near-term economic prediction. In our discussion, we keep the complications to a minimum by ignoring the entanglements of the particular equation and variable identification of the three models considered. We also give no attention to comparisons of the statistical results of time-series fitting of the models or to the econometric problems of model solution.

A Consensus Keynesian Model

In considering an econometric model of distinctly Keynesian lineage, several specific models could be chosen. Rather than focus on one particular model, we call upon our earlier discussion of the empirical explanation of consumer expenditures in Chapter 7, of business investment expenditures in Chapter 8, and of residential construction in Chapter 9 to construct a consensus Keynesian model for the explanation of product market expenditures. This structure represents several major Keynesian econometric models without exactly displaying any single model. As our earlier discussion pointed out, the empirical consensus obtained is based on common patterns found in the Wharton econometric model, the U.S. Commerce Department model, and the Brookings econometric model project.[1] In addition, the role of funds flow channels as given in Chapter 12 has been added to the consensus prod-

[1] For an explanation of the Wharton model, see M. Evans, *Macroeconomic Activity: Theory, Forecasting, and Control,* Harper & Row, New York, 1969. For an explanation of some recent findings from the Brookings econometric model project, see J. S. Duesenberry, G. Fromm, L. R. Klein, and E. Kuh, *The Brookings Econometric Model of the United States,* Rand McNally, Chicago, 1965. For an explanation of the Commerce Department, Office of Business Economics model, see the Department's *The Survey of Current Business,* May 1966. Another similar approach, associated with the University of Michigan, is found in D. B. Suits, "Forecasting and Analysis with an Econometric Model," *American Economic Review,* 52:1 (March 1962), pp. 104–132.

uct market demand structure to complete the monetary sector of the model. While this addition is not explicitly inspired by the models just referenced, each individual model has some mechanism for interrelating the real and monetary markets in the general fashion described by the *IS–LM* structure.[2] The results of combining the empirical models of consumer and investment spending with the funds flow channels of the banking system is shown in Figure 17–1. The upper right-hand part of the figure shows the consumer product market sector, while the upper left-hand portion shows the categories of gross private domestic investment. The center and lower part of the figure show the position of the banking system in the circular monetary and expenditure flow.

In consumer expenditures, the level of disposable income is a common determinant of expenditures in all three categories of consumer expenditures. Since disposable income is related closely to the GNP and is highly dependent upon it, the statistical relevance of disposable income in consumption verifies an empirical multiplier effect. In addition to this direct effect, flows of saving rise or fall with the GNP, add to consumer liquid asset accounts, and thereby affect expenditures on nondurables and services, since liquid assets are commonly found to be an important explanatory variable in consumption. Thus, the empirical multiplier effect emanating from the consumption function has both a real and a monetary facet in our consensus model. In addition, past stocks of automobiles and other durables are found to have important explanatory roles in new expenditures in these categories, leading to a longer period, time dynamic contribution to the multiplier effect that applies to a single period. Nondurables and services expenditures are also seen to be importantly influenced by population and by the standard-of-living effects of past expenditures.

In the investment sector, we find that private output (defined as GNP less government expenditures) influences both plant and equipment and inventory investment, both of which add directly to the GNP. But the level of private output is related by definition to the GNP. Thus, an accelerator-like effect is found to be statistically important in the Keynesian consensus due to the significance of the private output variable. In addition, plant and equipment investments are influenced by financial variables related to the cost of capital, including corporate cash flow, interest rates, and flows of long-term debt capital. Interest rates and capital flows emanate from the monetary sector of the model and reflect the interdependent impact of the monetary sector on plant and equipment outlays. Similar interest rate and

---

mortgage capital flows affect residential construction along with vacancy rates and construction prices. Inventories are influenced by unfilled orders for durables and by past patterns of inventory investment.[3]

Monetary effects contribute to the overall impact of expenditure changes upon the economy in the Keynesian consensus. The specific way this occurs is shown in the lower portion of Figure 17–1. Working downward, the sum of goods market expenditures adds to the GNP, influences national and personal income, and produces flows of consumer and business saving. The saving flow is channeled through financial institutions and influences the total flow of lending by banks and other institutions along with Federal Reserve policy. The velocity of this flow reflects the transactions demand for money. The bank lending flow along with anticipated demand for plant and equipment and residential construction expenditures essentially determines interest rates and flows of new capital lending. In turn, interest rates and the flow of new lending in these categories influence actual expenditures on plant and equipment and residential construction. In this way, changes in monetary conditions that exert an influence on capital lending by banks and other financial institutions directly affect flows of new investment expenditures. This feedback loop is the empirical counterpart of the IS–LM circular dependence of real and monetary markets.

In the model of Figure 17–1, changes in employment occur as a result of demand changes. This corresponds to the case described in the previous chapter as the under full employment, rigid wage case. It also corresponds to the result obtained when prices are considered fixed. Specifically, employment is seen as dependent upon the level of total aggregate expenditure, which is assumed equal to the GNP, i.e., the model explains equilibrium positions over time. This means that demand calls the tune in the Keynesian consensus insofar as changes in employment levels are concerned. In addition, a minor role at best is set forth for prices in influencing economic activity. All the expenditure and income relationships depicted in the figure can be thought of as being expressed in real terms. Thus, the absence of prices in the monetary sector indicates a departure from the endogenous (or model internal) role of prices described in the neo-Keynesian model of the previous chapter. In addition, there is no linkage in the model of Figure 17–1 between changes in the level of bank reserves (and thus the money supply) and expenditures on consumer goods. The impact of changes in bank reserve position that occur as a result of monetary policy fall entirely upon the bond market and, through it, upon investment spending. In this respect, the model is distinctly nonmonetarist.

These attributes of the Keynesian consensus distinguish it structurally from the monetarist model and from the expanded type of neo-Keynesian

---

[3] In particular models, time lags of various lengths are present in many of these relationships. We abstract from these time lags in our discussion for purposes of simplification.

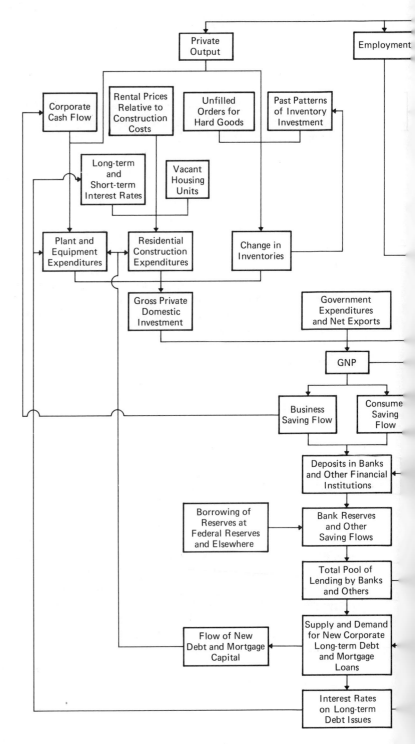

Figure 17–1

Consensus Keynesian Model

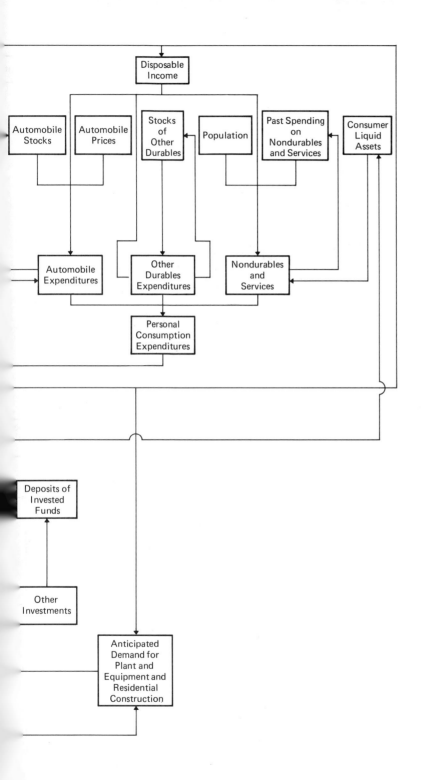

model presented in Chapter 16. It is to this latter type of model that our comparison now turns.

The FRB-MIT Model

A model developed jointly by the Federal Reserve Board and the department of economics of the Massachusetts Institute of Technology, known as the FRB–MIT model, provides an interesting illustration of the use of the techniques of econometric model building to explore a specific macroeconomic issue.[4] At the same time, the FRB–MIT approach reflects a rich development of the role of monetary variables in macroeconomic behavior. The specific purpose of the FRB–MIT model is to analyze the channels by which monetary policy actions influence product market activity and other related aspects of economic behavior. The model is divided into several sectors, each of which contains a number of equations describing activity in that sector. The most extensive sectors as well as the most important to the purpose of the model are the financial and the real sectors.

The financial sector links the instruments of Federal Reserve policy (open market actions, reserve requirement regulations, discount rate changes) with market interest rates and other financial variables. The response of interest rates in both money and capital markets to changes in Federal Reserve policy actions is laid out in detail in the financial sector of the model. The effect upon interest rates of bank portfolio adjustments similar to that discussed in Chapter 13 is incorporated into the explanatory equations in the financial sector. The impact of portfolio adjustments on the term structure of interest rates is measured in the model and found to be an important factor in near-term predictions. This aspect of the FRB–MIT results represents positive statistical support for a rational type of bank portfolio behavior in which the near-cash position of banks responds systematically to the spread on long- and short-term securities, thus influencing the market demand and supply for securities of differing maturities accordingly.

The result of the financial sector is to translate monetary policy actions into the entire relevant structure of money and capital market interest rates. In the real sector of the FRB–MIT model, the structure of interest rates is the basic conduit through which Federal Reserve monetary policy changes impact on product market expenditures. In this broad respect, the FRB–MIT model structure is consistent with the *IS–LM* scheme. However, several important departures are found in the FRB–MIT model from the world of *IS–LM*. Figure 17–2 shows diagrammatically the real sector of the model,

[4] For a presentation of this model, see F. deLeeuw and E. M. Gramlich, "The Channels of Monetary Policy: A Further Report of the Federal Reserve-MIT Model," *Journal of Finance,* 24 (May 1969), pp. 265–290.

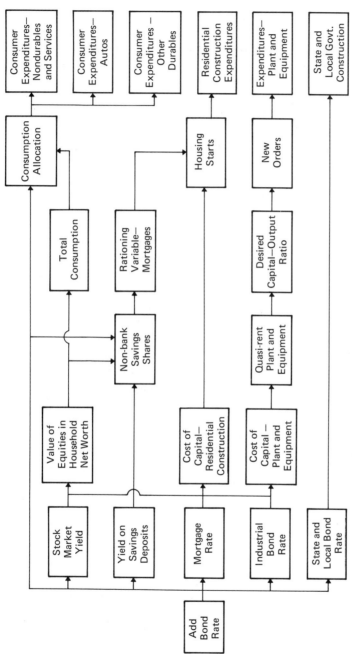

Source: Adapted from F. de Leeuw and E. M. Gramlich, "The Channels of Monetary Policy," *Journal of Finance* 24(May 1969):281.

Figure 17–2

FRB-MIT Model Structure—Basic Real Sector Effects

which illustrates some of these differences.[5] In the figure, the rate of interest on Aaa bonds (the most secure class of corporate bonds) is assumed to influence five diverse categories of investment: stock market yields, saving deposit yields, mortgage rates, the general industrial bond rate (for bonds of varying ratings), and the state and local bond rate. This model structure implies an orderly term structure in which changes in the basic Aaa rate bring about similar changes in the entire array of investment rates. It also suggests a sufficient level of speculative activity among alternative investment vehicles to maintain their yields in a regular configuration. The model then translates these yields into cost-of-capital effects, into decision variables, and finally into goods market expenditures. In the investment sector, the impact of both the mortgage rate (related to the financing of business structures) and the industrial bond rate (related to structures and equipment) is described as being upon the cost of capital similar to the discussion of that measure in Chapter 8. This impact affects the desired capital-output ratio, the level of new orders for capital goods, and the level of actual new plant and equipment expenditures. In the residential construction sector, the impact of mortgage rates is upon the cost of capital for construction, which in turn impacts on housing starts and construction expenditures. However, in addition to the cost of construction capital, the availability of funds is a factor in housing starts in the FRB–MIT approach.

The yield on savings deposits affects the level of nonbank savings shares, and through this channel affects the level of rationing that occurs in markets for mortgage capital, the same effect discussed in Chapter 13. This effect is incorporated into the model by formulation of a rationing variable that measures the existence and extent of rationing behavior in mortgage markets arising due to unfavorable interest rate spreads between mortgage rates and other rates. Unlike the assumption contained in the *IS–LM* formulation, the FRB–MIT model contains a channel by which interest rates impact upon consumer expenditures. This effect begins with the impact of yields on corporate stocks upon the value of equities held by households. The value of equities is a component in household net worth—thus, the yield on stocks impacts upon the net worth or wealth position of households. According to the general reasoning presented in Chapter 5, an enlarged wealth position enables the household to increase both current consumption and future consumption. The result of this is an increased level of consumer spending when yields on stocks are rising and a decreased level of consumer spending when stock yields are falling. This wealth effect on consumer spending was ignored in our discussion of the *IS–LM* model. We now see

---

[5] In this figure and our discussion of it, we abstract from the question of time lags. Several relationships operate with a time lag in the actual equations of the model.

that the FRB–MIT model-builders feel it is significant enough in its influence on consumer spending to use it in a predictive model.

Besides incorporation of the wealth effect, the FRB–MIT approach expands upon the conceptual framework of the *IS–LM* model by showing that several interest rates impact upon expenditure variables in ways that are not the same. This enables the model-builders to study the uneven effects of monetary policy actions on real markets, an illustration of which was discussed in Chapter 9 in connection with residential construction expenditures during times of monetary tightness. In addition, the FRB–MIT approach brings out an additional linkage not found at the level of generality of *IS–LM*. This is the intermediate role of cost of capital measures between market rates of interest and expenditure decisions. Although the primacy of the cost of capital to market interest rates was discussed in Chapter 8, later the expedient was taken of assuming the linkage to be constant. The FRB–MIT results suggest that value may attach to an explicit consideration of the intermediate role of the cost of capital in explaining the impact of interest rates upon investment expenditures.

There are a sufficient number of similarities between the financial aspects of the consensus Keynesian model and the FRB–MIT model to suggest that they are from the same basic species. The interest rate linkages are broadly the same, as is the effect of real wealth on consumption. This is not the case with the St. Louis model of the economy, to which our attention now turns.

The St. Louis Monetarist Model

Researchers at the Federal Reserve Bank of St. Louis developed a macroeconomic model in the late 1960s that reflects the general structure of the modern quantity theory of money.[6] As discussed in Chapter 14, the quantity theory relies primarily if not exclusively on fluctuations in the money supply to explain fluctuations in total aggregate income. This is the approach of the St. Louis model, and it leads to a considerably simpler structure than larger Keynesian-type models. The St. Louis model has only six equations and three identities to explain the nominal GNP, the price level, real output, long-term interest rates, short-term interest rates, and the rate of unemployment. By contrast, Keynesian models of the type incorporated into our earlier consensus model typically contain close to 100 equations and identities and involve complex solution procedures.

[6] For a full presentation of this model, see L. C. Anderson and K. M. Carlson, "A Monetarist Model for Economic Stabilization," *The Federal Reserve Bank of St. Louis Review,* 52:4 (April 1970), pp. 7–25.

Figure 17–3 shows the structure of the St. Louis model.[7] As seen, the change in the money stock and the change in federal government spending are relied upon to explain changes in the nominal GNP. The measure of government spending is called "high employment" because it includes transfer payments adjusted to remove the influence of variations in economic activity on unemployment payments as well as government expenditures on goods and services. Because of the use of both government spending and the money supply to explain nominal GNP, the authors of the St. Louis model describe the GNP equation as being consistent with either a quantity theory or a Keynesian-like approach. In this way, the judgment on whether both variables (or one and not the other) are crucial in the equation is left until after the statistical results can be analyzed. Our discussion of the quantity theory in Chapter 14 suggests that in a world that follows this model, a change in government expenditures unaccompanied by other changes should have no lasting effect on the nominal GNP. Of the two components of nominal GNP, the level of real output is set outside the realm of demand in product markets while the level of prices is controlled by the money supply. Thus, increases in government spending only crowd out other expenditures, leaving the total unaffected. On the other hand, fluctuations in the money supply should have an important and lasting effect on the nominal GNP, primarily by affecting the level of prices. The results of the St. Louis tests confirm this view. The money supply variable has a large and statistically significant impact on nominal GNP while the change in H.E. federal spending has a nearly zero and statistically insignificant effect. This result indicates that the change in federal expenditures could be dropped from the model with minimum loss in predictive power.

The determination of the nominal GNP in the St. Louis model leads to the determination of real output and prices. As Figure 17–3 shows, the relationship between the change in the actual nominal GNP and the potential GNP at full employment shows the closeness to full employment that occurs. This relationship is assumed to represent the demand related pressures on prices, which in turn determine the change in the price level. A level of actual GNP close to capacity results in intense demand pressures and leads to large increases in prices in the St. Louis model, whereas a large gap between actual and potential GNP leads to small price changes. The change in prices along with the previously determined nominal GNP determines the change in real GNP. This process shows real output in the St. Louis model to be a residual that derives by direct identity from the prior determination of both the nominal GNP and the level of prices. With large gaps between

---

[7] As with the earlier models, we abstract from time lags in this figure. Several of the equations employ distributed lags of up to 4 years past behavior in the case of interest rates and prices and 4 quarters in the case of the money supply-GNP relationship.

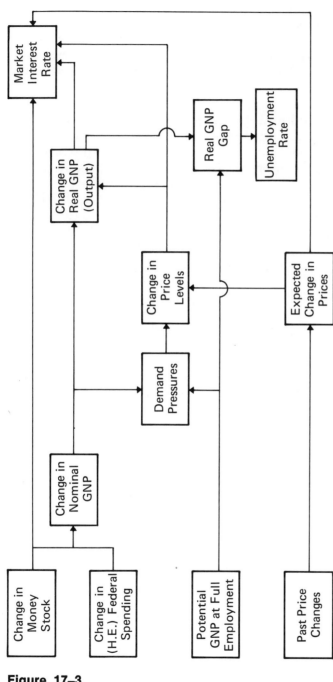

Figure 17–3

St. Louis Model

Source: Adapted from L. C. Anderson and K. M. Carlson, "A Monetarist Model for Economic Stabilization," *The Federal Reserve Bank of St. Louis Review 52,* 4(April 1970), p. 10.

actual and full employment GNP levels, changes in the nominal GNP lead to small price changes and therefore translate into nearly complete changes in real output. When actual GNP is close to the full employment level, the sharply rising prices absorb nearly all of a nominal GNP change, leaving real GNP little changed.

In addition to demand pressures, prices are influenced by expectations in the St. Louis model. Price expectations in turn are assumed to be based on the pattern of recent past prices. When prices have been rising rapidly for some period of time, this approach assumes they will be expected to continue to rise, which creates an environment in which actual price increases occur more readily.

The unemployment rate in the model is a product of the gap between the actual output level as measured by the real GNP and the potential output level as measured by potential real GNP. It accordingly has the same residual position in the model as the level of real GNP. When the level of real output and employment is low relative to full employment levels, a change in the nominal GNP leads to a nearly proportional change in employment. When the labor force is nearly fully employed, nominal GNP changes only result in higher prices and little employment changes.

Figure 17–3 shows interest rates to be a product of money supply changes, price expectations, and actual changes in both prices and real GNP. Interest rates are thus plainly the result of economic acitvity rather than a determinant of it. This view is consistent with our discussion in Chapter 14 of the role of interest rates in the quantity theory. Increases in the money supply increase the supply of funds available to money markets and thus lead to lower interest rates. Higher expected and actual prices affect the willingness of lenders to supply funds on money and capital markets. As prices increase at a more rapid pace, a given interest rate leads to less and less of a real return. Thus, higher actual and expected prices lead to higher interest rates. Increases in real GNP also lead to higher interest rates by placing greater demands on funds both for transactions purposes and to support higher levels of investment induced by real income increases. This role for interest rates is in sharp contrast with the two earlier models considered. In the St. Louis model, interest rates are the product of real market and price level behavior, but do not influence this behavior. Whether interest rates are high or low does not affect the level of nominal of real GNP or the level of prices.[8] In both earlier models, an important channel was defined running from interest rates to product market activity, particularly investment spend-

---

[8] From Chapter 8 it may be recalled that the only impact of increases in interest rates is to shift the composition of spending between consumer and investment sectors. However, the St. Louis model does not deal with a breakdown of GNP into consumer, investment, or other sectors, and accordingly can offer no evidence on this question.

ing. In the FRB–MIT model in particular, the role of interest rates on real market activity occupies the center of attention.

In our discussion of three approaches to the building of empirical macroeconomic models, we have now seen quite a contrast in model structure and in the theoretical apparatus involved. Although it is impossible to determine which approach is the most reasonable, it is possible to draw some impressions about the usefulness of varying models by comparing the extent to which models of varying theoretical origins can predict short-run movements in the economy. We now consider this topic.

The Forecasting Performance of Some Macroeconomic Models

Prediction is not the only test of a model. But it is an important way the correspondence between the model and the world can be judged. Comparing predictions obtained from different models must be done with care. It is not always clear that the smallest forecasting error means the superior model. To illustrate, suppose two models for the GNP are constructed. Model A requires the current interest rate as an exogenous input, while model B requires the population. Suppose model A shows the lowest prediction error under conditions where the exogenous variables are assumed known. Since interest rates are usually much more difficult to project in advance than the population, model A actually assumes much more than model B. The portion of model A's accuracy that is a result of this stronger assumption is an unknown but important factor in a comparison of the two. This ambiguity raises the question—Why not only consider comparisons between actual forecasts made in an environment where nothing can be assumed known in advance? The answer is that such a comparison mixes the skills of the model-builder with the inherent predictability of the model. For some purposes, it may be appropriate to view the forecasting system as truly a man-machine enterprise, such that comparisons of the average forecasting error of the model when actually used in forward projections is the final measure.[9] But for our purpose of drawing judgments about the applicability of various econometric models, the focus of attention is upon the predictability of the model structure rather than upon the skills of the model user. Under this premise, an objective comparison of the predictability of econometric models should be based on assumed knowledge of the exogenous variables and must also be based on a procedure that equalizes the strength of the assumed

[9] For an interesting comparison of simulated forecasts made cooperatively by several model-builders, see G. Fromm and L. R. Klein, "A Comparison of Eleven Econometric Models of the United States," *American Economic Review*, 63:2 (May 1973), pp. 385–393.

information. One possible procedure is to require that differing exogenous variables each be lagged sufficiently that they are known in advance for all models to be compared. In this way, the assumption about knowledge of differing exogenous measures is the same even though the exogenous information varies.

This approach has been taken in a recent comparison of the relative efficiency of a number of forecasting models.[10] This comparison includes the St. Louis model, a small Keynesian-type model developed by Irwin Friend and Paul Taubman (hereafter called the FT model), and several other approaches including so-called "naive" models that are essentially the projection of trends.[11] The FT model is of particular interest in our discussion because several comparisons of this model with larger models such as those included in our Keynesian consensus indicates the much smaller (five equation) FT model is approximately as effective in short-run predictions of the GNP as the much larger models. Thus, the FT model approximately reflects the effectiveness of Keynesian-type models in GNP predictions for the present purpose of comparing alternative model structures. The structure of the FT model used in the comparison is shown in Figure 17–4. As seen, the model explains the GNP as the sum of expenditures on consumer goods, plant and equipment investment, residential construction, inventory investment, net exports, and the level of government expenditures. Exogenous variables include the change in housing starts, the change in anticipated plant and equipment spending of business (based on a regular poll), the change in anticipated sales by business, the level of world trade, the change in government spending, plus various past values of variables in the model. A major multiplier-type feedback loop indicates the simultaneous determination of the various GNP components. The model contains no interest rates nor has it any role for the money supply in economic activity. It is thus similar to the crude version of the Keynesian model included in the four-sector model of Chapter 11.

According to our earlier discussion, each of the exogenous variables in the St. Louis, FT, and other models included in the comparison was lagged so its value would actually have been available to the forecaster at the start of the forecast period.[12] To obtain an absolute comparison as to the predictive accuracy of these model structures, two alternative forecasting models

[10] See J. W. Elliott, "A Direct Comparison of Short-Run GNP Forecasting Models," *Journal of Business*, 46:1 (January 1973), pp. 33–60.
[11] For a complete explanation of this small Keynesian model, see I. Friend and P. Taubman, "A Short-term Forecasting Model," *Review of Economics and Statistics*, 46:3 (August 1964), pp. 229–236.
[12] The single exception is the case of government expenditures, which were in each of the models compared and so were assumed exogenous and known in the forecast period.

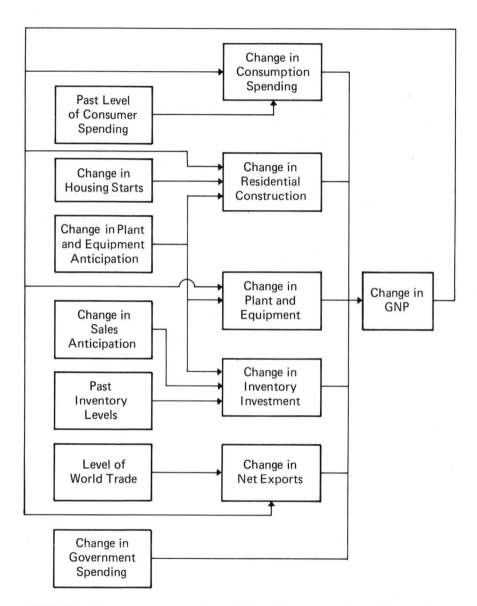

NOTE: This diagram represents the model used in a comparison of forecasting models. It differs from the original FT model in that net exports are not taken as exogenous but are predicted according to the level of world trade and the GNP level. For details, see Friend and Taubman or Elliott.

Figure 17–4

Basic Flows—Friend-Taubman Model

have been used, each of which is a product of trend extrapolation. They are

$$\text{NI}: \Delta\text{GNP}_t = 0 \qquad\qquad (17\text{--}1)$$

$$\text{NII}: \Delta\text{GNP}_t = \Delta\text{GNP}_{t-1} \qquad\qquad (17\text{--}2)$$

The NI model simply projects the absolute change in GNP in time period $t(\Delta\text{GNP}_t)$ to be zero for every period. The NII model predicts the rate of change in GNP to be zero (i.e., it predicts the change in the change to be zero).

Thirty-two forecasts were made of the change in real GNP with each of the models considered in the comparison, covering the quarterly time span from 1963.1 to 1970.4. Forecasts were made for one, two, and three quarters ahead for each of the models. Some of these results are summarized in Tables 17–1 and 17–2. In Table 17–1, the average forecasting error (disregarding the direction of the error) over the 32-quarter forecast period is calculated for the FT, St. Louis, NI, and NII models, for each of the one,

Table 17–1

GNP Forecasting Comparison

	AVERAGE ABSOLUTE FORECASTING ERROR (BILLIONS)		
	1 QUARTER AHEAD	2 QUARTERS AHEAD	3 QUARTERS AHEAD
FT	3.9	3.2	3.6
St. Louis	3.6	4.3	4.5
NI	6.6	6.7	6.7
NII	3.8	3.9	4.0

Source: J. W. Elliott, "A Direct Comparison of Short-Run GNP Forecasting Models," *Journal of Business*, 46:1 (January 1973), p. 50.

Table 17–2

GNP Tracking Comparison

	CUMULATIVE AVERAGE FORECASTING ERROR		
	AFTER ONE QUARTER	AFTER TWO QUARTERS	AFTER THREE QUARTERS
FT	3.9	4.1	4.4
St. Louis	3.6	6.7	9.0
NII	3.8	3.9	4.7

Note: Model NI has been omitted from this comparison because of its dominance by NII in earlier results.
Source: J. W. Elliott, "A Direct Comparison of Short-Run GNP Forecasting Models," *Journal of Business*, 46:1 (January 1973), p. 53.

two, and three quarters ahead forecasts. These results show that the FT, St. Louis, and NII models all yield comparable average absolute forecasting errors over the test period. For the two and three quarter ahead predictions, the FT model begins to show a perceptibly smaller standard error than the St. Louis model. For all three periods, the assumption of NII that the rate of change in the real GNP is constant proves to be a difficult standard to surpass, in terms of average error. Of course, such a naive model can never predict a change in direction in the series and is thus assured to be wrong at most of the critical points of economic activity.

Table 17–2 shows the cumulative error over the successively longer forecast periods. This additive error (sign included) reveals the tendency of each model to stray from the actual value in a systematic way. A model that shows no tendency toward larger and larger errors in this context is said to "track" well. Table 17–2 shows that the FT model tracks perceptibly better than the St. Louis model over the three-quarter period and shows a steady pattern of improvement relative to the St. Louis model over the one, two, and three period sequence. Taken together, the results of the two tables suggest that the FT model gives somewhat better results than the St. Louis model with the exception of one-quarter ahead forecasts where the two models are of approximately equal predictability.[13] Thus, our comparison somewhat favors the small, crude Keynesian model over the St. Louis monetarist model. Presumably, if we were to replace the FT model with the Wharton or Commerce model, the result would remain about the same or, if anything, lean more in favor of the Keynesian-type model. But, the St. Louis model makes an impressive show of predictive accuracy given its simplistic structure.

A Summing Up

It was not possible to include the FRB–MIT model in this comparison due to its size and complexity. However, a recent comparison of its forecasting properties compared to models such as NI and NII indicates its performance is comparable to such baselines in terms of average error.[14] Since this is also approximately the case for the Keynesian and St. Louis models, we are left with a rather unclear picture as to whether any of these three models has

[13] Three other models were also involved in the comparison, including a model based on NBER leading indicators, a model developed for the Federal Office of Management and Budget, and a model that is related to the Wharton model. The St. Louis and FT models were generally the best performing among the full group.

[14] See Charles Nelson "The Prediction Performance of the FRB-MIT-Penn Model of the U.S. Economy" Report 7117, Center for Mathematical Studies in Business and Economics, University of Chicago, April, 1971.

dominant predictive characteristics compared with the others. We cannot reliably point to one class of models as being clearly superior to all others for forecasting purposes. Nonetheless, we find many useful insights have been gained in the process of reaching this conclusion. Among these, the discipline of econometric model building forces a complete model structure and invites a flow chart type visibility for assumptions and structural stipulations that often escapes a narrative development of models. In addition, we find in the various model structures a way to locate the channel of influence for statistical variables and economic measures that previously had less significance. Further, in the flow chart descriptions of various models, a crude road map for analysis is presented. Nonstatistical forecasts made by a process of logical deduction can profit from the model structures presented by using them as a way to structure an analysis of the level of economic activity. To illustrate this, the consensus Keynesian model of Figure 17–1 contains an explicit role for variables such as corporate cash flow, vacancy rates, employment levels, and household liquid assets in current spending flows. In sizing up the future prospects for such spending flows, it is quite possible to use the structure of this or another model as a guide.

This chapter has illustrated an important use of macroeconomic theory —as the basis for the construction of predictive models of the economy. In the next two chapters, we consider additional applications of the theory now discussed. The next chapter takes up the question of the explanation of inflation in the context of our economic model. The last chapter considers the application of ideas from our model to the formulation of public policy.

Discussion Questions

1. What do you see as the essential differences between the Keynesian consensus and the FRB–MIT model structures?

2. Explain the differences in the role of interest rates in the determination of the GNP in the Keynesian consensus as compared to the St. Louis model.

3. Use the Keynesian consensus as a guide for forecasting the near-term (1-year) outlook for residential construction spending. What are the major inputs to your projection?

4. Using the St. Louis model as a guide, evaluate the predicted results of the period of high interest rates that occurred in the first half of 1974. Do you think the model would have predicted the results that actually occurred?

5. Each year during the latter several months, *Business Week* collects and publishes a variety of forecasts from econometric models and elsewhere, including some of those discussed in this chapter. Locate the last several of these write-ups, and make a current evaluation of which class of model has the best record in "before-the-fact" forecasts, using the advantage of now knowing what the actual value of the GNP turned out to be.

18

The Economy in Inflation

An inflation is a period of persistent and significant price level change. In this chapter, we consider several topics related to the operation of the economy during inflation. Among these, we first take up the nature of demand related and demand independent pressures on price levels. The combined effect of inflationary pressures is often to create an inflationary process throughout the economy. We consider the effect of an inflationary process on the working of the macroeconomic model. Finally, we consider the special problem of stability in interest rates during a time of general inflation.

Demand Factors in Price Level Change

In the United States, the majority of product prices are not determined impersonally in a market arena and changed in an auction fashion according to the dictates of current supply and demand. Instead, they are set by individual producers and typically are given to consumers on a take-it-or-leave-it basis. In industries dominated by a few sellers, the pricing decisions of individual firms are made in careful recognition of the possible reaction of rival producers. Whether or not a price increase will be "followed" is an important if not an overriding concern in decisions about price changes. These price-setting strategies are not characteristic of the operation of perfectly competitive market structures, in which the price rises and falls in direct response to changes in demand. Nonetheless, in the modified competitive environment of the United States, we may still expect sharply increased customer demand to cause producers to consider raising prices, particularly when productive capacity is largely utilized. If increased customer demand and high rates of capacity utilization are industry-wide, this feeling will most likely be shared among all producers, so that increased prices by some producers will likely be followed by increased prices by remaining producers. Under these circumstances, the potential risk (in terms of market share) of an individual producer posting a price increase is low. Thus, industry-wide increases in customer demand and diminished levels of excess capacity can be expected to create producer attitudes leading to price increases in the industry. Similarly, if a large number of industries in the economy are characterized by continued brisk demand and utilization rates approaching capacity levels, we may anticipate price increases on a widespread scale. This type of inflationary pressure is often referred to as *demand-pull* by economists, indicating the pressures of market demand and capacity production pulls prices up under such circumstances. Clear and straightforward illustrations of pure product market demand-pull inflationary pressures in the U.S. economy are not available, principally because they almost never occur in isolation. Other related pressures involving labor costs and materials prices usually complicate otherwise pure demand-pull circumstances, to produce a complex and interrelated structure of price level pressures.

When general increases in industry or aggregate demand occur, bringing with them direct upward pressures on prices, general increases in production levels are called forth. As production is increased in particular industries, all concerned producers have increased demands for labor. Labor markets tighten, initially in key low supply labor categories and eventually in all categories. Shortages of labor intitially result in more overtime at increased cost to producers. Producers may employ special financial or other incentives (e.g., relocation costs) to attract scarce labor, also at additional costs. These extra costs place immediate pressures upon profit margins.

Occurring concurrently with vigorously expanding product markets, shrinking profit margins produce additional producer incentive to raise prices and thus pass some of the increased labor cost through to the customer. These pressures add to product market influences on prices. If the market demand is persistent enough, it may have an impact on new major labor contracts, as management is in a reduced bargaining position during times of critical labor shortages.

As if product demand and labor cost forces weren't sufficient to translate market demand increases into inflationary patterns, still a third factor, having to do with the input-output interdependence of industry, usually intermingles and adds to the influence of the first two. Industries buy the output of other industries in the form of materials, components, and assemblies. For example, a portion of the output of the steel industry is purchased as a productive input by dozens of other industries such as automobiles, refrigerators, machine tools, building materials, and aircraft. When steel prices rise, costs rise for all using industries. Additional pressures are placed on profit margins of firms in these using industries. If they respond through price increases of their own, the steel industry effect is transmitted across the economy. Indeed, the steel industry may soon find that their profit margins are under increased pressures due to increased costs of machine tools and other products they purchase from other industries. If increased market demand applies to many industries, the effects of these industry input-output interrelationships upon input costs may be widespread, forcing up a large proportion of purchased parts and raw materials costs of producers in general and eroding profit margins.

Coupled with direct demand-capacity price pressures and related demand pressures on labor costs, the pressures of rising prices for materials and purchased parts complete an often powerful array of price pressures during times of advancing product market demand and high utilization of productive capacity.

Generally, economists feel that demand-pull and related pressures are greatly diminished if widespread underutilization of productive resources (e.g., high unemployment rates and excess plant capacity) accompanies the increase in product market demand. This is a view consistent with our discussion of price behavior in the underemployed, rigid wage economy in Chapter 16. For example, if the economy is making an initial expansion from a recession, increases in customer demand will have the immediate effect of reducing probably excessive inventory levels and propping sagging price structures. Under these circumstances, we may expect producers to be greatly concerned about sales and production levels, which are likely to be considered critically low relative to productive capacity. Producer's concern over output/sales levels can be expected to result in their reacting to customer demand increases principally through output changes accompanied by little if any price change.

If the business expansion continues, thereby absorbing excess plant capacity and reducing rates of unemployment, the reactions of producers can be expected to undergo a gradual change. As output/sales levels recover from recessionary levels, profit maximizing producers will have a reduced motivation to expand output levels and an increased motivation to consider higher prices, thereby widening profit margins to cover rising marginal costs. The result of this change is a general strategy of reacting to increased demand with both output increases and price increases.

If continued expansion in demand causes production of full employment and maximum plant utilization levels of output, producers' strategies can be expected to further shift toward a much heavier price reaction and a much smaller output reaction, exactly in the fashion discussed in Chapter 16 for the fully employed economy. In the proximity of the economy's full employment level, demand increases can be expected to precipitate proportional price level increases, with little or no output change. As this occurs, the operation of the product market, labor market, materials demand-pull forces now discussed become more pronounced, speeding up the overall rate of inflation.

So far we have exclusively discussed upward movements of prices and positive pressures upon prices. Historical observation of the U.S. economy does not suggest that our analysis applies equally to deflationary movements and pressures. Prices in the United States are less likely to fall during declining demand than they are to rise during increasing demand. This is due to an apparent tendency by many U.S. producers to accept declines in output more readily than declines in product prices during economic declines.[1] Thus, the primary impact of recessions upon U.S. price levels is typically not to cause prices to decline, but rather to halt or retard the rise in prices. Indeed, in the most recent two U.S. recessions—1960–1961 and 1970—price levels actually increased. (In 1970, the GNP price deflator rose over 5 percent.)[2] From our discussion of demand-pull influences, this experience indicates an inherent inflationary tendency in the United States. We now explore this tendency further.

Other Price Level Pressures

An additional factor intertwined with general demand-pull pressures on prices in the United States is the emergence during expansions of industry hot-spots. Typically, as the economy moves upward, some industries reach full utilization ahead of others. For these near capacity industries, demand-pull pressures are intense. Not only does product demand exceed productive capacity, but also the cost of labor has risen substantially as the slack has been absorbed from industry labor markets, thus eroding profit margins. We may expect a pattern of rising prices in these near capacity industries. This contributes to rising prices by providing an inflationary environment and a precedent for other industries. To the extent that the near capacity industries are important suppliers of material or products to other industries, the

---

[1] As our discussion of the rigid wage case in Chapter 16 implies, such a strategy is non-profit-maximizing. When wages are rigid, a decrease in demand should bring about a cut in prices in order to clear markets at profit maximizing production levels. Thus, a reluctance by producers to follow this course of action also shows a willingness to protect profit margins as much as possible from declines during output contractions, even though total profits are damaged in the process.

[2] At this writing, it also appears that 1974 can be added to this list as well, since a first quarter decline of nearly 6 percent in real output was accompanied by a rate of inflation in general prices of greater than 10 percent.

rising prices become cost increases for customer industries, stimulating price rises in these industries through declining profit margins.

A second way in which near capacity industries affect prices in other industries is through their impact on prices of labor and materials common to both. With their product prices rising, near capacity industries are willing to pay higher prices for materials and critical labor if necessary to assure continued high production. In some circumstances, the result may be a bidding up of prices in key input categories. The resulting rising input costs will be experienced by all customer industries regardless of demand conditions, causing shrinking profit margins and motivating price increases by producers in these industries, even though they may have excess capacity and sluggish customer demand.

The influences upon general price levels now outlined have resulted directly or indirectly from product demand-productive capacity relationships. They have largely been pressures produced by supply-demand imbalances. Other factors that apparently are largely independent of demand-capacity relationships have at times been important influences upon inflationary patterns in the United States. We now consider these factors.

Demand Independent Price Level Pressures

The U.S. economy in 1970 provided the first clear-cut example since inception of the GNP statistics (1929) of a clearly inflationary recession. Prices on the goods and services included in the GNP rose by better than 5 percent while real output declined during the year. The experience was perhaps traumatic for U.S. economic policy makers who had diligently steered a policy course during 1969 and early 1970 of cooling the economy, aiming at opening up a sufficient degree of unemployment and excess plant capacity to cause demand-pull and related inflationary pressures to subside. Yet, while unemployment rates grew steadily to over 6 percent by December 1970, general price increases continued unabated. By year-end, the accumulated evidence suggested that the main forces fueling the inflation were largely independent of output and employment levels, thus indicating the operation of a different set of explanatory forces than those associated with demand-pull. We now look at two such demand independent forces that appear to operate upon the U.S. economy.

Wage-Price Spiral

The first inflationary influence involves interactions between wages and prices under conditions of rigid strategies on the part of unions and management. To see the dynamics of this operation, assume the following:

(1) That decision makers of major labor unions are much more interested in higher wage rates than in full employment of union members, given a choice between the two.

(2) That decision makers of major price-setting producers are much more interested in preserving profit margins by price adjustments than in maintaining output at high levels, given a choice between the two.

When behavior of union and management decision makers approximates these assumptions, the potential of a wage-price spiral effect is created in the economy. It is of no consequence where we break into this spiral. For example, consider a key union demand for an 8 percent increase in wages, which after a long and costly strike is agreed to by management. Also, assume that increases in labor productivity (output per man-hour) of 3 percent make labor somewhat more efficient and offset part of this labor cost increase, causing approximately a 5 percent increase in labor costs per unit of output.[3] This unit cost increase reduces profit margins. If producers set prices to keep profit margins constant, we can expect approximately a 5 percent increase in prices to result according to our second assumption. If the union settlement set a pattern that became typical in the economy, then offsetting price increases would generally occur, producing a generally inflationary pattern. As prices rise and purchasing power of the dollar declines, union demands for higher wages intensify. The next round of wage negotiations can be expected to produce renewed settlements in excess of productivity, thus further increasing unit labor costs. These cost increases lead to further product price increases, and so forth.

The behavioral assumptions we have made about union and management decision strategies are the principal ingredients in this spiral. There seems to be no particular reason to assume that this behavior will be influenced by unemployment levels or rates of excess capacity unless these levels

---

[3] The arithmetic of this can be seen by focusing on the units of the two measures involved. Wages are (labor cost)/(man-hours) while productivity is (output)/(man-hour). Thus, dividing wages by productivity gives unit labor cost (labor cost)/(output). When wages rise faster than productivity, unit labor costs rise and profit margins decline. In fact, if wages are denoted by W and productivity by T, then unit labor cost is $W/T = ulc$. If W and T are initially at W_0 and T_0 (with ulc at ulc_0) and W rises by 8 percent while T rises by 3 percent, we have

$$\left(\frac{W}{T}\right)_1 = \frac{W_0(1.08)}{T_0(1.03)} = ulc_0(1.08/1.03) \cong ulc_0(1.05)$$

In general, we are approximately correct in subtracting the wage rate increase from the productivity increase to obtain the effect on ulc, e.g., $8\% - 3\% = 5\%$.

reach severe proportions. So, barring severe unemployment or excess plant capacity, the spiral we have outlined will operate effectively regardless of fluctuations in product market demand.

The U.S. economy of 1970 offers an example of this market demand independence. Labor union leaders were unimpressed by falling corporate profit margins, weak product markets, and production cutbacks. At the same time, they were greatly impressed by the sharply increasing cost-of-living as indicated by the consumer price index. As a result, union wage-increase demands typically approached 8–10 percent. Settlements of 8 percent or more were frequent. At the same time, with sales and production levels falling due to recessionary market conditions, and with profit margins under severe attack due to rapid increases in the cost of labor and other inputs, producers typically decided to ignore weak market conditions and increase product prices in an effort to recover former profit margins. This contributed to the cost-of-living rise, increased union demands and higher wage settlements, and produced further erosion of profit margins. Thus, prices rose briskly during the year while product demand slowed down, inventories piled up, and markets became increasingly sluggish.

Structural Wage-Productivity Imbalances

A new dimension in the understanding of wage-price inflationary processes has been added recently by William J. Baumol.[4] His analysis deals with relationships among prices, wages, and productivity in various segments of the economy having differing technological characteristics. To see the application of Baumol's argument to the United States, it is necessary to classify the U.S. economy into two sectors on the basis of technological characteristics. Sector A encompasses all industries whose product is such that more-or-less continuous increases in productive technique and related equipment occurs. Typically, industries that produce hard goods such as automobiles, appliances, and producer's durables are included in sector A. Also included are textiles, food products, and many other nondurable goods. In manufacture of sector A products, continual improvements in output-per-man-hour are possible through regular advances in the technological state. Sector A producers typically achieve regular labor productivity increases by employing more advanced equipment and techniques.

Sector B includes remaining industries that do not share this property. The nature of their products and services is such that advances in production techniques occur only infrequently on a sporadic basis, if at all. Typically, industries such as carpentry, bricklaying, plumbing, medical health, educa-

---

4 See W. J. Baumol, "Macroeconomics of Unbalanced Growth: The Anatomy of Urban Crisis," *American Economic Review*, 57 (June 1967), pp. 415–426.

tion, public services, and certain recreational productions may be thought of as being in sector B. In these productions, improvements in output-per-man-hour have not shown continuous patterns of increase. For example, in education, the output of productive services per educator man-hour employed is not subject to regular advance due to its basic nature. Sector B industries by definition are accompanied by approximately static productivity, while sector A industries enjoy dynamic productivity. For our present discussion, we shall presume we can classify all industries as sector A or sector B in nature. (In fact, this may present some difficult measurement problems.) Baumol now assumes two key behavioral properties of the economy:

1. Wages in both sector A and sector B move closely over time. In the United States, labor unions are important factors in both sectors. This means that settlements in certain key industries set goals for minimum acceptable settlements in other industries. In this way, it is assumed that pattern making settlements will spread through a sector and be transmitted to the other sector, causing a general leveling of wage gains throughout the economy.

2. Producers generally follow pricing strategies aimed at preserving profit margins at customary levels. Thus, when cost increases reduce profit margins, producers can be expected to respond by raising prices sufficiently to restore these margins.

To explore the implications of these classifications and assumptions, consider now the case where the wage settlements in the dynamic productivity sector A are approximately equal to the productivity increases in that sector. For illustration, assume both labor costs and output-per-man-hour rose by 4 percent with other costs constant. Total costs-per-unit would remain stable in sector A under these circumstances.[5] No profit margin motivation would exist to raise prices, and we may presume (per our second assumption) that they will remain stable in sector A.

In sector B, the effect of the 4 percent wage settlements in sector A industries is felt in the form of similar demands by sector B labor unions. According to our first assumption, we may expect the wage settlements in sector B to also approach 4 percent even though no increase has occurred in sector B productivity. As a result of higher labor costs and constant labor productivity, overall costs per unit rise in sector B by about 4 percent. Following our profit margin pricing assumption, this cost increase will be translated into an approximate 4 percent increase in prices of sector B products.

---

[5] Strictly speaking, the situation would have to apply to all industries in sector A. Otherwise, we would anticipate some increases and decreases in sector A prices. In this case, if downward price behavior is not symmetrical with upward price behavior, the effects may not be offsetting.

The sector B price increase will work back on sector A firms to the extent sector B products are inputs used in the production of sector A products. The effect will be to raise sector A firms' costs, leading to offsetting price increases by these firms.[6] Under the circumstances we have outlined, the overall effect is reasonable stability in prices in sector A due to the productivity gains in that sector, but price increases comparable to labor cost increases in sector B.

Seen over a period of several years, the impact of this process can be expected to produce continued increases in the prices of the products and services of sector B relative to those of sector A. Accordingly, prices of carpentry, plumbing, bricklaying, medical care, education, public service, etc., would rise relative to the prices of automobiles, refrigerators, T.V. sets, clothing, etc. Such a pattern can be seen in the recent structure of prices in the U.S. economy, particularly in the inflationary period of 1967–1974.

A continued rise in sector B prices relative to sector A prices means that an increasing percentage of national income is earned in producing sector B products. For those sector B products whose demand is sensitive to the price (price elastic), it also means that sales will fall off as prices increase, thus moving these products and services toward ultimate economic extinction. Examples of this process can be found in the production of handmade goods of various kinds, where the production technique is essentially fixed. As the wages required to retain producers in these employments rise with sector A wages, the resulting product price increases continually reduce the quantity demanded and produced. For sector B products having an inelastic demand, the effect of the continued price increase is to increase the proportion of the economy's resources committed to their production. As examples, education and medical care would be expected to command a growing share of national income if their production and supply is characterized by approximately constant technology. The same is true of many public services.

Baumol's analysis represents an inflationary influence that we may expect to operate in conjunction with the basic wage-price interactions previously discussed. As general prices are rising for reasons essentially associated with the wage-price spiral, Baumol's argument suggests that rises in sector B industries will be more pronounced than in sector A and will provide leadership for the inflationary increase. As with basic wage-price interactions, we find no reason to expect the dynamics of sector A–sector B inflationary processes to be importantly altered by demand conditions in markets for products and services. As with wage-price spiral assumptions, Baumol's two-key behavioral assumptions can be expected to hold during all but the most severe

---

[6] Of course, to the extent that some sector A products are inputs for sector B production, an additional cost will be retransmitted back to sector B, causing further price adjustments.

of recessions as effectively as they hold during conditions of near capacity production. Recent price data in the United States seems to support this expectation, as prices of services and other sector B products showed essentially the same pattern of increase in the recession of 1970 as in the preceding expansion, while many sector A products showed a much smaller increase.[7]

Inflationary Processes in the Economy

So far, our discussion of price level pressures has not dealt with the impact of such pressures upon economic equilibrium, or with the reaction of other nonprice economic variables back upon price levels during times of rapid price increases. We now consider inflation from this broadened perspective. To begin, we return to the model of goods, money, and labor markets of Chapter 16 and pose the question: How will the economy's markets respond to a pure demand-type inflation in a fully employed environment? Although we have already answered this question in the course of our discussion in Chapter 16, it will be profitable to review the result here with a focus on the movement of prices involved.

In Figure 18–1, we start with the economy in a stable full equilibrium situation with real income, y, at the full employment level, y_f, the LM function at $L_0 M_0$, the IS function at $I_0 S_0$, and the market interest rate, i_0, at the full equilibrium level. Now assume that an increased level of product market demand occurs. The IS shifts to $I_1 S_1$. The increased demand for goods and services increases transactions demand for money balances and places upward pressures on interest rates, which begin to rise toward i^*. The increased product market demand also puts pressures on prices, which begin to rise. The rising prices motivate expansion of output toward y^*, due to the falling real wage. But, a labor shortage appears, and the rising prices begin to reduce the real money supply. The labor shortage begins to produce an increase in the money wage rate, which starts to undo the motivation for producers to expand output levels further. The reduction in the real money supply starts an upward shift in the LM function, which motivates a further upward movement in interest rates from i^* toward i_1. Prices continue to rise as long as excess demand exists in product markets. Excess demand occurs as long as the IS–LM intersection lies to the right of the full employment level of real income. Thus, prices continue to rise until the contraction in the real money supply has shifted the LM function up to the location $L_1 M_1$. At this point, the level of demand has been reduced by the higher interest rates to the level of full employment supply, prices stop rising, and full equilibrium is again restored at higher but stable prices and

[7] This suggests that when demand pressures subsided during the year, the structural type influences remained to work a sector A–sector B effect on the economy.

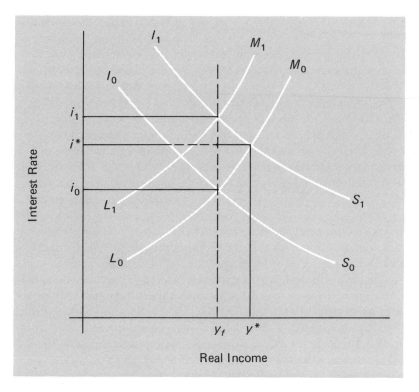

Figure 18–1

Inflationary Response

money wage rates. A crucial aspect of this process is that the increasing price level caused by excess demand in product markets set into motion a series of reactive forces that ultimately work back upon the product market excess demand conditions to eliminate the demand pressures and stop the price rise. The indication is that inflation set in motion by excess demand eventually burns itself out due to its effect on interest rates via the *LM* function. Does this mean we may rely upon the inherent characteristics of the economy to stop an inflationary pattern, without resort to governmental policy actions or monetary policy measures? While our present discussion shows the theoretical answer is yes, the practical answer is maybe. We now consider why.

Inflation and Interest Rate Stability

In Figure 18–1, the price increase stopped when the interest rate rose to i_1, a sufficiently high rate to level product market demand with full employment production. But, what if i_1 in the real world turns out to be unreasonable, say 21 percent? Our analysis makes no distinction as to whether the market-clearing full equilibrium interest rate is in a "reasonable" or an "unreasonable" range. Perhaps we should simply follow the prescription of Figure 18–1 and make no such distinction. If the economy needs a rate of interest of 21 percent to achieve a noninflationary equilibrium, then so be it. While economists may embrace such thoughts, it is difficult to envision decision makers at the Federal Reserve, the banking community, and the public in general being willing to stand by while interest rates climb to such extremely high levels. Indeed, the Federal Reserve normally maintains a policy of using their discretionary authority to support orderly debt markets. It seems likely that interest rates could rise to a point where the markets would be declared "disorderly," and expansionary monetary policy would be undertaken to bring rates down.

Bankers can also be expected to find a sharp increase in interest rates to extremely high levels undesirable. To mention but one adverse impact upon banks under such circumstances, the value of bank security holdings declines drastically, with rapidly rising interest rates such that normal bank liquidity needs may require portfolio adjustments resulting in the realization of capital losses in painful amounts. In addition, the housing market will in all likelihood not keep pace with sharply rising general interest rates with respect to adjustments in their borrowing and lending rates, if past experience with U.S. mortgage markets during periods of rising general rates is a useful guide. The result is below market interest rates on mortgages, a drying up of mortgage money, and a near depression in housing. Finally, there may be international repercussions, as our discussion in Chapter 11 indicated. A large gap between U.S. interest rates and those available in the rest of the world may draw foreign capital into U.S. investments in substantial proportions. While this improves the balance of payments, it is also similar to an injection of new monetary reserves into the economy. For a time, this effect could be expected to push market interest rates below the level needed to halt the inflation and restore stability. However, eventually, the continued high demand for (and shortage of) U.S. dollars on foreign exchange markets increases the price of the dollar (assuming flexible exchange rates) such that U.S. investments are no longer more profitable for foreign investors. At this point the international effect substantially dissipates.

This discussion indicates that a number of influences may combine to keep interest rates from rising to levels that may be required to bring about a full equilibrium condition and halt an inflationary condition. Figure 18–2 shows the consequences of such a situation. In this figure, the IS function intersects the full employment real income level, y_f, at an interest rate of 16 percent. When the LM function is at L_eM_e, a full equilibrium condition exists, the market interest rate is equal to the 16 percent full equilibrium rate, and prices and wages are stable. But, if the resulting market interest

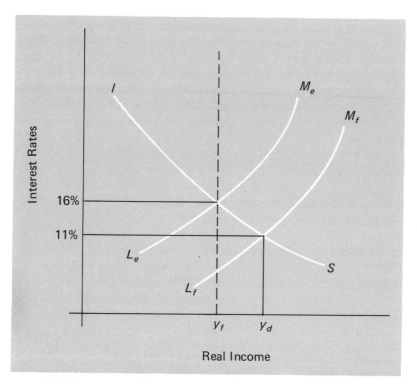

Figure 18–2

Impact of Stable Interest Rates

rate of 16 percent is seen as "too high," then monetary policy may be directed toward lowering the rate. Suppose the Federal Reserve engages in open market policy sufficient to shift the *LM* curve outward to $L_f M_f$. This brings the market interest rate down to 11 percent, which we assume for discussion is a maximum tolerable level for the Federal Reserve. However, at this level the demand for real output, y_d, exceeds the full employment supply, y_f. Inventories fall, and prices increase in response to the excess product market demand. Producers try to respond to the falling real wage by increasing their employment levels, but a labor shortage emerges, leading to rising wages. With no further Federal Reserve actions, the *LM* curve begins to shift back to the equilibrium level due to the reduction in the real money supply associated with the continued increase in prices. This increases interest rates back toward 16 percent. However, if the Federal Reserve is committed to a policy of holding interest rates in the region of 11 percent, they will continue to supply new reserves to the banking system to offset the tendency of the real money supply to shift leftward. As a result, the LM is maintained in the position L_fM_f. The inflation is not halted by the LM mechanism in this case, and the increase in prices and wages continues as long as the market interest rate is kept below the full equilibrium rate. We may now ask whether or not the inflation can go on indefinitely, under conditions where monetary policy keeps the market interest rate below the full equilibrium rate. We must again answer, maybe, depending on reactions in the real sector of the economy.

Inflationary Reactions in the Real Sector of the Economy

Following our discussion in the previous section, we continue to consider the case where the Federal Reserve maintains interest rates at a maximum level (say 11 percent) that is below the full equilibrium level. For simplicity, we assume the Federal Reserve is entirely successful in maintaining this rate constant at 11 percent by continual monetary expansion, which results in continued inflation. We now ask the question: Are there reactions in the real sector of the economy that will halt the inflation even with interest rates held at below equilibrium levels? Our analysis of this question is simplified by the assumption that interest rates are successfully held constant by Federal Reserve policy. In this case we can ignore monetary reactions and return to the crude Keynesian market sector model presented and discussed in Chapters 6–10, in which we need only be concerned with the supply and demand on markets for goods and services. The constant interest rate ceases to be a factor, as it has been neutralized by the Federal Reserve policy.

In Figure 18–3, a simplified two-sector model is shown that contains an investment and a consumer sector. To illustrate the present point, we show the diagram in nominal values rather than the real values with which our earlier analysis has been concerned. In addition, for simplicity we assume prices are constant for all output levels less than the full employment level (y_f) and that they rise in direct proportion to demand for levels of demand greater than full employment. We consider first the case in which consumers make their nominal consumption decisions based on nominal income changes. Their consumption function is expressed entirely in nominal rather than real terms. This indicates that consumers hold the so-called "money illusion" in which they react to price-induced nominal income changes in the same way they react to real-income-induced changes. In the nominal terms of Figure 18–3, this consumption function is given by the straight line pc, where p stands for the price level and the small letters stand for real quantities (c for real consumption, x for real investment, and y for real income/output). In contrast to the behavior of consumers, Figure 18–3 shows

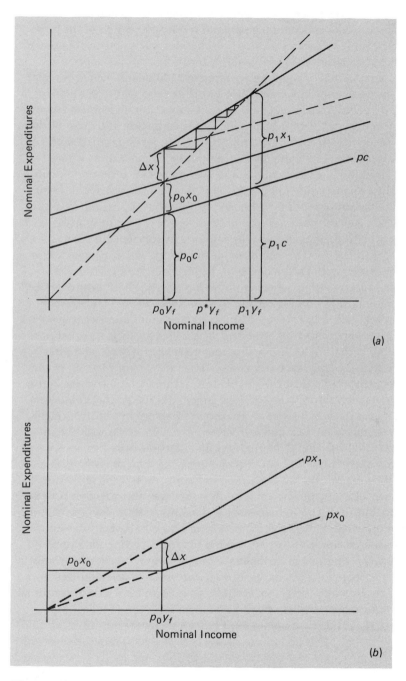

Figure 18–3

Reactions to Inflation

the case in which investors do not suffer the money illusion and demand a particular quantity of real capital goods and services regardless of the price level. Given a constant interest rate, we assume the real quantity of intended investment to be constant. Figure 18–3(b) shows that this assumption requires a rising nominal demand for investment as full employment is passed and prices begin to rise. The kinked line px_0 illustrates that to maintain a constant level of real purchases equal to x_0, nominal purchases must rise in proportion to demand once full employment is surpassed (the slope of the px_0 line passes through the origin, indicating a proportional relationship).

The upper part of Figure 18–3(a) shows the circumstances where the economy is initially in equilibrium at p_0y_f with nominal consumption equal to p_0c and investment equal to p_0x_0. Assume now that intended real investment rises by Δx to a level of x_1. The interest rate should rise, but it cannot, due to Federal Reserve policy. Thus, prices begin to rise in proportion to demand. But, due to the upward sloping nominal investment function, the effective slope of the nominal aggregate demand function is increased, as is the effective multiplier. This behavior by investors increases the new equilibrium position from p^*y_f (where it would have been if both consumers and investors transacted in nominal terms) to p_1y_f. Thus, we find the economy reaches a new (albeit inflated) equilibrium where the inflationary pressures cease. At this new equilibrium, investors have increased their nominal purchases enough to maintain their real purchases at the revised real output level, x_1. As a result, they are purchasing a larger (by Δx) proportion of the full employment supply than before the shift in intended investment. Since the full employment supply cannot be enlarged, this means that consumers must be acquiring less of a share of real output than before the investment shift, even though their nominal purchases have risen along with the increase in nominal income. (Nominal income increases from p_0y_f to p_1y_f.)

In this analysis, we find that the economy can tend to reestablish a new equilibrium position as a reaction to inflation, even if the interest rate is maintained at a subequilibrium level. But, we have also seen that such an equilibrium requires some demanders to be willing to settle for less real output so that other demanders can increase their real purchases. But, what if neither consumers nor investors are willing to accept a reduction in real output, during a time when the demand for real output by the two groups exceeds the supply? In this case, as long as interest rates are stabilized at below full equilibrium levels, the economy may be in for a case of continual, perhaps even runaway, inflation.

Figure 18–4 shows the case where neither consumers nor investors hold the money illusion. When prices are rising, both will maintain their level of intended real purchases in accordance with real income levels. The modified investment and consumption schedules are shown respectively in (b) and (c) of Figure 18–4. Each group changes their nominal demand proportionately in response to price changes that occur beyond full employment. Accord-

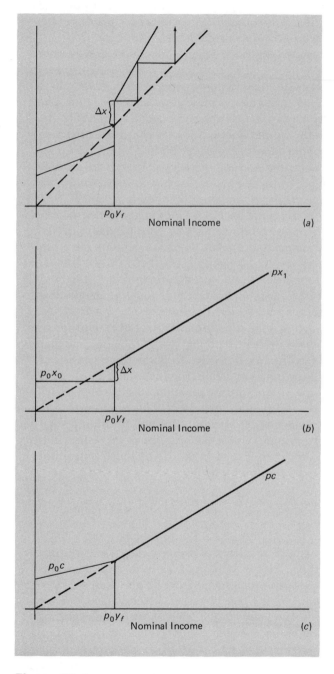

Figure 18–4

Runaway Inflation

ingly, each of these two upward sloping functions increases the slope of the aggregate demand function. The combined slope of the revised aggregate demand function is shown by the upper line in (a) of the figure. In the case shown, the slope of the revised aggregate demand function is greater than one. This is an unstable situation. If we continue to consider an increase in intended real investment of Δx, we find that a pattern of explosive growth in nominal demand occurs and prices increase at an increasing rate. The inflation does not dampen and cease as in the first case, but instead becomes explosive. The basic reason is quite simple. We have constructed the case where the level of full-employment real output is initially fully partitioned between consumers and investors and where both parties will not settle for a reduced share. A demand by investors for a larger share of real output results in a willingness on their part to increase their nominal demand accordingly. But, consumers will not settle for less. So they increase their nominal demand. This causes prices to rise faster, leading both parties to make further increases in their nominal demands. Runaway inflation has taken hold.

The upper part of Figure 18–4(a) shows that the runaway result is due to a combined nominal expenditure function that has a slope greater than one. This in turn depends on the effective slope of the investment and consumption functions in (b) and (c) in the region beyond full employment. In the case shown in Figure 18–4, the combined slope of the two functions is greater than one. In the earlier case of Figure 18–3, the combined slopes were less than one—thus the inflation damped out and the economy reached a new equilibrium position. Thus, whether an inflation supported by maintenance of a below full equilibrium interest rate will become runaway or not, by depending on the slope of the aggregate demand function beyond full employment, finally rests on the behavior patterns of demanders in the economy as reflected in the slopes of their respective intended expenditure functions.

Chapter Summary

In this chapter, we have considered demand pressures in price level changes and pressures on prices that have little if anything to do with demand. These provided a close-up view of the specific way in which product market demand and supply conditions produce increases in prices. Then our attention turned to the consideration of overall models of the economy during times of inflation. We found that monetary reactions are sufficient to bring inflationary movements in prices to a halt as long as interest rates are allowed to move to full equilibrium levels. Finally, we considered reactions in real markets to inflationary conditions under conditions where interest rates are held below full equilibrium levels by Federal Reserve policy. These concepts are important foundations of enlightened public policy toward the economy in inflation. But, in the consideration of policy, more is usually involved than the solution of one problem, since the solution of one problem in the economy as often as not creates or worsens another. It is to such questions that our attention turns in the next chapter.

Discussion Questions

1. Can you find reasons to expect demand type upward pressures on prices in an economy with less than full employment? Explain.

2. Consult statistical sources to define an industry in the United States that is a good example of a sector A industry. Now define a clearly sector B industry. Defend your choices by reference to your data sources. Has the price behavior in your two industries been in accord with the predictions of the sector A–sector B model? Explain.

3. Do you think the Federal Reserve in late 1973 and 1974 held interest rates artificially below full equilibrium levels by discretionary use of Federal Reserve policy? Defend your answer. Was it the right thing to do?

4. Overheard: "Although an inflation may be sustainable without excess demand, no inflation in the United States has ever started without excess demand being the primary cause." Comment on this statement in terms of the discussion of this chapter.

5. Develop statistical evidence on whether or not the statement in question 4 fits the facts of U.S. experience. On the basis of your evidence, do you agree or disagree with the statement?

Problem in Inflationary Policy

On February 26, 1974, the Chairman of the Board of Governors of the Federal Reserve System, Arthur Burns, warned that the United States seems headed for a Latin American style price spiral that could send interest rates soaring and ruin the chances for stable prosperity in the country. He contended that inflation is proceeding at a dangerous pace, while unemployment is rising. While Mr. Burns thought some improvement in the price situation was possible over the year, he was quite concerned with the consequences of the present trend. In a prepared statement, he cautioned that "if rapid inflation continues this year, it may undermine confidence, send interest rates soaring, and wreck our chances of regaining a stable and broadly-based prosperity in the near future."

Asked specifically about the outlook for interest rates over the year,

Mr. Burns said lending charges could decline if inflation is brought under control. But record rates will result if inflation continues surging, he said.

The price spiral may also destroy the gains recently made in strengthening the competitive position of the United States in world markets and in improving the nation's balance of payments.

Under questioning, Burns conceded that the Federal Reserve Board could stop the inflation dead in its tracks in a few months by severely tightening its grip on money and credit. "But, we have no intention of doing it," said Burns, because of the economic hardship it would cause. The economic stagnation and soaring unemployment that would result from a severe tightening of monetary policy can be avoided by a more gradual approach to controlling inflation, said Burns.

The Fed chairman indicated that he is against any immediate cut in the Reserve System's discount rate. Burns claimed that if this rate were lowered from its record level of 7.5 percent, then the Fed would be subsidizing commercial banks with bargain borrowing costs.

1. Using the data available in Mr. Burns's statement, what is the best estimate you can make of the precise rate of inflation at that time? Is this rate "soaring" by post-World War II standards?

2. What is the theoretical basis for Burns's connection between the rate of inflation and the level of interest rates? Given your inflationary projection in question 1, at what level should interest rates be?

3. What, if anything do domestic interest rate levels have to do with the country's balance of payments position?

4. How do you evaluate Burns's contention that a cut in the discount rate would represent a subsidy to commercial banks? Under what circumstances would this be true or untrue in your view?

19
Economic Policy

In this chapter, we consider topics related to the economics of public policy. In our discussion of macroeconomics throughout this book, a number of points have been found where governmental actions influence the course of economic activity. We saw that government purchases influenced the total level of product market demand. Tax policy was seen to influence the total saving flow in the economy and, through this channel, the level of product market demand. We found the supply of money to be importantly governed by governmental monetary management. These examples of circumstances where government actions have an impact on economic activity suggest the fundamental issues of economic policy. Should such policy actions by government be explicitly directed toward achieving desired economic goals? If so, can the actions have a predictable impact on the goals? How should we choose among alternative economic goals if we cannot achieve them all at once?

Our discussion of policy will be focused on such questions, with the purpose being to acquaint rather than enlist. We first consider the question of whether or not government should direct its activities toward economic targets in a discretionary way.

Public Actions and Economic Targets

The model developed in Chapters 4–16 leaves most readers with the strong indication that government actions can be directed toward discretionary

369

economic targets. We may assume with little controversy that relevant economic targets include fullness in production, minimum unemployment, price stability, and stability of the dollar in foreign exchange markets. Accordingly, it may seem reasonable that increases in government spending will bring an underemployed economy closer to full employment and that an increase in the money supply will have expansionary effects on real output and prices. Perhaps so, but Milton Friedman has argued strongly to the contrary.[1] Basically, Friedman's point is that the influence of monetary and fiscal policy on the economy is subject to a lag of varying and uncertain length and that the magnitude of the effect of policy on the economy is also difficult to predict. For example, Friedman suggests that an increase in the money supply may lead to an increase in output almost immediately in one instance and to little immediate increase in another instance. Similarly, a 1 billion increase in the money supply may associate with a 6 billion eventual increase in nominal GNP in one instance and a 1 billion eventual increase in nominal GNP in another instance. In Friedman's view, the impact of policy is highly unpredictable over the short-run period of several quarters or even a year. As a result, Friedman contends that public actions are quite likely to be ill-directed, producing immediate effects when delayed effects are needed and producing large effects on economic activity when small effects are called for. As a result, in Friedman's view, discretionary economic policy actions are as likely to move the economy away from its economic target as toward it.

As a result of this conclusion, Friedman has prepared a proposal designed to guide governmental actions in a way that contributes to maximum achievement of economic targets over the long-run, while disregarding attempts at short-run stabilization. The term long-run is crucial in understanding Friedman's proposal because he does not hold the same view about the impact of policy on economic targets over the long-run as he does over the short-run. Over the long-run, Friedman's position appears to be that most monetary effects are highly predictable while fiscal effects are largely nil (a view consistent with an essentially fully employed economy over the long-run). Accordingly, the thrust of Friedman's position is to remove the discretionary aspect of short-run government policy, replacing discretion with a set of rules. To eliminate discretion in the application of monetary policy, Friedman's proposal in its fullest form would do away with the U.S. concept of fractional reserves. Banks would be required to maintain 100

---

[1] Friedman's views originally appeared in "A Monetary and Fiscal Framework for Economic Stability," *American Economic Review*, 38 (June 1948), pp. 245–264. A later, much more streamlined version of Friedman's proposal can be gleaned from a series of lectures given at Fordham University in the late 1950s. See the published version of these lectures in M. Friedman, *A Program For Monetary Stability*, Fordham University Press, New York, 1960.

percent reserves, which effectively makes the level of outside money equal the total money supply and greatly increases the control the Federal Reserve would have over the money supply. In addition, discretionary open market policy actions by the Federal Reserve would be abolished. Government expenditures would be determined only by pressing social needs—never due to considerations of discretionary fiscal management. Transfer payments would be reformed so as to be uncoupled from the level of business activity, being put on more of a social security basis. Finally, the tax system would be overhauled such that the budgetary position could be maintained at a predetermined level. With these changes, discretionary governmental policy would be eliminated for all practical purposes. It would be replaced by a basic rule on the allowable rate of growth in the money supply. In Friedman's view, if the money supply were enlarged by, say, 4 percent a year, over the long-run the nation would closely approximate its economic targets, even though the course of economic activity would be uncertain in any particular year.

We do not have to subscribe to Friedman's proposal to appreciate the essential issue involved. The question of "rules versus discretion" remains an important one in the consideration of economic policy in the real world. We can replace Friedman's rules with others and still have the same question: Is the effect of government policy actions sufficiently predictable over the short-run that we should attempt to use policy for short-run adjustments toward our economic targets? Although we do not have a ready answer for this question, we shall proceed in our consideration of policy as if government actions have acceptably predictable effects on the economy. While this is not wholly satisfying, it moves the question from "whether to push policy buttons" to "which policy buttons to push and why," which is a somewhat less ambiguous avenue of inquiry.

From a broad perspective, our analysis in Chapters 15–16 of monetary effects upon real markets has indicated that the final impact of monetary actions in the fully employed economy is upon prices and not upon output. In the goods, money, and labor market model of Chapter 16, we found that the equilibrium level of real output was determined by either the full employment level, if the *IS–LM* intersection is to the right of full employment, or by demand conditions in the downwardly rigid wage case in which the intersection of the *IS–LM* equilibrium level of demand is less than full employment supply. Only in the underemployed rigid wage case does monetary action influence the level of equilibrium in real markets for products and services. Similarly, in the fully employed economy, the impact of fiscal policy (that shifts the *IS*) is basically upon interest rates and relatedly upon prices. An increase in demand for goods and services by government at full employment shifts the *IS* upward, increases the full equilibrium interest rate, and causes greater price increases to occur before the *LM* shifts back to the full equilibrium level. However, when excess capacity exists, fiscal policy can have effects on real markets, prices, and interest rates. Thus, when we confine our discussion to the case of an underemployed economy, we find the situation where both fiscal and monetary policy affect both prices and output levels. Since prices and output are both conventional economic targets, this implies a somewhat complicated situation for policy makers, since the impact of a given policy action may have both desirable and undesirable effects. It is made more complicated when we recognize that the Federal Reserve Board in the United States often sees itself as the primary guardian of price stability and thus often directs its policy actions toward this goal. By contrast, Presidential administrations and the Congress of the United States, who between them determine the final stance of fiscal policy, often are principally concerned with the goal of full employment. Accordingly, they often direct their budgetary and taxing actions largely toward full employment goals.

However, the actions of each policy setting group affect not only their own primary target but the primary target of the other policy group as well. Federal Reserve anti-inflationary policy (such as reducing the money supply) implies lower levels of employment. Similarly, governmental full employment policy (such as increased government expenditures) can mean higher rates of inflation. Thus, we may find the thrust of these two policy groups to be in conflict. What one is doing the other may be undoing.[2]

This discussion implies that full attainment of one economic target may have to be compromised on behalf of another target, in the case where the two are not fully compatible. The situation of price stability and full employment may be such an area where difficult public policy tradeoffs are necessary. We now turn to this question.

Full Employment and Price Stability

The classic study of the general nature of the tradeoff between full employment conditions and inflation was made by A. W. Phillips in a study of the relationship between the change in the money wage rate and the rate of unemployment in the United Kingdom.[3] In this study, Phillips found the two to be inversely related and relatively good substitutes in the sense that increases in one appear to be closely related to decreases in the other. Because

[2] Milton Friedman undoubtedly would find this possibility intriguing, as it suggests the possibility that the two together would produce a largely neutral effect on the economy that would at least not be destabilizing in its effect.

[3] See A. W. Phillips, "The Relationship Between Unemployment and the Rate of Change in Money Wages in the United Kingdom," *Economica*, 25:4 (November 1958), pp. 283–294. Additional studies after this time have been numerous. For an example using U.S. data, see W. G. Bowen and R. A. Berry, "Unemployment and Movements of the Money Wage Level," *Review of Economics and Statistics*, 45:2 (May 1963), pp. 163–172.

of the closeness of the relationship in the United States between money wage changes and price changes, the Phillips curve can be approximately reinterpreted in the U.S. case as the direct tradeoff between inflation and unemployment rates. Because our policy concern is directly with the level of prices relative to unemployment, we will focus on this reinterpretation in the present discussion. The relationship between price changes and unemployment rates in the United States on an annual basis over the period 1950–1973 is shown in Figure 19–1, with each point identified as to the year it

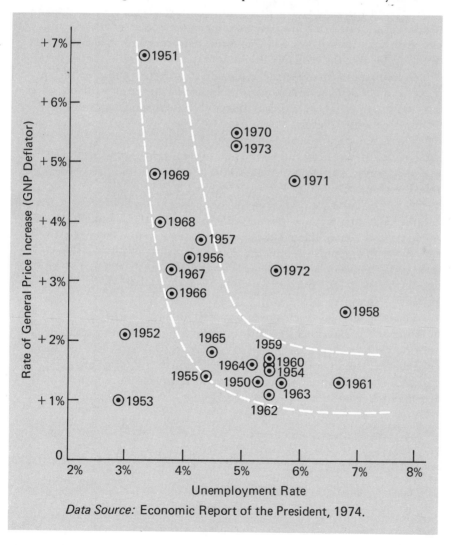

Data Source: Economic Report of the President, 1974.

Figure 19–1

Annual Price-Unemployment Relationships in U.S. 1950–1973

occurred. In a general way, the data in this figure show a pattern of substitution between price level change and unemployment rates over the period, as indicated by the predominant number of points that fall within the downward sloping trough described by the dotted lines. The points outside the dotted lines in Figure 19–1 are of particular interest. In 1952 and 1953, selective government price controls were imposed due to the Korean War. The price level changes in these 2 years are thus artificially low, accounting for their wide dispersion from the prevailing pattern. Two of the upward outlying points, 1958 and 1970, share a common property. Both were characterized by the onset of a business recession at the end of a vigorous business expansion. Accordingly, both years saw rising unemployment rates and a winding down of the economy from high capacity utilization rates. In both cases, the easing of demand capacity pressures apparently unveiled the operation of other demand independent inflationary pressures that kept prices rising at greater than normal levels during the year, even in the midst of declining real output levels.

The remaining three outlying points, 1971, 1972, and 1973, were all characterized in part or in full by the institution of price controls throughout the economy. The effect of these controls is difficult to judge, according to the President's Council of Economic Advisors.[4] It is not clear that the controls had any significant depressing effect on prices, particularly in 1973. But, it is likely that prices were somewhat lower than they would otherwise have been, and it is unlikely that they were higher.[5] In any event, the 3 years of controls resulted in outlying points on the high side—unlike the earlier 1952–1953 Korean experience with controls. In the absence of such controls, the 1971–1973 outliers would presumably be even further out of line on the high price side.

Focusing on these 3 years in more detail, we find that in 1971 the unemployment rate increased by a full percentage point. However, prices continued to rise at a 4.5 percent rate, even with controls instituted in September of that year. Rather than moving sharply downward in the manner of the dotted lines, the situation in 1971 shows a rightward movement of the price-unemployment relationship, as if the curve had shifted outward.

---

4 See *The Economic Report of the President,* U.S. Government Printing Office, Washington, D.C., 1974, Chapter 3.

5 However, it is possible to develop such a scenario. Suppose that many oligopolistic producers found that they could put larger price increases through the controls system than they could successfully "get away with" in their product markets in terms of the competitive reactions of rival producers. The allowable price increases under controls immediately become accepted industry-wide, eliminating the risk of competitive reactions. Thus, the controls organization becomes a proxy for a kind of oligopoly pricing cartel in this circumstance.

The combination of continued controls and a continued high unemployment rate (5.6 percent) apparently resulted in a cooling in the rate of inflation in 1972 to 3.2 percent. Although still considerably to the right of the bulk of post World War II experience, this result at least is in the direction called for by the Phillips curve relationship. The same is true for 1973, as a decline in unemployment from 5.6 percent to 4.9 percent associated with an upward movement in prices from a rate of 3.2 percent in 1972 to 5.3 percent in 1973, even with the continuation of controls throughout the year. However, it is difficult to believe that the controls that were in effect in 1973 had much to do with the rate of inflation that occurred during that year. The movements in 1972 and 1973 leave the impression that the U.S. price-unemployment relationship may well have shifted to the right, such that a given rate of inflation now associates with a higher unemployment rate than in the past.

The data in Figure 19–1 are annual averages and, as a result, they capture a broad pattern of price-unemployment rates. We can gain further impressions about the strength of this relationship by looking at data averaged over shorter periods. Figure 19–2 shows quarterly data from 1965–1973. As seen, the pattern is considerably blurred. It is impossible to construct a trough similar to that of Figure 19–1 due to the unclear pattern present in the figure. The conclusion seems clear that the appearance of some degree of stability in the annual price-unemployment curve breaks down substantially when viewed at quarterly data intervals.

In general, we are left with a less than conclusive picture about the strength and general usefulness of the price-unemployment relationship in the United States. The general fact that an inverse relationship exists in the annual data is evident. But, whether this pattern enables us to reliably translate unemployment levels into specific price level change counterparts is doubtful. Although a sparse sample, the 1958 and 1970 experience in the annual data of Figure 19–1 suggests that it depends somewhat upon how unemployment levels and economic activity are changing. This conclusion is strengthened by looking at the most stable portion of the period, 1962–1969, which was characterized by continuous and rather steady growth in output, with employment levels trending down and price levels trending up. During this period, the association between prices and unemployment rates is rather systematic and fully supportive of the Phillips curve concept. This suggests that where regular patterns of economic growth are underway and expected to continue, the price-employment curve may be useful in translating unemployment predictions into price level predictions and vice versa. However, the experience of 1971–1973 adds renewed uncertainty to the usefulness of the concept. If the curve has undergone a secular shift, then perhaps it is only necessary to learn the new parameters of the curve to employ the concepts usefully. However, if the 1971–1973 position of the curve is only

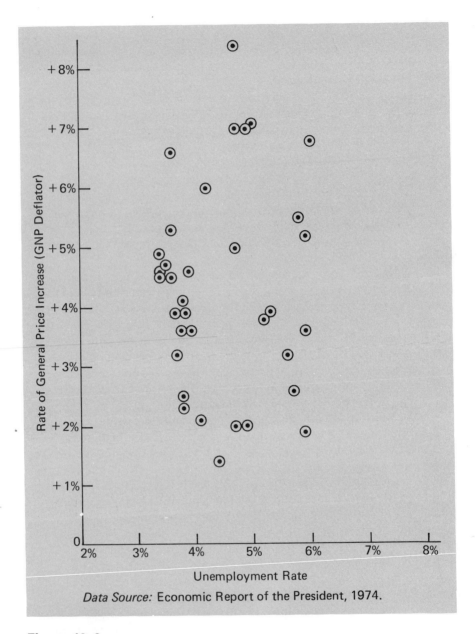

Figure 19–2

Quarterly Price-Unemployment Relationship in U.S. 1965–1973

temporary, transitory, or random, the notion of the curve as a component in economic planning suffers greatly, as it implies a high degree of nonsystematic behavior.

For economic policy, the conclusions are similar. Contractionary economic policy aimed at creating excess capacity and higher unemployment (in an effort to move down the Phillips curve to lower price level increases) must be formulated recognizing past and present patterns of capacity utilization and price change. Such policy must also take into account the related prospects that (1) the prime mover of the inflation may be demand independent forces, or that (2) the price-unemployment relationship may shift. For example, most analysts agree that the period of relatively high inflation beginning in 1967 was initially a product of the demand pressures that had built up in 1965–1966 in an increasingly fully utilized economy. However, once a full force inflation had churned up, it was impossible to ascertain whether or not these demand forces remained the prime mover of the inflation. The restrictive economic policy of 1969 essentially banked on the primacy of demand pressures in the inflation. But, as that policy delivered the sought after excess capacity and higher unemployment rates associated with the 1970 recession, it became apparent that the inflation was by now driven by demand independent forces. The general policy lesson of this and the 1958 experience is that demand independent influences of the type we have earlier discussed may develop once an inflation has gotten underway. Although our sample of 2 years is inadequate, it suggests that they can be expected to drive the inflation beyond the time when demand pressures subside.

Demand-Independent Inflationary Policy

If a stable price-unemployment relationship exists, then the tools of fiscal and monetary policy can bring about a change in the employment position of the economy in order to reach a desirable tradeoff between price stability and full employment. However, the tools of policy operate through the level of aggregate demand upon prices, rather than directly upon prices. Whenever a tax increase is instituted for anti-inflationary reasons, the assumption is implicitly made that the decrease in product market demand that results from the tax increase will produce lower prices. This was surely the assumption of the Nixon administration in 1969 when governmental policy tools were successfully directed toward generating the recession of 1970.

When the inflationary impetus is not closely related to product market demand, the tools of economic policy are largely ineffective in arresting the inflationary trend, for in these cases, retarding demand is far from retarding inflation. It was perhaps the realization of this circumstance in late 1970 by frustrated policy makers that contributed to the motivation for the price controls instituted during the next year.

The implicit recognition that inflationary pressures can be largely nondemand related actually began in the mid-1960s with the advent of the wage-price guidelines.[6] The wage-price guidelines was a system of organized government "jawboning" designed to make price and wage settlements highly visible and to publicly label wage and price actions as inflationary or noninflationary. The guidelines were organized around the following propositions:

1. That producers will in general follow pricing strategies designed to maintain constant profit margins.
2. That average wage increases equal to average productivity increases will leave profit margins intact on the average, i.e., other costs are ignored.

With these propositions, the guidelines stipulate that noninflationary wage settlements should not exceed the overall average gain in labor productivity, as this will leave unit labor costs and profit margins intact on the average and thus offer no rationale for price increases. For example, if average output-per-man-hour rises by 3 percent while average wages-per-man-hour rises also by 3 percent, then labor costs-per-unit remain constant as do profit margins at existing prices. This condition leads to price stability as long as other costs are constant and producers follow pricing strategies as identified in proposition 1.

Recognizing that some industries have less than average productivity gains while others have greater than average gains, the guidelines stipulated that wage settlements equal to average productivity increases should cause prices to rise in industries having below average productivity gains (where unit labor costs are consequently rising) and that prices should fall in industries where greater than average productivity gains reduce unit labor costs and improve profit margins. Under these circumstances, the price increases offset the price decreases, resulting in a general pattern of stable prices.

Although the concept of the guidelines evoked considerable debate among economists as to specific subtle aspects of the program and its application, there was considerable agreement on the basic logic of the scheme. However, the debate was largely unproductive as unions typically interpreted the guideline wage settlement as a minimum acceptable figure and worked actively and usually successfully to obtain settlements greater than this "minimum" figure. This dysfunctional aspect of the guidelines probably contributed as much as anything to the deemphasis of the guidelines by policy makers in the latter part of the decade of the 1960s.

The wage-price guidelines were a forerunner of the eventual price controls instituted in 1971, in the sense that both schemes were directed in sub-

---

[6] For an evolutionary explanation of the guidelines, the reader can consult *The Economic Report of the President* for the years in the middle and late 1960s.

stantial part toward demand-independent inflationary pressures. The controls of 1971 followed in the aftermath of the inflationary recession of 1970. When the controls were finally all removed in early 1974, there was nearly unanimous agreement that they had not been successful. Prices had risen rapidly during most of the period, as our earlier discussion indicated. In addition, the pressures brought about by controls did not work evenly upon producers. Large producers in highly visible industries were under the most pressure, while others had less difficulty moving prices to desired levels. The causes of the ineffectiveness of the controls of 1971–1973 will be the subject of debate for some time to come. However, the general administrative difficulty of such an undertaking could provide an adequate reason in and of itself. The administrative agency concerned with the controls was faced with the task of deciding which requests for price increases were justified on the basis of cost and profit margin positions and which were not. With the complexity of modern corporate accounting systems, and the flexibility in information processing and presentation they allow, evaluating such requests was undoubtedly a difficult undertaking. Other base period, list price, and special problems of particular industries combined to make the system of controls workable only with the wholehearted cooperation of those controlled, such as has characterized the U.S. economy during times of war. The lack of such a spirit undoubtedly contributed importantly to the lack of success of the controls program of 1971–1973.

Other Policy Questions

Our analysis of price-unemployment relationships suggests that the most appropriate concept of full employment may vary, depending upon the purpose of our policy discussion. In our discussion of labor market equilibrium in Chapter 16, full employment meant the situation in which the labor force was fully employed, to the point of a frictional minimum level of unemployment. In the United States, this frictional minimum has been defined variously to be between 3.5–4.5 percent of the labor force. However, our discussion of the price-unemployment relationship of Figure 19–1 suggested the possibility that at particular times a full employment rate of say 4 percent may associate with such a high rate of inflation that it is not a practical concept for policy purposes. To illustrate this, if we redraw the curve of Figure 19–1 to conform to the pattern of 1970–1973, we would find that prices begin to rise sharply when the rate of unemployment falls below about 5.5 percent. For purposes of price-unemployment tradeoffs, this higher rate of unemployment has more significance than the conventional labor-force related unemployment rate because it reflects the point where the economy begins to behave as if full employment conditions prevailed. With the curve

in the 1970–1973 position, policy prescriptions aimed at bringing the unemployment level much below 5.5 percent contain the potential for severe
inflationary consequences according to the appearance of Figure 19–1.

The relationship between prices and unemployment is complicated by
the particular policy followed by the Federal Reserve regarding interest
rates. To see this, we consider the (perhaps unlikely) case in which the Federal Reserve adopts the policy of maintaining interest rates at a constant
level regardless of fluctuations in product market demand. The situation is
depicted in Figure 19–3. The initial position of the economy is described by
L_eM_e and I_eS_e. Real income at full employment of the labor force is given
by y_f, so that the full equilibrium interest rate is i_e. Now, assume that product market demand is not static, but varies over time. When product market
demand is unusually high, it pushes the IS curve into the position I_pS_p.

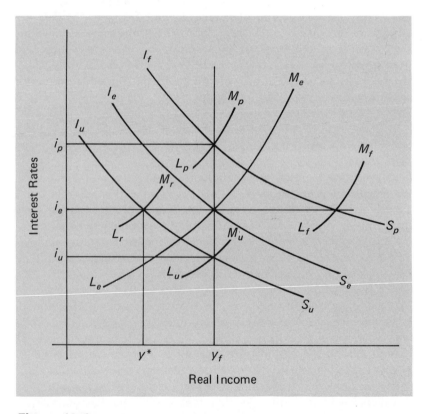

Figure 19–3
Interest Rate Policy

When product market demand is somewhat depressed, it moves the *IS* curve to I_uS_u.

Consider first the case where increasing demand shifts the *IS* curve to I_pS_p. Prices begin to rise, contracting the real money supply and motivating a rise in interest rates toward the new full equilibrium level of i_p, along with a shift in the *LM* curve to L_pM_p. But, the Federal Reserve moves against this trend by increasing the nominal money supply sufficiently to maintain interest rates at i_e. To do this, it is necessary to add sufficient reserves to shift the *LM* to L_fM_f, where the market interest rate remains at i_e. But this market rate is now too low for full equilibrium, and prices continue to rise, fueled in large part by the Federal Reserve increase in the money supply. Quite clearly, the goal of stable interest rates is in this case in conflict with the goal of price stability.

In the case where a fall in demand lowers the *IS* curve to I_uS_u, the situation is reversed. In this case, prices weaken and the real money supply begins to expand. With rigid wages, unemployment begins to appear, along with downward pressures on interest rates. The policy of interest rate stability now requires that the Federal Reserve move to sop up excess liquidity in money and capital markets by taking reserves out of the banking system to prop the sagging interest rates. By removing sufficient reserves to shift the *LM* curve back to L_rM_r, the market interest rate is maintained at i_e, a value higher than the new full equilibrium rate of i_u (which would occur if the *LM* was at L_uM_u). The result of this situation is to worsen the unemployment condition associated with the downwardly rigid wages as real income and output fall from Y_f to y^*. Thus, in this case, the target of interest rate stability conflicts with the target of full employment. This discussion further illustrates our earlier point that tradeoffs are necessary between the extent to which economic policy strives for orderly interest rates in money and bond markets on the one hand, and both full employment and price stability on the other. The policy stance taken on one target has repercussions on the others.

Applying Policy in the United States

In our discussion so far, we have considered the possible uncertainty associated with the short-run impact of policy actions. We have also considered the interaction among policy measures and the inescapable need for tradeoffs among the realization of conflicting economic targets. Even if these areas of uncertainty were completely resolved in the minds of policy makers, a simple but frustrating problem remains—those involved in the administration of both fiscal and monetary policy are not completely in control of their policy actions.

To consider this point, we first take the case of fiscal policy. We can think of the net fiscal policy stance of government as being the difference between total government expenditures and total taxes collected. Total government expenditures include state and local expenditures as well as federal expenditures. In recent years, more than half the total government purchases of goods and services are made by state and local governments. But state and local expenditures are not made in a way that responds to national economic targets. They are the sum of many thousands of municipal and local agencies' budgetary outlays. There is no reason to expect these expenditures to contribute to discretionary fiscal policy. The remaining portion, federal expenditures, is controlled by the joint actions of the president and the Congress. Federal expenditures are approved and made on a program-by-program basis, through the interaction of White House and congressional initiative. However, at present the total level of federal expenditure is not the subject of legal congressional or White House control, but is instead the sum of the expenditures made on all the individual programs that gained congressional and White House approval during the fiscal year. The total expenditure by the federal government is thus something that is more nearly discovered after the budgetary process is completed rather than being set in advance and given as a limitation on individual programs.

These realities make the fixing of the total level of government expenditures at some policy desired level a difficult if not impossible undertaking. Rather, the situation now described leads to the speculation that the total level of government spending is substantially independent of the economic policy targets of the nation's political and economic leaders.

Taxes are collected at the state and local level as well as at the federal level. As with state and local expenditures, we cannot consider the state and local tax flows to be influenced by economic policy targets. They are made in direct proportion to the expenditure needs of the locality involved. At the federal level, where more than half the total tax collections are made, tax policy has often been changed in direct response to the dictates of economic policy. Indeed, in practice, the burden of discretionary fiscal policy actions by the federal government has fallen largely on tax changes. Undoubtedly this is due in large part to the impossibility of implementing deliberate and timely policy oriented governmental spending actions.

However, the practical implementation of tax policy is not without its problems. One of the most important is the common politicization of tax policy in the United States. Political incumbents and hopefuls who campaign on the basis of tax cuts are likely to receive a boost from the electorate on this account. At the same time, incumbents who contribute to the passage of a tax cut as an election approaches are likely to benefit from it at the polls. In each case, the positive political result is likely to occur whether the tax cut was called for economically or not. In contrast, tax increases are likely to be seen as most politically desirable during the period just after major elections, as the effect has maximum time to "wear-off." Even if such political effects do not by themselves determine the timing of tax policy actions, they surely influence the timing of tax policy and often as not may lead to ill-timed fiscal policy acts, as portions of the post–World War II U.S. record attests.

In addition to the problem of inspiring the necessary political support for a tax policy change, there is substantial uncertainty in the time lag between the initiation of a tax action and the passage of the law. Hearings must be held, reports made, bills drawn up, and congressional action taken in both houses of Congress. The process can take a sufficiently long period of time that by the time the action is put into place the appropriate tax policy action may have changed.

With the net fiscal policy stance of government consisting of both expenditure and tax flows, our discussion has now indicated that important difficulties may exist in administratively placing the fiscal position in the stance required by policy targets in a timely fashion and to an adequate degree required by the nature of economic behavior in private markets. This indicates that short-run discretionary fiscal policy may be difficult if not impossible to administer in the real world of the twentieth-century United States.

The administration of monetary policy actions does not suffer from the lack of control of state and local fiscal actions that visits fiscal policy. But, it is confronted with a similar problem—that the creation of inside money by banks may occur in a manner independent of the policy stance of the Federal Reserve. In some respects, the Federal Reserve and the commercial banking establishment are naturally in conflict with each other in their organizational objectives. During times of rapidly expanding product markets accompanied by the threat of inflation, the Federal Reserve may initiate a contractionary open market policy to cool off the economy. In order for this stance to be fully effective, the level of new business loans must drop so that the level of investment spending contracts. But, during such times, the demand for new loans is likely to be unusually heavy and interest rates are likely to be rising. Most profit seeking banks will seek to enlarge rather than contract their level of outstanding loans under such circumstances. Therefore, commercial banks are motivated to work diligently to counteract the loss of reserves due to the restrictive Federal Reserve policy by more efficiently using available reserves, thus raising the ratio of inside to outside money. As a consequence, the total money supply will not contract in accordance with the contraction in the outside component brought about by the Federal Reserve policy. In fact, the commercial banking establishment will most likely cut their level of lending only as a last resort when all the existing slack has been taken from the banking system and other commercial bank options have been exhausted.

The Federal Reserve is motivated to expand the stock of outside money as a spur to the economy and generally in response to rising unemployment. During these times, the Federal Reserve is supportive of an increased level of business loans as they will increase investment spending and aid the unemployment condition. However, loan demand is likely to be weak during this type of period, as business firms may be reluctant to expand during recessions. In addition, loans are likely to be viewed as more risky by bankers due to recessionary conditions. Thus, banks may not be motivated to expand loans to the degree desired by the Federal Reserve. As a result, the ratio of inside money to outside money will drop with the Federal Reserve expansion of the outside money supply. As in the first case, the result of this policy is a response by the commercial banking establishment that buffers against the stance of the Federal Reserve and often makes the overall response of the money supply to the initiating Federal Reserve change sluggish.

This discussion indicates that moves by the Federal Reserve to either increase or decrease the growth rate in the money supply may not lead to an actual change in the money supply in the same proportion as the Federal Reserve change in the stock of outside money. This conclusion does not hold over extended periods of time. A limit exists to the increase in efficiency that the commercial banking establishment can generate during monetary contractions. When it is reached, commercial banks will be forced to maintain a constant (maximum) ratio of inside to outside money. In this case, Federal Reserve changes in outside money result in proportional changes in the total money supply. There is also a limit to which banks will allow their reserve position to build during periods of monetary expansion by the Federal Reserve. Increased investment in short- and long-term securities by banks is an outlet for such reserves, but an increased demand by banks for such securities will drive up their prices and lower their yields. With falling bond yields, loans will become a more attractive investment alternative, even given the higher risk associated with recessionary conditions. In this position, banks will tend to respond to Federal Reserve actions less sluggishly, so long as interest rates do not fall to such low levels that transactions costs absorb the yield on the investment.

Thus, the sluggishness (if not balkiness) in the short-run response of the total money supply to Federal Reserve policy actions does not appear to also characterize the long-run role of policy actions. A Federal Reserve policy stance taken and held over a period of several quarters is likely to bring about the desired response by the banking system and by the total money supply. On the other hand, we have found reasons to believe that short-run policy adjustments by the Federal Reserve may be of greatly reduced effectiveness in moving the economy toward the economic targets of the Federal

Reserve. Coupled with the earlier similar conclusion with respect to fiscal policy, we find reasons to believe that short-run adjustments (fine tuning) in both fiscal and monetary policy actions are likely to be difficult to bring about administratively with resultant uncertainty in their final effect. This raises questions about the practicality of the use of such tools in the art of administering close-up economic policy.

In this chapter, we have seriously unbalanced the conceptual scales by posing many more questions than answers. In discussing the slippery subject of economic policy, this is not only appropriate, it is required, since the number of questions exceeds the number of answers by a considerable margin when the subject turns to policy. In addition, we have avoided resolving the crucial tradeoffs such as those between stability in the purchasing power of millions of Americans and the employment of hundreds of thousands more American men and women in useful jobs. The resolution of such questions relies on individual values that are as unique as the personalities of individual students of macroeconomic analysis.

Discussion Questions

1. What evidence can you develop from published sources such as *Business Conditions Digest* on the applicability of Professor Friedman's contention that the results of short-run policy are difficult to predict? Explain.

2. Find the most recent data of the type included in Figure 19–1. Update this figure, and comment on possible reasons why the data occurred in the region of the curve you found.

3. What steps can the government take to reduce demand-independent inflation? Comment on the political feasibility as well as the economic properties of your solution.

4. Do you think stable interest rates are more important than inflation? Can they both be achieved? Focus on the tradeoff in as many different ways as you feel are relevant.

5. How could fiscal policy be made more manageable? What institutional changes are necessary?

6. How could short-term monetary policy be made more responsive? Discuss.

7. Was the Federal Reserve policy stance of early 1974 warranted? To answer this, develop a scenario of the price, interest rate, and employment conditions of this period. Now, judging from the money supply components, try to find out what kind of a policy the Federal Reserve followed during the period and whether or not it was appropriate, using the advantage of perfect hindsight.

A Problem in Economic Policy

On September 28, 1973, *The Wall Street Journal* reported on a press conference held by economist William Fellner shortly after his appointment as a member of the President's Council of Economic Advisors. Among the highlights of the press conference were Fellner's contentions that: (1) the system of price controls in the U.S. should be rapidly lifted, since they are both bad economics and bad politics; (2) attempts to get the unemployment rate under 5 percent by year-end would only fuel inflation; (3) the Federal Reserve Board and government budgetary authorities should clamp down on monetary and fiscal policies; (4) it was really a mistake for the Federal Reserve Board to ease monetary policy in mid-1972, thus contributing to overheating the nation's economy.

Using data sources such as the *Economic Report of the President,* organize the relevant economic statistics related to Fellner's contention, and develop a picture of the position of the economy at that point in time. Then, apply the economic theories presented thus far in the book to evaluate the correctness of Fellner's contentions. Which one is most highly debatable? Which do you find most agreeable?

A Problem in Monetary Policy

A conversation overheard between two would-be Federal Reserve Board members at lunch during a time of rapid output expansion and mounting pressures on prices.

W.B. Member A: "We must tighten money now. As long as we keep money easy, the pace of economic activity will proceed at an excessive rate."

W.B. Member B: "To tighten now would seriously disrupt business activity. It is nearly tax time, and firms must have liquidity to pay their taxes."

W.B. M. A: "We can provide temporary liquidity for that purpose, but I am talking about our policy stance for the next 6 months. We must make it impossible for the economy to grow at the present inflationary rate of 9 percent."

W.B. M. B: "What you are talking about is business failures. How do you get business to cut its output levels except by tightening money to the point that financial crisis is created?"

W.B. M. A: "By making it unattractive for business to borrow money to invest in new plant and equipment. That will dampen down the entire economy in a short while."

W.B. M. B: "And it will be inflationary as well. Don't you know that new plant and equipment ultimately *cut* the unit cost of business firms? You are talking about forcing business to produce with worn-out, inefficient capital assets."

W.B. M. A: "That effect, if there is one, which I doubt, will be swamped by the deflationary effect of declining investment and, ultimately, consumer spending levels. The net effect will be to cut prices."

W.B. M. B: "What's more, the higher interest rates your tight money policy will create add to the financing costs of business even more, and put pressures on product prices. And, the sector that will be hit hardest will be home-building. Families with small children and little savings will be prohibited from building new homes. Is that what you really want?"

W.B. M. A: "No doubt that home-building will suffer from my tight money proposal, but a cutback in these expenditures will help dampen the excessive current rate of output expansion."

W.B. M. B: "Have you no heart? You are ignoring the people who would have lived in those unbuilt houses. What's more, the tight money is bound to lead to a stock market decline. The value of stocks held by U.S. families will decline. Capital losses will be suffered. Is that part of your plan also?"

W.B. M. A: "Stock prices may indeed fall, but this will have a contributing effect to the dampening of excessive demand. As households' wealth position is eroded, they will in all likelihood reduce their spending on consumer goods. Thus, the level of demand and the level of output will be further reduced to healthier levels."

W.B. M. B: "Your idea of 'healthy' is positively scary. To you, a healthy economy is one where the business sector is in a severe liquidity crisis, where new investment is being choked off and artificially retarded, where home-building is greatly depressed and disrupted, and where the value of security holdings is eroded away. If this is healthy, I'd like to know what constitutes economic ill-health."

W.B. M. A: "Your bleeding heart overlooks one crucial fact. If we do not act to tighten money right now, we will be ratifying the current inflationary rate of economic growth. The responsibility will be ours when product prices begin to rise at 10 to 15 percent rates. Starving elderly people on social security and widows on fixed incomes will have us to thank for their misery. Families on tight budgets will have us to blame when inflation erodes their food budget to the point of meat only once a week. That is what it is all about, my friend."

W.B. M. B: "I don't buy it. There must be another way to ease inflationary pressures."

W.B. M. A: "I'm listening."

1. How could "tight money conditions" be created if *W.B. M. A's* plan prevails, i.e., what actions are necessary to create tight money?

2. What does *W.B. M. A* mean about "ratifying the current inflationary rate" by board policy?

3. Consult data sources such as the *Economic Report of the President, Business Conditions Digest,* or the *Survey of Current Business* to attempt to provide statistical support for the various propositions of both the would-be board members as to the effect of tight money. The 1968–1969 period may be a useful reference framework.

4. Which argument do you find more appealing and why? Which side would you be on?

5. Can you suggest another way to ease inflationary pressures?

Index